Sentence Processing in East Asian Languages

Sentence Processing in East Asian Languages

edited by
Mineharu Nakayama

CSLI
PUBLICATIONS
Center for the Study of
Language and Information
Stanford, California

Copyright © 2002
CSLI Publications
Center for the Study of Language and Information
Leland Stanford Junior University
Printed in the United States
06 05 04 03 02   5 4 3 2 1

Library of Congress Cataloging-in-Publication Data

Sentence processing in East Asian languages /
[edited by] Mineharu Nakayama.
   p.   cm. — (CSLI lecture notes ; 122)
Includes bibliographical references and index.
   ISBN 1-57586-308-1 (pbk. : alk. paper)
   ISBN 1-57586-307-3 (alk. paper)
   1. Ambiguity. 2. Semantics.
 I. Nakayama, Mineharu.   II. Series.
   P325.5.A46 S47   2001
   401'.43—dc21   2001025224

∞ The acid-free paper used in this book meets the minimum requirements of the American National Standard for Information Sciences—Permanence of Paper for Printed Library Materials, ANSI Z39.48-1984.

CSLI was founded early in 1983 by researchers from Stanford University, SRI International, and Xerox PARC to further research and development of integrated theories of language, information, and computation. CSLI headquarters and CSLI Publications are located on the campus of Stanford University.

CSLI Publications reports new developments in the study of language, information, and computation. In addition to lecture notes, our publications include monographs, working papers, revised dissertations, and conference proceedings. Our aim is to make new results, ideas, and approaches available as quickly as possible. Please visit our web site at
http://cslipublications.stanford.edu/
for comments on this and other titles, as well as for changes and corrections by the author and publisher.

Contents

Contributors   vii

Preface   xi

1   Timing Issues in Lexical Ambiguity Resolution   1
    KATHLEEN AHRENS

2   Resolution of Reanalysis Ambiguity in Japanese Relative
    Clauses   31
    YUKI HIROSE

3   The Nature of Categorical Ambiguity and Its Implications for
    Language Processing   53
    CHU-REN HUANG, CHAO-JAN CHEN AND CLAUDE C.C. SHEN

4   Syntactic and Positional Similarity Effects in the Processing of
    Japanese Embeddings   85
    RICHARD L. LEWIS AND MINEHARU NAKAYAMA

5   Lexical Ambiguity in Sentence Processing   111
    PING LI, HUA SHU, MICHAEL YIP, YAXU ZHANG AND YINGHONG TANG

6   Costs of Scrambling in Japanese Sentence Processing   131
    REIKO MAZUKA, KENJI ITOH AND TADAHISA KONDO

7   Sources of Difficulty in Processing Scrambling in Japanese   167
    EDSON T. MIYAMOTO AND SHOICHI TAKAHASHI

8   Processing Filler-gap Constructions in Japanese   189
    TSUTOMU SAKAMOTO

9   Effects of Accentual Phrasing on Adjective Interpretation in Korean   223
    AMY J. SCHAFER AND SUN-AH JUN

10 Center-embedding Problem and the Contribution of Nominative Case Repetition   257
    KEIKO UEHARA AND DIANNE C. BRADLEY

Subject Index   289

Contributors

KATHLEEN AHRENS: Graduate Institute of Linguistics, National Taiwan University, 1 Roosevelt Road, Section 4, Taipei 106, Taiwan, Republic of China.
ahrens66@hotmail.com

DIANNE C. BRADLEY: Ph.D. Program in Linguistics, Graduate Center of The City University of New York, 365 Fifth Avenue, New York, NY 10016, U.S.A.
dbradley@gc.cuny.edu

CHAO-RAN CHEN: Maison de l'Italie, 7A, Bd. Jourdan, 75014 Paris, France.
chen_chaojan@yahoo.com.tw

YUKI HIROSE: Department of Computer Science, The University of Electro Communications, 1-5-1 Chofugaoka, Chofu, Tokyo, 182-8585, Japan.
hirose@cs.uec.ac.jp

CHU-REN HUANG: Institute of Linguistics, Academia Sinica, 130, Yanjiuyuan Rd., Nankang, Taipei 115, Taiwan, Republic of China.
churen@sinica.edu.tw

KENJI ITOH: Department of Speech and Cognitive Sciences, School of Medicine, The University of Tokyo, Tokyo, 113-0033, Japan.
kitoh@m.u-tokyo.ac.jp

SUN-AH JUN: Department of Linguistics, University of California, Los Angeles, CA 90095-1543, U.S.A.
jun@humnet.ucla.edu

TADAHISA KONDO: NTT Communication Science Laboratories, NTT Corporation, 3-1, Morinosato-Wakamiya, Atsugi, Kanagawa, 243-0198, Japan.
kondo@avg.brl.ntt.co.jp

RICHARD L. LEWIS: Department of Psychology, University of Michigan, 525 East University, Ann Arbor, MI 48109-1109, U.S.A.
rickl@lsa.umich.edu

PING LI: Department of Psychology, University of Richmond, Richmond, VA 23173, U.S.A.
pli@richmond.edu

REIKO MAZUKA: Department of Psychology, Duke University, Durham, NC 27708-0085, U.S.A.
mazuka@duke.edu

EDSON T. MIYAMOTO: Graduate School of Information Science, Nara Institute of Science and Technology, 8916-5 Takayama, Ikoma, Nara, 630-0101, Japan.
etm@is.aist-nara.ac.jp

MINEHARU NAKAYAMA: Department of East Asian Languages and Literatures, The Ohio State University, Columbus, OH 43210, U.S.A.
nakayama.1@osu,edu

TSUTOMU SAKAMOTO: Department of Linguistics, Faculty of Humanities, Kyushu University, 6-19-1 Hakozaki, Higashi-ku, Fukuoka, 812-8581, Japan.
sakamoto@lit.kyushu-u.ac.jp

AMY J. SCHAFER: Department of Linguistics, University of Hawai'i at Manoa, Honolulu, HI 96822, USA.
aschafer@hawaii.edu

CLAUDE C.C. SHEN: Mandarin speech recognition, Philps Research East Asia, 24FB, 66, Sec. 1, Chung Hisao W. Rd, Taipei 100, Taiwan, Republic of China
claude.shen@philips.com

HUA SHU: Department of Psychology, Beijing Normal University, Beijing, People's Republic of China.
shuh@bnu.edu.cn

SHOICHI TAKAHASHI: Department of Linguistics and Philosophy, E39-245, 77 Massachusetts Avenue, MIT, Cambridge, MA 02139, U.S.A.
s_t@mit.edu

YINGHONG TANG: Department of Psychology, Beijing Normal University, Beijing, People's Republic of China.
tang@bnu.edu.cn

KEIKO UEHARA: Ph.D. Program in Linguistics, Graduate Center of The City University of New York, 365 Fifth Avenue, New York, NY 10016, U.S.A. Department of English, School of Education, Gunma University, 4-2 Aramaki, Maebashi, Gunma, 371-8510, Japan.
kuehara@edu.gunma-u.ac.jp

MICHAEL YIP: Department of Psychology, Open University of Hong Kong, Hong Kong, People's Republic of China.
myip@ouhk.edu.hk

YAXU ZHANG: Department of Psychology, Peking University, Beijing, People's Republic of China.
yxzhang@pku.edu.cn

Preface

This volume is a collection of papers on sentence processing in East Asian languages. Many papers were presented at the International East Asian Psycholinguistics Workshop held at The Ohio State University on August 4, 1999. However, this volume should not be regarded as the proceedings as it includes papers solicited after the Workshop and each article has been reviewed for this publication.

The "East Asian" languages discussed in this volume are Cantonese, Japanese, Korean, and Mandarin Chinese. This book is the first of its kind that solely focuses on sentence processing issues in these languages. The contributors explore the effects of homophones on lexical ambiguity in Chinese, the effects of word order, thematic roles, and short-term memory in Japanese, and the impact of prosody on structural ambiguity in Korean. Although the issues taken up by each paper and in different East Asian languages vary, many of them can easily be identified and investigated in other East Asian languages.

The findings presented in this volume have important implications for sentence processing and cognitive processing models, and by extension contribute toward the construction of a universal theory of human language processing. Many researchers in the fields of linguistics, psychology, cognitive science and neuroscience believe that such a theory could possibly assist in the understanding of how the human brain works. Since much research has been performed on sentence processing in English and other Indo-European languages, I am pleased to present this volume to the public. This book will certainly serve as a rich resource of future investigations in experimental and theoretical linguistics, psycholinguistics, computational linguistics, psychology, neuroscience, and cognitive science, among others.

This project has been supported by different agencies and several units at The Ohio State University. By listing their names below, I would like to express my gratitude for their generous support: The Japan Foundation, the Korea Research Foundation, and The Ohio State University: Center for Cognitive Science, College of Humanities, Department of Computer and Information Science, Department of East Asian Languages and Literatures, Department of Linguistics, Department of Speech and Hearing, the East Asian Studies Center, the Institute for Japanese Studies, Foreign Language Center, National Foreign Language Resource Center, and Office of International Studies.

I would like to thank anonymous reviewers of this volume for their comments, and Kim Lewis Brown and Christine Sosa of CSLI for their assistance. Finally, I would like to thank Jennifer and Serino for their patience and understanding.

Mineharu Nakayama
Columbus, Ohio, U.S.A.

1

Timing Issues in Lexical Ambiguity Resolution*

KATHLEEN AHRENS

1 Introduction

Many words have multiple senses. People do not, however, consciously register all the senses of a word when they hear it in a particular context. The word *port* in English, for example, is ambiguous between the senses of 'harbour' or a 'bottle of wine'. But when people hear the sentence "The captain steered the ship safely into the *port* before the storm hit" they know that the sense of 'harbour' is intended. They might not even register that 'port' has another sense. However, many on-line sentence processing studies have shown that the alternate sense of an ambiguous word is accessed immediately along with the contextually appropriate sense (e.g. Swinney 1979, Tanenhaus et al. 1979, Onifer and Swinney 1981, Swinney and Love 1996).

---

* The author gratefully acknowledges support from the National Science Council during 1998-1999 (#87-2411-H-002-030-M7) and during 1999-2000 (#88-2411-H-002-051-M8). I also thank Florence Yi-ping Chang for running the experiments, Hui-Ru Hsiung and Chu-Ren Huang for the linguistic judgements in Section 3, and Vicky Tzu-yin Lai for help in formatting the final version of this paper. I would also like to thank Chu-Ren Huang, Tracy Love, Li Ping, Amy Schafer, and Dave Swinney for their comments on the work presented here. Remaining errors are my sole responsibility.

Sentence Processing in East Asian Languages.
Mineharu Nakayama (ed.).
Copyright ©2002, CSLI Publications.

This finding, seemingly opposite to what our intuition tells us should be the case, has important implications for sentence processing models as well as cognitive processing models in general. If all available senses are accessed at an ambiguous word, even when the context is biased towards one particular sense, then it indicates that access of lexical meaning is independent of sentential context. This is evidence for the modularity hypothesis, which postulates that cognitive modules conduct their internal operations without outside influence.

What is an example of a cognitive module? In terms of language, for example, there are at least six levels or subsystems: the phonological, morphological, lexical, semantic, syntactic and discourse levels. The rules and representations that describe the relevant linguistic phenomena are different for each level, and thus are considered to be structurally autonomous levels or modules.[1]

For example, the module in charge of access of lexical meaning (i.e. a lexical-level module) is postulated to be independent of the module responsible for comprehending preceding sentential context (i.e. a discourse-level module). That is, when processing is going on in one module, other modules cannot interact or interfere. Once processing is completed, however, and an output is generated, then it can interact with an output from another module. Two arguments for modularity are that it is more efficient because fewer mistakes are made, and that it is safer because the source of the input can be adequately discriminated (Fodor 1983).

There is another point of view, however, known as the interaction view, which is more closely reflects our intuition concerning lexical access of ambiguous words. This view also has empirical support from on-line sentence processing studies (e.g. Li and Yip 1996, Li and Yip 1998, Simpson 1981, Tabossi, Columbo, and Job 1987, Tabossi 1988, Tabossi and Zardon 1993). Under the interaction hypothesis, the cognitive processing system is not made up of functionally autonomous modules. Instead, the modules can interact and share information across levels at the same time that processing is going on in a particular level (Marslen-Wilson and Tyler 1980, McClelland 1987). One argument for an interactionist account is that permitting higher-level constraints to guide lower-level processes lowers the amount of noise in the processing system.

Although the modularity hypothesis and interaction hypothesis can be tested in a variety of linguistic and cognitive processing situations, it has been tested extensively in the paradigm explained at the beginning of this

---

[1] It is also possible, of course, that modules may exist within a particular linguistic level. However, because of the structural autonomy that exists between the linguistic subsystems, it is straightforward to minimally postulate a different module for each level.

paper, namely: Can preceding sentential context influence lexical access of an ambiguous word? It is clear from conscious introspection that the appropriate meaning of a lexically ambiguous word is selected, but the critical question is: when does that selection take place? Does it take place after all available senses have been accessed? Or is the information in the discourse module able to tell the lexical module that it only needs one particular sense, and to access only that sense? In addition, do the answers to these questions vary with respect to the languages under study?

Since researchers' findings have varied on the answers to these questions, it is the goal of this paper to examine the linguistic and methodological issues involved in lexical ambiguity resolution during on-line sentence processing. In Section 2, I first lay out the different models available within the modularity hypothesis and within the interaction hypothesis. In Section 3, I turn to the language specific characteristics of the language under study in this paper, Mandarin Chinese. In particular, I will look at the degree of homophony in Mandarin as well as its grammatical characteristics.

The issue of degree of homophony was raised by Li and Yip (1998). They suggest that Mandarin Chinese is extensively homophonous. They give an example where the character *yi4* has ninety meanings listed in the dictionary. Moreover, they suggest that this extensive homophony should cause problems for the modularity hypothesis because all the meanings could not possibly be accessed. Thus, they postulate that lexical ambiguity resolution in Mandarin Chinese might be better dealt within an interactionist account, which is, in fact, what their experiments (in Cantonese) show. However, I look at the linguistic data available from the Sinica Corpus, a five-million word balanced corpus of Mandarin Chinese, and find that this extensive homophony is not as prevalent in Mandarin as Li and Yip suggest. Although I conclude that homophony in Mandarin is not as extensive as has been hypothesized, I point out that certain grammatical aspects of Mandarin indicate that lexical ambiguity resolution might need to be resolved more quickly in Mandarin (once all meanings have been accessed) than in other languages such as English.

In section 4, I present two critical methodological issues: immediacy of lexical access, and automaticity of lexical access. Immediacy of lexical access has to do with the time course of lexical access. There is a time window for accessing lexical meaning and once that window has closed, other processes are post-lexical (Prather and Swinney 1989). Automaticity of lexical access has to do with the processing strategies involved in completing the task. Intentional strategies or problem-solving routines compromise automaticity. If automaticity is compromised, then modularity may also be compromised. I postulate that the reason that Li (1998) and Li and Yip (1998) find evidence for the interaction hypothesis is because immediacy and automaticity of lexical access were compromised in their experiments in Cantonese.

In the fifth section, I set forth my predictions for an on-line lexical ambiguity resolution experiment in Mandarin Chinese and present the experiment itself. I find that when the sentential context is biased towards the secondary meaning of the ambiguous word, both the primary and secondary meanings are accessed at the offset of the ambiguity. This finding is not what a strong version of the interaction hypothesis would predict, but is in line with the predictions of the modularity hypothesis. In the sixth section, I discuss the implications of the findings for lexical ambiguity resolution models, and suggest areas for future research.

2 Processing Models

The modularity hypothesis and interaction hypothesis, which are hypotheses concerning cognitive processing, also have specific models related to their predictions in linguistic processing. The context-independent models are language processing models that are in line with the assumptions and predictions of the modularity hypothesis. There are two types of context independent models that will be presented below in Section 2.1. The two context-dependent models, on the other hand, follow the predictions of the interaction hypothesis; namely, that context can influence lexical access.

2.1 Context-Independent Models

There are two types of context-independent models. One is the exhaustive or multiple-access account. This model is a form-driven account, since access is obtained through the form of the word and not through the context that precedes the ambiguity. The multiple-access account predicts that all meanings will be immediately accessed regardless of the sentence's contextual bias, or the relative frequency of each meaning (e.g. Swinney 1979, Onifer and Swinney 1981, Ahrens 1998a). By 1500 milliseconds downstream, after lexical access has occurred, only the contextually appropriate meaning is left available (e.g. Swinney 1979, Tanenhaus et al. 1979, Onifer and Swinney 1981, Swinney and Love 1996). Thus, the context preceding an ambiguous word does not influence lexical access, as both meanings are accessed at the point of lexical access, but context will aid in choosing the appropriate meaning once access has occurred. The conclusion drawn is that lexical access is "an exhaustive and autonomous subroutine of the sentence comprehension process" (Onifer and Swinney 1981). "Exhaustive" means that all meanings are accessed, and "autonomous" refers to the fact that lexical access is not driven or guided by semantic information that preceded lexical access. Thus, word meaning in the multiple-access model is accessed independent of preceding contextual information.[2]

The second context-independent model hypothesizes that the order of access of a word's meaning is related to its frequency ranking (Hogaboam and Perfetti 1975).[3] Under this ordered-access account, access of lexical meaning is also not influenced by preceding sentential context. Instead, the most frequent meaning is retrieved and if it is compatible in the context, access is completed. If it is incompatible, then the next most frequent meaning is retrieved and tested, until a match is found. An ordered-access model predicts that if the sentential context is biased towards the most frequent meaning, that will be the only meaning retrieved. However, if the context is biased towards a less frequent meaning, all meanings up to and including that particular meaning will be retrieved, in descending order of frequency (i.e. from the most frequent meaning to the least frequent meaning). Thus, context biased towards a more frequent sense should be resolved faster.

Although this account makes different predictions from the multiple-access account, it still falls within the modular theory of language processing because lexical access is not influenced by sentential context. The difference between this account and the multiple-access account is the way lexical access occurs, i.e. a word's meaning is either accessed in order of its frequency, or all the word's meanings are accessed at once. Of course, once lexical access has occurred, context will select the contextually appropriate meaning under either account.

2.2 Context-Dependent Models

There are traditionally two types of context-dependent accounts. The first I will refer to as the "strictly selective-access account" following Ahrens (1998a). A strictly selective-access account postulates that context alone is enough for the processor to select the appropriate meaning of an ambiguous word (Simpson 1981). Under this account, if the context is biased towards the dominant meaning of the word, then only the dominant meaning is accessed. Moreover, if the context is biased towards the subordinate meaning of a word, then only the subordinate meaning is accessed.

---

[2] However, that this does not mean that the processor is necessarily serial. It is possible for the processor to be both parallel and modular.

[3] Hogaboam and Perfetti (1975) had not run an on-line study when they first proposed this model. On-line evidence for this model comes from Tabossi, Columbo and Job (1987) and Tabossi and Zardon (1993), who preferred to explain their findings within a context-dependent account. However, as discussed in Section 2.2, a context-independent explanation is also possible.

The context-dependent model is compatible with an interactionist account of cognitive processing because the preceding context allows only the contextually appropriate meaning to be accessed.

The second type of model traditionally viewed as a context-dependent model I will call a "modified selective-access account" again following Ahrens (1998a). A modified selective-access account predicts that when the context is biased towards the most frequent meaning, only that meaning is accessed. However, when the context is biased towards the subordinate meaning, both meanings can be detected as being accessed.

Note that this account makes the same predictions as the ordered access account for words with exactly two meanings, which means that the same prediction, if true, would support two different models. In this connection, it is useful to note that, although Tabossi and colleagues have claimed to find evidence for a context dependent model in a series of experiments in Italian (Tabossi, Columbo and Job 1987, Tabossi 1988, Tabossi and Zardon 1993), their evidence is, by their own admission, far from conclusive. An alternate interpretation of Tabossi and Zardon's findings put forth in Ahrens (1998a) is that both meanings were accessed when biased towards the most frequent (e.g. dominant or primary meaning), but that the experimental technique they used was not sensitive enough to capture what was taking place.[4]

Another possibility is that what Tabossi and Zardon found is evidence for the ordered-access account within the context-independent model. In this case, it would be necessary to tease apart the difference between the two accounts (i.e. the modified selective-access account and the ordered-access account). Ahrens (1998a) points out that it might be possible to distinguish between the two accounts if words with more than two meanings were used as stimulus items:

> In cases where there are more than two meanings, it is possible that the modified selective-access account will again make the same prediction as the ordered-access account; namely, if any subordinate meaning is picked, all more dominant meanings will also be accessed. However, the modified selective-access account could also predict that only the contextually appropriate subordinate meaning (e.g. M_4, the fourth meaning), and the most dominant meaning (e.g. M_1, the first meaning) will be accessed. (Ahrens 1998a: 13)

---

[4] Ahrens (1998a,b) points out that both the length of time the visual target was presented in Tabossi and Zardon (1500ms) and the task used (a go/no-go task) both could have limited the sensitivity of the reaction time measurements.

The latter possibility, called the "frequency and context account" suggests that the frequency of meaning and sentential context both play a role in lexical access, such that the most frequent meaning is always accessed. However, sentential context can influence the access of a particular subordinate meaning (i.e. the fourth meaning) of an ambiguous word when it is biased towards that particular meaning, and in addition the most dominant meaning is also accessed.

It is important to note that the other two subordinate meanings (i.e. the second and third meanings) are not accessed. This instance represents a clear-cut case of where context influences access of a subordinate meaning, at the same time that the dominant meaning is always accessed. This model then, accounts for frequency and context both playing a role in lexical access, as opposed to the ordered-access account which would predict that all meanings up to and including the fourth meaning were accessed. Thus, the frequency and context account is the only explanation that would be compatible with a context-dependent model of language processing.

To summarize, there are two context-independent models -- the multiple-access account and the ordered-access account. I place the "modified selective-access account" within the context-independent model for two reasons. First, Tabossi and Zardon's (1993) explanation of their account hypothesizes that both meanings receive initial activation, which is the main spirit of a context-independent account. Second, it makes the same predictions as the ordered access account for ambiguous words with two meanings. There are also two context-dependent models -- the strictly selective-access account and the frequency and context account. The latter account must be tested on ambiguous words that have more than two meanings.

3 Chinese

Recent work in lexical ambiguity resolution has been carried out in Mandarin Chinese and Cantonese (Ahrens 1998a, Ahrens 1998b, Li and Yip 1996, Li 1998). Both the Mandarin and Cantonese languages are tonal languages; individual tones are associated with each syllable. Both languages also use characters to write a particular syllable, and not an alphabetized system, for writing.[5] However, these languages are not mutually intelligible in their spoken form. They are somewhat mutually intelligible in their written form, since most content words and some function words are etymologically related and are written with the same characters. In what follows, the term

---

[5] Note that these characters are not ideographs. Characters may carry both phonological and semantic information. This semantic information, moreover, is no longer in pictorial form.

"Chinese" will be used to encompass characteristics of both Mandarin Chinese and Cantonese.

3.1 Degree of Homophony

Li and Yip (1998) emphasized the fact that the Chinese language "has a massive number of homophones on the lexical-morphemic level even with tonal distinctions. In English and other Indo-European languages, homophony is a relatively low frequency event. In Chinese, homophony is extensive" (p. 224).

They go on to give an example from the Modern Chinese Dictionary (1985) of the syllable *yi* which in the fourth tone has 90 different characters associated with it.[6] Each character has a unique meaning associated with it. Li and Yip ask:

> Upon hearing *yi* in a sentence, do Chinese speakers activate all 90 or more meanings of the syllable? The exhaustive access hypothesis predicts that they should, because lexical access is a modular, autonomous, and capacity-free process. The context-dependency hypothesis predicts that they activate only the contextually appropriate meaning with aid from prior sentence context. (Li and Yip 1998: 225)

There are several reasons, however, to question the validity of their assumptions. First, speakers are not expected to access all *dictionary* meanings of a word. After all, they cannot access a meaning that they do not have.

Second, the authors are confusing the notion of morpheme and lexeme. A morpheme may carry meaning, but it is not an independent unit. It cannot stand by itself. A lexeme is an independent unit in the language. It can stand alone. All characters in Chinese are morphemes, while only a subset of these individual morphemes are lexemes, or individual lexical items. Other lexemes are made up of more than one morpheme. As Chao (1938: 143) defines the difference: "A morpheme which can be uttered alone is free (F), and one which always occurs without pause with another morpheme in an utterance is bound (B)." A bound morpheme, then, is not a lexeme.[7]

---

[6] The Modern Chinese Dictionary is a dictionary of Mandarin Chinese compiled in Mainland China.

[7] If lexical access includes morphemic access, as it seems to be assumed by Li and Yip, then English is not different from Chinese because English also has morphemes such as (-)a(-), (-)in(-), which may have as many meanings as *yi4*. Whether morphemic access is valid lexical access is beyond the scope of this paper. I will keep to the standard view of lexical access in this paper.

I asked a linguistically trained native speaker of Mandarin Chinese analyzed the 90 morphemes in the 1996 version of the Modern Chinese Dictionary according to the criteria of Chao (1938). Of these 90 characters, she concluded that only 13 were independent lexemes. Thus, even in the case where 90 potential homophones exist, 77 of those homophones are bound morphemes that must occur with another character. A second linguistically trained native speaker then looked at this list of 13 independent lexemes and concluded that none of them could be classified as individual lexemes because they either occurred in classical phrases, i.e., they were not individual lexemes in the modern language, or they occurred in abbreviations, or they were in fact bound forms (as in the case of two resultative verbs). Thus, it is not clear that any of the ninety characters associated with the syllable *yi4* are individual lexical items. But as can be seen from the above discussion, the distinction between free and bound morphemes, even for linguistically trained speakers, is not always clearcut.[8] One solution that could be applied in this case would be to run an off-line experiment.

The experiment would consist of playing an audiotape that had monosyllabic as well as multisyllabic words on it (with adequate time in between the presentation of each word). Each subject is asked to write down as many words as they can think of for each item they hear on the tape. Then they are asked to write down as many meanings as they can think of for each word, in the order they think of them. They are also asked to write down a sentence that uses that particular meaning of the word in the sentence. This last step serves two purposes. It gives the independent judgers additional data for them to use when they are evaluating if the meanings that an individual subject gave were distinct. It also allows the judger to check if (especially in the monosyllabic instances) the character was used in a bound form with another character.

Boundedness can be checked by searching for that character in a large-scale corpus such as the Sinica Corpus, and using the tools in that corpus to determine the mutual information value of the two characters in question. If the mutual information value is above 2, then the character sequence in question is highly collocational and considered to be bound (e.g. Sproat and Shih 1990, Huang, Ahrens and Chen 1998, Huang 2000). If this is the case, it means that the character that the subject wrote down is not a lexeme, but is instead a morpheme. If the mutual information value is below 2, it means that the character is a free form lexeme. Once the judgers have ascertained the number of lexical entries (or meanings) a phonemic representation has for each subject, then they can evaluate which meanings are shared by all

---

[8] See Huang, Ahrens and Chen (1998) for further discussion on how to distinguish between free and bound morphemes with the aid of computational linguistic tools.

the subjects, which meanings are shared by at least 75% of the subjects, etc. Only in this way can the number of lexical entries for a phonemic representation be determined for a subject population.[9]

Third, Li and Yip (1998) assume that Mandarin Chinese is a monosyllabic language, but modern Mandarin Chinese is in fact, a multisyllabic language, and not a monosyllabic one. An analysis of the 146,787 word lexicon extracted from the five million-word Sinica Balanced Corpus (i.e. an analysis by type) reveals that only 3% of the lexemes are monosyllabic, while 46% are disyllabic, 32% are trisyllabic, 10% are made up of four syllables, and 9% are made up of five syllables or more. Thus, 97% of the lexicon is made up of words that are multisyllabic. However, in terms of tokens (i.e. the number of times the words appear in the corpus itself), monosyllabic words appear 45% of the time, disyllabic words appear 47% of the time, and trisyllabic words appear 6% of the time, with four and five-syllable words both appearing 1% of the time (Huang, Chen and Sher 2001). The perception that Mandarin Chinese is a monosyllabic language may come from the fact that these monosyllabic words are highly frequent, though even in terms of frequency, they are less than disyllabic words.

Moreover, these monosyllabic words perform in the corpus (i.e., as tokens) primarily as function words (69%) as opposed to content words (31%) (i.e., nouns, verbs and adjectives). The disyllabic words that appear in the corpus, on the other hand, consist of 83% content words and only 17% function words (Huang et al. 2001). While it will be important to look at the effect of context on these monosyllabic content words in the future, it is the disyllabic content words that are occurring more frequently. A perusal of an alphabetized pinyin-based dictionary such as DeFrancis (1996) shows that homophony is rare among lexemes of two are more syllables (i.e., cases where a disyllabic word has matching tones and syllables with another disyllabic word that is made up of two different characters). Thus, it is not correct to argue that 'homophony is extensive' in Mandarin Chinese.[10] That is not to say, however, that ambiguity does not exist. Lexemes can, and do, have more than one meaning. In section 5, I will present an experiment that looks at lexical ambiguity resolution in Mandarin Chinese for disyllabic lexemes.

---

[9] Note that "lexical entry" is referring to the sense of the lexeme. Some lexemes have more than one sense (lexical entry), while some only have one. A different character usually indicates a different sense of a word, with certain exceptions (i.e. some characters have variant forms that mean the same thing).

[10] A fourth point, albeit not a linguistic one, is that Fodor (1983), in setting forth the modularity hypothesis, did not stipulate that it was a capacity-free process. Fodor's nine principles of a modular system are given in Section 4.

3.2 Grammatical Characteristics

However, although Mandarin is not excessively lexically ambiguous, it does have grammatical characteristics that indicate that context could play an important role in listening comprehension.

For example, Ahrens (1998b) argued that the different grammatical properties of a language could influence how on-line lexical ambiguity resolution is handled. She proposed a language-driven hypothesis, which says that if contextual information is often used to interpret utterances in a language, it will also be able to affect lexical access in that language. The language-driven hypothesis is formulated as in (1).

(1) Language-driven hypothesis:
If a language is context-prominent, then context will be able to influence lexical access immediately and automatically. (Ahrens 1998b: 18)

Ahrens (1998a) defines a language as being context-prominent "if contextual information plays a prominent role in interpreting a sentence." For example, languages which allow dropping of the subject, or of the object, need context in order to interpret the missing information. For example, in Mandarin both the subject and object can be omitted in situations where context allows the information to be reconstructed. For example, if someone asks: *Ni xihuan bingqiling?* ('Do you like ice cream?') one can respond with a simple *Xihuan* ('Like'). In Mandarin, the previous sentence is enough to "fill in" for both the speaker and the hearer who is doing the liking, and what is liked.

Moreover, even though in Mandarin subjects and objects are structurally encoded as in English, when topicalization occurs, a subject and object can switch their surface position without changing the dominant interpretation (i.e. Ahrens 1998b, examples (4) and (5)). Thus, Mandarin Chinese can rely on contextual information to assign interpretations, instead of structural information which may either be missing or unreliable. Thus, if the language-driven hypothesis is plausible then context should influence ambiguity resolution in Mandarin Chinese because Mandarin relies on contextual information for semantic and propositional interpretation.

This hypothesis was tested on nouns at the onset position in Mandarin Chinese when the ambiguity was biased towards the secondary meaning (Ahrens 1998b). However, both meanings of the ambiguity were still accessed, which does not support the Language-driven Hypothesis. However, in the experiment that is presented in this paper we look at lexical ambiguity resolution under the same conditions in Mandarin, but we look at the offset of the ambiguity. One reason for doing so is because Li and Yip (1996) found that in Cantonese both meanings were accessed at the onset of the ambiguity, but that only the contextually appropriate meaning was accessed at the offset of the ambiguity. Another possibility, then, is that the context-prominence of the language speeds up *selection* of the appropriate meaning, once all meanings have been accessed, as is postulated in (2).[11]

(2) Speeded-selection hypothesis:
    If a language is context-prominent, then the language processor will select the contextually appropriate meaning faster (once all meanings have been accessed) than it would in languages which rely less heavily on context for interpretation. (Ahrens 1998b)

English, on the other hand, which is not postulated to be a context-prominent language, is expected to have both meanings accessed at the offset of the ambiguity, which is what researchers have found (Swinney 1979, Tanenhaus et al. 1979, Onifer and Swinney 1981, Swinney and Love 1996). The Speeded-selection hypothesis, moreover, is not at odds with the modularity hypothesis because it postulates that selection is made faster, but only after all meanings have been accessed.

In Section 5, I will present an experiment that looks at lexical ambiguity resolution at the offset of the noun in Mandarin Chinese. Since Ahrens (1998a,b) found that both meanings were accessed at the onset, if only the contextually appropriate meaning is accessed at the offset, one possible explanation could involve the Speeded-selection hypothesis.

4 Methodological Issues

On-line sentence processing studies on lexical ambiguity resolution have been run for the past twenty years since Swinney (1979). Yet, as can be seen from the discussion in Section 2, there has been no consensus to date on the results or the models to explain these results. This is surprising given the fact that the researchers' general approach has been quite similar; i.e., to determine whether preceding sentential context can influence lexical access. Moreover, although earlier experiments were criticized for not having strongly enough biasing contexts (so as to adequately challenge the modularity hypothesis), later experiments all made sure that the contexts are

---

[11] The Speeded-selection hypothesis is one possible explanation for Li and Yip's (1996) findings at the onset and offset of the ambiguity in Cantonese. I will present another possible explanation concerning methodological issues in the next section.

strongly biasing using off-line tests.[12] But as we will see below, slight variations in other methodological areas have led to differing results.

These variations in methodology, which include modality of presentation, experimental task, position of visual probe, and timing (i.e., length of presentation of visual probe), relate to two fundamental issues in lexical ambiguity resolution: automaticity and immediacy. Any variations in experimental methodology that infringe upon the immediacy and automaticy of lexical access may also interfere with modular processing and therefore cannot be considered an adequate test of the modularity hypothesis.

The concepts of automaticity and immediacy are not new. Fodor (1983) listed them as two of his nine properties that are required for a modular system, although he used the different terms. The summary of the nine properties of modules are that they: are domain specific, are mandatory, allow only limited central access to computations of the module, are fast, are informationally encapsulated, have shallow outputs, are associated with fixed neural architecture, show characteristic and specific breakdown patterns, and exhibit a characteristic pace and sequencing in their development. Automaticity has to do with the fact that the operation of the input systems is mandatory, i.e., "they are constrained to apply wherever they can apply" (Fodor 1983: 53), while immediacy means that the processing must be fast. Obviously, any violation of one of the above nine principles would mean that the conditions for modularity had been violated. My point is that the lexical ambiguity resolution experiments that argue that their findings do not support the modularity hypothesis have, in particular, unknowingly violated these two particular conditions.

Prather and Swinney (1989) also touched upon the issues of immediacy and automaticity, although again under different terms. They write:

> [Lexical] ambiguity resolution is a complex function of at least four general types of issues: (1) The nature of temporal processing requirements during perception (e.g. speed of utterance, speed of required response, etc.). (2) The nature of the available "contextual" information in which the ambiguity occurs. (3) The nature of the processing strategies recruited for analysis (e.g. automatized routines, intentional strategies, linguistic/perceptual vs. problem solving routines, etc.). (4) The nature of the response required of the processing system, or in experiments, of the experimental situation (e.g. passive comprehension, rapid recognition, use of the ambiguity in a novel manner, etc.). The complex-

---

[12] For example, this paper (along with Ahrens (1998a,b)) follows Tabossi's (1987) guidelines for determining a strongly biasing context, and Li and Yip (1998b) follow Marslen-Wilson and Welsh (1978).

ity and interactivity of these issues cannot be overrated. (Prather and Swinney 1989: 290)

Immediacy here relates to the issues brought up in (1), that is, relates to issues of speed. Automaticity relates to the issues mentioned in (3) and (4), namely: are the processing strategies and responses required allowing normal processing to unfold, or are other intentional strategies interfering with the usual processing routines? In the discussion that follows, I will discuss how the modality of presentation, the experimental task, the ambiguous word position, and the presentation time of the visual target relate to either the principle of immediacy or automaticity or to both.

4.1 Modality

Sentence comprehension can occur in two modalities: auditory and visual. Some researchers have conflated these modalities when evaluating lexical ambiguity resolution results (i.e. Simpson 1994). Ahrens (1998b) points out that conflating the auditory and visual modalities is inappropriate for four reasons. First, different areas in the brain deal with different types of incoming stimuli (i.e. the occipital lobe contains the visual cortex and the temporo-parietal lobes contain the auditory cortex), and these different stimuli may be handled with different time courses from one another. Second, speech production and comprehension is learned earlier than reading. Third, speech is the basis for learning how to read. Fourth, reading is carried out at a slower speed than listening. This slower rate means that it is possible in reading experiments that both meanings are first accessed, and then a selection is made, but that the only data that is captured in the reaction times is after the selection has been made. Such data is not evidence for the interaction model (and against the modularity hypothesis) because it is not measuring immediate and automatic access, and the modularity hypothesis only claims to be true for these types of access. In addition, speaking rates below a normal rate of speech would also not be adequate tests of the modularity hypothesis, because slower speaking rates could cause interference with normal listening processes (such as immediate and automatic access of lexical meaning).

Thus, when comparing evidence for and against the competing models, it is necessary to specify the modality of presentation and the rate of speed of auditory presentation, as Ahrens (1998a) does: "To what extent do higher level semantic representations constrain the activity of a lower process (in this case the identification of a word) in natural speech comprehension?"[13]

---

[13] The question asked in Ahrens (1998a) was revised from a question asked in Simpson (1994).

In this paper, I will concentrate on experiments that deal with lexical ambiguity resolution in on-going speech comprehension.

4.2 Task

Cross-modal lexical priming experiments gather precise reaction time data, while allowing the subject to listen to on-going natural speech comprehension. Cross-modal priming experiments consist of a subject listening to a sentence over headphones and making either a lexical decision to a visual target that appears on the screen (cross-modal lexical decision task) or by naming the visual target that appears on the screen (cross-modal naming task). All the sentences that are heard by the subject have been previously recorded to tape or computer by a native speaker of the language, who is speaking at a normal rate of speed. No pause occurs in the auditory presentation of the sentence when the visual target appears on the screen. The subject hears a complete, natural sounding sentence.

The cross-modal priming technique has four advantages. First, subjects are listening to natural sounding sentences just as they would in a non-experimental setting. Second, the position of presentation of the visual target can be synchronized with the audio presentation, allowing for a fine-grained time course analysis of lexical ambiguity resolution. Third, the speed of natural speech does not allow time for conscious reflection on the possible relationship between the words they are hearing in the sentences over the headphones and the visual target (Nicol, Fodor, and Swinney 1994, Swinney and Love 1996). However, this last point applies only to sentence-medial cross-modal naming or cross-modal lexical decision experiments. Testing at the sentence-final position means that sentential wrap-up effects may interfere with priming. In addition, the sentence-final position is not an adequate test of what is happening in *on-going* sentence processing because the subject is naming or making a decision only *after* the entire sentence has been heard. Fourth, the priming task indicates whether the meaning of the word has been accessed or not. Other tasks, such as interference tasks (Glucksberg et al. 1986) do not necessarily reflect lexical access.

Within these tasks, however, there is some variation in methodology. For example, the experiments in Italian use a go/no-go method in their lexical decision tasks (Tabossi et al. 1987, Tabossi 1988, Tabossi and Zardon 1993). A lexical decision task usually means that the subjects press one button if the word they see on the screen is a word, and a different button if the word they see on the screen is a non-word. But in the go/no-go method, the subjects only pressed a button if the string of letters flashing on the screen was a word, and were not supposed to press anything if the string of letters was not a letter. Ahrens (1998b) has pointed out that this means the subjects are not automatically performing an action upon seeing the stimulus. Instead they must make a decision about whether to perform the action or not, which could inhibit the automaticity of the decision. In fact, Tabossi and her colleagues found that only the contextually appropriate meaning was available when the context was biased towards the primary meaning of the ambiguity, but that both meanings were available when the context was biased towards the secondary meaning of the ambiguity. The fact that only the contextually appropriate meaning was found when the context was biased towards the primary sense of the ambiguity indicated to the authors that the modularity hypothesis does not hold. But Ahrens (1998b) questioned their interpretation of their results, since the task they used could have compromised immediacy and automaticity of lexical access. Once immediacy and automaticity is compromised, then the conditions for modular access no longer exist.

Li and Yip (1998) used a different type of cross-modal task, a cross-modal gating task, to look at whether context was able to influence what word was perceived in the gating task and how quickly it was perceived. In this task subjects heard sentences up to the ambiguous word and then heard a portion of the ambiguous word. The subjects wrote down their best guess at the word (which was in fact a one-syllable word) and then listened to the sentence again, this time, with a slightly longer portion of the gated word. They concluded that context played an important role in the processing of Chinese homophones because the gated word was guessed with less than half the acoustic phonetic information.

However, this again is not evidence against the modularity hypothesis because automatic access is not being tested. The gating task is designed to force the subject to integrate preceding information in order to make a guess at the gated word. It is natural that when asked to guess at a word, subjects use preceding context to do so. But it is not a test of modularity since the prerequisite of automatic access is missing. Automatic access takes place without the subject consciously thinking about it. But the gating task used in Li and Yip requires a conscious processing strategy so that the subject can guess the final syllable of a sentence.

In short, when testing whether or not sentential context can influence lexical access, the task must be allow for immediate and automatic access in natural on-going speech comprehension. Any interruptions in the automaticity of access, such as in the go/no-go task or in the gating task, will mean that modularity is not being tested.

4.3 Position of Visual Probe

In this and the next subsection, I will discuss immediacy of access. The first issue involving immediacy has to do with the position of the visual target. Research has shown that a delay of 120ms after the offset of the visual target shows evidence for context influencing lexical access (Simpson 1981). However, since there was a delay from the offset of the ambiguous word, it is not clear that the experiment tested immediate access.

Experiments that positioned the probe at the onset of the ambiguous word such as Ahrens (1998a,b) and Li and Yip (1996) found that both senses were accessed.[14] Experiments that have positioned the probe at the offset of the ambiguous words have been divided in their findings. Ahrens (1998a) looked at the previous literature and found that the results divided along language lines, with work in English indicating that both meanings were access at the offset (e.g. Swinney 1979, Tanenhaus et al. 1979, Onifer and Swinney 1981, Seidenberg et al. 1982, Swinney and Love 1996). However, work in Italian showed that both senses were accessed only when the context was biased towards the secondary sense, but only the contextually-appropriate meaning was accessed when the context was biased towards the primary sense (Tabossi, Columbo and Job 1987, Tabossi 1988, Tabossi and Zardon 1993). Ahrens (1998b) postulated that language differences might be driving these findings (cf. the discussion in Section 3.2). However, her experiment on lexical ambiguity resolution in Mandarin Chinese did not support this hypothesis. She suggested that the other difference between the Italian and English experiments had to do with the length of the visual target demonstration, which we will turn to next.[15]

4.4 Timing

In the experiments run in English, the visual probes were present for either 300ms or 750ms or 1000ms or until the subject responded, whichever was shorter (e.g. Swinney 1979, Tanenhaus et al., 1979, Onifer and Swinney 1981, Seidenberg et al. 1982, Swinney and Love 1996). However, in the

---

[14] Li discounted the 1996 results at the onset of the ambiguous word in Li (1998). He pointed out that since a cross-modal naming task was used, naming the visual target could interfere with listening to the ambiguous word. If that was the case, however, it is still difficult to explain why the primary and secondary naming reaction times were faster than the reaction times to the control words at the onset of the ambiguity.

[15] In addition, she noted that the combination of the task issue (i.e., using the go/no-go lexical decision task) in combination with the length of presentation of the visual target could also be a factor. However, as will become apparent in Section 5, length of visual presentation alone may have driven the results Tabossi and colleagues got.

Italian experiments, the visual probes were presented for 1500ms or until the subject responded (Tabossi, Columbo and Job 1987, Tabossi 1988, Tabossi and Zardon 1993). In all these experiments, the probe was presented at the offset of the ambiguous word. In the Cantonese experiment (Li and Yip 1996) the visual probe was presented for 2000ms or until the subject named the target at either the onset or the offset of the ambiguity. In both the Italian and Cantonese experiments, the contextually appropriate meaning was selected when the context was biased towards the secondary meaning of the ambiguity at the offset of the word. But in the English experiments, both meanings were available even when the context was biased towards the secondary meaning. Moreover, both meanings were available in Cantonese at the *onset* of the ambiguous word.

I hypothesize that it is the length of the presentation (in combination with the position of presentation) of the visual target that created the discrepancy between the findings in English and Italian/Cantonese. That is, in the Italian and Cantonese cases, the *immediacy* of access was compromised by the fact that the visual target was displayed for so long at the offset. This immediacy was not compromised at the onset in Cantonese however, because the position of presentation was earlier. The point is that there is a window of opportunity to view the process of lexical access. Once this window shuts, all that can be viewed are post-lexical-access effects. Under this scenario, what happened in Li and Yip (1996) was that flashing the visual target for up to 2000ms at the offset allowed the window of opportunity to view lexical access to close, while in Swinney and Love (1996) flashing the visual target for only 300ms allowed us to see into that processing window of time.

This is not to say that the subjects' reaction times were slowed at the offset because of the length of presentation of the visual target. It would be difficult to compare such a metric across languages and across subjects. My point is that when the visual target flashes only for 300ms, the subjects are on the edge of their processing capacities. They need to be on the edge in order to glimpse immediate and automatic access. They have already heard the completion of the word and have by this point, at the latest, accessed its meaning.

Needless to say, pushing subjects beyond the edge of their processing capacities would lead to other (artificial) processing strategies which is not useful either. What we need is the window in which to see if modular processing is taking place. It is only through a careful review of previous work that we can gain an insight on where to locate this processing window.

In conclusion, after examining the literature that has argued against the modularity hypothesis, I have found that they compromised either the immediacy or automaticity of lexical access, and as such, cannot be considered adequate data against modularity. I revise the question asked in Ahrens (1998b) to include the concepts of immediacy and automaticity to ask: "To what extent do higher level semantic representations constrain the activity of a lower process (in this case the *immediate and automatic* identification of a word) in natural speech comprehension?"

5 On-line Lexical Ambiguity Resolution Experiments in Mandarin Chinese

In this section, I present the results from two experiments that explore the issue of immediacy. I use a cross-modal lexical decision task and place the ambiguity sentence-medially in order to ensure automaticity. The sentential bias is towards the secondary meaning of the ambiguity. In experiment #1, the visual target is displayed for 300ms, and in experiment #2 it is displayed for 1500ms. If the issue of immediacy is as critical as I hypothesize, then both meanings of the ambiguity should be available when the visual target is presented for 300ms, but only the sententially appropriate meaning should be available when the visual target is presented for 1500ms. This finding would be in line with the modularity hypothesis because it would mean that both available meanings were first accessed and one was later selected. On the other hand, if the interactive hypothesis is correct, then only the sententially appropriate meaning should be available at both the 300ms and the 1500ms visual target presentation.

5.1 Subjects

All subjects used in the pretests and the on-line tests are native speakers of Mandarin Chinese, have lived in Taiwan since birth, and are undergraduate or graduate (M.A. level) students of a national university.[16] In Taiwan, there is usually another language spoken in the home in addition to Mandarin, such as Taiwanese, Hakka, or an Austronesian language. In order to keep the subject pool as homogenous as possible in terms of language background, all subjects used in the following experiments were exposed not only to Mandarin, but also to Taiwanese in the home before the age of seven. In addition, they had no exposure to other dialects or languages before seven.

Subjects were also screened for any brain injury, learning disability, visual impairment, or auditory impairment. All subjects were paid NT$100

---

[16] Mandarin Chinese is the official language that is spoken throughout China and Taiwan by the majority of speakers, who may in addition, speak another regional dialect. In this paper, I focus on the Mandarin Chinese that is spoken in Taiwan.

(equivalent to US$3.60) for their participation, which took approximately one-half hour. The actual number of subjects used in each pretest or experiment is given in each of the appropriate sections below.

5.2 Pretest for Ambiguity Bias

Thirty undergraduates in National Chung Cheng University were presented with ninety disyllabic words (52 nouns, 38 verbs), which had at least two meanings based on the judgments of two linguistically trained native speakers. The words were presented auditorially from an audiotape, since words often have different auditory and visual biases. For each word, subjects were asked to provide first meaning that came to their mind, and then to provide any additional meaning or meanings that came to mind in their respective orders. Tallies of the numbers of the first and second choice for each meaning of the words were carried out.

For the present study, 16 nouns were chosen which had a preference for the primary interpretation (i.e. the primary meaning was given as the first-choice meaning for speakers over 75% of the time); and in addition, the secondary meaning was given as the second-choice meaning for speakers over 60% of the time.

5.3 Pretest -- Visual Probes

Probes for the Primary and Secondary meaning of the ambiguity were chosen by using one of the three most frequently provided associates from the previous pretest above. The following restriction applied: if these associates were not disyllabic, a disyllabic word closely related to the most frequent associate was used. A large number of words equated to the 'related' associates on the bases of frequency, length and form class were included with experimental/related associated words in an isolated lexical decision task. The purpose of the isolated lexical decision task is to determine the lexical decision times of the words *a priori* to running the cross-modal experiment.[17]

Twenty-two subjects from National Taiwan University participated in this experiment. After screening for errors and language exposure, data from twenty subjects were analyzed. The average reaction time for each word in the list was calculated over all subjects. After the average for each word was calculated, a "matched" control word was chosen for each "related" associate for each meaning of the ambiguity (i.e. Primary and Secondary). Over-

---

[17] Although I had reaction time data from National Chung Cheng University students, which was reported in Ahrens (1998b), I ran the reaction time study again at National Taiwan University because I was in a new lab, and because I wanted to the *a priori* reaction time data to come from the same student population as the cross-modal experiment.

all, the mean reaction times for the Primary experimental and control condition was 581ms and for the Secondary experimental and control conditions was 577ms. In addition, the experimental and control conditions were matched across individual items for syllable length, and the frequency of the control conditions was always higher than for the experimental conditions overall. This works against our hypothesis since higher frequency words are more likely to be accessed more quickly. The frequency data was based on written norms (CKIP 1993).

5.4 On-line Cross-modal Experiment with 300ms Visual Target Presentation

5.4.1 Creation and Pretest of Sentential Materials

Experimental sentences were created according to the following criteria. First, the context of each sentence was strongly biased toward the secondary, non-dominant meaning of the ambiguous word tested. Subjects were given the actual experimental sentence up to the point just before the ambiguity and asked to complete the sentence. Following Tabossi et al.'s (1987) criterion for the existence of a strong bias towards one meaning of the ambiguous word, an item was accepted for use in the main experiment only if the completions supplied by at least 75% of all 21 subjects exhibited the contextually favored interpretation. A sample experimental sentence can be found in (3), and the experimental and control visual targets for primary and secondary meanings are given in (4).

(3) tonghua gushi li de wangzi ru yao yingqiu bei kun zai chengbao
 fairy tale story in DE prince if want win BEI confine in castle

 nei de gongchu shi ta bishu guo chongchong de **jiguan** cai neng
 in DE princess when he must pass multiple-level DE **trap** then can

 cong ermo shou zhong qiu hui ta de xinshangren,
 from devil hand middle rescue back he DE loved-one

 yushi congci yihou guo zhe xinfuquaile de rezi.
 then from after live particle happy DE days

 'In a fairy tale, when a prince wants to rescue a princess that is locked up in a castle, he must overcome serious traps in order to rescue the one he loves from evil, so that the two of them can live happily ever after.'
 (Ahrens 1998a: (6a))

(4) Ambiguous word: *jiguan*

	Experimental visual target	Control visual target
Primary meaning (institution)	xingchen 'administration'	xiaoshi 'hour'
Secondary meaning (trap)	xianjin 'trap'	shumian 'report in writing'

(Ahrens 1998a: (6b))

Overall, the number of characters before the ambiguous word ranged from 28 to 40, and the average was 32. The number of characters after the ambiguous word ranged from 25 to 33, and the average was 27.

5.4.2 Design

A script was designed with a total of 42 sentences, 16 experimental sentences and 26 filler sentences. The filler sentences were of approximately the same complexity as the experimental ones in order to deter subjects from creating any sort of strategy while the experiment was progressing. Four lists were constructed so that no one visual probe was linked to a condition more than once to avoid repetition effects. There were 21 non-words and 21 words in each list. The 64 visual probes were matched and rotated through each of the four lists.

5.4.3 Stimulus Presentation

The 42 sentences were recorded by a female speaker to the hard drive of an IBM-compatible Pentium computer with the aid of the Creative Wave sound card using the Creative Wave program. The time from the beginning of the sentence to the offset of the ambiguous word was measured using the same program. This information was then entered into a control list that associated the time of presentation along with each respective sentence and visual probes. At the time of the offset of the ambiguous word, a visual target was flashed on the screen for 300 ms. An internal dedicated CPU in the button box measure the time from the presentation of the visual target until a response was made on the button box or 2000 ms had passed, whichever was earlier. The measurements themselves were made to the nearest millisecond. The sentences occurred in random order, and there was a four second delay between sentences.

5.4.4 Procedure

Subjects sat in front of a computer monitor in a quiet room and were told that they had two tasks. The first task was to listen to and understand the sentences that they heard over headphones. They were told that they would be tested on the comprehension of the sentences at the end of the experiment. The second task was to watch the computer screen and when they saw Chinese characters appear on the screen, they had to decide if the characters made up a word or not. They were told to press the right hand button ('word' button) if they thought it was a word, and to press the left hand button ('non-word' button) if they thought it was not a word. They were asked to keep their fingers on the buttons at all times and to respond as fast and accurately as possible. The auditory presentation of the sentences continued on without interruption even when the visual probe appeared and when subjects were making their decision. The computer screen was covered with a piece of dark gray cardboard with a rectangle cut out of its center so that subjects' attention would be on the center of the computer screen. At the end of the experiment, the subjects were given 10 sentences printed on a sheet of paper and asked to mark which sentences they had just heard.

5.4.5 Subjects

Eighty-four subjects participated in the on-line cross modal lexical decision task. These subjects were all undergraduate students of National Taiwan University. All subjects were screened as described in Section 5.1.

5.4.6 Results

It was determined a priori that the following subjects would be excluded from the data analysis: 1) those who were exposed to both Mandarin and Taiwanese before the age of 7; 2) those who had brain injury, learning disability or other abnormal mental behavior; 3) those who had more than 15% errors on the experimental items (including no response); 4) those who had more than 20% errors on comprehension test. In all, 84 subjects were run in the experiment. Based on the *a priori* decisions described above, 44 subjects were excluded from the data analysis—9 had errors over 15% on the experimental items and 36 had errors over 20% on comprehension test (i.e. more than 2 wrong out of 10 questions).[18] The data from 40 valid subjects were tallied and means were calculated below in Table 1.

---

[18] The percentage of errors on comprehension test was higher than expected. We attributed this result to a possible factor that no practice sentences were presented to the subjects beforehand to help them be more familiar with how the experiment was going. We therefore added a practice section in the second experiment.

Meaning of the ambiguity	Visual Target 300ms	
	Related	Control
Primary	754*	811
Secondary	743*	801

*significant difference between related and control

Table 1: Mean reaction times in ms

There was a main effect of experimental of experimental vs. control groups, $F(1,36) = 12.592$, $p < .001$. This effect was examined for two *a priori* comparisons between the experimental and control conditions for the primary meaning as well as for the secondary meaning. There was a significant effect for the primary condition $F(1,36) = 6.045$, $p < .01$. There was also a significant effect found for the secondary condition $F(1,36) = 6.300$, $p < .01$.

5.4.7 Discussion

The evidence found in this experiment supports the hypothesis that both meanings are accessed even in the face of a contextually-biased preceding sentential context when the presentation of the visual target is 300ms at the offset of the ambiguity. This is evidence in support of a context-independent model of lexical access. We next look at whether or not both meanings are accessed when the preceding context is biased, and the length of presentation of the visual target is 1500ms at the offset.

5.5 On-line Cross-modal Experiment with 1500ms Visual Target Presentation

5.5.1 Subjects

Fifty-three subjects participated in this experiment. In addition to the language and education screening that was determined in experiment 1, it was also determined that these subjects had not participated in experiment 1 or any other preliminary experiments.

5.5.2 Methodology

The sentences, stimulus presentation and procedure was the same as for experiment 1, with two differences. The first difference was that subjects were given a practice session of 5 sentences before the actual experiment in order to familiarize themselves with the procedure.

Second, the visual probe flashed onscreen for 1500ms. This is the critical difference. In the first experiment, the visual probe flashed for only 300 ms. We are hypothesizing that the longer probe time is giving context a chance to select a meaning from the ones already accessed. If this is true, it would explain why some researchers found for context effects, namely because the visual target was around long enough for it to select a meaning *after* both meanings had been accessed. It would argue against the proposal that context allowed only the contextually appropriate meaning to be accessed, because as we have seen in Experiment 1, both meanings are available when the visual target is presented for 300ms.

5.5.3 Results

Fifty-three subjects were run in the experiment. Based on the screening decisions described in 5.4.6, 13 subjects were excluded from the data analysis— 1 had errors over 15% on the experimental items, 1 was exposed to three languages before the age of seven, and 10 had errors over 20% on comprehension test (i.e. more than 2 wrong out of 10 questions). 1 subject did not finish the experiment. The data from 40 valid subjects were tallied and means were calculated as below in the righthand column in Table 2.

Meaning of the ambiguity	Visual Target 1500ms	
	Related	Control
Primary	788	810
Secondary	748*	810

*significant difference between related and control

Table 2: Mean reaction times in ms

There was a main effect of experimental of experimental vs. control groups, $F(1,36) = 12.727$, $p < .001$. This effect was examined for two *a priori* comparisons between the experimental and control conditions for the primary meaning as well as for the secondary meaning. There was no effect for the primary condition $F(1,36) = 1.751$, $p = .1$ There was, however, a significant effect found for the secondary condition $F(1,36) = 15.251$, $p < .001$.

5.5.4 Discussion

The results demonstrate that when the length of the presentation probe is 1500ms, only the contextually appropriate meaning is still available. Since I showed in the first experiment that both meanings were available at the offset of the ambiguity when the visual probe was presented for 300ms, the fact that only the contextually appropriate meaning was available at 1500ms indicates that the non-contextually appropriate was initially available, but then faded. This is precisely what a context-independent model of lexical ambiguity resolution predicts.

6 Conclusion

In this paper I presented the particular models that are associated with either the context-dependent or context independent account. I also discussed the evidence that pertains to each model. In addition, I argued that extensive homophony was not a unique design characteristic of Mandarin, although Mandarin did have certain grammatical characteristics that might argue for the necessity of speeding up the decision-making process at a lexical ambiguity. I also pointed that the issues of immediacy and automaticity must be taken into consideration when evaluating and designing lexical ambiguity resolution experiments.

I proposed that timing issues relating to the presentation of the visual probe are at the crux of the current stalemate between researchers who argue for either a context-dependent or context-independent view of language processing. I tested this hypothesis by looking at ambiguity resolution in Mandarin Chinese. I tested for the activation of both meanings at the offset position when the sentential context is biased toward the secondary meaning of the ambiguity. Using a cross-modal lexical decision experiment, I demonstrated that both meanings of an ambiguity are semantically primed when the visual target is presented for 300ms, but only the contextually appropriate meaning is accessed when it is presented for 1500ms. This supports the hypothesis that timing issues are critical in determining whether or not lexical access can be influenced by context. In short, I have found evidence that the multiple access account within a context independent model is supported when lexical access is immediate and automatic. Moreover, I did not find evidence that the grammatical characteristics of Mandarin Chinese, which indicate that context is necessary for propositional interpretation, need to be invoked to explain the processing findings. Instead, Mandarin Chinese is behaving similarly to English in terms of lexical ambiguity resolution.

In future research, it will be necessary to test if the multiple-access model or the ordered-access model is more appropriate. This question can be tested by biasing the sentential context towards the primary meaning of the word. Finding that both meanings are accessed when the context is biased towards the dominant meaning is strong evidence for the multiple-access hypothesis. However, finding that only the contextually appropriate meaning is accessed would be evidence for either the ordered-access model or the frequency and context model. In the latter case, it would then be necessary to look at ambiguous words with more than two meanings to distinguish between these two accounts, as I discussed at the end of Section 2.2.

In sum, the evidence points to modularity as the underlying design characteristic of immediate and automatic lexical access. However, this is not to say that the entire language processing system is necessarily run by the principles governing modularity. Li and Yip (1998) demonstrated that context does play an critical role when the subject is guessing a gated, ambiguous word. This task, while not conforming to the principles underlying modularity, can tell us about the conscious decision-making processes that the language processor goes through to solve a particular linguistic problem. Thus, the questions that face researchers in the future should no longer be: is lexical access modular? Instead, they should be: under what conditions does modularity hold? Under what conditions does interaction take place? And, what do these results indicate for understanding the millisecond-by-millisecond time course of language processing?

References

Ahrens, K. 1998a. Lexical Ambiguity Resolution of Verbs in On-line Sentence Comprehension. *International Conference on Chinese Linguistics.* Paper presented for the IACL Young Scholar Award, June 26-28, Stanford University. To appear in the *Journal of East Asian Linguistics.*

Ahrens, K. 1998b. Lexical Ambiguity Resolution: Languages, Tasks and Timing. *Sentence Processing: A Crosslinguistic Perspective,* ed. D. Hillert. San Diego: Academic Press.

CKIP. 1993. *Corpus-Based Frequency Count of Words in Journal Chinese.* Taipei: Academia Sinica, Chinese Knowledge Information Processing Group.

Chao, Y.-R. 1938. *A Grammar of Spoken Chinese.* UC Berkeley Press.

DeFrancis, J. ed. 1996. *ABC Chinese-English Dictionary.* University of Hawaii Press.

Fodor, J. 1983. *Modularity of the Mind.* Cambridge: MIT Press.

Glucksberg, S., R. Kreuz, & S. Rho. 1986. Context Can Constrain Lexical Access: Implications for Models of Language Comprehension. *Journal of Experimental Psychology: Learning, Memory & Cognition* 12:323-335.

Hogaboam, T. & C. Perfetti. 1975. Lexical Ambiguity and Sentence Comprehension. *Journal of Verbal Learning & Verbal Behavior* 14:265-274.

Huang, C.-R., C.-R. Chen, & C. C.C. Shen. 2001. The Nature of Categorical Ambiguity and Its Implications for Language Processing: A Corpus-based Study of Mandarin Chinese. *Sentence Processing in East Asian Languages,* ed. M. Nakayama. Stanford: CSLI Press.

Huang, C.-R. 2000. From Quantitative to Qualitative Studies: Developments in Computational and Corpus Linguistics of Chinese. *Sinological Studies* 18:473-509.

Huang, C.-R., K. Ahrens & K.-J. Chen. 1998. A Data-driven Approach to the Mental Lexicon: Two Studies on Chinese Corpus Linguistics. *Bulletin of the Institute of History and Philology*. Taipei: Academia Sinica.

Li, P. & M. Yip. 1996. Lexical Ambiguity and Context Effects in Spoken Word Recognition: Evidence from Chinese. *Proceedings for the 18th Annual Meeting of the Cognitive Science Society*. Hillsdale, NJ: Earlbaum.

Li, P. 1998. Crosslinguistic Variation and Sentence Processing: The Case of Chinese. *Sentence Processing: A Crosslinguistic Perspective*, ed. D. Hillert. San Diego: Academic Press.

Li, P. & M. Yip. 1998. Context Effects and the Processing of Spoken Homophones. *Reading & Writing: An Intedisciplinary Journal* 10:223-243.

Marslen-Wilson, W. & A. Welsh. 1978. Processing Interactions and Lexical Access During Word Recognition in Continuous Speech. *Cognitive Psychology* 10:29-63.

McClelland, J. 1987. The Case for Interactionism in Language Processing. *Attention and Performance XII: The Psychology of Reading*, ed. M. Coltheart. Hillsdale, NJ: Earlbaum.

Nicol, J., J. D. Fodor, & D. Swinney. 1994. Using Cross-modal Lexical Decision Tasks to Investigate Sentence Processing. *Journal of Experimental Psychology: Learning, Memory & Cognition* 20.5:1229-1238.

Onifer, W. & D. Swinney. 1981. Accessing Lexical Ambiguities During Sentence Comprehension: Effects of Frequency of Meaning and Contextual Bias. *Memory & Cognition* 15:225-236.

Prather, P. & D. Swinney. 1988. Lexical Processing and Ambiguity Resolution: An Autonomous Process in an Interactive Box. *Lexical Ambiguity Resolution: Perspectives from Psycholinguistics, Neuropsychology and Artificial Intelligence*, eds. S. Small, G. Cottrell, & M. Tanenhaus. San Mateo: Morgan Kaufmann Publishers.

Seidenberg, M., M. Tanenhaus, J. Leiman, & M. Bienkowski. 1982. Automatic Access of the Meanings of Ambiguous Words in Context. *Cognitive Psychology* 14:489-537.

Simpson, G. 1981. Meaning Dominance and Semantic Context in the Processing of Lexical Ambiguity. *Journal of Verbal Learning & Verbal Behavior* 20:120-136.

Simpson, G. 1994. Context and the Processing of Ambiguous Words. *Handbook of Psycholinguistics*, ed. M. Gernsbacher. San Diego: Academic Press.

Swinney, D. 1979. Lexical Access During Sentence Comprehension: (Re)consideration of Context Effects. *Journal of Verbal Learning & Verbal Behavior* 18:645-660.

Swinney, D. & T. Love. 1996. Co-reference Processing and Levels of Analysis in Object-relative Constructions: Demonstration of Antecedent Reactivation with the Cross-modal Priming Paradigm. *Journal of Psycholinguistic Research* 25:5-29.
Sproat, R. & C. Shih. 1990. A Statistical Method for Finding Word Boundaries in Chinese Text. *Computer Processing of Chinese Oriental Languages* 4:336-351.
Tabossi, P. 1988. Accessing Lexical Ambiguity in Different Types of Sentential Context. *Journal of Memory & Language* 27:324-340.
Tabossi, P., L. Colombo & R. Job. 1987. Accessing Lexical Ambiguity: Effects of Context and Dominance. *Psychological Research* 49:161-167.
Tabossi, P. & F. Zardon. 1993. Processing Ambiguous Words in Context. *Journal of Memory & Language* 32:359-372.
Tanenhaus, M., J. Leiman, & M. Seidenberg. 1979. Evidence for Multiple Stages in the Processing of Ambiguous Words in Syntactic Contexts. *Journal of Verbal Learning & Verbal Behavior* 18:427-440.
Xiandai Hanyu Cidian. 1985. [Modern Chinese Dictionary]. Beijing: Commercial Press.

2

Resolution of Reanalysis Ambiguity in Japanese Relative Clauses: Early Use of Thematic Compatibility Information and Incremental Processing*

YUKI HIROSE

1 Introduction

This paper is an ongoing analysis of a series of studies on relative clause processing in Japanese, which is assumed to involve temporary ambiguity not only in the first-pass stage but also in the reanalysis stage. Particularly, we consider the proposal made by Hirose and Inoue (1998) that in resolving a structural ambiguity in reanalysis, information regarding the possible thematic role that the head noun can play in the candidate structures is used prior to, or as early as the decision made by the structure-driven preference principle or strategy. In this paper we will first review the previous studies

---

* This research is part of the doctoral dissertation of the author (Hirose 1999). I thank the members of my dissertation committee and the audience at the International East Asian Psycholinguistics Workshop. The experimental program was developed at Ohio State University. I thank Hiroko Yamashita and Mineharu Nakayama for making it available for this study. I thank Satoru Nakai at Doshisha University and Kazuhiko Kakehi at Nagoya university for their support in obtaining subjects.

Sentence Processing in East Asian Languages.
Mineharu Nakayama (ed.).
Copyright ©2002, CSLI Publications.

by Hirose and Chun (1998) and Hirose and Inoue (1998) about the early influence of the thematic factor and then pose the question of whether thematic cues are *always* a necessary basis for structural decisions. The discussion will then address issues of strict incrementality in reanalysis, which is the chief concern of this paper.

The studies under discussion here concern the contrast in processing difficulty between sentences such as (1) and (2) discussed in Mazuka and Itoh (1995).

(1) Yoko$_i$-ga   kodomo-o [e$_i$ e$_j$ koosaten-de   mikaketa] takusii$_j$-ni
    Yoko-Nom child-Acc   intersection-Loc saw   taxi-Dat

   noseta.
   put on

   'Yoko put the child into the taxi she saw at the intersection.'

(2) Yoko-ga [e$_j$ kodomo-o koosaten-de   mikaketa] takusii$_j$-ni
    Yoko-Nom   child-Acc intersection-Loc saw   taxi-Dat

   donatta.
   yelled at

   'Yoko yelled at the taxi which/whose driver saw the child at the intersection.'

Standard serial processing models assume that a parser had initially favored a single clause analysis of the material up to the initially encountered verb *Yoko-ga   kodomo-o koosaten-de mikaketa* which would generate the meaning 'Yoko saw the child at the intersection'. Reanalysis is initiated when the subsequent head noun (e.g. *takusii*, 'taxi') indicates such an analysis is incorrect. However, a further temporary ambiguity arises regarding the type of relative clause to compute: The sentence could be analyzed as one having a structure such as (1) or (2), depending on the position the relative clause gap must be postulated. The relative clause gap is postulated in the subject position in (2), whereas it is postulated in the object position in (1) in which the empty category in the subject position is supposed to be an empty pronoun associated with the matrix subject.[1] This

---

[1] As Hirose and Inoue note, it may be possible to interpret the empty category in the subject position in (1) to be the relative clause gap, and the empty category in the object position to be

ambiguity will eventually be resolved by type of other noun phrases or matrix verb encountered. In (1), the matrix verb requires an *o*-marked direct object; therefore it becomes apparent that *kodomo-o* is a matrix clause constituent. On the other hand, the matrix verb *donatta* in (2) does not take an *o*-marked NP as its object, and thus it becomes obvious that *kodomo-o* must be an object of the relative clause verb.

Mazuka and Itoh (1995) propose that in sentences such as (2), reanalysis is not costly because only the subject NP "must be taken out of the lower clause" (p. 307) while reanalysis in (1) is costly because "both the subject and the object NPs need to be taken out of the lower clause" (p. 307) where "the lower clause" refers to the originally constructed clause. Based on Mazuka and Itoh's characterization, we will henceforth refer to structures such as (2) as *Subject Reanalysis* (or SR) structures and to structures such as (1) as *Subject and Object Reanalysis* (or SOR) structures. This terminology is convenient, although such terms imply movement of the subject and object out of the original clause.[2]

In some models (although assumption about the mechanism varies: Gibson 1991, Lewis 1993, Fodor and Inoue 1994, 1998, Gorrell 1995a, 1995b), the nature of the SR/SOR contrast is characterized as one between processable structures and structures that are unprocessable by the normal processing routine; SOR is predicted to be a severely difficult structure. This type of accounts which attribute severe difficulty to the SOR analysis may be called *parse-failure accounts*. For other models (Inoue 1991, possibly Frazier and Clifton 1998, Sturt and Crocker 1996), SOR is difficult at the sentence-final disambiguation only (or primarily) because it is not selected when the SR/SOR ambiguity first arises, and hence must be created by reanalysis operations when the need for SOR becomes apparent later. These models assume an initial preference for SR that derives from some structure-based processing principle or strategy. Such a principle may be a least-effort principle which favors SR *because* it is associated with a lower processing cost. Such accounts of SR/SOR structures can be referred to as *garden-path accounts*.

---

an empty pronoun coindexed with the matrix object. However, such reading is not readily obtainable to all native speakers. At present, we do not consider this possibility.

[2] For some theories assuming that a single clause is initially constructed in processing of (1) and (2), this may not accurately describe the process by which a relative clause structure is established (e.g., Gorrell 1995, Sturt and Crocker 1996, who describe the operation by which a relative clause structure is obtained as "tree lowering").

2 Previous Studies

Hirose and Chun (1998) and Hirose and Inoue (1998) argue that the difficulty associated with SOR types can be diminished by changing its lexical content as shown in (3).

(3) Yoko$_i$-ga   kodomo-o [e$_i$ e$_j$ hiroba-de   mikaketa] buranko$_j$-ni
     Yoko-Nom child-Acc   square-Loc   saw   swing-Dat

     noseta.
     put on

     'Yoko put the child onto the swing she saw at the square.'

In (3), the head noun *takusii* 'taxi' is replaced with *buranko* 'swing' and to maintain plausibility, 'intersection' is replaced with 'square'. Let us compare this with (1). At the point of the parse at which 'taxi' in (1) is received, and recognized as a head noun, its semantic content allows it to be interpreted not only as an object of the verb 'see' but also as a subject, metaphorically meaning 'the driver of the taxi'. That is, 'taxi' can be either AGENT (EXPERIENCER) of 'see' and hence associated with a subject gap in the relative clause, as was shown in (2), or THEME of 'see' and hence associated with an object gap.

A difference in the position of the gap often correlates with a difference in the position of the left edge of the relative clause boundary, i.e., which items in the word string belong to the relative clause and which to the matrix clause. In particular, in the SR/SOR ambiguity, a gap in subject position entails that the overt subject phrase must be in the matrix clause, no longer a clause-mate of the overt object phrase. A gap in object position implies that both the overt subject and the overt object are matrix constituents. The left boundary of the relative clause follows the subject in SR, and follows the object in SOR. The construction can thus be disambiguated in principle either via gap position or via clause boundary position. If the parser is sensitive to the thematic relation between the head noun and the embedded verb, it can decide at 'swing' in (3) that both the subject and the object should be analyzed as being outside the relative clause (SOR). In (1), however, at the head noun 'taxi', the parser cannot decide between the two possible reanalyzes, one which reanalyzes only the subject (SR) and the other which reanalyzes both the subject and the object (SOR).

Thus, temporary structural ambiguity in reanalysis can be resolved at the head noun in (3) but not in (1), if the parser can make use of lexical information about a head noun, e.g. its animacy. This information can determine the plausibility of the noun's fit to the thematic roles that the relative clause verb can assign. We call this *thematic compatibility information* (to be distinguished from thematic information in the sense of the set of thematic roles selected by a verb). As we discussed, for animate head nouns and a relative clause verb of the appropriate kind, there is more than one plausible thematic role the noun could be assigned. We refer to this situation as one involving thematic-role-ambiguity. On the other hand an inanimate noun cannot usually (if non-metaphoric) take an AGENT role, but only THEME or some adjunct type.

A whole-sentence reading time experiment reported in Hirose and Chun (1998) shows that (i) an SOR sentence such as (3) was read notably faster than (1), and (ii) no significant difference in reading time was found between an SOR sentence such as (3) and an SR sentence such as (2), which contains the same head noun but a different sentence-final matrix verb. The facilitating effect of a plausibility mismatch between the head noun and the subject role of the embedded verb is also discussed in Sturt and Crocker (1996).

The results led to a suspicion that it is incorrect to assume that severe difficulty is inevitably associated with the processing of SOR sentences and that it may not be difficult to compute the SOR structure when it is clear from the outset that SOR is required, i.e., when only SOR is thematically acceptable at the head noun. Based on these results, Hirose and Chun support garden-path accounts over parsing-failure accounts which claim that SOR is not merely unpreferred, but inherently problematic and perhaps unprocessable by the normal parsing routines. For theories presenting garden-path accounts of the additional difficulty of SOR processing (e.g., Frazier and Clifton 1998, Inoue 1991, Sturt and Crocker 1996), the contrast in reading times at the matrix verb depending on the ambiguity of the noun is explicable as long as it is assumed that the parser prefers SR to SOR at the head noun and this would have to be a structure-based preference in garden path models. An SR choice at the role-ambiguous noun would lead to a problem when the matrix verb disambiguates toward SOR, hence garden path at the matrix verb. However, Hirose and Chun's study does not identify specific points in the sentence, if any, which identify the origin of the contrast.

An experiment presented in Hirose and Inoue (1998) attempted to determine the point at which the effect of thematic compatibility is reflected in reading times; i.e., at the site at which the thematic compatibility information first becomes available, or later where the SR/SOR is finally disambiguated. Sentences of the same three types used in Hirose and Chun were constructed, and were tested in a frame-by-frame self-paced reading experiment. (4a-c) below illustrates the example sentences divided into frames.[3]

(4)   Frame 1   Frame 2   Frame 3   Frame 4 ...
       roojin-ga   sutego-o   atikoti kiite   sagasita
       old man-Nom orphan-Acc by asking in various places looked for

    a.   ...Frame 5   Frame 6   Frame 7   Frame 8
        bokusi-ni   tootoo   takusukotonisita   ○
        priest-Dat   finally   decided to entrust

'The old man finally decided to entrust the orphan to the priest who he looked for by asking in various places.'

    b.   ...Frame 5   Frame 6   Frame 7   Frame 8
        sisetu-ni   tootoo   takusukotonisita   ○
        orphanage-Dat   finally   decided to entrust

'The old man finally decided to entrust the orphan to the orphanage which he looked for by asking in various places.'

    c.   ...Frame 5   Frame 6   Frame 7   Frame 8
        bokusi-ni   tootoo   aukotonisita   ○
        priest-Dat   finally   decided to meet

'The old man finally decided to meet the priest who looked for the orphan by asking in various places.'

In the comparison between SOR and SR sentences with role-ambiguous head nouns, e.g., (4a) versus (4c), the outcome was consistent with Hirose and Chun. These pairs were identical except for the matrix verb, and the positions of interest were therefore restricted to the end of the sentence. At the matrix verb, Frame 7, where the ambiguity as to relative clause type is resolved, no significant difference between SR and SOR sentences emerged, nor was any significant difference evident at the following maru (the Japanese equivalent of the English period symbol) frame.

---

[3] Rated plausibility of the content expressed by the three types of sentences used in the experiment did not show any reliable difference. For details of these experiments, see Hirose (1999).

The major comparison of our interest here is one between SOR role-ambiguous and SOR role-unambiguous sentences, e.g. (4a) versus (4b).[4] This is illustrated in Figure 1 below (adopted from Hirose and Inoue).

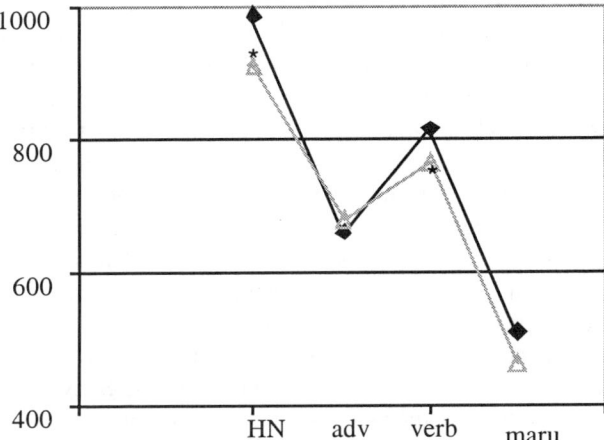

Black: Head noun role-ambiguous
Gray: Head noun role-unambiguous
(Final disambiguation to SOR at the matrix verb)

Figure 1. Mean reading times (in milliseconds) per frame, as a function of sentence type

This comparison showed that at Frame 5 (the head noun) thematic-role ambiguity led to significantly longer reading times. At the following AdvP position, Frame 6, no reliable difference in reading times was found but at the matrix verb position, Frame 7, and the subsequent maru position, Frame 8, SOR sentences with a role-ambiguous head noun again yielded significantly longer reading times than those with an unambiguous head noun. Arguably the effect observed at the head noun and the matrix verb positions must have independent sources, since reading times did *not* differ at the adverb position which intervened between these.[5]

---

[4] The lexical items used as head nouns were not matched in frequency within items. Instead, a separate experiment was conducted to ensure that the average reading times for role-ambiguous and role-unambiguous nouns used in the main experiment did not differ significantly when they were presented out of the sentential contexts.

5 One could argue for some alternative accounts of these findings which need to be considered. Some parallel models (e.g., Just and Carpenter 1992, MacDonald, Pearlmutter,

The results observed at the role-ambiguous and unambiguous head noun position ((4a,c) vs. (4b)) pose a question to standard garden path accounts. In fact, an ambiguity-induced cost at the very site of ambiguity is quite unexpected in standard garden path theories (Frazier 1978). These models posit that when deciding which type of relative clause to build (SR or SOR), in the absence of any syntactic disambiguation, the parser's priority is to base its decision on structurally-grounded reanalysis principles or strategies. That is, a candidate structure would be initially selected without reference to head noun content. Thematic compatibility information would be used only subsequently in a follow-up assessment of the candidate's viability. Sturt and Crocker's (1996) "tree-lowering" model of reanalysis, among others, is an instantiation of this procedure.

This ordering of parser priorities does not lead to an account of the experimental results that head noun content has an *immediate* consequence, with role-ambiguous head nouns being read more slowly than role-unambiguous head nouns. Role-ambiguous head nouns, by design, have semantic content that is compatible with both SR and SOR structures; thus, processing of the head noun should go through smoothly regardless of what structural decision was made, since a thematic check will discover a plausible interpretation whichever structure was selected. Role-unambiguous nouns, by design, fit the SOR structure and are incompatible with the SR structure; thus, processing would be disrupted if the parser's structural choice were SR when the implausible interpretation detected by the second-stage check (e.g., 'an orphanage looking for something') results in rejection of the SR structure. Therefore, it is role-unambiguous nouns that will be predicted to induce processing disruption, the opposite of the reading time pattern observed. The observed cost of ambiguity is thus not explained.

Hirose and Inoue thus propose that when syntactic information is absent, the parser tries to select an appropriate relative clause structure by *first* (before applying structural preference principles) consulting thematic compatibility information that enables it to assess which thematic roles the noun can plausibly fit. When the head noun allows only one thematic role, the parser can simply accept the structure that is thematically indicated.

---

and Seidenberg 1994) would predict that the parser carries out parallel computation of both possible relative clause analyses in the case of sentences with a role-ambiguous head noun, and that this is the cause of their greater processing cost for the role-ambiguous noun than for the role-unambiguous noun. However, this is not compatible with the fact that no reading time difference was observed at the adverb position following the head noun. The temporal separation of the processing costs at the head noun (Frame 5) and the matrix verb (Frame 7) suggests that two different phenomena are occurring. At least by the adverb, it seems that a choice between relative clause structures has been made.

However, when the head noun is role-ambiguous, i.e., compatible with more than one thematic role, thematic compatibility information necessarily fails to specify a unique analysis. If parsing is incremental, the parser needs to make a decision, but in this situation it has neither syntactic nor thematic information as a basis for that decision. In order to settle on one relative clause structure it must find some other criterion to apply. Thus, encountering a role-ambiguous head noun would result in a period of indecisiveness while encountering a role-unambiguous head noun would not.

In fact, a somewhat different evaluation of alternatives can be implied if it is assumed instead that thematic information and structural preferences are applied simultaneously in resolving ambiguity. This assumption is consistent with constraint-based account (Juliano and Tanenhaus 1994, MacDonald 1994, Tanenhaus, Carlson, and Trueswell 1989) although at present we are limiting our discussion to the issue of ambiguity resolution in reanalysis. Under this approach, it might be possible to explain the longer reading times evinced at the ambiguous head noun in Hirose and Inoue's experiment as a product of the competition between two opposed preferences applied simultaneously. In order to correctly predict not only the competition at the role-ambiguous head noun but also the absence of competition at the role-unambiguous head noun, we would have to assume that the latter combination (ii), i.e., a thematic-driven preference toward AGENT (or EXPERIENCER), and some other source of preference toward SOR. No such preference is supported by any existing theories under consideration. However, it is possible to argue for a structure-based preference toward SOR in a number of ways. For example, if Sturt and Crocker (1996) assumed a language-universal bottom-up search strategy for node insertion, the SOR structure would be predicted as preferred. Hirose and Inoue (1998) also note a possible processing advantage for SOR arising from the fact that the matrix subject and the relative clause subject are co-indexed, thus creating a 'parallel-subject' structure. If some such basis for SOR preference can be assumed, the competition between the two biases would be manifested in elevated reading times at the role-ambiguous head noun. By contrast, no such competition should arise at the role-unambiguous (THEME-only) noun, for which the two constraints are compatible in reanalysis preference.

The results of Hirose and Inoue do not distinguish between the thematic-indecisiveness account and the competing-preferences account proposed above. This question remains open in this paper, and we will focus on the matter of when these decision principles (whatever are the right ones) are initiated.

3 Questions about Incrementality in Relative Clause Processing

Given the proposal that reanalysis decision is primarily influenced by thematic consideration, our next question addresses whether SR/SOR reanalysis decisions *need* to be driven by thematic-compatibility information.

Most models that we have considered assume that parsing is strictly incremental (Inoue and Fodor 1995, Gorrell 1995a, Sturt and Crocker 1996, Frazier and Clifton 1998, among others), i.e., that every item is given its place in the current partial phrase marker (CPPM) as it is encountered. An incremental full-attachment (non-delay) parser thus circumvents the enormous delays of semantic interpretation, given that in Japanese the verb is not normally encountered until the very end of the clause. This contrasts with a head-driven model (Pritchett 1991, 1992) in which structure building is delayed until the head of that category is processed. A number of studies have argued for attachment of argument and adjunct NPs to VP and IP nodes before the verb (the head of the clause) is encountered (Yamashita, 1994, Inoue and Fodor 1995, Mazuka and Itoh 1995, Hirose 1995, Kamide 1998). These observations support the incrementality of phrase structure assignment to the input word string. However, none of these studies has focused specifically on the issue in the context of reanalysis, although it seems more than natural to assume that the incrementality applies to the reanalysis stage as well. But there is a case which may present a challenge to such an assumption.

Consider the pair of sentences in (5a, b) below. These are modified version of the two types of SOR sentence previously studied in Hirose and Chun and Hirose and Inoue. In both sentences types, as in the first two conditions in the previous experiments, the final verb provides disambiguation in favor of SOR, and one type has a thematically ambiguous head noun, while the other has a thematically unambiguous (THEME-only) head noun. However, unlike the items in the previous experiments, the head nouns are preceded by an adjective which is able to modify either animate or inanimate nouns, and hence which does not disclose the thematic status of the head noun.

(5) a. roojin-ga   sutego-o   atikoti kiite   sagasita
        old man-Nom orphan-Acc by asking in various places looked for

   ryoosintekina bokusi-ni   tootoo   takusukotonisita.
   good   priest-Dat finally   decided to entrust

   'The old man finally decided to entrust the orphan to the good priest who he looked for by asking in various places.'

b. roojin-ga   sutego-o   atikoti kiite   sagasite
    old man-Nom orphan-Acc by asking various places looked for

   ryoosintekina   sisetu-ni   tootoo   takusukotonisita
   good   orphanage-Dat   finally   decided to entrust

   'The old man finally decided to entrust the orphan to the good orphanage which he looked for by asking in various places.'

In a head-driven parsing a relative clause construction is not postulated at the adjective, because the relative clause is a constituent of a complex NP, whose head (the head noun) has not yet been encountered. Thus no reanalysis of the single-clause analysis to a relative clause structure is activated at the adjective.

For an incremental full-attachment parser, the syntactic cue for relative clause reanalysis in these examples is the adjective, since it indicates that a head noun will follow. The first question that we raise is whether the parser attempts to build a particular relative clause structure upon encountering the post-verbal adjective. Even if a relative clause construction can be recognized at the adjective because the adjective predicts a noun category (which in this case must be the head noun of a relative clause), the decision as to what kind of relative clause should be built could be postponed until the head noun is received, if the parser tries to make its reanalysis decision on the basis of thematic information carried by the head noun when syntactic disambiguation is lacking. The head noun might provide the thematic information which the adjective in these sentences fails to provide, so even an incremental parser might sacrifice its incrementality in order to wait and see if such information may be provided. Such a strategy is not necessarily inconsistent with some theories of reanalysis, because reanalysis, by its nature, involves operations on an already computed phrase-marker, over which processing of all the other sources of information including thematic information have had an opportunity to run. On the other hand, if the parser is strictly incremental, regardless of whether thematically related information is present or absent, the parser will be constrained to create a relative clause at the adjective in (5). The decision about the type of relative clause - or a decision about its gap position (and which NPs are in the matrix versus relative clause) - is forced, and this decision must be made by means other than either syntactic or thematic information. If the parser has a preference toward either SR or SOR, the decision will be made accordingly.

Between SR and SOR, SR would be a reasonable choice according to most theoretical proposals about structure-based parsing preferences (Inoue 1991, Sturt and Crocker 1996, Frazier and Clifton, 1998). SR would also be the most likely choice if the parser's preference is thematically based, since it is often observed that the AGENT role ranks higher than other roles such as THEME, for items compatible with both. However, we noted that an SOR preference must be postulated as competing with an AGENT preference on the competing-preferences account discussed above.

Thus the incremental approach predicts that the same factors should be at work at the adjective in sentences like (5) as at the noun in the experiment in Hirose and Inoue.[6] Thus, the absence of syntactic or thematic disambiguation should make processing harder (the ambiguity cost of Hirose and Inoue), but an SR preference should emerge (in at least a substantial number of cases).

This should cause easier processing of a subsequent animate noun than of an inanimate noun which is incompatible with the SR reading. If, on the other hand, no SR/SOR decision is made at the adjective, the pattern of reading times at the head noun and at subsequent positions should not differ from those in the experiment reported in Hirose and Inoue: An ambiguity

---

[6] There is a possible difference, that is of interest. Arguably, the adjective in (5) is *neutral* (not ambiguous) with respect to the animacy of a noun that can follow, and in the absence of animacy information, the default principle which links animacy to probable thematic roles is not activated. Therefore, unlike the head nouns in Hirose and Inoue (which we take to be *ambiguous* between specific thematic roles), it could be that the adjectives in examples (5) do not even speak to evaluation of what role would be possible for the head noun. Examples in English of this kind of neutrality are adjectives like *good*, *strange*, or *tall*, which can be applied appropriately to persons and objects. By contrast, adjective such as *kind* or *wooden* apply exclusively to animate and inanimate entities respectively. It is reasonable to assume that an inanimate-only adjectives such as *semakurusii* 'cramped, unspacious' could bias the parser toward an SOR decision. (Strube, Hemforth, and Wrobel 1990, claim that thematic information can occur at a prenominal adjectives in English; they found a processing cost for an animate-preferring adjective such as *blond* in an ambiguous context favoring an INSTRUMENTAL role, e.g., *Peter watched the girl with ...*) But animacy-neutral adjectives might fail to activate any thematic evaluation, so they would not present the parser with an SR/SOR choice. If so, then possibly no thematic default would be applied, in which case any structural default would show up clearly in the absence of competition. This is a possibility that deserves to be pursued in future research but we will not discuss it further here.

cost at the animate noun, followed by a garden-path at the matrix verb (SOR disambiguation) for sentences with a role-ambiguous (animate) head noun.

4 Experiment

A frame-by-frame self-paced reading task was employed to measure processing load at different positions in sentences modeled on the two types of SOR sentence employed in the experiment in Hirose and Inoue (see (4a) and (4b), earlier): One type has a thematically role-ambiguous head noun, and the other a thematically role-unambiguous (THEME-only) head noun. The construction of materials differed from the previous experiment only in that an adjective was inserted which modified the head noun, e.g. 'ryoosintekina' (good, conscientious). The adjective was presented in a separate frame occurring between the relative clause verb and the head noun. The adjectives in the present experiment were selected to be equally natural as modifiers of animate and inanimate nouns.

4.1 Method

4.1.1 Subjects

Twenty-four undergraduate students from Doshisha University and Nagoya University participated successfully in the experiment, twelve in each of the two versions of the experiment. All were native speakers of Japanese, and naive with respect to the purpose of the experiment. Subjects typically took twenty to thirty minutes to complete the experiment.

4.1.2 Materials and Design

The experimental sentences were constructed to form pairs, differing only in their head nouns (animate/inanimate), and were identical to the two types of SOR sentences used in Hirose and Inoue except for the presence of an adjective preceding the head noun.[7] The sentences were divided into nine frames, as illustrated in (6a-b) below. Frames 1 through 5 were identical across the two sentence types. The positions at which reading times are of interest were Frame 6, the head noun; Frame 7, an adverbial or prepositional phrase; and Frame 8, the matrix verb. Frame 9 was a maru.

---

[7] One might suspect that some adjectives used in the experiment (as the one in the example) had a bias toward an AGENT and also that the head nouns that were intended as inanimate noun allowed animate interpretation, like 'orphanage' as implying the administration of the institution. It is possible that the intended contrast was weakened, and so were the observed effects.

(6)   Frame 1   Frame 2   Frame 3   Frame 4
         roojin-ga   sutego-o   atikoti kiite   sagasita
         old man-Nom orphan-Acc by asking in various places looked for

    a.   Frame 5   Frame 6   Frame 7 Frame 8   Frame 9
        ryoosintekina   bokusi-ni tootoo   takusukotonisita o
        good   priest-Dat finally   decided to entrust

       'The old man finally decided to entrust the orphan to the good priest who he looked for by asking in various places.'

    b.   Frame 5   Frame 6   Frame 7 Frame 8   Frame 9
        ryoosintekina sisetu-ni   tootoo   takusukotonisita o
        good   orphanage-Dat finally decided to entrust

       'The old man finally decided to entrust the orphan to the good orphanage which he looked for by asking in various places.'

There were twenty-four such sentence pairs, and the two sentences in each pair differed only in the identity of their head noun (e.g. *bokusi/sisetu*), one of which was role-ambiguous and the other compatible only with THEME role. The adjectives appearing in Frame 5 were selected to be equally compatible with the role-ambiguous (animate) head nouns and their role-unambiguous (inanimate) counterparts appearing in Frame 6. This was checked informally by consulting three native speakers.[8,9]

---

[8] Informants were asked to judge if the modification of each noun in a pair by the adjective was either 3 ("natural"), 2 ("neither natural nor weird (in between)"), or 1 ("weird"). Only those pairs in which both combinations of adjective and noun were predominantly judged to be "natural" were used as experimental items.

[9] An additional frame-by-frame self-paced experiment was conducted which was intended to rule out the possibility that any systematic difference in goodness-of-fit between the adjectives and the two types of the nouns used in the experiment that might affect reading time. As examples (ia-b) below illustrate, the experimental items were simplex sentences with the same matrix verbs and matrix arguments as the corresponding sentences in the main experiment.
(i)a.   Frame 1   Frame 2   Frame 3   Frame 4
       roojin-ga   ryoosintekina   bokusi-ni   tootoo
       old man-Nom   good   priest-Dat   finally
       Frame 5   Frame 6
       sutego-o   takusukotonisita   o
       orphan-Acc   decided to entrust
       'The old man finally decided to entrust the orphan to the good priest.'

There were sixty-six filler sentences in total including twenty-four SR-type sentences to avoid biasing subjects toward the SOR reading, since all the experimental items were SOR-type relative clause constructions in this experiment. An example SR filler sentence is shown in (7) below.

(7) itamae-ga ryoori-o kiniiranakatta joorenkyaku-ni   ikinari donatta
     chef-Nom dish-Acc disliked   customer-Dat   suddenly yelled at
     'The chef suddenly yelled at the customer who disliked the dish.'

The experimental materials (twenty-four pairs, thus forty-eight items) were distributed over two versions of the experiment in a counterbalanced design, so that the twenty-four experimental items within each version were made up of twelve instances of each of two conditions, without repetition of sentential content.

For all sentences used in the experiment (including fillers), comprehension questions were prepared to which a YES/NO response was required.

4.1.3 Procedure

The sentences were presented on a computer screen, one frame at a time, each ending with a *maru*, under the control of a custom-made Hypercard program on a Macintosh computer. Each sentence and question was displayed at a fixed central position on the liquid-crystal screen of a Macintosh Powerbook.

Presentation of the first frame of a sentence was initiated when the subject first pressed the return key on a standard computer keyboard, which was labeled 'YES' in English; with each subsequent key press, a new frame immediately replaced the previous display. The key press following the final display (*maru*) initiated display of a question about the content of the sentence, to be answered by pressing either the YES key or the tab key labeled 'NO'. The time between the onset of presentation of any frame and the key press initiating the next frame was recorded as reading time, in

b.	Frame 1	Frame 2	Frame 3	Frame 4
	roojin-ga	ryoosintekina	sisetu-ni	tootoo
	old man-Nom	good	orphanage-Dat	finally
	Frame 5	Frame 6		
	sutego-o	takusukotonisita	o	
	orphan-Acc	decided to entrust		

'The old man finally decided to entrust the orphan to the good orphanage.'

No significant difference between the two types of sentences was found at the adjective frame, or any frame that followed it. Details of this experiment are described in Hirose (1999).

milliseconds.

Some consideration was given to the speed of performance, given that the reading times reported in Hirose and Inoue were somewhat slow. The experimenter supervised the practice trial of each subject individually, and advised subjects to try to perform the reading task at a reasonable speed.[10]

4.1.4 Data Treatment

Reaction times greater than 3000 milliseconds were rejected as outliers, and this trimming procedure affected 0.9% of the data. Also, any data point that was less than 100 milliseconds was similarly rejected. Finally, values falling beyond cutoffs established for each subject at mean plus-or-minus two standard deviations were replaced with those cutoff values.

4.2 Results and Discussion

Table 1 below shows the mean reading times for the five frames that were relevant, i.e. Frames 5 through 9, for each SOR sentence type.

Frame	5 Adj	6 Head N	7 AdvP	8 MatrixV	9 maru
Head Noun Type					
Ambiguous	572	590	413	662	416
Unambiguous	570	623	486	586	367

Table 1. Mean reading times (in milliseconds) per frame, as a function of head noun type

The comparison between role-ambiguous and unambiguous SOR sentences showed that at Frame 6 (head noun), thematic-role ambiguity led to reading times that were, overall, thirty-three milliseconds shorter than those for thematically unambiguous head nouns, though the difference did not reach significance ($F_1(1,22) = 2.30$, $p > .10$, $F_2(1,22) = 1.13$, $p > .10$). At the following Frame 7 which presented an adverbial phrase (AdvP), sentences with ambiguous head nouns yielded reading times seventy-three milliseconds shorter than those with unambiguous head nouns, and the effect was highly significant ($F_1(1,22) = 11.61$, $p < .005$, $F_2(1,22) = 9.48$, $p <$

---

[10] If a subject's performance was unexpectedly slow and unlike normal reading behavior, an additional instruction was offered (in Japanese) as follows: 'You look as if you were trying to memorize each word to be able to answer the question. However, the questions will be simple enough so that most of the time you will be able to answer without having to memorize the sentence word-by-word. Actually, other people typically go a little faster. You can proceed as if you were reading the sentences under normal circumstances.'

.01). At the matrix verb position, Frame 8, the direction of reading time differences reversed; now, SOR sentences with an ambiguous head noun yielded reading times longer by 76 milliseconds than those with an unambiguous head noun ($F_1(1,22) = 9.54$, $p < .01$, $F_2(1,22) = 8.25$, $p < .01$). A difference in the same direction was found at the maru position ($F_1(1,22) = 9.19$, $p < .01$, $F_2(1,22) = 6.30$, $p < .05$). The RT data are shown in Figure 2 in a plot together with the data from Hirose and Inoue for comparison.[11]

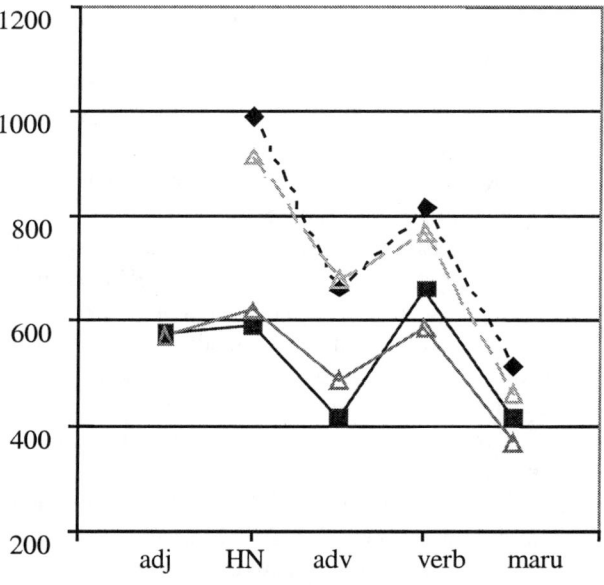

Solid lines: Results of the present Experiment
Dotted lines: Results of Hirose & Inoue's experiment
Black: Head noun role-ambiguous
Gray: Head noun role-unambiguous
(Final disambiguation to SOR at the matrix verb)

Figure 2. Mean reading times (in milliseconds) per frame, as a function of sentence type

---

[11] The reading times of the present experiment are generally faster than those of Hirose and Inoue's experiment. This appears to be a reflection of the fact that we gave a special instructions to the subjects whose performance in the practice session seemed slow. (See footnote 13.)

The reading times at the matrix verb (Frame 8, with spillover onto the *maru*) showed the same pattern as in Hirose and Inoue's experiment: Head-ambiguous SOR sentences were associated with longer reading times than head-unambiguous SORs. This can be interpreted as a garden path effect resulting from the parser's prior commitment to SR. However, reading times at the head noun (Frame 6) and the adverb (Frame 7) did not show the same pattern as the Hirose and Inoue study. Overall, the pattern of costs associated with thematic-role ambiguity of a head noun that was found in Hirose and Inoue's experiment was not replicated in the present experiment, in which the input first signaling the relative clause structure was not the head noun itself but rather an adjective modifying the head noun, appearing in a preceding frame. That is, it was *not* the case that ambiguous head nouns led to slower reading at early stages of the relative clause analysis: Hirose and Inoue's "ambiguity cost" was absent. Instead, the longer reading times at the adverb position following an *unambiguous* noun suggest that the parser did not delay relative clause reanalysis until the head noun was received, but made a commitment at the adjective to SR.

Let us consider further the longer reading times observed for the adverbial phrase following an unambiguous THEME-bias head noun, compared to the same phrase following an ambiguous head noun. It can reasonably be assumed, since the content is identical, that the reading time difference found at this position is a delayed effect of the preceding head noun. Similar "delayed" garden path effects are frequently reported in self-paced reading studies (e.g. Yamashita, Stowe, and Nakayama 1993) and even eye-movement studies (e.g. Traxler, Pickering, and Clifton 1998). Thus we conclude that an unambiguous THEME head noun causes more difficulty than an ambiguous noun. This is consistent with the parser's making an SR choice at the prior adjective position on at least some proportion of trials. Whenever an SR analysis was selected at the adjective, it would turn out to be incompatible with the thematically unambiguous head noun which allows only the SOR analysis; there would be no such incompatibility between an SR decision at the adjective and a following ambiguous noun.

4.3 General Discussion

The critical finding of the present experiment is that when the head noun was preceded by an adjective signaling a relative clause but not its gap position, reading of the noun was faster for role-ambiguous head nouns than for role-unambiguous (THEME-only) nouns.

If reanalysis decisions regarding the type of relative clause were always deferred until the head noun is available, the reading time pattern at the head noun and the final matrix verb would not have differed from that of the experiment in Hirose and Inoue: i.e., reading time for the ambiguous head noun should have been longer than that for the unambiguous head noun. Thus we conclude that the reanalysis decision was made at the adjective.

The current results indicate that not only initial parsing decisions but also reanalysis decisions are made without delay. As soon as the incorrect initial single-clause analysis of a relative clause is falsified, a reanalysis decision is made concerning the relative clause structure including the position of the relative clause gap. It could be expected that the parser would find it helpful to wait just a word or two for more relevant information such as thematic compatibility information provided by another modifier and/or the head noun. (Of course there is no *guarantee* that these later words will be any more informative than the initial animacy-neutral adjective, but there is a good probability that they will.) Thematic compatibility information, as we have seen, can be very useful in deciding on the correct relative clause structure and it is in fact in many cases the only useful cue for doing so. The fact that the parser does *not* wait for such information suggests that its decision making is strongly incremental.

5 Conclusion

We started with the question of whether plausibility relations between nouns and thematic roles is the cause of informally observed difficulties in processing SOR relative clause structures. In Hirose and Inoue, it was shown that this complicating effect of thematic role ambiguity arises at the very site of ambiguity, i.e., the head noun, suggesting that the SR/SOR reanalysis decision is being made there. In contrast, in the present experiment, the ambiguity cost disappeared when the head nouns were preceded by a thematically uninformative adjective. Based on these outcomes together, we argued that the parser makes use of thematic compatibility information when it is available, no later than the application of structure-based preference principles (if any). Thus, one conclusion is that structure-based preferences are not the primary means of resolving relative clause ambiguity in Japanese.

Another conclusion to be drawn which is important is that, when thematic compatibility does not select a unique reanalysis, the parser does not delay its reanalysis decision-making (until the next word). As we have demonstrated, temporary structural ambiguity abounds in Japanese not only in the initial parsing phase but also in reanalysis. Thematic compatibility information is a very useful cue especially in this language in which availability of syntactic cue is considerably low. Our question was whether the parser sacrifices its incrementality when the useful thematic compatibility information is predicted to be provided shortly. Our results suggest that parsing is strictly incremental in the reanalysis stage as well as in the first-pass stage.

We have discussed possible candidate factors which affect the reanalysis choice in processing Japanese relative clauses. These include structure-based SR preferences such as least-effort principle, a thematic-based preference favoring an AGENT role rather than THEME for the relative clause gap, and some structure-based SOR preference as discussed in Hirose & Inoue. At present, we cannot offer a definitive conclusion as to what are the exact factors at play, but it is apparent from the present study that the answer is probably quite complex. In fact, additional factors have been found in other studies. For example, in speech, relative clause ambiguity can often be resolved by means of prosodic information which signals the presence of a clause boundary, as has been shown in Uyeno, Hayashibe, Imai, Imagawa, and Kiritani (1980). Hirose, Inoue, Fodor, and Bradley (1999) recently observed that constituent length of the sentence-initial noun phrase also has an influence on SR/SOR ambiguity resolution which they propose is an effect of prosodic phrasing of the silently-read sentences. In the future research, consideration of these other factors would be essential.

References

Fodor, J. D. & A. Inoue. 1994. The Diagnosis and Cure of Garden Paths. *Journal of Psycholinguistic Research* 23:407-434.

Fodor, J. D. & A. Inoue. 1998. Attach Anyway. *Reanalysis in Sentence Processing*, eds. J. D. Fodor & F. Ferreira, 101-141. Dordrecht: Kluwer Academic Publisher.

Frazier, L. 1978. On Comprehending Sentences: Syntactic Parsing Strategies. Doctoral dissertation, University of Connecticut, Storrs. Distributed by the Indiana University Linguistics Club, Bloomington.

Frazier, L. & C. Clifton, Jr. 1998. Sentence Reanalysis and Visibility. *Reanalysis in Sentence Processing*, eds. J. D. Fodor & F. Ferreira, 143-176. Dordrecht: Kluwer Academic Publisher.

Gibson, E. A. F. 1991. A Computational Theory of Human Linguistic Processing: Memory Limitations and Processing Breakdown. Doctoral dissertation. Carnegie Mellon University.

Gorrell, P. 1995a. *Syntax and Parsing*. Cambridge: Cambridge University Press.

Gorrell, P. 1995b. Japanese Trees and the Garden Path. *Japanese Sentence Processing*, eds. R. Mazuka & N. Nagai, 331-350. Hillsdale: Erlbaum.

Hirose, Y. 1995. Garden Paths and Minimal Everything Principles in Japanese Relative Clauses. Poster presented at the 8th Annual CUNY Conference on Human Sentence Processing, University of Arizona, Tucson.

Hirose, Y. 1999. Resolving Reanalysis Ambiguity in Japanese Relative Clauses. Doctoral dissertation, The City University of New York.

Hirose, Y. & S. Chun, 1998. Attachment Ambiguity in Head Final Languages. *Japanese and Korean Linguistics* Vol 7, eds. N. Akatsuka et al., 311-327. Stanford: CSLI. Distributed by Cambridge University Press.

Hirose, Y. & A. Inoue. 1998. Ambiguity of Reanalysis in Parsing Complex Sentences in Japanese. *Syntax and Semantics 31: A Cross-linguistic Perspective*, ed. D. Hillert, 71-93. New York: Academic Press.

Hirose, Y., J. D. Fodor, A. Inoue, & D. Bradley. 1999. Evidence for an Effect of Implicit Prosodic Phrasing on Ambiguity Resolution in Reanalysis. Paper presented at the 12th CUNY conference on Human Sentence Processing, The City University of New York.

Inoue, A. 1991. A Comparative Study of Parsing in English and Japanese. Doctoral dissertation, University of Connecticut.

Inoue, A. & Fodor, J. D. 1995. Information-paced Parsing of Japanese. *Japanese Sentence Processing*, eds. R. Mazuka & N. Nagai, 9-63. Hillsdale: Lawrence Erlbaum Associates.

Juliano, C. & M. K. Tanenhaus. 1994. A Constraint-based Lexicalist Account of the Subject/object Attachment Preference. *Journal of Psycholinguistic Research* 23:459-471.

Just, M. A. & P. A. Carpenter. 1992. A Capacity Theory of Comprehension: Individual Differences in Working Memory. *Psychological Review* 99:122-149.

Kamide, Y. 1998. The Role of Argument Structure Requirements and Recency Constraints in Human Sentence Processing. Doctoral dissertation, University of Exeter.

Lewis, R. L. 1993. An Architecturally-based Theory of Human Sentence Comprehension. Doctoral dissertation, Carnegie Mellon University.

MacDonald, M. C. 1994. Probabilistic Constraints and Syntactic Ambiguity on the Processing of Syntactic Ambiguity. *Cognitive Psychology* 24:56-98.

MacDonald, M. C., N. J. Pearlmutter, & M. S. Seidenberg. 1994. The Lexical Nature of Syntactic Ambiguity Resolution. *Psychological Review* 10:676-703.

Mazuka, R. & K. Itoh. 1995. Can Japanese Speakers Be Led Down the Garden Path? *Japanese Sentence Processing*, eds. R. Mazuka & N. Nagai, 295-329. Hillsdale: Lawrence Erlbaum Associates.

Pritchett, B. 1991. Head Position and Parsing Ambiguity. *Journal of Psycholinguistic Research* 20:251-270.

Pritchett, B. 1992. *Grammatical Competence and Parsing Performance*. Chicago:

University of Chicago Press.
Strube, G., B. Hemforth, & H. Wrobel. 1990. Resolution of Structural Ambiguities in Sentence Comprehension: On-line Analysis of Syntactic, Lexical, and Semantic Effects. *The 12th Annual Conference of the Cognitive Society*, 558-565. Hillsdale: Erlbaum,
Sturt, P. & M. Crocker. 1996. Monotonic Syntactic Processing: A Cross-linguistic Study of Attachment and Reanalysis. *Language & Cognitive Processes* 11:449-494.
Tanenhaus, M. K., G. N. Carlson, & J. C. Trueswell. 1989. The Role of Thematic Structures in Interpretation and Parsing. *Language & Cognitive Processes* 4:211-234.
Traxler, M. J., M. J. Pickering, & C. Clifton, Jr. 1998. Adjunct Attachment Is Not a Form of Lexical Ambiguity Resolution. *Journal of Memory & Language* 39:558-592.
Uyeno, T., H. Hayashibe, K. Imai, H. Imagawa, & S. Kiritani. 1980. Comprehension of Relative Clause Construction and Pitch Contours in Japanese. *Annual Bulletin of Research Institute of Logopedics and Phoniatrics* 14:225-236.
Yamashita, H. 1994. Processing of Japanese and Korean. Doctoral dissertation, Ohio State University.
Yamashita, H., L. Stowe, & M. Nakayama. 1993. Processing of Japanese Relative Clause Constructions. *Japanese and Korean Linguistics* Vol. 2, ed. P. Clancy, 248-263. Stanford: CSLI. Distributed by Cambridge University Press..

3

The Nature of Categorical Ambiguity and Its Implications for Language Processing: A Corpus-based Study of Mandarin Chinese[*]

CHU-REN HUANG, CHAO-JAN CHEN AND CLAUDE C.C. SHEN

1 Introduction

Ambiguity is a "design characteristic" of the human cognitive system, even though scientific endeavors generally regard ambiguity as an evil that must be avoided at all cost in a representation system. Ambiguities are also costly to resolve in any psychological or computational model of language processing (e.g. Small et al. 1988, Gorfein 1989, Schutz 1997, Ahrens 1998). However, the understanding of ambiguity may hold the key to the understanding of human cognition.

In this paper, we take an empiricist approach toward a descriptive account of the nature of categorical ambiguity in Chinese. The two assump-

---

[*] The authors would like to thank Kathleen Ahrens for her helpful comments on various versions of this paper. The comments of the participants of the 1999 International East Asian Psycholinguistics Workshop as well as colleagues at CKIP, Academia Sinica, are appreciated. The research conducted here was partially supported by grant 89-2420-H-001-002 from the National Science Council of Taiwan, ROC. Any remaining errors are, of course, our own responsibility.

Sentence Processing in East Asian Languages.
Mineharu Nakayama (ed.).
Copyright ©2002, CSLI Publications.

tions of this study are that i) categorical ambiguity is lexical by nature, i.e. a word is categorically ambiguous only when it is assigned multiple categories in the lexicon; and that ii) lexical representation of grammatical categories must be attested by actual use.

Based on the above assumptions and given the fact that it is still impossible to enumerate contents of any individual mental lexicon (Huang 1995), we base our exploration on the information of an annotated corpus: the 5 million word segmented and tagged Sinica Corpus (Chen et al. 1996). A lexicon of over 140,000 entries is compiled based on the corpus. Any entries that are assigned more than one category in the corpus are considered categorically ambiguous. We will answer the following questions based on the data:

a) What is the degree of categorical ambiguity in a natural running text?
b) Will the size of category sets affect the degree of ambiguity?
c) Are some natural classes more ambiguous than others (Gentner 1981)?
d) Is there always a strong default in categorical ambiguities?

Results reported here will have important implications for both computational and psycholinguistics, as well as the fundamental issue of knowledge representation in cognitive science.

2 Background

2.1 Premises

We will show in this paper that corpus-based approaches are highly relevant to the study of human language processing and have important insights to offer to its theory. In particular, we will show that corpus-based approaches allow us to study ambiguity globally and systematically as an integral part of human grammatical representation. Such approaches, we claim, lead to better understanding of the nature of ambiguity as well as of the human linguistic system.

Our three premises are that:

a) ambiguity is a "design characteristic" of the human cognitive system,

b) corpora offer reliable empirical data of active ambiguity in human language processing, and
c) ambiguity must be introduced lexically.

First, resolution of ambiguity is a recurring topic in studies of both psychological and computational language processing (e.g. Small et al. 1988, Schutz 1997). It is also a central issue in linguistic semantics (e.g. Lyons 1977, Pustejovsky 1995). In contrast, artificial languages, including those intended to be spoken by people, tend to be ambiguity-free. To truly understand the human cognitive system, we feel that it is inadequate to take discovery and accounting of strategies or algorithms of ambiguity resolution as theoretical aims. If the observation that ambiguity is one of the defining features of human grammatical representation is correct, then it is theoretically more pertinent for language processing studies to account for why ambiguity exists rather than how to resolve it. And of course, knowing the "why's" should help us to implement the "how's" in a principled way with better results.

Second, if ambiguity is taken to be a design characteristic of human language, then it is the role that ambiguity plays in a grammatical system that is critical to the theory of language and cognition. In other words, we want to know what conceptual or representational issues in human language and cognition induce ambiguity in grammar. To answer this essential question, we must study a complete grammar and make generalizations over all possible ambiguities. However, current psycholinguistic experiments allow us to study ambiguity only locally. In addition, since it is not possible to describe directly and completely the mental grammar of any given person, it is also not possible to extract formal properties from such grammatical systems.

Huang (1994) argues that "a grammar of language X" cannot be defined in the Chomskyan sense as the final mental states of individual language acquisition. Adopting Chomsky's (1995) UG-type definition, assuming that speaker of the same language share a grammar, it leads to the conclusion that a child acquires the grammar of his/her parents. However, since our parents acquired the grammar of their parents, and so on, the argument implies that contemporary Chinese share the same grammar as first century (or earlier) Archaic Chinese, which is a simple and straightforward fallacy.

On the other hand, if each individual mental grammar is taken to be different, there is still a need to describe the "sameness" of the set of "grammars" that form the "language" as shared by a given speaker community, such as English or Chinese. If this "sameness" is to be defined according the

Chomskyan mental grammar, then we will lead to the same fallacy as above.[1]

Huang (1994) concludes that "(t)he grammar of any given language L is the set of shared (linguistic) knowledge of the speakers of L". If this position is adopted to account for the notion of "the grammar of language L", then the only realistic alternative to study grammar of a language L is to study a comprehensive subset of actual language use shared by speakers of a language. We claim that corpora offer such a fragment. In particular, since a balanced corpus contains language production produced by a wide range of speakers and accepted for comprehension by the majority of speakers, we assume that it contains reliable empirical data of active ambiguity in the language. By "active" ambiguity, we refer to the ambiguities that are instantiated in language uses. In other words, study of ambiguities in a corpus allows us to approximate the nature of ambiguity in a grammatical system.

Third, in order to study ambiguity, we need to know the sources of ambiguity. Although linguists talk about different types of ambiguity such as lexical ambiguity, structural ambiguity, and contextual ambiguity, it is a simple fact of the grammar that no meaning can be accessed unless it is represented in the mental lexicon. Even for the so-called structural ambiguity (e.g. PP attachment), it is a prerequisite that the words involved in the structures are lexically encoded to allow either interpretation.[2] In other words, it is the lexicon that provides the full range of ambiguities. The ambiguity-inducing contexts (lexical collocation, structure, discourse contexts etc.) actually restrict ambiguity to certain alternatives. To sum up, in accordance with a lexicalist and modular view of grammar, ambiguity is representational in nature and must be introduced lexically.

2.2 Goals

In this study, we concentrate on categorical ambiguity. This is because 1) grammatical categories are better defined and 2) category-tagged corpora are available for study. Based on the above premises, we identify the goals for this study as: first, to establish the distribution of categorical ambiguity

---

[1] Note that this cannot be accounted for by invoking the langue/language distinction of Saussure. If the distinction were between individual language use and the system of langue, then we will induce that there is only one langue for all human beings, again contradicting Saussure's original definition of langue as the grammatical system shared by speakers of a given language (i.e. English or French).

[2] It is worth noting that, similar to Pustejovsky (1995) we take ambiguity to be a representational and interpretational issue, not a processual issue. In other words, a linguistic item is only ambiguous when its representation allows multiple interpretations. Constructions such as garden path sentences allow only one interpretation. Thus, while being misleading and costly processing-wise, they are not ambiguous.

in the language. This includes how often categorical ambiguity occurs in the language, as well as the distribution of the categories involved when ambiguity does occur. One of the expected results of this study will be the baseline performance benchmark of categorical ambiguity resolution. In practice, we will take the expected performance of ambiguity resolution with lexical information alone as the baseline. This benchmark can be used then to measure the success of a computational category tagging or ambiguity resolution algorithm. It can also be used as a parameter to measure whether an ambiguity resolution task is successfully completed in a human language processing experiment. Second, in order to better understand the nature of categorical ambiguity in human languages, we will extract generalizations involving categorical ambiguity. In particular we would like to establish correlations between categorical ambiguity data and lexical factors. For instance, we will look into the correlation between categorically ambiguity and frequency, categories, syllabic length, etc. Third, our ultimate goal is to model the lexical representation of categorical ambiguity. Our first steps towards a theoretical model will include the description and account of default category, as well as a comparative study of the effect of the size of the categorical set on degree of ambiguity.

3 Methodology

As mentioned above, since it is not possible to examine a complete individual mental lexicon, we extract our data from a corpus instead. A corpus is treated as collective language use of the population for the following two reasons. First, a corpus is the collection of the language production of all the authors/speakers involved. And second, a corpus, especially a balanced one, is a representative sample of language comprehension data received by the majority of the speakers. In the first sense, a corpus is the instantiation of the collection of individual active lexicons. In the second interpretation, a corpus is the instantiation of a shared passive lexicon of the language. In this study of categorical ambiguity, we assume the second interpretation in our account.

As a logical consequence to our corpus-based approach, we take an empirical definition of categorical ambiguity. In other words, all and only forms which have attested instantiation with more than one category in the corpus are considered categorically ambiguous. While we cannot rule out the possibility of un-instantiated lexical ambiguity, such rare un-instantiated instances will have at most a marginal effect on the result of our statistical characterization of the entire corpus.

Based on the above assumption, each instance of the categorically ambiguous lexical item in the corpus represents an instance of successful resolution of the lexical ambiguity. Thus, our task is straightforward: to examine all such instances in the corpus, and to extract generalizations that will shed light on the nature of categorical ambiguity as well as its interaction with other grammatical elements.

3.1 Data

The corpus we use is Sinica Corpus 3.0., i.e., version 3.0. of the Academia Sinica Balanced Corpus for Modern Mandarin (Chen et al. 1996). It was completed in 1995 and contains 5 million words of modern Taiwan Mandarin. The data includes mostly written texts as well as a small portion of transcribed spoken texts. These texts are mostly from the 80's and early 90's. Each text is segmented to mark word boundary and each word is tagged with grammatical category. The segmentation and tagging were machine-aided. In other words, automatic segmentation and tagging were performed by machine to give human taggers the raw material to work with. The human taggers then either accept the machine-given default or assign a new boundary/category according to his/her analysis. Each tagged and segmented text is crossed-checked by both human and machine to eliminate inconsistency and human error. In addition to local versions, Sinica Corpus is available on the web for search and use: http://www.sinica.edu.tw/ftms-bin/kiwi.sh.

3.2 Tagset: The Set of Grammatical Categories Chosen

There are forty-six (46) categories used in the Sinica Corpus for tagging. This category set is a modified version based on Chao (1968), and described in CKIP (1995). The number of categories is of the same scale as many modern day corpora in other languages. Hence it allows altogether 2,070 (=46x45) possible pairs of two-way ambiguity. However, only 1,375 pairs are attested in the corpus. The number of non-attested pairs is 695. We will be looking into these pairs in the future to decide which of them are genuinely impossible, as well as if there is any linguistic motivation or explanation for the absence of such types of ambiguity.

In addition, when the Sinica Corpus data was used in constructing a digital museum/library site, the category set was reduced to thirteen for the general public that we expect to reach. Linguists as well as elementary school teachers were involved in deciding the set of thirteen categories such that they are both linguistically felicitous and pedagogically intuitive (Huang 1999). The thirteen generalized categories and their corresponding subcategories are listed below in Table 1. Please see Chen et al. (1996), as well as online help at the Sinica Corpus website, for a definition of the complete category set.³

Generalized Tag	Category Name	Equivalent Complete Categories
1. A	Adjective	A
2. C	Conjunction	Caa, Cbb
3. ADV	Adverb	Da, Dfa, Dfb, Dk, D
4. ASP	Aspect (marker)	Di
5. N	Noun	Na, Nb, Nc, Ncd, Nd, Nh
6. DET	Determiner	Neu, Nes, Nep, Neqa
7. M	Measure (word)	Nf
8. T	Particle	I, T, DE
9. P	Preposition	P
10. Vi	Intransitive Verb	VH, VA, VB, VI
11. Vt	Transitive Verb	VAC, VC, VCL, VD, VE, VF, VG, SHI, VHC, VJ, VK, VL, V-2
12. POST	Postposition	Ng, Neqb, Cab, Cba
13. FW	Foreign Word	FW

Table 1. Generalized and complete category sets for Sinica Corpus

The variation in the categorical sets brings up the issue of the psychological reality of sets of grammatical categories. While the psychological reality of a single category is easy to justify with either distributional/linguistic data or with psychological experiments, it is far more difficult to justify a complete system of categorization, such as the system of grammatical categories. We are not aware of any previous empirical attempt to justify the choice of a system of grammatical categories. The usual practice is simply to adopt an established linguistic account. However, we observe that corpus and computational linguistics often adopts a category set much larger than that adopted by psycholinguistic work. The size that a computational work adopts varies from 40 to 100. For instance, the British National Corpus has sixty-five parts of speech, while a recent French corpus under construction adopts over forty categories (Abeille 1998). On the other hand, a typical category set a psycholinguistic work adopts is between ten and twenty. For instance, Redington et al. (1995) justified their reduction of the Sinica Corpus category set to eleven by mentioning that the typical

---

³ FW (Foreign Word) is theoretically speaking not a grammatical category. However, it is a necessary corpus tag especially in this age of high tolerance of multi-lingualism and frequent code-switching. The generalized category set will contain twelve categories, and the complete set forty-five categories, if FW is not counted.

number of grammatical categories used in psycholinguistics is less than a score.

While it is beyond the scope of this current study to test for the validity of a given system of grammatical categories, we would still like to shed some light on the observed disparity of categorical set size chosen by psychological and computational linguists. Take Redington et al. (1995) for example again, the paper and other related simulation work proved that a simple distributional learning mechanism can acquire grammatical categories from unanalyzed linguistic data. However, since no categorical set has been independently verified as psychologically real and as the goal of language acquisition, it is justifiable to ask if the same result can be obtained when a different categorical set is adopted, especially one that differ substantially in scale. In this current study of categorical ambiguity, we will compare the data involving both the generalized and the complete category sets of Sinica Corpus. Since these two sets are both linguistically well-motivated and one subsumes the other, it can be argued that their only difference is in their size. Thus, the result of the comparative study will tell us if the choice of size of category set affects the nature of categorical ambiguity.

3.3 Basic Distribution

To sum up the introductory section, we would like to clarify the basic facts regarding syllabification of Mandarin Chinese. On one hand, Chinese is often claimed to be a monosyllabic isolating language. Even though this may be historically true, the modern language is definitely not monosyllabic. On the other hand, it has also been repeatedly claimed recently that Mandarin Chinese is undergoing disyllabification and disyllabic words are dominant in modern usage. This also proves to be overexaggeration. Our complete statistics of token and type distribution of Sinica Corpus shows that while disyllabic words dominate the lexicon (i.e. type distribution), they do not exceed 50% (Diagram I). While disyllabic words take up 46.06% of all lexical entries, monosyllabic words take up a mere 2.73%.

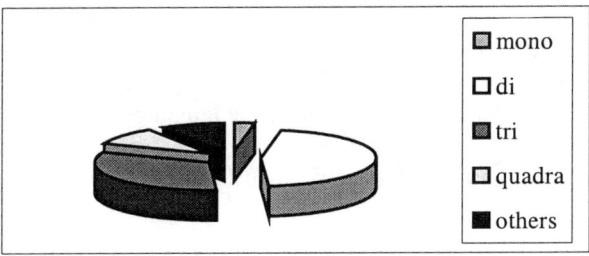

Diagram Ia. Distribution of word types in Sinica Corpus by syllable length

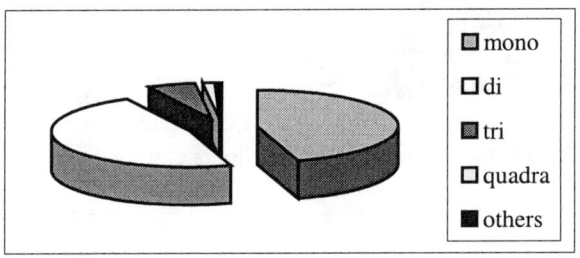

Diagram Ib. Distribution of word tokens in Sinica Corpus by syllable length

Syllabicity	Type	Token
monosyllabic	2.73%	45.33%
disyllabic	46.05%	47.25%
tri-syllabic	32.41%	5.57%
quadra-syllabic	10.05%	1.29%
all others	8.75%	0.56%

Diagram I also shows that while mono-syllabic words takes up a small percentage in the lexicon, they tend to be highly frequent and occur almost as frequently as disyllabic words as a group in actual use. Total occurrences (i.e. token frequency) of monosyllabic and disyllabic words are roughly equivalent, with disyllabic words at 46.83% and monosyllabic words at 45.83%. The above corpus data can be used to explain the conflicting claims of mono- and disyllabicity of Chinese. The highly frequent use of monosyllabic works enhances the cognitive saliency of monosyllabic words in Chinese.[4] However, on the other hand, the large number of disyllabic entries leads to the impression that Mandarin is a disyllabic language. While the truth is that these two tendencies are both at work and dominant at the type and token levels respectively. Words of higher syllabicity, however, do occur and represent substantial fragments of the language.

Distribution of nouns and verbs are given in Diagram II and Diagram III respectively to show that syllabic distribution varies from category to category.

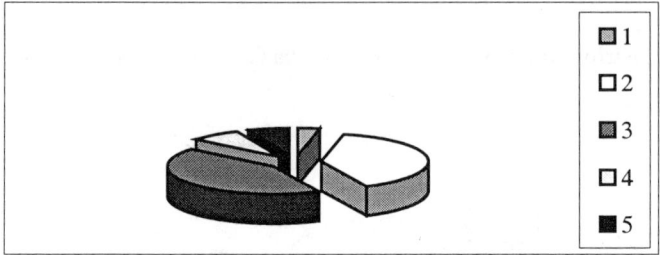

Diagram IIa. Distribution of noun types in Sinica Corpus by syllable length

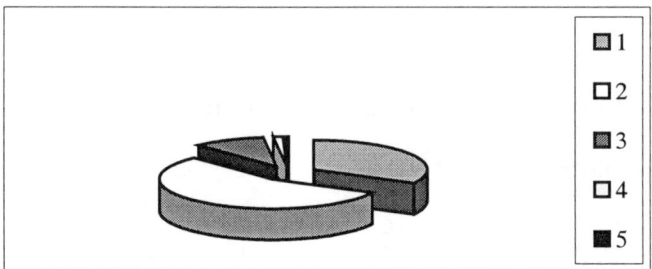

Diagram IIb. Distribution of noun tokens in Sinica Corpus by syllable length

Syllabicity	Type	Token
monosyllabic	3.30%	32.84%
disyllabic	39.67%	55.03%
tri-syllabic	42.97%	10.17%
quadra-syllabic	7.79%	1.37%
all others	6.27%	0.59%

---

[4] Eighty-six of the one hundred most frequent words in this corpus are monosyllabic, the other fourteen are disyllabic. And the most frequent disyllabic word was ranked eighteenth overall (Huang et al. 1998c).

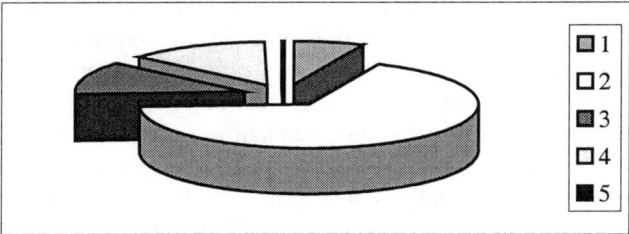

Diagram IIIa. Distribution of verb types in Sinica Corpus by syllable length

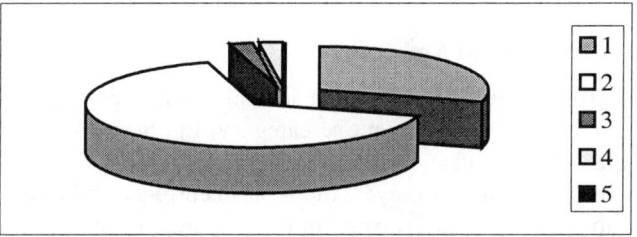

Diagram IIIb. Distribution of verb tokens in Sinica Corpus by syllable length

Syllabicity	Type	Token
monosyllabic	6.72%	29.36%
disyllabic	67.33%	66.10%
tri-syllabic	12.22%	2.39%
quadra-syllabic	13.42%	2.13%
all others	0.31%	0.02%

The above diagrams show that verbs and nouns have different distributional properties based on their syllable length. Although verb types are predominantly disyllabic (over 67%), there are actually more noun types which are tri-syllabic (almost 43%) than disyllabic (close to 40%). This can be explained by the pragmatic fact that Chinese names are predominantly tri-syllabic (monosyllabic family plus disyllabic given name). It is also worthwhile to point out that even though monosyllabic words represent only a small fraction of the verbal and nominal entries, they are used more frequently than any other syllabic type. For instance, the token distribution of monosyllabic nouns is ten times bigger than their type distribution. This means that monosyllabic nouns have an average frequency ten times bigger than the average frequency of all nouns. Similarly, monosyllabic verbs are more than four times as likely to be used than an average verb. In contrast, disyllabic nouns and verbs have a close to average distribution, while all the other longer syllabic types occur much less often than average. One last observation involves the quadra-syllabic verbs. Although lexical types and tokens in Chinese tend to become less frequent as syllabic length increase, quadra-syllabic verbs are actually slightly more than tri-syllabic ones in terms of types and roughly equivalent in terms of tokens. This can be attributed to the popularity of Cheng2yu3, four syllable idiom chunks, in Chinese. Cheng2yu3 are typically used as an intransitive predicate in Chinese.

4 Categorical Ambiguity and Distributional Factors

4.1 Degree of Categorical Ambiguity

Only 4.298% (6316/146,929) of all the lexical entries represented in the corpus are assigned with more than one category. In other words, these are the words that call for categorical ambiguity resolution when they are encountered in processing. However, the total occurrences of these lexical entries take up 54.59% of the corpus. In other words, even though only a small portion of the lexicon is categorically ambiguous, their usage represents more than half of the corpus. In natural language processing terms, the small number of lexical items involved means that the lexical knowledge of categorical ambiguity can be dealt with exhaustively and heuristically. In addition, regarding on-line ambiguity resolution, the high percentage of potential ambiguity implies that human resolution of categorical ambiguity is highly principled and efficient, since human language processing would be prone to mistakes and highly inaccurate otherwise. This fact also suggests that there is a high correlation between frequency and ambiguity, which will be looked at in more detail in the next section.

Another way to look at degree of categorical ambiguity is to find out the distribution of the number of possible categories for all ambiguous words. We found that of all ambiguous lexical types, two-way ambiguous types dominate and represent roughly half of all types (49.478%). In addition, three-way ambiguous types represent 9.832% of all types, and percentage of higher multi-way ambiguity gets progressively lower. Because of the near majority of the two-way ambiguous types, and because all higher order ambiguity can be factorized into several two-way ambiguous types, our current study will focus on binary contrasts as the basic type.

4.2 Categorical Ambiguity and Lexical Frequency

We observed in the last section that categorically ambiguous words represent only a small portion of the lexicon but take up more than half of the corpus in actual use. To illustrate a possible correlation between frequency and categorical ambiguity, complete data from the 5 million words corpus is used to plot Figure 1. Degree of ambiguity is calculated according to intervals of frequency ranking. For instance, 320 of the 500 most frequent words are categorically ambiguous, thus the degree of ambiguity of this interval is 64%; while only 62 of the 500 words ranked between 10,001 and 10,500 are ambiguous, with a degree of ambiguity of 12.4%.[5]

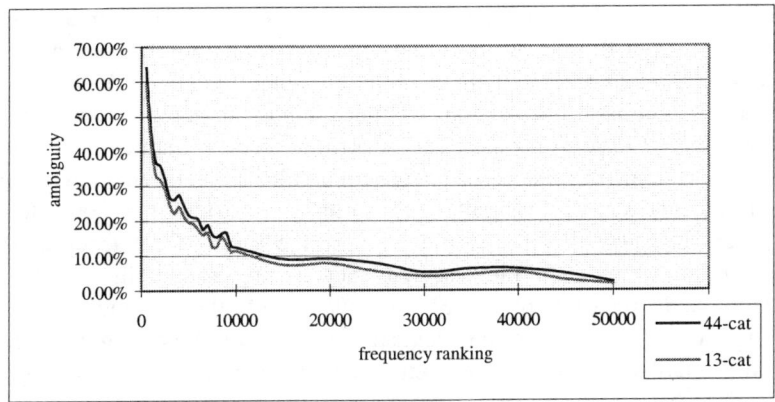

Figure 1. Frequency ranking and categorical ambiguity

Figure 1 shows that there is a high correlation between frequency ranking and categorical ambiguity. This diagram also shows distinct areas of correspondence: First, from the top rank to the rank around 1,000, the correlation is highly regular and ambiguity level descends acutely. Second, between the rank of roughly 1,000 to 10,000, the decrease is less acute and seems to fluctuate more. Lastly, for the rank above 10,000, the degree of ambiguity is so low that the frequency ranking does not seem to have any significant effect.

It is interesting to note that these three areas seem to correspond to commonly used criteria to define "frequent", "less frequent", and "infrequent" lexical entries. In Huang et al.'s (1998c) statistics based on Sinica

---

[5] In this section, we will restrict our discussion to the data involving either the thirteen or the complete forty-four categories, although the data are sometimes shown together. The contrast between the complete and generalized thirteen categories will be discussed later in Section 5.

Corpus, the accumulated frequency of the top 456 words just surpasses 50%, the top 1,000 words cover nearly 60%, while the top 10,000 words cover 85.87%. In terms of lexical frequency, the 456th word has a frequency of 0.0259%, the 1,000th word 0.0128%, and the 10,000th word 0.000896%.

Theoretically, however, we need to measure degree of ambiguity directly against lexical frequency in order to understand the nature of the relation between frequency and ambiguity. The above result is inadequate since frequency ranking is only a second order representation of lexical frequency. Methodologically, however, we have a problem to overcome before the frequency-ambiguity relation can be studied. Note that lexical frequency is the attribute of an individual lexical item and that each lexical item is either ambiguous or unambiguous. In other words, degree of ambiguity of a lexical item is either 1 or 0. In order to have a degree of ambiguity data, we need to define a sub-set of lexical items that share similar frequency features and calculate the number of ambiguous words among them. A significant way to achieve this is to group lexical items according to their frequency ranking. Thus lexical items in each group will share similar lexical frequency, while their frequency will differ significantly from other lexical items outside of the group. Hence it will be justified to take the average frequency of the whole group as their shared lexical frequency, and to examine its correspondence to the degree of ambiguity of the group. One further technical detail is that logarithmic representation of lexical frequency will be adopted, following well-established tradition to better demonstrate frequency variations. Figure 2 is the result of plotting degree of ambiguity against their average frequency for each 500 lexical items arranged according to descending frequency rank (i.e. from the least frequent to the most frequent).

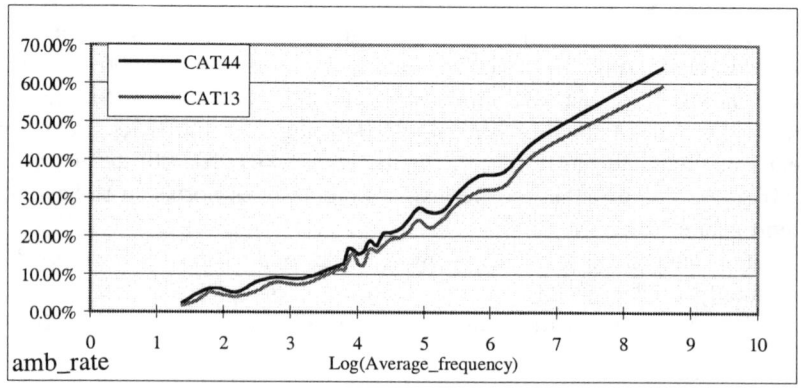

Figure 2. Lexical frequency and degree of ambiguity

The correlation between lexical frequency and degree of ambiguity is succinctly represented by Figure 2. The figure shows unequivocally that there is a direct proportional relationship between frequency and degree of ambiguity. The more frequent a lexical item is, the more likely for it to be categorically ambiguous. This is another instantiation of Zipf's law (see Manning and Schutze (1999) for an interpretation).

The evolutionary view on language (Cavalli-Sforza 1994, Cavalli-Sforza and Wang 1986) offers a possible explanation of the above correlation between frequency and categorical ambiguity. It is widely accepted that gene mutations are highly correlated to the rate of its reproduction. In other words, the more often a gene is copied, the more likely it is to mutate.

With regard to linguistic categories, we can treat each use of a lexical item in a context similarly to an instance of gene copying. In other words, each is an instance of instantiation of an archetype. Hence, as the frequency of use of a lexical item rises, so does its chance to change, including to a shift in its grammatical category. Of course, frequency of use does not guarantee change, just as frequent reproduction does not guarantee mutation either. It is simply that the statistical probability rises significantly. We expect this account to receive future support from the pioneering research on the evolution of language.[6]

4.3 Grammatical Categories and Categorical Ambiguity

An interesting theoretical question to ask is if ambiguity is category-dependent. If words belonging to a certain grammatical category are more ambiguous than others, then it is natural to follow up with the question of whether the defining features of that particular category directly lead to its tendency for categorical shift. Hence study on categorical dependency of ambiguity could offer crucial evidence for human cognitive system; particularly if it is shown that the propensity for ambiguity is driven by the same cognitive/conceptual characteristics defining a category. Initial data that degree of ambiguity do range widely (from just over 5% to over 60%) by categories seem to suggest a correlation between categorical ambiguity and categorical classification, as listed below in Table 2:

---

[6] Note that this account is also compatible with the lexical diffusion theory for language change and language variation (Wang 1969, 1991).

Category	Amb.Entry/Total Entry	Percentage
Noun	4727/93295	5.067%
Verb	3939/44241	8.904%
Adjective	430/1912	22.490%
Interjection	22/76	28.974%
Adverb	935/2664	35.098%
Preposition	180/306	58.824%
Particle	48/78	61.538%

Table 2. Degree of ambiguity for lexical categories

However, there are two theoretical issues which indicate that the above data alone are not sufficient to lead to the conclusion that ambiguity is category-dependent. The first involves the assignment of a 'primary' category to a lexical item. The identification of a primary category is crucial in order to establish the correlation between category and ambiguity, since all the categorically ambiguous lexical items are assigned with more than one category in the corpus and lexicon. Is there a general and principled way to assign the primary categorical affiliation of a categorically ambiguous word and hence attribute ambiguity to that category? The answer is a qualified no. Etymology and speaker perception are two obvious ways to determine primary category for a lexical entry. However, based on past experience as well as our pilot analyses, they often conflict with each other and there do not seem to be any principled ways to resolve the conflicts. On the other hand, even if a "primary" category can be assigned with consensus, it is still not valid to make the deduction that the lexical categorical ambiguity be attributed to it. One could as easily argue that a lexical item shifts to a secondary category simply because it has some of the characteristics of that category. Thus, can the categorical ambiguity could be attributed to the characteristics of the secondary (or tertiary, etc.) category.

To overcome the above potential problems, we take a naïve but non-discriminatory approach for the current study. That is, any lexical item that is assigned multiple categories is counted towards the statistics of each and every category it is assigned to. In other words, if a word is assigned 3 possible categories, than it is added to the ambiguous word list for all the three categories. This way, we can avoid making arbitrary decisions to rule out the contribution of any category. And since all attested categories are counted, there is also no danger of any specific category being given privilege over others.

The second problem is that, as shown in the last section, ambiguity is highly dependent on frequency. It is also known that lexical frequency varies greatly from category to category. For instance, the closed categories tend to have a smaller number of members that are more frequently used. Hence the claim that such categories are more ambiguous may be misleading since their ambiguity can actually be attributed to the frequency effect. To overcome the possible influence of frequency effect and yet investigate the correlation between category and categorical ambiguity, we need to compare two categories that are versatile and have the same wide range of distribution. Two of the categories that meet these requirements are verbs and nouns.

It is interesting to note that nouns and verbs happen to be at the center of dispute over the so-called mutability issues. Genter (1981) first observed that verbs are consistently more polysemous than verbs across different frequency ranges in English. Genter and France (1988) offered the account that verbs are more mutable than nouns. This claim was challenged by S. Huang (1995) and received a qualified support and revisions from Ahrens (1999), both based on Mandarin Chinese data. Genter and France's (1985) original cognitive claim was that verbs are less concrete and therefore more susceptible to change. S. Huang's (1995) work based on counting sense entries in a dictionary raises the issue that this motivation may be language-dependent. Ahrens's (1999) off-line experiments on native speakers are more strictly controlled regarding syllable length and frequency. However, none of the above studies were able to do an across-the-board look of the data from a language. The Sinica Corpus data offers a chance for us to have a comprehensive look at contrasts between verbs and nouns across all frequency ranges.

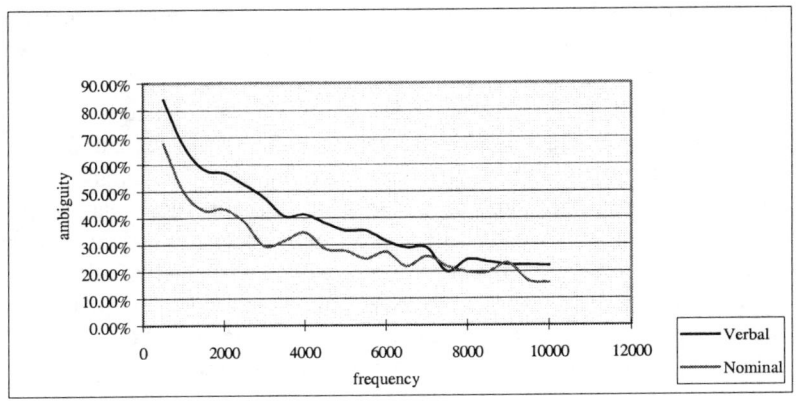

Figure 3. Comparison of verbal and nominal ambiguity (44 categories)

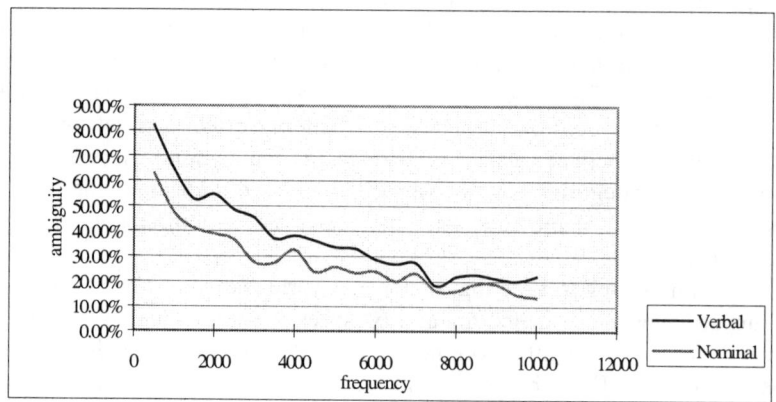

Figure 4. Comparison of verbal and nominal ambiguity (13 categories)

In Figures 3 and 4 above, we see a consistent gap between the degree of ambiguity between nouns and verbs at every frequency range. Thus verbs are more likely to be categorically ambiguous than nouns. An interesting observation can also be made when comparing Figures 3 and 4 with Figure 1. It is shown that the degree of ambiguity of both nouns and verbs are higher than the average degree of ambiguity of all categories. In other words, these two 'substantive' categories are more likely to be categorically ambiguous than others. This actually supports Ahrens's (1999) position that verbs and nouns are both mutable but for different reasons.[7] Thus, we offered empirical evidence to show that categorical ambiguity is indeed dependent on categorical identity. Whether such dependency can be shown to be driven by the same conceptual or cognitive motivations for categorical classification will be an interesting research topic for future study.

Recalling our discussion on frequency ranking and lexical frequency earlier, even though the above frequency ranking data give us good indication that verbs are more likely to be categorically ambiguous than nouns, it is more interesting to show direct correspondence between lexical frequency and degree of ambiguity. In the current study, the danger of distortion is even greater since verbs and nouns may differ in individual frequency, even when they belong to the same frequency range. Following the methodology established earlier, we plot (logarithmic) average frequency against their

---

[7] The proposal is that a verb is more likely to change in situations when the change is not crucial to its meaning. On the other hand, a noun is more likely to change in a situation when the change brings a more specific interpretation.

degree of ambiguity according to frequency ranking range of every 100 words, for both nouns and verbs.

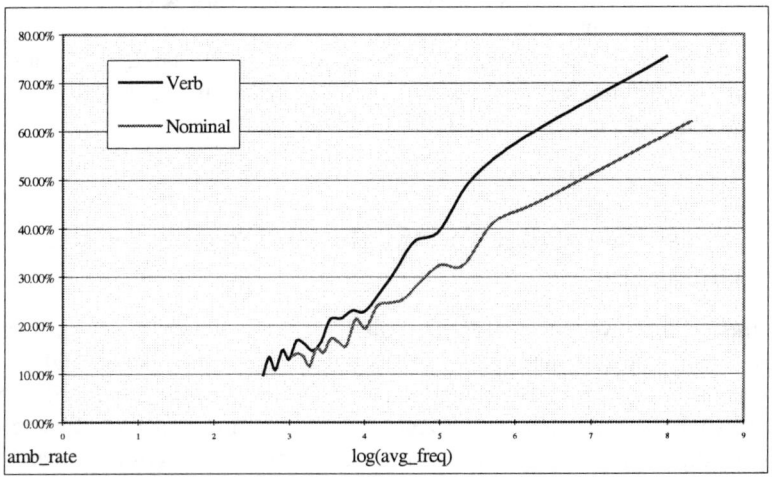

Figure 5. Noun-verb frequency-ambiguity correspondence contrast (44 categories)

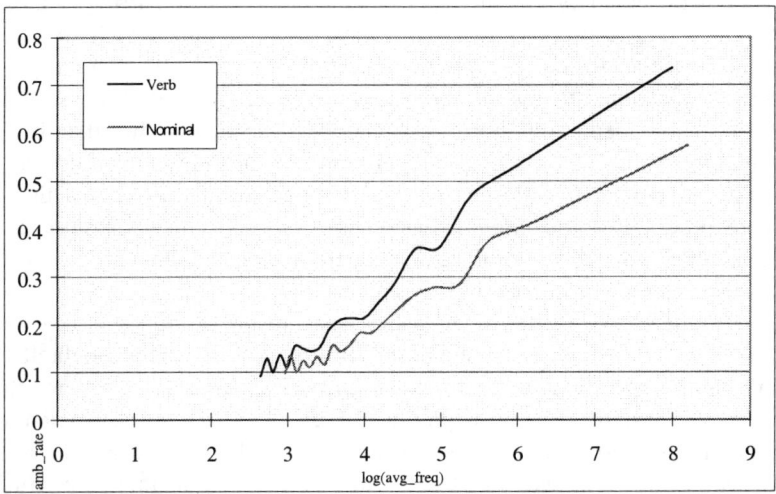

Figure 6. Noun-verb frequency-ambiguity correspondence contrast (13 categories)

Figures 5 and 6 both show two important generalizations. First, they show that the direct proportional relationship between frequency and degree of ambiguity holds for individual categories too (i.e. for nouns and verbs). Second, They show unequivocally that verbs are more likely to be categorically ambiguous than nouns given that they have the same frequency. In addition, the figures also show that the categorical ambiguity disparity between verbs and nouns grows when frequency increases.

5 Lexical Knowledge and the Resolution of Categorical Ambiguity

In this section, we will explore the role lexical knowledge plays in the resolution of categorical ambiguity. In particular, we would like to find out the distribution of all possible categories for a lexical form. If the distribution is somewhat random, then categorical ambiguity is not constrained by lexical knowledge and is totally dependent on contextual rules. On the other hand, however, if generalizations on categorical distribution can be extracted for all lexical entries, then how to represent such generalizations in the lexicon becomes a crucial issue.

In a model where all possible categories of a ambiguous word are accessed with equal probability, one would predict that, barring contextual coercion, all possible categories will have similar frequency. It would also predict that the difficulty of ambiguity resolution of any lexical entry is directly proportional to the number of available categorical choices. Neither of the above predictions bore out. A look at the data shows that 1) Most lexical forms have a dominant category in terms of frequency of use, as will be discussed later in this section. 2) Assuming the modular view that language production and comprehension presupposed correct assignment of grammatical categories to all lexical items, native speakers rarely, if ever, makes mistakes in category assignment.

An alternative model, without having to resort to the yet controversial issue of lexical encoding of stochastic information, is where a default category can be specified for each lexical entry. Lexical default ensures that a category is assigned in a principled way even when there is insufficient contextual information. Such a default mechanism will allow the speaker to beat the statistical odds without going through complex calculation. Such a model will also provide the baseline performance standard for computational tagging (i.e. categorical assignments), to be discussed in the next subsection.

5.1 Categorical Default

In this study, we follow the standard practice and lexically encode the most frequently instantiated category of each word form as its default category. We assume that a speaker's null hypothesis is to assign the default category to each instance of the word form unless context information indicates otherwise. In this model, categorical assignment and ambiguity resolution does not start with either zero or statistical ambivalence. It starts with all the correct prediction based on lexical knowledge. Lexical knowledge can provide correct categorical assignments in two ways: First, it automatically assigns the correct category when a lexical item is unambiguous. This happens to nearly half of the tokens in Sinica Corpus. Second, when there is categorical ambiguity, lexical knowledge makes the correct prediction when the actual category is the lexical default. The Sinica Corpus data also shows that lexical default holds true for 88.37% over all ambiguous tokens. Taking the two scenarios together, a purely lexical approach to categorical ambiguity resolution and assignment will have very good results according to our corpus data. The frequencies of the default category being instantiated are shown in Table 3 according to both syllable length and number of possible categories.

Syllable Number	Freq. (by type)	Freq. (by token)
1	80.21%	88.86%
2	78.34%	86.87%
3	73.73%	89.70%
4	69.98%	81.82%
5	69.02%	80.02%
6	65.01%	74.35%
7	65.15%	83.33%

No. of Categories	Freq. (by type)	Freq. (by token)
2	77.65%	91.21%
3	77.71%	88.39%
4	74.21%	89.50%
5	73.83%	92.43%
6	73.46%	86.09%
7	68.51%	86.09%
Total	77.36%	88.37%

MEAN = 77.3556%
DEV = 17.2175%

Table 3. Frequency of default category

However, it is interesting to observe that if the precision rate of assigning the default category is calculated for each lexical form, and the average precision rate of all lexical types is actually only 77.36%, much lower than the overall precision rate. The only possible explanation for such discrepancy is that the default precision rate for more frequent lexical types is higher than less frequent ones.

Another observation of Table 3 is that default categorical precision does not seem to correlate with either syllable length or number of possible categories. We will discuss the implications of the two observations at the conclusion section.

5.2 Estimating the Baseline Performance Categorical Ambiguity Resolution

Given the model of lexical assignment of default categories as well as the data from Sinica Corpus, we will construct a baseline model of categorical ambiguity resolution in this subsection. This model will assume that a speaker starts his/her task of ambiguity resolution with lexical knowledge alone. Post-lexical, including structural and contextual, information will then be incorporated to improve on the result of lexical resolution. Thus, we can estimate baseline performance of categorical ambiguity resolution by using the lexical default frequency data. As mentioned earlier, lexical categorical assignment and ambiguity resolution is successful in two scenarios: where there is no ambiguity and where ambiguity goes to the default category. The baseline performance is very important in two fields of language processing studies: In computational linguistics, it represents the benchmark that any automatic tagging/ambiguity resolution program must surpass. In psycholinguistics, it represents the benchmark for valid subject performance as well as for evaluating model simulation.

A rough estimate of the performance can be given before our computational simulation. As mentioned above, 54.59% of the tokens in the corpus are categorically ambiguous, and the average default precision for all ambiguous tokens is 88.37%. Based on these two numbers, and assuming that there is no unknown word, we estimate the precision rate of lexical category assignment at 93.65% (100%-54.59%+(54.59%x88.37%)). This is actually higher than most of the results reported by automatic tagging programs.

To simulate human ambiguity resolution, however, it is not adequate to simply obtain the statistics from a complete corpus. In actual language use, a speaker's task is to successfully process a text. A text could be a natural segment of a running dialogue or a natural segment of a written document. To simulate actual linguistic tasks, we take marked and segmented texts from Sinica Corpus as natural units of ambiguity resolution and category assignment. Since we are testing the simple lexical resolution and assignment algorithm, there is no speaker variation except in individual mental lexicons. Since we do not have individual mental lexicons, we will simply assume that a complete lexicon compiled from the corpus is a shared passive lexicon of all speakers. In other words, the only variation lies in the texts, and the experiment will show how well lexical resolution of categorical ambiguity resolution will perform assuming a perfect lexicon. We estimate the expected performance based on the average of all texts. In this experiment, we randomly picked one hundred and twenty (120) texts from Sinica Corpus. The length of texts ranges roughly from 900 to 90,000 characters (roughly from 500 to 50,000 words). These texts represent different topics, genres, styles, etc. We assume that there are no unknown words. Some of the typical results as well as the average results of the 120 texts are given below in Table 4.

File name	Ambiguity	Default precision	Baseline res. Accu.
Nroot.tag	54.7556%	79.8791%	88.9788%
Ointer.tag	61.8716%	92.3125%	95.2436%
Okuo2b.tag	59.9797%	84.2452%	90.5661%
Opinyi1.tag	67.8163%	87.3529%	91.4232%
Opinyi2.tag	64.8642%	84.5382%	89.9708%
Tsa.tag	43.2161%	91.2791%	96.2312%
Ywcomp.tag	52.7599%	93.0657%	96.3415%
Ywsubs.tag	45.6564%	91.2732%	96.0157%
AVERAGE	54.4011%	89.0696%	94.0537%
Corpus	54.59%	88.37%	93.65%

Table 4. Experiment baseline performance of default category assignment

The lowest and highest number from this experiment are highlighted with underline to show the range of variation. The average mean of testing 120 texts are given right above the result obtained from the complete corpus (as if it were a single text) for contrast. The results show that even though degree of ambiguity (based on token frequency) in a text can vary, from as low as 43.21% to as high as 67.82%, it is somehow compensated by the changes in the frequency and dominance of default categories. Similarly, frequency of default category also varies widely, from a little under 80% to over 93%. There is a clear tendency for more ambiguous texts to also show high frequency of default category. The result is a fairly stable range of baseline ambiguity resolution performance that averages at 94.05% but ranges, roughly, only from a little under 90% to a little over 96%.

The variation in degree of ambiguity as well as in dominance of default category is expected, as they are obviously dependent on the length, topics, etc. of each text. The stable baseline performance is surprising given the above variations. However, the surprising results itself lends strong support for a ambiguity resolution model based on lexical default. A human language cognition model would expect predictably good result of such basic linguistic task as category assignment, since a model that does not have good performance would predict frequent linguistic failure. And a model that allows too much fluctuation would predict that linguistic ability is highly context-dependent. Neither is correct. The fact that lexical default category assignment predicts the desirable result of categorical ambiguity resolution strongly suggest that it is the right model.

6 Categorical Sets and Categorical Ambiguity

In a random stochastic system, the distribution of samples is clearly dependent on the number of classes involved. This leads to an interesting question regarding categorization in human languages. Intuitively, there seems to be a 'universal' set of categories such that different languages can be compared with the same category set. And an identical grammar can be constructed by all speakers of the same language. However, in practice, we observe that different linguists often adopt different category sets that may vary widely in its size, from a score to a hundred. In addition, theoretical linguists often find it necessary to refer to the notion of sub-categories in accounting for linguistic facts. Thus, before asking the crucial question of if there is any cognitive or conceptual foundation of linguistic categorization, we need to ask if there is an optimal size of sets of categories.

The data involving categorical ambiguity offers the strictest test for the hypothesis that there is an optimal number of categories in human linguistic categorization. Again, in a simplistic formal system assuming no conceptual dependencies among categories, the probability for a given category to shift to any other category is the same. Hence degree of ambiguity will most likely be dependent upon the number of possible shifts, i.e. the number of categories. Furthermore, this model predicts that the number-of-classes effect on degree of ambiguity will show up as long as there is no complete dependency between two category sets of different sizes. In other words, if no sets of categories are optimal, then their size should play a role in the degree of categorical ambiguity. Thus, the number-of-classes effect will disappear only when one category set is optimal (or is a logically necessary reduction towards the optimal set by the larger set).

Sinica Corpus can be interpreted with two different category sets of either thirteen or forty-four categories, as introduced earlier. Hence it offers the opportunity to compare degree of ambiguity with different category sets as well as testing the hypothesis that there be an optimal number for the size of linguistic categories. In the following figure, two frequency-ambiguity correspondence lines based on the forty-four-category and thirteen-category tagging are put together for comparison. Note that this figure is slightly different from Figure 2 since a smaller frequency range of 100 is taken, and hence the figure is less smooth, though the positive dependency remains identical.

Figure 7. Frequency-ambiguity correspondence comparison category sets of 44 and 13

Figure 7, as well as all the other figures involving two different category sets: Figures 2, 3, 4, 5, and 6, tell the same story. It contradicts naïve static intuition to find that the correspondence is essentially the same regardless of whether the data is taken from tagsets of forty-four or thirteen categories.

As mentioned earlier, the thirteen category set subsumes the forty-four category set. In other words, the forty-four category set can be regarded as the elaboration of the thirteen category sets with subcategories. The most plausible explanation for this contradiction to normal stochastic distribution is that the thirteen categories represent the conceptually primary, hence optimal, categories. Hence all bona fide categorical ambiguity exist among these categories, whereas the added categories in the forty-four categories sets are subcategories that are mostly motivated by distributional difference. Since distributional differences are complementary by nature, there are few, if any, additional instances of categorical ambiguity among these subcategories themselves.

To sum up, our study involving two different category sizes lends strong support to the conceptual primacy and psychological felicity of the small (thirteen) category set. We find that this set is likely to represent the optimal size of category set (for Chinese). This finding also strongly suggests that categorical ambiguity is conceptually based, since pure structural categorization (i.e. subcategories added in the set of 44) surprisingly failed to increase categorically ambiguity. Thus it lends further support for future study to look for conceptual/cognitive foundation of categorical ambiguity.

7 Future Studies: the "Hard" Problems in Categorical Ambiguity Resolution

In Section 3 above, we showed that there is a strong tendency towards a default category for categorically ambiguous items. In this penultimate section, we would like to find out if there are lexical items where such defaults do not exist. In other words, are there lexical items where ambiguity resolution must be dependent primarily on contextual information. We will refer to these items as *Categorically Ambivalent*. The essential distributional data involving potentially ambivalent words are given below in Table 5.

$P_{default}$	No. of Words	% by Type	% by Token	% in Corpus
0.51	132	3.14	1.95	1.06
0.52	164	3.90	2.09	1.14
0.53	210	4.99	2.31	1.26
0.54	254	6.04	2.64	1.44
0.55	299	7.11	2.80	1.53
0.56	335	7.96	3.08	1.68
0.57	355	8.44	3.16	1.72
0.58	399	9.48	3.41	1.86
0.59	448	10.65	3.69	2.01
0.60	506	12.02	4.75	2.59

Total Number of Ambiguous Words with Frequency Over 10 = 4,208

Table 5. Statistics of ambiguous words with low default category

The statistics given above show that only a small portion of all lexical items are categorically ambiguous. And among this small set, only a small portion is ambivalent. Since the effectiveness of lexical default model lies in the clear advantage it offers for choosing the default category, the potentially problematic cases are when choosing the default offers no clear advantage. For instance, if a default category has a frequency of 55%, then it could be only 10% stronger than a competing category. If its frequency is 60%, it can be only 20% stronger than a competing category. If 55% is taken as the cut-off point, then there are only 299 words that are ambivalent. In addition, they take up only 2.80% of all ambiguous words, and 1.53% of all corpus. The small number of ambivalent words as well as their limited representation in actual use suggest a lexicon-driven model for category ambiguity is still possible. In other words, even if each ambivalent word requires a different set of heuristic rules to resolve its ambiguity, they can still enumerated and be treated as lexical idiosyncrasies.

In future studies, we will concentrate on these ambivalent words to find out if there is any cognitive motivation for the lack of a strong lexical default, as well as if such cognitive motivation can render ambiguity resolution cost-effective in context. Three representative examples are given below to suggest the kind of conceptual dependencies that may be involved.

(5) Categorically ambivalent words
    a. 像 *xiang4* freq.=4414   1. prep. 'like' 2342
                                            2. verb 'to be like' 2022
                                              3. noun 'likeness(=image/statue)' 50
    b. 影響 *yin3xiang3* freq.=2397 1. noun '(the) influence' 1291
                                              2. verb 'to influence' 1106
    c. 自然 *zi4ran2* freq.=2164   1. noun 'nature' 1012
                                              2. adverb 'naturally' 781
                                            3. adjective 'to be natural' 371

8 Conclusion

In conclusion, we have shown that lexical knowledge is crucial in categorical ambiguity representation and resolution. We also showed ambiguity is dependent on frequency and categorical identity. On the other hand, we showed that degree of ambiguity is not dependent on the size of categorical sets. Based on the fact that increase in number of categories does not noticeably increase degree of ambiguity, we argue that there is an optimal size of grammatical categories, probably around thirteen. Based on the fact that distributional subcategories do not contribute to categorical ambiguity and that verbs are more likely to be categorically ambiguous than nouns, we suggest that categorically ambiguity might be primarily motivated by conceptual necessity. In terms of processing, we also established the baseline performance for categorical ambiguity resolution for Chinese, as well as identify the small number of lexical items that are hard problems for ambiguity resolution.

There are three important directions for future studies to take: first, we need to develop a default inheritance model for lexical representation that can both felicitously account for categorical ambiguity as well as offer an efficient algorithm for ambiguity resolution. Second, we need to find explanatory accounts for categorically ambivalent words, and hope that generalizations can be reached from these accounts to give them conceptual and cognitive motivation. Last, based on the above results, we need to explore the relationship between categorical ambiguity and semantic ambiguity. We suspect that conceptual basis can be found for both kinds of ambiguity, with the difference being that categorical ambiguity involves highly grammaticalized concepts, i.e. the linguistic categories.

References

Abeille, A., L. Celement, & R. Reyes. 1998. TALANA Annotated Corpus: the First Results. *Proceedings of First Conference on Linguistic Resources*, 992-999. Grenade, Spain.
Ahrens, K. 1998. Lexical Ambiguity Resolution: Languages, Tasks and Timing. *Sentence Processing: A Cross-linguistic Perspective*, ed. D. Hillert, 11-31. New York: Academic Press.
Ahrens, K. 1999. The Mutability of Noun and Verb Meaning. *Chinese Languages and Linguistics V: Interactions in Language*, eds. Y. Yin, I. Yang, & H. Chan, 335-371. Taipei: Institute of Linguistics, Academia Sinica.
Briscoe, T., V.d. Paiva, & A. Copestake. eds. 1994. *Inheritance, Defaults, and the Lexicon*. Cambridge: Cambridge University Press.
Cavalli-Sforza, L. L. 1994. An Evolutionary View in Linguistics. *In Honor of William S-Y. Wang. Interdisciplinary Studies on Language and Language Change*, eds. M. Y. Chen & O. J-L. Tzeng, 17-28. Taipei: Pyramid.
Cavalli-Sforza, L. L, & W. S-Y. Wang. 1986. Spatial Distance and Lexical Replacement. *Language* 62:38-55.
Chao, Y.-R. 1968. *A Grammar of Spoken Chinese*. Berkeley: University of California Press.
Chen, K.-J., C.-R. Huang, L. Chang, & H.-L. Hsu. 1996. Sinica Corpus: Design Methodology for Balanced Corpora. *Proceeding of the 11th Pacific Asia Conference on Language, Information and Computation*, eds. B.-S. Park & J.B. Kim, 167-176. Seoul: Kyung Hee University.
Chen, C., S. Tseng, C.-R. Huang, & K.-J. Chen. 1993. Some Distributional Properties of Mandarin Chinese: A Study Based on the Academia Sinica Corpus. *Proceedings of the Pacific Asia Conference on Formal and Computational Linguistics*, 81-95. Taipei: R.O.C. Computational Linguistics Society.
Chinese Knowledge Information Processing (CKIP) Group. 1995. An Introduction to Academia Sinica Balanced Corpus for Modern Mandarin Chinese. *CKIP Technical Report* 95-01. Nankang: Academia Sinica.
Chomsky, N. 1995. *The Minimalist Program*. Cambridge: MIT Press.
Gentner, D. 1981. Some Interesting Differences Between Verbs and Nouns. *Cognition & Brain Theory* 4.2:161-178.

Gentner, D. & I. France. 1988. The Verb Mutability Effect: Studies of the Combinatorial Semantics of Nouns and Verbs. *Lexical Ambiguity Resolution*, eds. S.I. Small, W.C. Garrison, & M.K. Tanehaus, 343-382. San Mateo: Morgan Kaufmann. 1988..

Gorfein, D.S. 1989. ed. *Resolving Semantic Ambiguity.* New York: Springer Verlag.

Huang, C.-R. 1994. Corpus-based Studies of Mandarin Chinese: Foundational Issues and Preliminary Results. *In Honor of William S-Y. Wang. Interdisciplinary Studies on Language and Language Change*, eds. M. Y. Chen & O. J-L. Tzeng, 165-186. Taipei: Pyramid.

Huang, C.-R. 1999. *SouWenJieZi* 搜文解字:A Linguistic KnowledgeBase Anchoring Chinese Digital Museums. Presented at Digital Museum Seminar and AP Digital Library Consortium Joint Meeting 1999. July 21-23. Taipei.

Huang, C.-R., Z. M. Gao, C. C.-C. Shen, & K.-J. Chen. 1998a. Quantitative Criteria for Computational Chinese Lexicography: A Study Based on a Standard Reference Lexicon for Chinese NLP. *Proceedings of ROCLING XI*, 87-108.

Huang, C.-R., K.-J. Chen, Z. M. Gao, F. Y. Chen, & C. C.-C. Shen. 1998b. Word Frequency Dictionary. *CKIP Technical Report* 98-01. Nankang, Taipei: Academia Sinica.

Huang, C.-R., K.-J. Chen, Z. M. Gao, F. Y. Chen, & C. C.-C. Shen. 1998c. Accumulated Word Frequency in Sinica Corpus. *CKIP Technical Report* 98-02. Nankang, Taipei: Academia Sinica.

Huang, S. 1994. Chinese as a Metonymic Language. *In Honor of William S-Y. Wang. Interdisciplinary Studies on Language and Language Change*, eds. M. Y. Chen & O. J.-L. Tzeng, 223-252. Taipei: Pyramid.

Lyons, John. 1977. Semantics. Cambridge: Cambridge University Press.

Manning C. D. & H. Shutze. 1999. *Foundations of Statistical Natural Language Processing*. Cambridge: MIT Press.

Meng, H. & C. W. Ip. 1999. An Analytical Study of Transformational Tagging for Chinese Text. *Proceedings of ROCLING XII*, 101-122. Taipei: Association of Computational Linguistics and Chinese Language Processing.

Pustejovsky, J. 1995. *The Generative Lexicon*. Cambridge: MIT Press.

Redington, M., N. Chater, C.-R. Huang, L.-P. Chang, S. Finch, & K.-J. Chen. 1995. The Universality of Simple Distributional Methods: Identifying syntactic categories in Mandarin Chinese. Paper presented at the International Conference on Cognitive Science and Natural Language Processing. July 7-11. Dublin City University.

Schutz, H. 1997. *Ambiguity Resolution in Language Learning: Computational and Cognitive Models*. Stanford: CSLI Publications.

Small, S.I., W.C. Garrison, & M.K. Tanehaus. eds. 1988. *Lexical Ambiguity Resolution*. San Mateo: Morgan Kaufmann.

Wang, W. S-Y. 1991. *Explorations in Language*. Taipei: Pyramid.

Wang, W. S-Y. 1969. Competing Changes as a Cause of Residue. *Language* 45.1:9-25.

4

Syntactic and Positional Similarity Effects in the Processing of Japanese Embeddings[*]

RICHARD L. LEWIS AND MINEHARU NAKAYAMA

1 Introduction

This study addresses a fundamental issue in human language processing: the nature of limited working memory in comprehension. Our work is based on

---

[*] Different portions of this paper have been presented at the International East Asian Psycholinguistics Workshop at The Ohio State University, Institute for Cognitive Science in Seoul National Univ., the Graduate Program in Linguistics in Kanda Univ. of International Studies, and the Psychology Department at Michigan State Univ. We would like to thank the participants of those talks, in particular, Nobuko Hasegawa, Chungmin Lee, Yoshihisa Kitagawa, Kazumi Matsuoka, Reiko Mazuka, Edson Miyamoto, Tsutomu Sakamoto, Shoichi Takahashi, Keiko Uehara and Shravan Vasishth, and anonymous reviewers for their helpful comments. Furthermore, we would like to thank Yoko Matsudaira and Mitsuko Shimoda of Kobe Shoin Women's University, Noriko Yoshimura, Kaori Mizuno, and Atsushi Fujimori of the University of Shizuoka, and Masatoshi Koizumi of (then) Tohoku Gakuin University for their assistance in the data collection and Koichi Sawasaki for his statistical assistance. All shortcomings are of course ours. This research was supported by a grant-in-aid by OSU College of Humanities to the second author and a targeted interdisciplinary seed grant by OSU Office of Research and Graduate Studies to both authors.

Sentence Processing in East Asian Languages.
Mineharu Nakayama (ed.).
Copyright ©2002, CSLI Publications.

the hypothesis that similarity-based interference is a general principle that holds across all types of human working memory, including working memory for linguistic structure in parsing. The specific area of sentence processing that is most deeply related to working memory limitations is the difficulty of comprehending center-embeddings (Miller 1962, Miller and Chomsky 1963). Consider the well-known double center-embedded object relative clause in English:

(1) The salmon that the man that the dog chased smoked fell off the grill.

The problem faced by the parser in a center-embedding is that it must temporarily set aside the partial products of working on the initial part of a constituent while it parses another embedded constituent, then retrieve those earlier partial products to finish the parsing. The connection to computational theory is significant: one of Chomsky's earliest results was a formal proof that arbitrary center-embedding is precisely the property of a grammar that moves it outside the scope of any finite memory device (Chomsky 1959).

The original insights of Miller and Chomsky concerning center-embedding led to a rich line of work on resource-limited parsing, but it has been surprisingly difficult to produce models and metrics that are empirically adequate, particularly when considered against a broad range of cross-linguistic embeddings. Furthermore, there has been little independent psychological motivation for the proposed memory structures (e.g., stacks, lookahead buffers) and their associated limitations (Lewis 1996).

As an example of the kind of empirical hurdle faced by any theory of syntactic working memory, consider a fact established by Cowper (1976) and Gibson (1991) in their seminal work: a metric based purely on the amount of center-embedding does not account for many difficulty contrasts in English and other languages. Consider (2):

(2) a. That the food that John ordered tasted good pleased him.
    b. What the woman that John married likes is smoked salmon.

Though both constructions involve two levels of center-embedding of sentential structures (and (2b) even involves center-embedding of relative clauses), neither causes the dramatic difficulty associated with the classic structure in (1).

Although increasing center-embedding certainly increases difficulty, another important observation is that increasing the similarity of the embedded constituents increases difficulty, and making constituents more distinct or dissimilar in some way helps processing (e.g., Bever 1970, Miller and

Chomsky 1963, Kuno 1974). Why is this observation significant? Similarity-based interference is a principle that holds of working memory in general. Lewis (1996) reviews evidence for a range of working memory types subject to selective, type-specific interference, including verbal, spatial, odor, kinesthetic, and sign language. The robust result across domains is that when to-be-remembered items are followed by stimuli that are similar along some dimensions, the original items are more quickly forgotten.

Building on these results, and the work cited earlier by Cowper (1976) and Gibson (1991), Lewis (1993, 1996) hypothesized that similarity-based interference is a principle that applies to syntactic working memory as well. Lewis described a computational model that embodies retroactive, type-specific syntactic interference, and accounts for a range of cross-linguistic data on difficult center-embeddings. The model posited a simple buffer that could index no more than two constituents under a particular syntactic relation (see also Stabler 1994).

The type specificity of the limitation is crucial to the empirical success of the model. To see why, consider the comprehensible Japanese construction in (3) below (Lewis 1993):

(3) Jon-wa   Biru-ni Mari-ga   Suu-ni   Bobu-o   syookaishita to itta.
    -Top   -Dat   -Nom   -Dat   -Acc introduced that said
    'John said to Bill that Mary introduced Bob to Sue.'

Such sentences do not cause the difficulty associated with (1), despite stacking up five NPs. A crucial difference is that (3) requires buffering no more than two NPs of any particular syntactic function: at most two subjects, two indirect objects, and a direct object.

What this theory suggests is that we should add "syntactic" to the list of immediate memory types that exhibit type-specific interference and decreased performance with increased similarity. Just as there is the well-known phonological similarity effect, there is also a "syntactic similarity effect", and one way this effect manifests itself is difficulty with center-embedding. Lewis (1998) reformulates this theory to combine both retroactive and proactive interference into a measure of working memory load. The new theory increases the empirical coverage and yields moment-by-moment predictions of processing load. We discuss this model below in §2.

Assuming an interference based processing model raises a number of important questions, such as: What precisely are the features that contribute to similarity interference? For example, does semantic similarity or positional similarity count? Is interference alone sufficient to account for the data, or is there still some role for level of embedding or locality? We have begun a set of empirical studies to explore some of these issues, using embedded structures in Japanese. The head-final syntax and overt case-marking of Japanese make it particularly useful for teasing apart some of the factors contributing to processing complexity. (See Nakayama (1999) for an overview of Japanese syntactic characteristics and sentence processing.) In this paper, we report the results of several experiments using a difficulty rating task under different presentation modes. These experiments identify more precisely what makes complex syntactic embeddings difficult (or easy) to process, in particular, investigating syntactic and positional similarity interference. The first three experiments test the effects of positional similarity and stacking when controlling for level of embedding. The fourth and fifth experiments examine scrambling as a device for modulating positional similarity. The results of these experiments support the hypothesis that the *syntactic and positional similarity* of overt NP arguments contributes to the difficulty of sentence processing in Japanese.

The organization of this paper is as follows: The next section presents some background and discussion of Lewis's (1998) processing theory, and a pilot study to set the stage for the five experiments. Experiments I–III and IV–V will be discussed in Sections 3 and 4, respectively. Finally, concluding remarks will be provided in Section 5.

2 Theoretical Background

2.1 Syntactic Interference in Parsing

Lewis (1998) posited a metric that predicts processing load based on the combined effects of retroactive and proactive interference on syntactic attachments. Consider the abstract schema in (4) below:

(4) $\phi_1 \phi_2 \ldots \phi_n X \rho_1 \rho_2 \ldots \rho_m Y$

Suppose that Y is the current word, and that a syntactic relation must be established between a constituent projected from Y and a constituent headed by a prior word X. For example, Y might be a verb and X an argument of that verb. This attachment may suffer from retroactive interference from the intervening items $\rho_1 \ldots \rho_m$ and proactive interference from the prior items $\phi_1 \ldots \phi_n$ that are still active in the parse. The theory asserts that the critical factor determining the amount of interference is the similarity of the interfering items to the to-be-retrieved (to-be-attached) item X. This assumption follows considerable empirical work on multiple kinds of short-term and working memory (reviewed in Lewis 1996). We will operationalize similarity as syntactic similarity, determined by the structural role to be assigned element

X. The focus on syntactic similarity is functionally motivated, assuming that an important task of the sentence processor is uncovering the structure of the input string. (In Lewis (1996), a standard ontology of X-bar structural positions was assumed, though that commitment is not critical for the studies presented here).

For example, if X is to be assigned the structural position of a subject, then we expect proactive interference from those items in $\phi_1 \ldots \phi_n$ that have not yet been attached and may also fill subject position.[1] And we expect retroactive interference from those items in $\rho_1 \ldots \rho_m$ that were potential subjects. As a simplifying first approximation, we will assume that the similarity metric is all-or-nothing, so that items with identical potential syntactic positions interfere with each other, and items with distinct positions do not.

Consider how to apply the metric to the two Japanese embedded structures in (5):

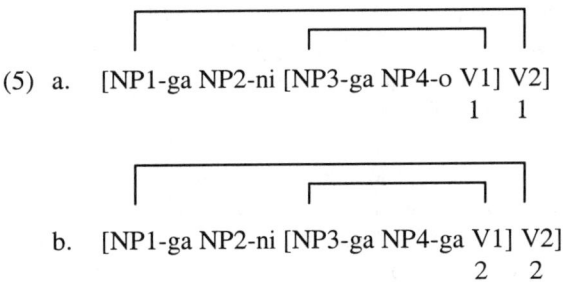

(5) a. [NP1-ga NP2-ni [NP3-ga NP4-o V1] V2]
        1   1

b. [NP1-ga NP2-ni [NP3-ga NP4-ga V1] V2]
        2   2

Focus on the subject attachment for the first (embedded) verb, V1. The item to be retrieved is the third noun phrase, marked with nominative -*ga* (NP3-*ga*). The set of items potentially contributing retroactive interference is only NP4-*o*, but since it is accusative marked and cannot appear in subject

---

[1] To simplify the presentation, we will assume here that NP arguments are left unattached before the verbs are encountered. This assumption is probably incorrect in general for head-final constructions (e.g. Frazier 1987, Bader and Lasser 1994, Inoue and Fodor 1995, Koniecnzy, Hemforth, Scheepers, and Strube 1997). However, the processing account can be reformulated assuming a fully-connected structure is maintained throughout the parse with predicted categories. In that case, there is a choice of retrieval/attachment cues to use. Under one scheme, the syntactic features of the incoming lexical items are used to retrieve the matching predicted categories. For example, a verb would not directly set retrieval cues for its unattached subject and object, but would set cues for the matching predicted transitive category. In another scheme, the predicted categories are associated with exactly the same retrieval cues used in the more head-driven approach described in the text. In that case, the verb sets retrieval cues for a subject and object, which activates the predicted category. For present purposes, the two approaches can be taken as equivalent.

position, it should not cause interference.[2] The set of items potentially contributing proactive interference is NP1-*ga* NP2-*ni*. Of these, only NP1-*ga* should contribute interference, since its nominative marking indicates that it is a potential subject. The subject attachment of V2 is the symmetrical case: retrieving NP1-*ga* suffers no proactive interference, but is retroactively interfered with by NP3-*ga*. Thus, in both cases, there is one unit of interference for the subject attachments (indicated by the 1 below each verb).

Why should the attachment of V2 to NP1 suffer from retroactive interference from NP3, if NP3 has already been attached? While NP3 is not an active competitor for the subject role of V2 at the time V2 is encountered, the encoding of NP3 as a potential subject is assumed to interfere with the representation of NP1 as a potential subject. Even if NP3 is later retrieved and removed from active consideration as a subject before NP1 must be retrieved, the damage has been done at the time of encoding NP3. Thus (in these examples) retroactive interference results from *encoding* or *storage* interference, and proactive interference results from *retrieval* interference.[3] We will take RI and PI as descriptive terms that happen to map onto storage and retrieval interference respectively in these materials (though the mapping need not always be that straightforward).

The structure in (5b) is also a singly embedded structure with four stacked NPs, but now the embedded clause is a double nominative construction with a stative verb V1 taking a -*ga* marked subject and a -*ga* marked object. The potential subject-hood of NP4-*ga* increases the retroactive interference for the subject attachments of both V1 and V2.[4] Thus, V1 suffers from one unit of retroactive interference and one unit of proactive (total two), and V2 suffers from two units of retroactive interference (total two). We are adopting the initial simple assumptions that retroactive and proactive interference contribute equally to retrieval difficulty, and that the amount of interference increases linearly with the number interfering items.

---

[2] Assuming that the embedded object NP-*o* contributes no interference seems to put the model at odds with the finding reported by Babyonyshev and Gibson (1999) that embedded transitive clauses are more difficult than embedded intransitives. However, the incorrect prediction follows from the simple all-or-nothing similarity metric. Under a more graded similarity metric, the object NP would contribute some retroactive interference and the transitive–intransitive contrast follows.

[3] For example, retrieval interference is likely to be a function of overlapping retrieval cues, while storage interference will be a function of overlapping features of the item representation.

[4] More precisely, we assume that it is the preferred interpretation of NP-*ga* as occupying subject position (e.g. Inoue and Fodor 1995) that contributes the interference. That is, if it was possible to change the interpretive bias for the NP to a nominative object, then the interference should be reduced. Our present materials do not distinguish between interference due to identical case marking, and interference due to preferred structural position.

We expect that both assumptions will require modification; see Gibson (1998) for discussion of non-linear interference and decay functions.

Because this metric yields interference values for each word in a sentence, a natural and detailed behavioral correlate is on-line reading times. However, for the present set of studies, we are concerned with global judgments of processing difficulty, and, following Gibson (1998), we will assume that these global judgments reflect the *maximum* level of difficulty experienced in the sentence. That is, the word-by-word metric can be used to predict global acceptability by taking the maximum value over all the words in the sentence. Again, this is an initial simplifying assumption, and other plausible mappings are possible, including average difficulty, or, more likely, an averaged weighted by some non-linear recency function.

2.2 An Exploratory Pilot Study

The syntactic characteristics of Japanese make it possible to keep the level of embedding and amount of stacking constant, while changing the number of syntactically similar NP arguments, as in (5), repeated below as (6):

(6) a. [NP-ga NP-ni [NP-ga NP-o V] V]
       (level of embedding=1, stacking=4, maximum interference=1)
    b. [NP-ga NP-ni [NP-ga NP-ga V] V]
       (level of embedding=1, stacking=4, maximum interference=2)

To explore the possible effects of stacking, embedding, and interference, we conducted a pilot questionnaire rating study with forty students from Kobe Shoin Women's University in Japan using a variety of sentential complement structures, along with single-clause controls. Subjects rated the difficulty of comprehending the sentences on a scale of 1 (easy) to 7 (very difficult) (e.g., see Uehara 1996, for similar designs). There were twenty different structural types, which varied along the three dimensions above. The level of embedding ranged from 0 (a single verb and its arguments) to 1 (a matrix verb taking a sentential complement, verb, and one embedded clause); the number of stacked NPs ranged from 1 to 5; and the level of maximum interference ranged from 0 to 2, according to the metric discussed above. A fully factorial design was impossible with this range of levels (e.g., it is impossible to stack five NPs in a single clause), but collapsing subranges of the levels into "high" and "low" permitted an ANOVA of these two factors. Table 1 shows the ratings as a function of NP stacking and syntactic similarity interference.

	Low stacking (1–3 NPs)	High stacking (4 and 5 NPs)
Low interference	1.3	2.3
High interference	4.5	4.2

Table 1. Difficulty ratings as a function of amount of syntactic similarity interference and NP stacking in the pilot study.

The predicted effect of interference was confirmed. Although interference appears to be more important than stacking as a determinant of difficulty in these materials, and there is a significant stacking × interference interaction ($p < 0.001$), the ordinal nature of the metric means that we should not take the interaction and the difference in the size of the stacking and interference effect too seriously. What the data do suggest is that both stacking and interference have independent effects on the difficulty ratings.

To gain a better understanding of the effects in this study, we performed a number of exploratory regressions, using level of embedding, amount of stacking, and interference as predictors of the average rated difficulty on the twenty different structures. Neither embedding level nor stacking were good predictors of difficulty alone ($R^2=0.036$ and $R^2=0.15$, respectively). Figure 1 shows the rated difficulty as a function of stacking. Interference was a much better predictor ($R^2=0.55$, see Figure 2). However, adding one more component to the similarity metric, *positional similarity*, improves the fit dramatically to $R^2=0.73$ (the regression equation is *difficulty* = 2.07 + 0.40*SyntacticInteference + 0.21*PositionalSimilarity, where positional similarity is simply the number of adjacent syntactically similar NPs). In other words, when syntactically similar NPs are closer together, there is a substantial increase in the perceived complexity of the structure. This replicates an effect noted by Uehara (1996, 1999).

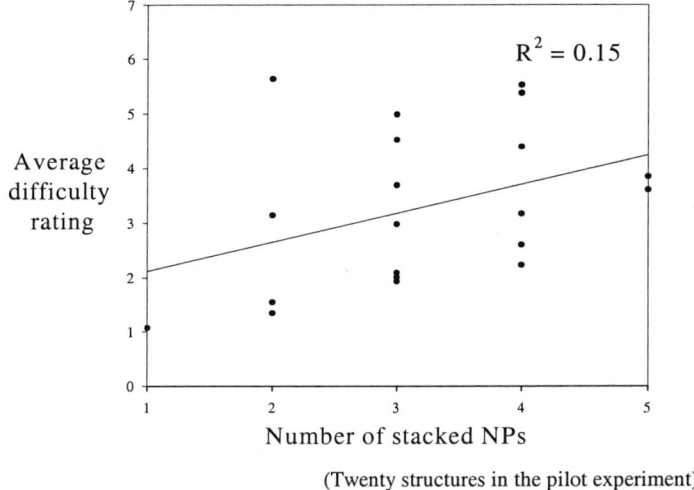

(Twenty structures in the pilot experiment)

Figure 1. Rated difficulty as a function of number of stacked NPs

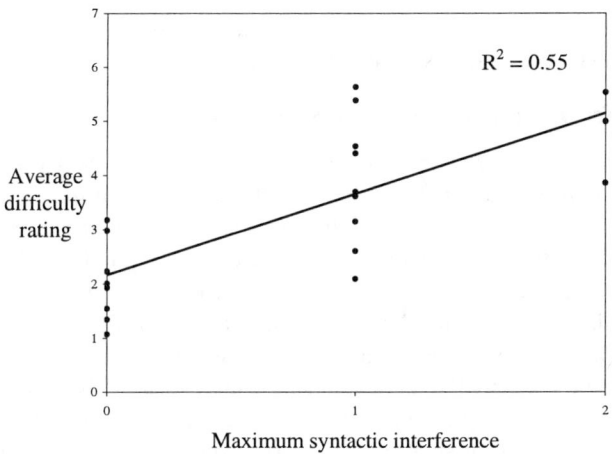

(Twenty structures in the pilot experiment)

Figure 2. Rated difficulty as a function of maximum similarity-based syntactic interference

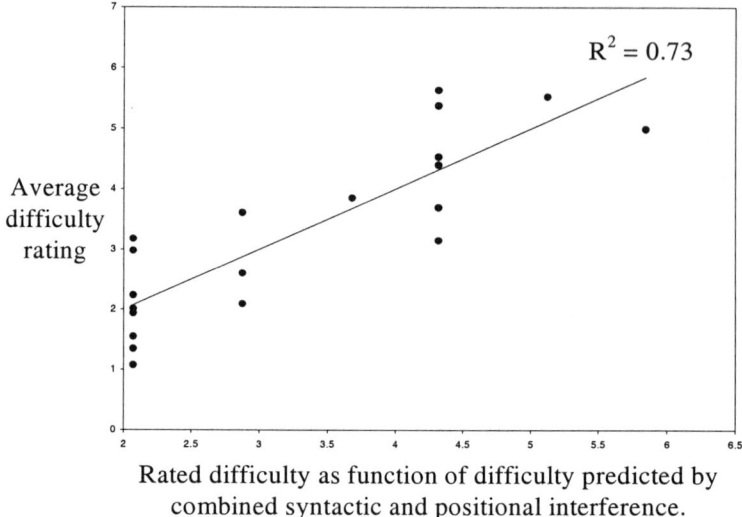

Rated difficulty as function of difficulty predicted by combined syntactic and positional interference.

(Twenty structures in the pilot experiment)

Figure 3: Rated difficulty vs. difficulty predicted from combined maximum syntactic and positional interference

2.3 Interference due to Positional Similarity

To see why positional similarity may exert a strong effect on processing difficulty, consider again the NP1–V2 attachment required in (5) above. Both NP1 and NP3 are syntactically marked as potential subjects. In the absence of any further basis on which to discriminate the NPs, the only way that the parser knows that NP1, and not NP3, is to be attached to V2 (and similarly, that NP3, and not NP1, is to be attached to V1) is the relative *serial positions* of the two candidate NPs. (Japanese disallows crossed embeddings, so the alternative attachments are not syntactically viable.)

A substantial body of on memory for serial order has established that positional confusions arise as a function of distance: the closer together two items are, the more likely their serial positions will be confused (e.g. Estes 1972, see Henson 1998 for a recent review). If we adopt this principle as a property of working memory for parsing, then it follows that placing otherwise syntactically indiscriminable NPs adjacent to one another will increase processing difficulty, just in those cases where the correct attachment of the

NPs depends on their relative positions. We call this the *positional similarity* effect.

Positional similarity can be understood to be another kind of similarity-based retrieval interference. At the point of attachment, the correct NP must be retrieved on the basis of positional information as well as item information (the syntactic features associated with the item.) Just as retrieval interference arises as a function of the syntactic similarity of candidate items, interference also arises as a function of the positional similarity of candidate items. Furthermore, serial position itself provides a natural, graded, similarity metric for positional interference, and one that receives considerable empirical support from existing work in verbal short term memory. Our initial results from the pilot study suggest that positional similarity plays an important role in working memory for parsing as well.

3 Experiments I–III: Testing the Effects of Positional Similarity and Amount of Stacking

To test the new processing metric in which positional similarity plays an important role, we designed the following experiment. Level of embedding was kept constant at one embedded clause. We independently varied the amount of stacking (STACK) and the number of syntactically and positionally similar NP arguments (POS). Consider the schematic sentences below.

(7) a. *Type DI*
[NP-ga NP-ni [NP-ga V-to] V]   (POS 0, STACK 3)
 b. *Type TT*
[NP-ga [NP-ga NP-o V-to] V]   (POS 2, STACK 3)
 c. *Type DT*
[NP-ga NP-ni [NP-ga NP-o V-to] V]   (POS 0, STACK 4)
 d. *Type TD*
[NP-ga [NP-ga NP-ni NP-o V-to] V]   (POS 2, STACK 4)

Sentence type (7a) contains a ditransitive verb in the matrix clause and an intransitive verb in the embedded, complement clause (DI). Sentence type (7b) has a matrix transitive verb and an embedded transitive verb in the complement clause (TT). Sentence type (7c) is similar to (7a) in that it also includes a matrix ditransitive verb, but it is different from (7a) in that it has a transitive verb in the complement clause. Sentence type (7d) is similar to (7b) in that it contains a matrix transitive verb, but different in that its complement clause includes a ditransitive verb. Thus, sentence types (7a)–(7d) all have the same level of embedding, and sentence types (7a) and (7b) have three NPs, and (7c) and (7d) four NPs. Only (7b) and (7d) contain two adjacent overt subject NPs with the same case marker *-ga*.

Experiments I–III all contained the sentence types described above.[5] They were all 2 × 2 designs with two levels of stacking (3 NP and 4 NP) and two levels of positional similarity (adjacent subject NPs and non-adjacent subject NPs), holding constant level of embedding. Each subject saw four versions of the four experimental types (sixteen total experimental sentences) interspersed with thirty-four fillers, for a total of fifty sentences.

3.1 Design and Procedure

Experiment I was a paper-and-pencil questionnaire study, where participants were asked to rate the difficulty of a sentence on a seven point scale, as in the pilot study. Experiment II employed the same test material as in Experiment I, but was an on-line non-cumulative moving window study implemented in Psyscope (Cohen, MacWhinney, Flatt, and Provost 1993) on a Macintosh Powerbook G3. The participants were asked to rate the difficulty of a sentence on a seven point scale as in Experiment I. Participants read the sentences one word (or *bunsetsu*, i.e., NP-*ga/o/ni*) at a time by pressing the space bar. Each time the subject hit the space bar, the next word was uncovered on the screen and the previous word was hidden with a string of dashes. At the end of the sentence there was a period, and as soon as the participant hit the space bar, the period disappeared and the screen presented the instruction to rate the difficulty of the sentence just read. Then, the subject typed in a number from one to seven. Experiment III used the same on-line moving window task as in Experiment II, but, as explained below, the test sentences were slightly different from those in   Experiments I and II. The same number of test sentence types and filler sentences were included in all three experiments.

All test sentences in Experiments I and II were constructed using common nouns with familiarity rating from 1.14 to 2.5 (SD .11) and verbs from 1.29 to 2.36 (SD .22) (where 1=very familiar (see/hear very frequently) and 7=very unfamiliar (not see/hear at all) in the 1–7 scale). These ratings were the average ratings of the word familiarity test independently given to fourteen native speakers of Japanese in Columbus, Ohio, and Tokyo, Japan, prior to conducting this experiment. Each individual test sentence was balanced as much as possible with the noun and verb ratings so that a particular sentence did not contain only less familiar words: The mean ratings for the nouns in DI, TT, DT, and TD were 2.06, 2.06, 2.15, and 2.15, the mean ratings for the verbs were 1.6, 1.87, 1.76, and 1.76, and the mean ratings for

---

[5] Experiment I was first presented in Lewis and Nakayama (1999).

all items (i.e., nouns and verbs; SD .10) were 1.89, 1.98, 2.02, and 2.02, respectively. Although the familiarity was controlled, the number of mora and letters were not controlled. Appropriate characters (i.e., *hiragana, katakana, kanji* and *romaji*) were used in order to avoid reading difficulties. All nouns used in the test sentences were human common nouns, but those in the filler sentences contained inanimate and proper nouns. Test sentences in Experiment III contained proper nouns (names) instead of common nouns. These proper nouns were not controlled in terms of the familiarity ratings because of the unavailability of their ratings, but they were judged to be familiar names by one of the authors (Nakayama), a native speaker of Japanese. They were either 3 or 4 morae long, but represented by two *kanjis*. The verbs used in the test sentences included both native Japanese and Sino-Japanese verbs (i.e. Verbal Noun+*suru*). Matrix verbs were all past-tense while the embedded verbs had a counter-balanced number of present and past tenses (i.e. two non-past and two past tense sentences). Five matrix verbs in Experiment III were different from those used in Experiments I and II in order to avoid the unnaturalness resulting from the uses of the individual names. Verbs with familiarity rating from 1.29 to 2.36 were used in Experiment III: The mean ratings for DI, TT, DT, and TD were 1.6, 1.94, 1.78, and 1.84 (SD.24). The mean familiarity ratings of the four types were not significantly different from one another. Examples are shown below. For instance, the DI sentence contained three NPs with a matrix ditransitive verb and an intransitive embedded verb, i.e., zero similar consecutive NPs (POS 0) with three stacked NPs (STACK 3).

(8) a. DI   (POS 0, STACK 3)
    Experiments I and II
    Ani-ga   sensei-ni   onna-no-ko-ga asondeiru-to
    elder brother-Nom teacher-Dat girl-Nom   playing that

    renrakushita.
    Notified

    'My older brother notified the teacher that a girl was playing.'

    Experiment III
    Yamada-ga Uehara-ni Fukuzawa-ga asondeiru-to renrakushita.
    'Yamada notified Uehara that Fukuzawa was playing.'

b. TT   (POS 2, STACK 3)
   Experiments I and II
   Haisha-ga   daitooryoo-ga tsuuyaku-o   yonda-to
   dentist-Nom president-Nom interpreter-Acc called that

   oboeteita.
   remembered

   'The dentist remembered that the President called the interpreter.'

   Experiment III
   Koyama-ga   Miyamoto-ga Takeuchi-o   yonda-to oboeteita.
   'Koyama remembered that Miyamoto called Takeuchi.'

c. DT   (POS 0, STACK 4)
   Experiments I and II
   Kyooju-ga   shachoo-ni   daihyoo-ga   kookoosei-o
   professor-Nom president-Dat representative-Nom   h.s. student-Acc

   shinsasuru-to yakusokushita.
   examine that promised

   'The professor promised the company president that the representative would examine the high school student.'

   Experiment III
   Kosaka-ga Ogihara-ni Miyazawa-ga Morita-o shinsasuru-to yakusokushita.
   'Kosaka promised Ogihara that Miyazawa would examine Morita.'

d. TD   (POS 2, STACK 4)
   Experiments I and II
   Seito-ga   kooshi-ga   repootaa-ni   sakka-o
   student-Nom lecturer-Nom   reporter-Dat   author-Acc

   shookaishita-to kizuita
   introduced that noticed

   'The student noticed that the lecturer introduced the author to the reporter.'

Experiment III
Misawa-ga   Hagimoto-ga   Watanabe-ni   Matsui-o
shookaishita-to kizuita.
'Misawa noticed that Hagimoto introduced Matsui to Watanabe.'

According to the interference theory outlined in §2 above, the POS 0 sentences should be easier than those with POS 2. Furthermore, if there is some encoding or storage interference from any NP regardless of case-marking, then STACK 3 sentences should be easier than those with STACK 4. That is, if STACK is an independent determinant of processing complexity, (8a) and (8b) should be easier than (8c) and (8d). If POS is an independent determinant of processing complexity, then (8a) and (8c) should be easier than (8b) and (8d). If both are contributing factors, (8d) should be the most difficult sentence type.

Sixty female participants (between 19–22 years old) from Kobe Shoin Women's University participated in Experiment I. Each participant was given a questionnaire and asked to rate the sentences in class. They were also asked to make the sentences easier with slight changes if they found them to be difficult. Because of this rewriting, the experiment took about thirty to forty minutes. In Experiment II, thirty-five female subjects with normal vision or corrected vision (between 19–39 years old) from Kobe Shoin Women's University participated. They were all different from those who participated in Experiment I. In Experiment III, thirty male and female Japanese native speakers with normal vision or corrected vision (25–40 years old) participated. Half of them were Japanese elementary and junior high school teachers who had just arrived from Japan to observe elementary and junior high school classes in Ohio, and the other half were the Ohio State University students or students' spouses. In both Experiments II and III, all participants were paid volunteers and tested individually. The experiments took about twenty to thirty minutes per person.

3.2 Results

Results show that the DI sentences evoked the easiest and the TD sentence the most difficult ratings among the four sentence types in all three experiments. Table 2 shows the summary of the average ratings of the four sentence types in Experiment I.

| | POS | |
STACK	0	2
3	3.02 ± 0.26 (DI)	5.07 ± 0.24 (TT)
4	4.2 ± 0.25 (DT)	5.22 ± 0.24 (TD)

Table 2. Mean ratings of the four sentence types in Experiment I (paper-and-pencil questionnaire), with 95% confidence intervals.

The STACK 3 sentences (DI and TT) were significantly easier to understand than the STACK 4 sentences (DT and TD) ($F1(1, 59)=31.68$, $p<.001$; $F2(1, 12)=10.20$, $p<.008$) and the POS 0 sentences (DI and DT) were significantly easier than the POS 2 sentences (TT and TD) ($F1(1, 59)=106.89$, $p<.001$; $F2(1, 12)=54.94$, $p<.001$). There is a significant interaction of STACK and POS ($F1(1, 59)=25.35$, $p<.001$; $F2(1, 12)=6.10$, $p<.029$). However, because the difficulty scale used here is ordinal (and may not be interval), this interaction may not be meaningful. Sentence type DI is significantly easier than DT, TT, and TD, and DT is significantly easier than TT and TD (by a post-hoc Tukey HSD test at family $\alpha=0.05$, for both item and subject means).

Table 3 shows the summary of the average ratings of the four sentence types in Experiment II.

| | POS | |
STACK	0	2
3	2.77 ± 0.28 (DI)	3.89 ± 0.28 (TT)
4	3.91 ± 0.30 (DT)	4.43 ± 0.28 (TD)

Table 3. Mean ratings of the four sentence types in Experiment II (moving-window), with 95% confidence intervals.

Again, the STACK 3 sentences were significantly easier to understand than the STACK 4 sentences ($F1(1, 34)=37.49$ $p<.001$; $F2(1, 12)=12.38$, $p<.004$) and the POS 0 sentences were significantly easier than the POS 2 sentences ($F1(1, 34)= 27.47$, $p<.001$; $F2(1,12)=11.76$, $p<.005$). There was no significant interaction of STACK and POS. Sentence type DI is significantly easier than DT, TT, and TD at the .05 level (by a post-hoc Tukey HSD test at family $\alpha=0.05$, for both item and subject means).

Table 4 shows the summary of the average ratings of the four sentence types in Experiment III.

	POS	
STACK	0	2
3	3.16 ± 0.30 (DI)	4.19 ± 0.30 (TT)
4	4.05 ± 0.33 (DT)	5.23 ± 0.29 (TD)

Table 4. Mean ratings of the four sentence types in Experiment III (moving window, with proper nouns), with 95% confidence intervals

The same patterns holds with sentences using proper nouns: the STACK 3 sentences were significantly easier to understand than the STACK 4 sentences (F1(1, 29)=81.32, p <.001; F2(1, 12)=13.75, p<.003) and the POS 0 sentences were significantly easier than the POS 2 sentences (F1(1, 29)=44.42, p<.001; F2(1, 12)=18.09, p<.001). There is no significant interaction of STACK and POS. Sentence types DI and DT are significantly easier than TD (by a post-hoc Tukey HSD test at family α=0.05, for both item and subject means).

The results of these three experiments demonstrate that the number of argument NPs and their positional and syntactic similarity contribute to the difficulty of the sentences across quite different presentation paradigms and across different sentences with common and proper nouns. Increasing the discriminability (decreasing the similarity) of the NP arguments clearly makes processing easier. If this finding is correct, scrambling should also in some cases reduce the difficulty of processing. We will look at the effect of scrambling below.

4 Experiments IV and V: Using Scrambling to Reduce Interference Due to Positional Similarity

The experiments above suggest that the difficulty of comprehending sentences is a function, in part, of similarity-based syntactic and positional interference. This section examines the similarity interference hypothesis in scrambled sentences. According to the simplest hypothesis in which scrambling per se introduces no additional cost (Yamashita 1997, see also Nakayama 1995), scrambling that reduces positional similarity should make sentences easier to process. Japanese is a language that allows us to test this prediction.

Two experiments were conducted testing the following sentence types. Level of embedding was kept constant at one embedded clause and both matrix and embedded verbs were transitive verbs (i.e., three NP arguments for the entire sentence). Consider the following examples.

(9) a. *Type Sso* (STACK 3, POS 2)
Keikan-ga ryooshin-ga kodomo-o sagasu-to kangaeta
policeman-Nom parents-Nom child-Acc look for that thought
'The policeman thought that the parents would look for their child.'

b. *Type soS* (STACK 2, POS 0)
Ryooshin-ga kodomo-o sagasu-to keikan-ga kangaeta.

c. *Type Sos* (STACK 3, POS 0)
Keikan-ga kodomo-o ryooshin-ga sagasu-to kangaeta.

All three sentences in (9) contain the same number of words and the same nouns and verbs, but word orders are different. Sentence (9a) is the canonical word order while both (9b) and (9c) contain scrambled constituents. In (9b), the entire complement clause is scrambled while in (9c) the object is scrambled in the complement clause. Because of the different word orders, the positional similarity (POS) levels are different: only the Sso type has POS 2, because there are consecutive overt subject NPs with the same case marker –*ga*. If scrambling per se carries no processing cost, i.e., the processing cost is determined only by the effects that scrambling has on interference, it should be possible to scramble NPs or complement clauses and actually reduce working memory costs. Therefore, (9b) and (9c) are predicted to be easier than (9a).

4.1 Design and Procedure

Experiments IV and V both contained the same test material as described above. However, they were different in that Experiment IV was a paper-and-pencil questionnaire study while Experiment V was a moving window study, as in Experiments I and II, respectively.[6] Similar to the experiments above, all test sentences were constructed using nouns and verbs with similar familiarity ratings. Nouns with familiarity rating from 1.14 to 2.43 (mean 1.98, SD .10) and the verbs from 1.36 to 2.36 (mean 1.88, SD .24) were used (the mean item rating = 1.94, SD .12). Three versions of each sentence (corresponding to the three conditions) were constructed from each set of nouns and verbs, so there was no lexical variability across conditions. Appropriate characters (*hiragana, katakana, kanji* and *romaji*) were used in

---

[6] Experiment IV was reported in Nakayama and Lewis (2000).

order to avoid reading difficulties. All nouns used in the test sentences were human common nouns, but the filler sentences contained inanimate and proper nouns. The verbs used in the test sentences included both native Japanese and Sino-Japanese verbs (i.e., Verbal Noun+*suru*). Matrix verbs were all past-tense. In the test material, each sentence type was represented by four sentence tokens, and there were thirty-eight filler sentences, for a total of fifty sentences in the experiment. Three different lists of experiments were prepared so that each subject saw only one version of each sentence. Each list was given to the same number of the subjects in each experiment.

Sixty male and female Japanese natives (20–25 years old) from Tohoku Gakuin University participated in Experiment IV and 30 female subjects with normal vision or corrected vision (18–28 years old) from Kobe Shoin Women's University and University of Shizuoka participated in Experiment V. They were asked to rate the difficulty of each of these sentence types on a 7 point scale in the questionnaire (Experiment IV) or in the moving window presentation (Experiment V). The subjects in Experiment V were tested individually and paid nominal fees. Experiment IV took about thirty minutes while Experiment V took about twenty to thirty minutes.

4.2 Results

Results show that the soS sentences (with a scrambled clause) evoked the easiest and the Sos sentence (with a scrambled object in the complement clause) the most difficult ratings among the three sentence types in both experiments. Table 5 shows the summary of the average ratings of the three test sentences in Experiments IV and V.

Structure type	Experiment IV (paper questionnaire)	Experiment V (moving window)
Sso, STACK 3, POS 2 (no scrambling)	4.53 ± 0.19	3.90 ± 0.35
soS, STACK 2, POS 0 (scrambled clause)	3.59 ± 0.22	3.05 ± 0.35
Sos, STACK 3, POS 0 (scrambled object in complement clause)	5.20 ± 0.17	4.38 ± 0.37

Table 5. Mean ratings of the three sentence types in Experiments IV and V (scrambling), with 95% confidence intervals.

As predicted by the similarity interference theory, the soS type sentences like (9b) are the easiest.[7] The soS type sentences are significantly easier than the Sso and the Sos ((9a) and (9c) respectively) sentences in (by a post-hoc Tukey HSD test at $\alpha=0.05$, for both item and subject means). However, the Sos (9c) sentences are not easier than the Sso (9a) sentences, contrary to the theory's predictions. Why? One explanation is that it is unnatural to have scrambling within the complement clauses in the sentences with the overt matrix subjects. Because the complement clauses were not direct quotes, it is odd to prepose the object within the complement clause. This unnaturalness might have overcome the reduced positional similarity and evoked the high score in the difficulty rating. Another possibility is that there is a kind of garden path effect in (9c) resulting from the initial subject NP and object NP being structured together in the same clause. There is considerable independent evidence that such structuring takes place before the verb in head-final languages (e.g. Bader and Lasser 1994, Inoue and Fodor 1995). Thus, the Sos sentences may incur the additional processing cost of reanalyzing the second NP from object of the main clause to object of the embedded clause (see Mazuka, Itoh, and Kondo 2001, Miyamoto and Takahashi 2001, and Nakano, Felser, and Clahsen, 2000; cf. Yamashita 1997). Either of these possibilities provides an independent reason for the difficulty of the Sos structure. Thus, we believe that the results of the experiments are consistent with the prediction of the theory that positional similarity of NP arguments will be a significant determinant of processing difficulty. What clearly remains to be done is to integrate this metric with a comprehensive processing model that includes reanalysis from garden paths.

5 Conclusion

The results of all the studies confirm the prediction of the similarity-based interference theory (Lewis 1996, 1998) that syntactic similarity of NP arguments will be a significant determinant of processing difficulty in unambiguous embedded constructions, even when controlling for level of embedding and amount of stacking. We have furthermore extended this account to include positional interference. All five experiments confirm the prediction that increasing the positional similarity of syntactically indiscriminable NPs will increase processing difficulty. Our results are similar to Uehara's

---

[7] There is also a difference in level of center-embedding between the soS sentences and Sso sentences (9a); i.e., level of embedding is confounded with interference. Thus, a theory based only on level of center-embedding could also account for this difference. However, such a theory could not account for the results of Experiments I–III, which controlled level of embedding while varying amount of interference.

(1999), who came to the conclusion that it is repetitive nominativeness that causes the difficulty in parsing (but see below); we are interpreting this result in the theoretical framework of similarity-based interference. Thus, we continue to have empirical support for the idea that working memory for syntactic processing is governed by the same processing principles that govern other kinds of working memory, even if the underlying representational codes used are different across different tasks.

Are there viable alternative explanations for the positional similarity effects? The evidence we have presented here comes exclusively from repeated NP-*ga* sequences, and therefore the difficulty could have arisen from a number of sources not related to positional similarity. Let's consider briefly three such possibilities:

a) Is the difficulty due to the functional ambiguity of the *–ga* marker—perhaps a kind of garden path effect? Independent evidence suggests that the multiple functions of *–ga* (focus, subject marker, and object marker of the statives) do not account for the processing difficulty. Such sequences are effectively taken as two subjects belonging to two separate clauses (Uehara 1999, Uehara and Bradley 2001), which is the correct interpretation for all five of our experiments.

b) Is the difficulty due to the phonological repetition of the *–ga* marker? Apparently not: similar findings are reported in Korean using phonologically distinct nominative markers (Uehara and Bradley 1996).

c) Is the difficulty due to repetitive nominative marking, as Uehara (1999) suggests? Apparently not: Vasishth (2000) reports studies in Hindi that show that adjacent NPs marked by the dative *–ko* also lead to difficulty.

Although much works remains to be done, we believe the studies to date point to the need to include some effect of positional similarity in models of parsing.[8] This is a natural extension to a model already based on similarity-modulated interference, and receives support from the fact that positional similarity (or temporal distinctiveness; Neath and Crowder 1990, Neath and Knoedler 1994) is known to affect recognition and recall in a variety of verbal short-term memory paradigms. More generally, we believe

---

[8] The item separating the two *ga*-marked NPs was a dative-marked NP in Experiments I-III. Apparently, it does not have to be the argument NP. We have tested the sequences separating two *ga*-marked NPs with a dative-marked NP and an adjunct locative PP (NP-*de*) in another experiment. Both sentence types evoked similar difficulty ratings.

the theoretical framework and studies reported here will pave the way to a better understanding of how serial position information is encoded in sentence comprehension, and provides the opportunity to establish close ties between sentence processing theory and accounts of serial order in other more general theories of memory.

References

Bader, M. & I. Lasser. 1994. Processing: Evidence for Immediate Attachment, in., *Perspectives in Sentence Processing*, eds. C. Clifton, L. Frazier, & K. Rayner. Hillsdale, NJ: Erlbaum.

Bever, T. G. 1970. The Cognitive Basis for Linguistic Structures. *Cognition and the Development of Language,* ed. J. R. Hayes. New York: Wiley.

Baddeley, A. D. & G. J. Hitch. 1974. Working Memory, *Recent Advances in Learning and Motivation* Vol. 8, ed. G. A. Bower. New York: Academic Press.

Chomsky, N. 1959. On Certain Formal Properties of Grammars. *Information & Control.* 2:137-167.

Cohen, J. D., B. MacWhinney, M. Flatt, & J. Provost. 1993. PsyScope: A New graphic Interactive Environment for Designing Psychology Experiments. *Behavioral Research Methods, Instruments & Computers* 25.2: 257-271.

Cowper, E. A. 1976. Constraints on Sentence Complexity: A Model for Syntactic Processing. Doctoral dissertation, Brown University.

Estes, W. 1972. An Associative Basis for Coding and Organisation in Memory. *Coding Processes in Human Memory*, eds. A.W. Melon & E. Margin, 161–190. Washington, D.C: Winston & Sons.

Gibson, E. A. 1991. A Computational Theory of Human Linguistic Processing: Memory Limitations and Processing Breakdown. Doctoral dissertation, Carnegie Mellon University.

Gibson, E. A. 1998. Linguistic Complexity: Locality of Syntactic Dependencies. *Cognition* 68:1-76.

Henson, R. N. 1998. Short-term Memory for Serial Order: The Start-End Model. *Cognitive Psychology* 36:73-137.

Hawkins, J. A. 1994. *A Performance Theory of Order and Constituency.* Cambridge: Cambridge University Press.

Inoue, A. & J. D. Fodor 1995. Information Paced Parsing of Japanese. *Japanese Sentence Processing*, eds. R. Mazuka & N. Nagai, 9-64. Hillsdale, NJ: Lawrence Erlbaum Associates.

Just, M. A. & P. A. Carpenter. 1992. A Capacity Theory of Comprehension: Individual Differences in Working Memory. *Psychological Review* 99:122-149.

Konieczny, L., B. Hemforth, C. Scheepers, & G. Strube. 1997. The Role of Lexical Heads in Parsing: Evidence from German. *Language & Cognitive Processes*

12: 307–348.
Kuno, S. 1974. The Position of Relative Clauses and Conjunctions. *Linguistic Inquiry* 5:117-136.
Lewis, R. L. 1993. An Architecturally-based Theory of Human Sentence Comprehension. Doctoral dissertation, Carnegie Mellon University.
Lewis, R. L. 1996. Interference in Short-term Memory: The Magical Number Two (or Three) in Sentence Processing. *Journal of Psycholinguistic Research* 25.1:93-115.
Lewis, R. L. 1998. Interference in Working Memory: Retroactive and Proactive Interference in Parsing. Talk presented at the Twelfth Annual CUNY Sentence Processing Conference, San Diego.
Lewis, R. L. & M. Nakayama. 1999. Determinants of Processing Complexity in Japanese Embeddings: New Theory and Data. Paper presented at the International Ease Asian Psycholinguistics Workshop, The Ohio State University.
Mazuka, R. K. Itoh, & T. Kondo. 2001. Costs of Scrambling in Japanese Sentence Processing. *Sentence Processing in East Asian Languages*, ed. M. Nakayama. Stanford: CSLI.
Miller, G. A. 1962. Some Psychological Studies of Grammar. *American Psychologist* 17:748-762.
Miller, G. A. & N. Chomsky. 1963. Finitary Models of Language Users. *Handbook of Mathematical Psychology* Vol.II, eds. D. R. Luce, R. R. Bush, & E. Galanter. New York: John Wiley.
Miyamoto, E. & S. Takahashi. 2001. Source of Difficulty in the Processing Scrambling in Japanese. *Sentence Processing in East Asian Languages*, ed. M. Nakayama. Stanford: CSLI.
Nakano, Y., C. Felser, & H. Clahsen 2000. Antecedent Priming at Trace Positions in Japanese Long-distance Scrambling. *Essex Research Reports in Linguistics* 31, 45-76.
Nakayama, M. 1995. Scrambling and Probe Recognition. *Japanese Sentence Processing*, eds. R. Mazuka & N. Nagai, 257-273. NJ: Lawrence Erlbaum Associate.
Nakayama, M. 1999. Sentence Processing. *The Handbook of Japanese Linguistics*, ed. N. Tsujimura, 398-424. Boston: Blackwell.
Nakayama, M. & R. L. Lewis. 2001. Similarity Interference and Scrambling in Japanese. *Injiguahak Jakop* [Journal of Cognitive Science] 1:39-53. Institute for Cognitive Science, Seoul National University.
Neath, I. & R. G. Crowder. 1990. Schedules of Presentation and Temporal Distinctiveness in Human Memory. *Journal of Experimental Psychology: Learning, Memory & Cognition* 16:316-327.
Neath, I. & A. J. Knoedler. 1994. Distinctiveness and Serial Position Effects in Recognition and Sentence processing. *Journal of Memory & Language* 33:776–795.

Stabler, E. P. 1994. The Finite Connectivity of Linguistic Structure. *Perspectives in Sentence Processing*, eds. C. Clifton, L. Frazier & K. Rayner. Hillsdale, NJ: Erlbaum.

Vasishth, S. 2000. Processing Hindi Center-embeddings. Talk presented at Department of Linguistics, The Ohio State University.

Uehara, K. 1996. The Effect of *-ga* Sequences on Judged Processing Load in Japanese. Poster presented at the 9th Annual CUNY Conference on Human Sentence Processing, New York.

Uehara, K. 1999. Center-embedding Problem and the Contribution of Nominative Case Repetition. Paper presented at the International East Asian Psycholinguistics Workshop at The Ohio State University.

Uehara, K. & D. Bradley. 1996. The Effect of *-ga* Sequences on Processing Japanese Multiply Center-embedded Sentences. *Language, Information & Computation*, eds. B.-S. Park & J.-B. Kim. Seoul: Kyung Hee University.

Uehara, K. & D. Bradley. 2001. Similarity-based Interference in Japanese Double versus Single Center-embedding. Poster presented at the 14th Annual CUNY Conference on Human Sentence Processing, Philadelphia.

Yamashita, H. 1997. The Effects of Word-order and Case Marking Information on the Processing of Japanese. *Journal of Psycholinguistic Research* 26:163-188.

Appendix A

Instructions for the questionnaire:

I am investigating how Japanese natives perceive Japanese sentences while hearing/reading them. Please read the following sentences and rate how easy they are to understand. If the sentence is very easy to understand, write numeral 1, if it is average, 4, if it is very difficult to understand, write 7 in ( ). If the sentence is difficult to understand, please write under the sentence how you would say it. Thank you very much for your cooperation.

Examples:
   a) Zaisei-koozoo-ga   kawaru.
      economic structure-Nom change
      'The economic structure will change.'
      (1) (= very easy to understand)
   b) Keeki-o jon-ni biru-ga inu-ga daidokoro-de tabeteiru-to itta.
      cake-Acc John-Dat Bill-Nom dog-Nom kitchen at eating that said
      'Bill told John that the dog was eating the cake in the kitchen.'
      (7) (= very difficult to understand)
      (These examples were the same in both experiments.)

Appendix B

Experiments I & II: Test Sentences

The number before each sentence indicates the order of presentation in the experiments.

DI 3. Ani-ga sensei-ni onna-no-ko-ga asondeiru-to renrakushita.
    17. Kantoku-ga josei-ni picchaa-ga ganbatta-to kotaeta.
    36. Shoogakusei-ga otoosan-ni hito-ga ita-to shiraseta.
    45. Oya-ga kyaku-ni musume-ga neteiru-to chuuishita.

TT 12. Haisha-ga daitooryoo-ga tsuuyaku-o yonda-to oboeteirta.
    21. Untenshu-ga kyokan-ga tomodachi-o korosu-to shinjiteita.
    28. Suponsaa-ga buchoo-ga shijo-o shootaisuru-to kimeta.
    38. Haha-ga chichi-ga tsuma-o mushishita-to nayandeita.

DT 9. Ryooshin-ga hitobito-ni puro-ga satsujinhan-o sagasu-to happyooshita.
    24. Anaunsaa-ga juumin-ni keikan-ga daigakusei-o shirabeta-to hoosooshita.
    30. Chuugakusei-ga OL-ni seijika-ga otooto-o tsukatta-to itta.
    42. Kyooju-ga shachoo-ni daihyoo-ga kookoosei-o shinsasuru-to yakusokushita.

TD 6. Seito-ga kooshi-ga repootaa-ni sakka-o shookaishita-to kizuita.
    15. Ashisutanto-ga kakari-ga hannin-ni kodomo-o watasu-to shitteita.
    33. Keisatsukan-ga gakusei-ga yuujin-ni imooto-o uru-to kangaeta.
    48. Otoko-no-ko-ga hahaoya-ga isha-ni akachan-o miseta-to omoidashita.

Appendix C

Experiment III: Test Sentences

DI 3. Yamada-ga Uehara-ni Fukuzawa-ga asondeiru-to renrakushita.
    17. Nonaka-ga Matsuyama-ni Nagashima-ga ganbatta-to kotaeta.
    36. Natsume-ga Ootsuka-ni Miyazaki-ga ita-to shiraseta.
    45. Nizuno-ga Yamanaka-ni shindoo-ga neteiru-to chuuishita.

TT 12. Koyama-ga Miyamoto-ga Takeuchi-o yonda-to oboeteita.
    21. Ogawa-ga Fujiwara-ga Nishimura-o korosu-to shinjiteita.
    28. Shiono-ga Kobayashi-ga Moriyama-o shootaisuru-to kanjita.
    38. Tanaka-ga Shimamoto-ga Yamaguchi-o mushishita-to nayandeita.

DT 9. Suzuki-ga Nakamura-ni Nishiyama-ga Tanabe-o sagasu-to tsutaeta.
    24. Shimada-ga Nakazawa-ni Nishimoto-ga Takano-o shirabeta-to henjishita.
    30. Nakata-ga Shinohara-ni Miyashita-ga Takei-o tsukatta-to itta.

42. Kosaka-ga Ogihara-ni Miyazawa-ga Morita-o shinsasuru-to yakusoku-shita.

TD 6. Misawa-ga Hagimoto-ga Watanabe-ni Matsui-o shookaishita-to kizuita.
15. Shimoda-ga Yoshimoto-ga Morisawa-ni Satoo-o watasu-to handanshita.
33. Yoshino-ga Nishizawa-ga Yoneyama-ni Sakata-o uru-to kangaeta.
48. Ueda-ga Yoshimura-ga Kurosawa-ni Komiya-o miseta-to omoikonda.

Appendix D

Experiments IV & V: Test Sentences (unscrambled version)

3. Sensei-ga otooto-ga hahaoya-o shinsasuru-to kimeta.
6. Koshi-ga gakusei-ga ashisutanto-o tsukatta-to kookaishita.
10. Untenshu-ga kyooshi-ga tomodachi-o korosu-to shinjiteita.
15. Haha-ga chichi-ga tsuma-o mushishita-to nayandeita.
18. Keikan-ga ryooshin-ga kodomo-o sagasu-to kangaeta.
21. OL-ga otoosan-ga isha-o hihanshita-to kanashinda.
24. Oya-ga kyooju-ga musume-o otosu-to kanjita.
29. Repootaa-ga seito-ga hito-o mitsuketa-to omotta.
33. Daigakusei-ga keisatsukan-ga bujinesuman-o shiraberu-to shitteita.
38. Josei-ga puro-ga yuujin-o kangeishiteita-to kizuita.
43. Haisha-ga daitooryoo-ga tsuuyaku-o yobu-to omoidashita.
48. Suponsaa-ga buchoo-ga shijo-o shootaishita-to oboeteita.

5

Lexical Ambiguity in Sentence Processing: Evidence from Chinese[*]

PING LI, HUA SHU, MICHAEL YIP, YAXU ZHANG AND YINGHONG TANG

1 Introduction

Lexical ambiguity has been the focus for the study of context effects in word recognition in the past twenty-five years (Small, Cottrell, and Tanenhaus 1988, Onifer and Swinney 1981, Simpson and Krueger 1991, Swinney 1979, Tabossi 1988). Most of this literature has been concerned with the study of Indo-European languages, in particular, English. However, the phenomenon of lexical ambiguity is pervasive in almost all languages, and it surfaces particularly strongly in Chinese. Thus, the study of lexical ambiguity in the processing of East Asian languages is important, especially given that the previous findings in this domain are claimed to be relevant to fundamental problems of language processing. In this study, we set out to ex-

---

[*] Preparation of this article was made possible by a Faculty Research Grant from the University of Richmond and in part by a grant from the National Science Foundation (#BCS-9975249) to Ping Li. Michael Yip received a postgraduate fellowship support from the Chinese University of Hong Kong, and Hua Shu, Yaxu Zhang, and Yinghong Tang received support from the National Science Foundation of China (#39670254). Correspondence concerning this paper should be addressed to Ping Li, Department of Psychology, University of Richmond, Virginia 23173, USA. Email: pli@richmond.edu.

Sentence Processing in East Asian Languages.
Mineharu Nakayama (ed.).
Copyright ©2002, CSLI Publications.

amine the processing of lexical ambiguity in Chinese, a language that has a massive number of homophones at the lexical and morphemic level.[1]

It is without doubt that listeners, in most instances, arrive at a unique semantic representation of an ambiguous word during the comprehension of a sentence in discourse. That is, they resolve the ambiguity at some point in time during comprehension. It is rather undesirable from a discourse processing perspective that listeners/readers should allow competing meanings of the same word to linger on through the sentence (see Simpson and Adamopoulos, in press, for a discussion of this point). Of course, just when lexical ambiguity is resolved is the issue at stake. The major debate concerns whether the access and selection of a contextually appropriate meaning from among several possible meanings depends on the prior sentence context, and how early, if at all, context can influence the access and selection process. Two competing hypotheses have emerged in the past twenty-five years from research with psychological, linguistic, and computational perspectives (Glucksberg, Kreuz, and Rho, 1986, Grosjean 1980, Marslen-Wilson 1987, 1990, Onifer and Swinney 1981, Small, Cottrell, and Tanenhaus 1988, Simpson 1981, Simpson and Kang 1994, Simpson and Krueger 1991, Swinney 1979, Tabossi 1988). First, the exhaustive or multiple access hypothesis argues that all meanings of an ambiguous word will be accessed momentarily following the occurrence of the word, and that sentence context can only help to select the appropriate meaning at a post-access stage. This hypothesis is based on the premise that language processing is a modular, bottom-up process in which non-lexical, sentential information does not penetrate lexical access (Fodor 1983). A contrasting hypothesis, the context-dependency or selective access hypothesis, argues that the contextually appropriate meaning of an ambiguous word can be selectively accessed early on if the preceding sentence context provides a strong bias to the appropriate meaning. This hypothesis assumes that language processing is operated by an interactive mechanism in which information can flow both bottom-up and top-down and that lexical access and sentential context can mutually and simultaneously interact with one another at a very early stage (McClelland 1987). In either case, researchers believe that the time course of lexical ambiguity resolution reflects the general mechanisms of language processing.[2]

---

[1] In this article we use "Chinese" as a generic term to refer to all dialects of Chinese, including Cantonese and Mandarin. In the discussion of specific experiments, however, we will refer specifically to Cantonese or Mandarin Chinese.

[2] Note that there are also hybrid models between the two competing hypotheses. In particular, the re-ordered access model (e.g. Rayner et al. 1994) argues for an interaction effect of meaning frequency and context: the dominant meaning is always activated irrespective of

As a major Sino-Tibetan language, Chinese differs significantly from most Indo-European languages in its phonological, lexical, and syntactic structures, which offer unique properties for psycholinguistic investigations of lexical and sentence processing (see Li, Bates, and MacWhinney 1993, Li 1996a, 1998, for a review). In particular, Chinese has a massive number of homophones at the lexical-morphemic level. According to *the Modern Chinese Dictionary* (Institute of Linguistics 1985), 80% of the monosyllables (differentiated by tones) in Chinese are ambiguous between different meanings (with different characters), and 55% have five or more homophones. The single syllable *yi* with the dipping tone has up to ninety homophones (e.g. skill, justice, benefit, discuss, intention, translate, hundred-million, etc.).[3] Upon hearing *yi* in a sentence, do Chinese listeners access all ninety homophonic meanings of the syllable? The strong version of the multiple access hypothesis would predict so, according to which lexical access is an autonomous and capacity-free process. However, the context-dependency hypothesis predicts that only the contextually appropriate meaning(s) will be accessed.

Because of the unique cross-linguistic properties of Chinese and the important role that lexical ambiguity plays in sentence processing, recently, research from our laboratories has been concerned with testing the above-mentioned competing hypotheses in Chinese. In particular, Li and Yip (1996, 1998) and Li (1998) have explored the processing of Chinese homophones, using cross-modal and gating paradigms (Grosjean 1980, Li 1996a, b) to examine the effects of sentence context, homophone frequency, homophone density, and lexical tonal information on native Cantonese speakers' access and selection of homophone meanings. Our cross-modal experiment showed that context effects take place immediately following the occurrence of the spoken homophone, and the gating experiment showed that listeners can recognize the contextually appropriate meaning with less than half of the acoustic information of the homophone. These experiments indicate that Chinese speakers are sensitive to the contextually biased meaning at an early stage, probably within the acoustic boundary of the word. Our results have also been confirmed by other studies in Mandarin Chinese. For example, Chen and Cui (1997) tested Mandarin speakers in Beijing in a reading task and their results showed that prior sentence contexts affect the different levels of activation of the dominant (the more frequent meanings) versus the subordinate meanings (the less frequent meanings) of ambiguous words:

---

context, and context can only help in elevating the activation level of the subordinate meaning. We will return to this model in General Discussion.

[3] This number would increase to 171 if identical syllables with different tones were considered as homophones.

dominant meanings have faster and stronger activation than subordinate meanings. Ahrens (1998) tested Mandarin speakers in Taipei in a cross-modal lexical decision task and her data indicate that the context-biased meaning receives significantly more priming than the meaning not biased by the sentence context.[4]

In the present study, we extend this line of research by using the cross-modal priming technique to examine the processing of homophones in both Cantonese and Mandarin Chinese. Experiment 1 extends the study of Li and Yip (1996, 1998) and examines Cantonese speakers' processing of homophones more systematically, taking into consideration word-gating results in the selection of ISI (inter-stimulus-interval). Experiment 2 investigates Mandarin speakers' processing of homophones, using a cross-modal priming method in a lexical-decision task. Converging results from the two experiments would allow us to select between the competing hypotheses in the processing of lexical ambiguity in sentences.

2 Experiment 1

2.1 Method

2.1.1 Participants

One hundred and forty-four native Cantonese speakers who reported no speech or hearing deficits participated in this experiment. All participants were students at the Chinese University of Hong Kong. They took part in the experiment as a laboratory requirement for credits in an introductory psychology course.

2.1.2 Materials

Thirty monosyllabic spoken homophones in the same tone were selected, each with at least two different meanings (syllables with different tones are not considered homophones in this experiment). Each homophone was embedded in three different sentences with prior context biased to different meanings. There was a total of ninety test sentences (thirty biased to the dominant meaning, thirty to the subordinate meaning, and thirty neutral). A

---

[4] But Ahrens (1998) had a different interpretation of the data, on the basis of which she argued against the context-dependent hypothesis. Our examination of her data reveals that the data are compatible only with the predictions of the context-dependent hypothesis. Note that there is *no* significant priming for the related probes for the primary meaning, contrary to her report (the *p* value of $F(1,44) = 3.01$ would be above and not below the .05 significance level).

separate group of twenty native Cantonese speakers was asked to judge the degree of constraint of the prior context on the target homophone. They were given the sixty test sentences with the prior biasing context (excluding the thirty neutral test sentences) but without the homophone, and were asked to fill in the word. They were told to think of a Chinese word that would naturally complete the sentence. Their responses were scored on a 1-4 scale, based on the scale proposed by Marslen-Wilson and Welsh (1978): 1 was given for a word identical to the test word, 2 for a synonym, 3 for a related word, and 4 for an unrelated word. Responses were pooled across the twenty judges, and the mean rating was 1.6 (s.d.= 0.43). This score was above the high constraint condition in Marslen-Wilson and Welsh (1978). An effort was also made to have prior sentence context of equal length, and the average length of the test sentences, counting the target homophone, was fourteen syllables (ranging from twelve to seventeen syllables). In addition, we tried to eliminate potential intrasentential associations between words in the sentence context and the target words, as such associations could lead to possible priming effects (Moss and Marslen-Wilson 1993).

Five independent variables were manipulated in this experiment:

(a) *Context type*: The preceding semantic context was (i) biased to the dominant meaning of a homophone, or (ii) biased to the subordinate meaning of the homophone, or (iii) neutral (i.e., compatible with both meanings).
(b) *Dominance*: The visual probe was related to either the dominant meaning of the homophone, or to the subordinate meaning of the homophone. The dominance information was based on the frequency counts in Ho and Jiang's (1994) analyses of Cantonese speech. In the example given below, the 'window' meaning of *coeng* has a higher frequency count than the 'gun' meaning of *coeng*, and therefore the former was the dominant meaning of the homophone while the latter the subordinate.
(c) *ISI*: The visual probe occurred at three interstimulus-intervals relative to the acoustic offset of the spoken homophone: the isolation point (ISI=IP), the acoustic offset of the homophone (i.e. ISI=0ms), or 300ms after the acoustic offset (i.e. ISI=300ms). The IP point for each homophone was derived from a separate study using the gating method (Yip & Li 1997). The IP point varies from word to word, and the average IP for the words used in this study was 54% (s.d. = 22%, range = 28%-79%) of the acoustic length of the word.
(d) *Relatedness*: The visual probes were either semantically related to the spoken homophone or unrelated controls.

(e) *Homophone Density*: A given homophone had either many potential competitors (four or more alternative meanings) or few competitors (two to three alternative meanings).

An example *coeng* (window/gun) and the three corresponding test sentences are given below.

(1) a. Sentence context biased to the dominant meaning
Gaan uk gam guk nei faaidi zau heoi hoi sai di **coeng**.
This room so muggy you quick walk go open all these window
'This room is so muggy that you should rush to open all the *windows*.'

b. Sentence context biased to the subordinate meaning
Gwanfo zyungaa waa ledi cyunbou dou hai zan **coeng**.
Military expert say these every all be real gun
'Military experts said that all of these are real *guns*.'

c. Ambiguous sentence context
Ngo jiu neidei yigaa zikhak zau heoi hoi **coeng**.
I order you now immediate walk go fire/open gun/window
'I order you to go immediately to fire/open your *guns/windows*.'

The four visual probes to *coeng* in these sentences are: *men* 'door' (related-dominant), *dan* 'bullet' (related-subordinate), *yi* 'clothes' (unrelated-dominant), and *ji* 'set' (unrelated-subordinate). All the visual probes were selected on the basis of a semantic relatedness judgment task from another separate group of 20 native Cantonese speakers. They were asked to think of three Chinese single characters that have the same or closely related meaning to each homophone, and their most frequent response was selected as the related visual probe for the homophone. The unrelated visual probes were randomly selected from the same source.

2.1.3 Design

The participants were divided into three groups of forty-eight according to the three context types. Context type was treated in a between-subject design, and all other variables were in a within-subject design. Within each context condition, the forty-eight participants were randomly assigned to twelve groups of four. Each group randomly received an equal number of sentences for each context condition in the 3 (ISI) x 2 (dominance) x 2 (relatedness) x 2 (homophone density) design. This yielded a total of twenty-four different experimental conditions. The order of presentation for the sentences was pseudorandomly arranged such that the visual probes did not consecutively bias spoken homophones. The order of presentation was counterbalanced across participants. No participant heard the same homophone twice.

2.1.4 Experimental Apparatus

The test sentences were read by a native Cantonese speaker at a normal conversation rate, and were tape-recorded and then digitized into a PowerMac computer. The presentation of the auditory and visual stimuli was controlled by the PsyScope program (Cohen, MacWhinney, Flatt, and Provost 1993). Participants' naming latencies were recorded and calculated (counting from the onset of the visual probe) by the CMU button-box (Cohen et al. 1993). A unidirectional microphone to register listeners' vocal responses was connected to the button-box through the box's voice-activated relay. Listeners' response accuracy was also recorded over a remote-controlled SONY tape-recorder by the experimenter in another room.

2.1.5 Procedure

Before the experiment began, the experimenter explained the task in Cantonese to the listener. Listeners were told that they would be hearing a Cantonese sentence on a pair of headphones, and immediately afterwards they would see a single Chinese character (visual probe) on the computer screen. Their task was to name the visual probe aloud into the microphone as accurately and quickly as possible. Listeners were given a maximum of two seconds to respond, counting from the onset of the visual probe. This length of time was sufficient for most participants to give their responses while at the same time putting them under time pressure. All participants did the experiment individually. Before the actual test began, they were given a practice session in which they heard a separate set of similar sentences. The whole experiment took about twenty minutes.

2.2 Results

Mean response latencies, counting from the onset of the visual probe to the participant's vocal response, are presented in Table 1. We conducted three separate statistical analyses on the data from neutral sentence context, sentence context biased to the dominant meaning, and sentence context biased to the subordinate meaning.

First, in the neutral context, a 3 (ISI) x 2 (dominance) x 2 (relatedness) x 2 (homophone density) repeated-measure ANOVA revealed a main effect of dominance, $F(1,47) = 23.34$, $p < .01$. Collapsed over other variables, the mean response time to access the dominant homophone meaning was 697ms and that to the subordinate meaning was 722ms. This result indicates that the most frequent meaning of a given homophone will be activated first if no biasing contextual information is available. There is also a main effect of ISI, $F (2,94) = 52.26, p < .01$. Collapsed across other variables, the mean response times to the three ISI conditions were 738ms (IP), 725ms (0ms), and 666ms (300ms), respectively, with the fastest response latencies occurring at the 300ms condition. This result indicates that when no strongly biasing context is available, the access of a given meaning occurs relatively late (300ms after the homophone's offset). No other effects are significant.

Context type	Dominant**		Subordinate	
	Related	Unrelated	Related	Unrelated
Biased to dominant				
IP	690	695	699	701
0 ms	667	670	663	690
300 ms	657	635	611	665
Biased to subordinate				
IP	704	741	761	739
0 ms	699	707	717	723
300 ms	638	646	700	750
Neutral				
IP	728	746	734	743
0 ms	706	689	745	738
300 ms	644	650	659	711

*Because the effect of homophone density was absent in our data, data for this variable were not included here.

** Dominant vs. Subordinate means whether the visual probe was related to the dominant meaning or the subordinate meaning (see discussion in Method). Same in Table 2.

Table 1. Response latencies (ms) as a function of context type, dominance, ISI, and relatedness in Experiment 1*

Second, in the sentence context that was biased toward the dominant meaning, a 3 x 2 x 2 x 2 repeated-measure ANOVA also revealed the main effects of dominance and ISI, similar to the conditions of the neutral sentence context. However, a post hoc comparison (Tukey HSD) shows that the ISI main effect was due to the significance difference between the IP level and the 0ms level ($p < .05$), and there was no significant difference between the 0ms level and the 300ms level ($p > .01$). This result is in contrast to that in the neutral context, where the difference between the IP level and the 0ms level was relatively small, while the difference between the 0ms level and the 300ms level was relatively large. Such a contrast suggests that the sentence context is playing an earlier role (i.e., within the acoustic boundary of the word) in this case than in the neutral context case.

Third, in the sentence context that was biased toward the subordinate meaning, a 3 x 2 x 2 x 2 ANOVA revealed again the main effects of dominance and ISI. When data from the two biased context conditions were compared, we found that sentence contexts biased to the dominant meaning produced stronger priming effects than contexts biased to the subordinate meaning, $F(1,94) = 3.9$, $p = .05$. A full five-way factorial analysis with type of contexts as an independent variable further confirmed that there was an interaction of context type by ISI by dominance, $F(2,188) = 8.11$, $p < .01$. These results show that when sentence context is biased toward different homophone meanings, the processing time will differ under different ISI levels: at the 0ms and the 300ms conditions (but not the IP point), the dominant meaning was accessed significantly faster than the subordinate meaning.

Finally, we conducted a separate analysis to compare the processing times in biased versus neutral sentence contexts, collapsing the two biasing context types. There was a clear effect of context, as revealed by ANOVA, $F(1,94) = 4.09$, $p < .05$. The average response latency in the biasing sentence contexts was 670ms and that in the neutral sentence context was 709ms. This shows that the access of homophone meanings occurs much earlier in the biasing context than it does in the neutral context. In sum, our data indicate an early context effect and its mutual interaction with word frequency during sentence processing, providing further evidence to the context-dependency hypothesis.

In this experiment, we examined the processing of homophones in Cantonese. To further corroborate the results, we conducted a similar but slightly different experiment in Mandarin Chinese, Experiment 2. In contrast to Experiment 1 in which monosyllabic homophones were tested, Experiment 2 investigates the processing of bisyllabic homophones.[5]

---

[5] Although both experiments used the cross-modal task, they are not exact replicates of each other, because the testing materials are different, and some information (e.g., dominance information, or IP information) that is available in Cantonese may not be available in Mandarin, and vice versa.

3 Experiment 2

3.1 Method

3.1.1 Participants

Eighty native Mandarin speakers who reported no speech or hearing deficits participated in this experiment. All participants were students at Beijing Normal University, and were paid for taking part in the experiment.

3.1.2 Materials

Twenty-four disyllabic spoken homophones were selected, each with two different meanings. Each homophone was embedded in two different sentences with prior context biasing either the dominant meaning or the subordinate meaning. There was a total of twenty-four test sentences (twelve biasing dominant meaning and twelve subordinate meaning). We also used twenty-four control sentences that were made up by replacing the homophone in each of the test sentences with an unambiguous word.

Four independent variables were manipulated in this experiment:

(a) *ISI*: The visual probe occurred at two interstimulus-intervals relative to the acoustic offset of the spoken homophone: the acoustic offset of the homophone (i.e., ISI=0ms), or −150ms before the acoustic offset (i.e., ISI=-150ms). We did not use the IP point ISI because no gating results were available for Mandarin homophones. However, the −150ms ISI can roughly approximate the function of the IP point, since for most of the disyllables in our experiment −150ms is at the beginning of the second syllable, which is comparable to the 54% for the IP of the monosyllables (see Experiment 1).
(b) *Context type*: The preceding semantic context was (i) biased to the dominant meaning of a homophone, or (ii) biased to the subordinate meaning of the homophone.
(c) *Dominance*: The visual probe was related to either the dominant meaning or the subordinate meaning of the homophone. The dominance information was determined by asking a separate group of thirty-one students to listen to the sentences and write down the homophone (the last word of the sentence). The dominant meaning of the homophone would elicit twenty-five or more written responses in this task, and the subordinate meaning would elicit five or fewer responses.

(d) *Prime type*: The prime (last word of the sentence) was either the homophone or an unrelated control word, matched to the frequency of one of the meanings of the homophone. The control words were all unambiguous words.

An example *fayan* (speak/infect) and the corresponding test sentences are given below.

(2) a. Sentence context biasing the dominant meaning
Homophone:
Qunchang dunshi bian-de anjing qilai, yinwei xianzai yijing
place   suddenly become quite up   because now already

kaishi **fayan**.
start speech

'The place suddenly became quiet because it's time to begin the *speech*.'

Control:
Qunchang dunshi bian-de anjing qilai, yinwei xianzai yijing
place   suddenly become quite up   because now already

kaishi **fangying**.
start show

'The place suddenly became quiet because it's time to begin the *show*.'

b. Sentence context biasing the subordinate meaning
Homophone:
Yisheng gei bingren kai-le   xie zhenyao, yinwei xianzai yijing
doctor give patient give–LE some medicine because now   already

kaishi **fayan**.
start infection

'The doctor gave the patient some medicine since there was already *infection*.'

Control:
Yisheng gei bingren kai -le   xie   zhenyao, yinwei xianzai yijing
doctor give patient give –LE some medicine because now already

kaishi **jiangwen.**
start colder

'The doctor gave the patient some medicine since there was already *lower temperature.*'

The visual probes to sentences in the (a) conditions are *jianghua* 'talk' and to sentences in the (b) conditions are *huanong* 'fester', if they were designed to relate to the dominant meaning. When the visual probes were supposed to relate to the subordinate meaning, the conditions in which the above two probes occur would switch. All the visual probes were selected on the basis of a semantic relatedness judgment task from another separate group of forty-four native Mandarin speakers. They were asked to evaluate the relatedness of the homophones and the visual probes on a 9-point scale, and all twenty-four visual probes that were selected had an average rating of 8 or above.

3.1.3 Design

The participants were divided into two groups of forty according to the two ISI conditions. ISI was treated in a between-subject design, and all other variables were in a within-subject design. Within each ISI condition, materials were arranged according to a Latin-square design so that each of the forty participants received 24 sentences in the 2 (context type) x 2 (dominance) x 2 (prime type) design and another 24 sentences that contained control words and no homophones. The order of presentation for the sentences was counterbalanced across participants. No subject received the same target word or the visual probe twice.

3.1.4 Experimental Apparatus

The auditory materials were read by a native Mandarin speaker at a normal conversational rate, and were tape-recorded and then digitized into a PC. The presentation of the auditory and visual stimuli was controlled by the Vmaster and Dmaster programs developed by Kenneth Forster at the University of Arizona (Forster and Forster 1990).

3.1.5 Procedure

Before the experiment began, the experimenter explained the task in Mandarin Chinese to the listener. Listeners were told that they would be hearing a Chinese sentence on a pair of headphones, and immediately afterwards they would see a Chinese word (two characters) on the computer screen. Their task was to, as accurately and quickly as possible, decide whether the characters on the screen were true Chinese words (lexical decision). They should press the 'Yes' key if these would make up true words, and the 'No' key if they were not Chinese words. The non-words were two randomly scrambled characters. All participants did the experiment individually. Before the actual test began, they were given a practice session in which they heard a separate set of twelve similar sentences. The whole experiment took about fifteen minutes.

3.2 Results

Mean response latencies, counting from the onset of the visual probe to the participant's key press, are presented in Table 2. We conducted two separate statistical analyses on the data from the 0ms ISI condition and the data from the –150ms ISI condition.

First, in the 0ms ISI condition, the homophone elicited faster (though not statistically significant) responses than the unrelated control word when the biasing context and the visual probe were consistent, that is, when the context biased the dominant meaning of the homophone and the visual probe was related to the dominant meaning, or when the context biased the subordinate meaning and the visual probe was related to the subordinate meaning. A priming of 28 ms ($t(39) = 1.84$, $p > .05$) and 33 ms ($t(39) = 1.74$, $p > .05$) were obtained for the two consistent conditions, respectively. When the biasing context and the visual probe were inconsistent, the homophone and the unrelated control word elicited similar responses ($p > .10$). Although none of the paired differences between homophones and the controls reached statistical significance, it is clear that at 0ms ISI sentence context already started to play a role to influence the access of the homophone meanings. Unfortunately, a potentially interesting condition, 300ms ISI (comparable to Experiment 1), was not manipulated in this study. We would expect, on the basis of our results from Cantonese, that the priming effects would become more significant at relatively later stages of processing.

	Dominant**		Subordinate	
Context type	Homophone	Control	Homophone	Control
Biased to dominant				
0 ms	545	573	600	617
-150 ms	581	616	631	639
Biased to subordinate				
0 ms	553	572	567	600
-150 ms	586	606	613	610

Table 2. Response latencies (ms) as a function of context type, dominance, ISI, and relatedness in Experiment 2

Second, in the -150ms ISI condition, we found that only if the context biased the dominant meaning of the homophone and the visual probe was related to the dominant meaning, the homophone elicited significantly faster responses than did the unrelated control word (a priming of 35ms, t(39) = 2.52, p < .05). In all other situations there were no significant differences between the homophone and the control word (p > .10). This indicates that at an earlier stage, context effects influence the access of only the dominant meaning of the homophone, and does not influence the access of the subordinate meaning. We can compare the absence of difference here with the presence of a 33ms priming when ISI was 0ms in the subordinate conditions, which shows clearly that it takes time for the subordinate meaning to become activated. This result is also consistent with results from Experiment 1 that there was a significant interaction between context type and dominance, and that in the neutral context condition, the dominant meaning was accessed first.

4 General Discussion

Much of our existing knowledge about lexical ambiguity in sentence processing has been limited to English and other Indo-European languages. The present study is an attempt to broaden this knowledge base by examining this important phenomenon in one of the major East Asian languages, following our previous work in Chinese language processing. We used the cross-modal method to examine the processing of ambiguous words in both Cantonese and Mandarin Chinese. The two comparable experiments have yielded converging evidence on how Chinese speakers face the massive homophony problem during sentence processing.

Our results indicate that in both Cantonese and Mandarin, listeners make early use of prior sentential context in the resolution of lexical ambiguity. Sentence contexts aid the processing of Chinese homophones from early on, probably within the acoustic boundary of the ambiguous word in natural speech. This claim pushes the effect of sentence context to a much earlier stage than what has been proposed by the multiple access hypothesis, e.g., about 1.5 seconds after the word offset (see Onifer and Swinney 1981). The converging results from the two experiments provide further support to the context-dependency or selective access hypothesis. They are consistent with findings from other studies (Ahrens 1998, Chen and Cui 1997), as well as our own previous findings (Li 1998, Li and Yip 1996, 1998).

One important finding from the current set of experiments is that sentence context effects interact closely with frequency/dominance effects. In Experiment 1, we found that when there was no biasing context available (the neutral context condition), the dominant meaning elicited significantly faster responses than the subordinate meaning. However, when there was biasing context, dominance and context type had a complex interaction, along with ISI. In Experiment 2, we found that only the dominant and not the subordinate meaning of the homophone elicited priming effects when the ISI was at −150ms, but both dominant and subordinate meanings elicited priming effects when the ISI was at 0ms. These results seem to require a more complex explanation than a simple version of the context-dependency hypothesis, an explanation that emphasizes the interaction between context and frequency. To account for this type of interaction, we turn to the reordered access hypothesis (Hogaboam and Perfetti 1975, Simpson 1981, Simpson and Burgess 1985, Rayner et al. 1994), a model that considers both context and frequency effects in lexical ambiguity processing.

The reordered access hypothesis assumes that the access of ambiguous words is frequency-based: the dominant or primary meaning of the word is accessed first, irrespective of context, followed by the access of the subordinate or secondary meaning. Context can help in elevating the activation level of the subordinate meaning, but has limited role in the case of dominant meaning. Our data from both experiments support this general claim. However, this hypothesis would be indistinguishable from the context-dependent hypothesis when one looks at the sentence context that biases the dominant meaning, in which case both hypotheses predict that only the dominant meaning would be activated. This is true with our results from Experiment 1, in which the dominant meaning was accessed faster than the subordinate meaning and with results from Experiment 2, in which only the dominant meaning elicited priming. However, the re-ordered access hypothesis may also be indistinguishable from the multiple access hypothesis when one looks at the sentence context that biases the subordinate meaning, in which case both hypotheses predict that subordinate as well as dominant meanings would be activated; the dominant meaning is activated because of frequency, and the subordinate meaning is activated because of context according to the re-ordered access hypothesis. With regard to contexts biased to the subordinate meaning in our data, Experiment 1 shows that the dominant meaning is in general activated faster than the subordinate meaning, both at early and late stages of processing, although the subordinate meaning elicits priming effects at later but not early stages. In Experiment 2, similarly, the subordinate meaning elicits priming only at the later stage (0ms), but not at the early stage (-150ms). Thus, these data indicate that there is a time course to the effects of frequency and context: both frequency and context are important early on, but contexts take precedence over frequency at later stages. In addition, our data show that the frequency of homophone meanings can operate relatively early (probably within the word boundary), in contrast to the assumption that frequency effects can occur only at a later selection stage (see Onifer and Swinney 1981, Swinney 1979).

Note that there were no effects of relatedness or homophone density in Experiment 1. The absence of these effects may be due to two problems. First, there have been no semantic associate norms for Cantonese, and we approximated the variable of relatedness by using a separate semantic relatedness judgment task (see Method). As mentioned before, we selected the most frequent responses as the related visual probes while randomly selected other characters as the unrelated probes from the same source of the characters proposed by the participant judges. Therefore, the unrelated items might still have served to activate meanings related to the homophone, though to a lesser extent. Second, the lack of a good control for the frequency of the visual probes might be a source of confound in the current study, thereby obscuring the density effects.

To conclude, results from the present study along with our previous findings suggest that the successful recognition of spoken homophones depends on the continuous on-line interaction between contextual and lexical (including frequency) information in the sentence. These results are consistent with interactive models at large, as discussed in Kawamoto (1993), Marslen-Wilson (1987), McClelland (1987), and McClelland and Elman (1986), according to which language processing is a highly interactive form of information processing, and that prior sentence context can influence lexical access at an early stage.

References

Ahrens, K. 1998. Lexical Ambiguity Resolution: Languages, Tasks and Timing. *Sentence Processing: A Crosslinguistic Perspective*, ed. D. Hillert, 11-33. San Diego, CA: Academic Press.

Chen, Y-M., & Y. Cui. 1997. Hanyu Qiyiju de Jiagong. [The Processing of Chinese Ambiguous Sentences]. *Xinli Xuebao [Acta Psychologica Sinica]* 29:1-7.

Cohen, J. D., B. MacWhinney, M., Flatt, & J. Provost. 1993. PsyScope: A New Graphic Interactive Environment for Designing Psychology Experiments. *Behavior Research Methods, Instruments, & Computers* 25: 257-71.

Fodor, J. A. 1983. *The Modularity of Mind: An Essay on Faculty Psychology*. Cambridge, MA: MIT Press.

Forster, K. I., & J. C. Forster. 1990. User's Guide to the DMASTR Display System [Software Manual]. Tucson, AZ: University of Arizona.

Glucksberg, S., R. J. Kreuz, & S. H. Rho. 1986. Context Can Constrain Lexical Access: Implications for Models of Language Comprehension. *Journal of Experimental Psychology: Learning, Memory, & Cognition* 12:323-35.

Grosjean, F. 1980. Spoken Word Recognition Processes and the Gating Paradigm. *Perception & Psychophysics* 28:267-83.

Ho, H.-H. & Y.-H. Jiang. 1994. *Word Frequency in Hong Kong in the 90's*. Research Institute of Humanities, Chinese University of Hong Kong.

Hogaboam, T., & C. Perfetti. 1975. Lexical Ambiguity and Sentence Comprehension. *Journal of Verbal Learning & Verbal Behavior* 14:265-74.

Institute of Linguistics, The Academy of Social Sciences. 1985. *Xianda Hanyu Cidian* [Modern Chinese Dictionary]. Beijing: Commercial Press.

Kawamoto, A. H. 1993. Non-linear Dynamics in the Resolution of Lexical Ambiguity: A Parallel Distributed Processing Account. *Journal of Memory & Language* 32:474-516.

Li, P. 1996a. The Temporal Structure of Spoken Sentence Comprehension in Chinese. *Perception & Psychophysics* 58:571-86.

Li, P. 1996b. Spoken Word Recognition of Code-switched Words by Chinese-English Bilinguals. *Journal of Memory & Language* 35:757-74.

Li, P. 1998. Crosslinguistic Variation and Sentence Processing: The Case of Chinese. *Sentence Processing: A Crosslinguistic Perspective*, ed. D. Hillert, 33-51. San Diego, CA: Academic Press.

Li, P., & M. Yip. 1996. Lexical Ambiguity and Context Effects in Spoken Word Recognition: Evidence from Chinese. *Proceedings of the 18th Annual Conference of the Cognitive Science Society*, ed. G. Cottrell, 228-32.

Li, P., & M. Yip. 1998. Context Effects and the Processing of Spoken Homophone. *Reading & Writing: An Interdisciplinary Journal* 10:223-43.

Marslen-Wilson, W. D. 1987. Functional Parallelism in Spoken Word Recognition. *Cognition* 25:71-102.

Marslen-Wilson, W. D. 1990. Activation, Competition, and Frequency in Lexical Access. *Cognitive Models of Speech Processing*, ed. G. T. Altmann, 148-172. Cambridge: The MIT Press.

Marslen-Wilson, W. D., & A. Welsh. 1978. Processing Interactions and Lexical Access during Word Recognition in Continuous Speech. *Cognitive Psychology* 10:29-63.

McClelland, J. L. 1987. The Case for Interactionism in Language Processing. *Attention and Performance XII: The Psychology of Reading*, ed. M. Coltheart, 3-36. Hillsdale, NJ: Erlbaum.

McClelland, J. L., & J. Elman. 1986. Interactive Processes in Speech Perception: The TRACE Model. *Parallel Distributed Processing: Explorations in the Microstructure of Cognition* (Vol. I & II), eds. J. L. McClelland, D. E. Rumelhart, & the PDP Research Group, 58-121. Cambridge: The MIT Press.

Onifer, W., & D. A. Swinney. 1981. Accessing Lexical Ambiguities during Sentence Comprehension: Effects of Frequency of Meaning and Contextual Bias. *Memory & Cognition* 9:225-36.

Rayner, K., J. M. Pacht, & S. A. Duffy. 1994. Effects of Prior Encounter and Global Discourse Bias in the Processing of Lexically Ambiguous Words. *Journal of Memory & Language* 33:527-44.

Simpson, G. 1981. Meaning Dominance and Semantic Context in the Processing of Lexical Ambiguity. *Journal of Verbal Learning & Verbal Behavior* 20:120-36.

Simpson, G., & A. Adamopoulos. In press. Repeated Homographs in Word and Sentence Contexts: Multiple Processing of Multiple Meanings. *On the Consequences of Meaning Selection*, ed. D. S. Gorfein. Washington, DC: American Psychological Association.

Simpson, G., & C. Burgess. 1985. Activation and Selection Processes in the Recognition of Ambiguous Words. *Journal of Experimental Psychology: Human Perception & Performance* 11:28-39.

Simpson, G. B., & H. W. Kang. 1994. Inhibitory Processes in the Recognition of Homograph Meanings. *Inhibitory Processes in Attention, Memory, and Language*, eds. D. Dagenbach & T. H. Carr, 359-381. San Diego: Academic Press.

Simpson, G.B., & M. A. Krueger. 1991. Selective Access of Homograph Meanings in Sentence Context. *Journal of Memory & Language* 30:627-43.

Small, S., G. Cottrell, & M. Tanenhaus. 1988. *Lexical Ambiguity Resolution: Perspectives from Psycholinguistics, Neuropsychology, and Artificial Intelligence.* San Mateo: Morgan Kaufmann Publishers.

Swinney, D. A. 1979. Lexical Access during Sentence Comprehension: (Re)Consideration of Context Effects. *Journal of Verbal Learning & Verbal Behavior* 18:645-59.

Tabossi, P. 1988. Accessing Lexical Ambiguity in Different Types of Sentential Contexts. *Journal of Memory & Language* 27:324-40.

Yip, C.W., & P. Li. 1997. Processing Homophones Interactively: Evidence from Chinese. Paper presented at the *International Symposium on Cognitive Processes of the Chinese Language,* University of Hong Kong, Hong Kong, September.

6

Costs of Scrambling in Japanese Sentence Processing*

REIKO MAZUKA, KENJI ITOH AND TADAHISA KONDO

1 Introduction

During the past decade, research in Japanese sentence processing has established that the syntactic properties of Japanese pose a special challenge for models of on-line language processing (cf. Mazuka and Nagai 1995, Nakayama 1999, for overview). Three syntactic properties are considered to be the main sources of these difficulties; viz, the left-branching, head-final nature of phrases, the productive usage of empty categories, and the presence of scrambling (Inoue and Fodor 1995, Mazuka and Itoh 1995, Berwick and Fong 1995).

---

* The research reported in this paper was funded in part by grants from NSF (SBR-9357893) and from NIMH (R29-MH51655) to the first author, and a Grant in Aid for Scientific Research from Japan Society for the Promotion of Science (1680836) to the second author. Part of the research was conducted while the first author was an invited researcher at NTT Communication Science Research Laboratories.

An earlier version of this paper was presented as a poster at the Eleventh Annual CUNY Conference on Human Sentence Processing Conference in 1998. We thank Masaki Tojo of Toho University, Noriko Nagai of Ibaraki University, and Toshisada Deguchi and Akiko Hayashi of Tokyo Gakugei University for their assistance in data collection. We would also like to thank Edoson Miyamoto, Shoichi Takahashi, Hiroko Yamashita, and Mineharu Nakayama for helpful discussions. All remaining errors, however, are our own.

Sentence Processing in East Asian Languages.
Mineharu Nakayama (ed.).
Copyright ©2002, CSLI Publications.

These properties make the syntactic structure of Japanese sentences highly ambiguous until the very end of each sentence. Consequently, any commitment as to how an incoming string should be parsed runs the risk of being incorrect in the ultimate analysis of the sentence. Thus, in order to avoid committing errors, decisions may be delayed until disambiguating information becomes available. However, it is also known that it is costly to hold incoming lexical items without making parsing decisions (Miller 1956).

Computationally, various solutions are possible. One can propose that Japanese sentences are processed incrementally without delay. If such were the case, the resulting parsing decisions would have a high probability of being incorrect. Such a model would require an assumption that most mistakes can be corrected without much disruption. We call this type of model an "incremental model" (cf. Inoue and Fodor 1995).[1] Alternatively, one can propose to delay parsing decisions until they can be made safely. This way, the likelihood of misanalysis is minimized, even though the cost of holding onto unanalyzed items may increase. We call this type of model a "delay model" (cf. Weinberg 1993, Gorrell 1995).

Another alternative is to propose that parsing decisions are made when certain types of information become available. A grammatical head is an ideal candidate for such processing, since it is the grammatical head that provides the information as to how its complements are to be attached to the phrase structure. We call this type of processing a "head-driven model" (cf. Pritchett 1988, 1992).

Using a computational model based on the Government and Binding theory of syntax (Chomsky 1981), Berwick and Fong (1995) have argued that the presence of scrambling, especially in combination with the presence of empty categories, contributes significantly to the computational difficulty of processing Japanese sentences. To date, however, experimental studies that investigated scrambled sentences have failed to find significant psychological costs associated with scrambled word order in Japanese.

If scrambled word order is indeed not associated with any processing cost in comprehension, it has far-reaching implications for models of Japanese sentence processing. Therefore, we should make sure that the failure to find effects of scrambling is not due to some limitation of the experiments. It is possible that if we used a more sensitive measure of processing cost, we might be able to detect the processing cost associated with scrambled sen-

---

[1] The individual proposals that have been put forth in the articles sited here are much more sophisticated, and contain detailed subsystems that are designed to deal with a wide range of issues on Japanese sentence processing. It is beyond the scope of this paper to discuss them here. The very simplified accounts we adopt in our discussion are not necessarily an accurate description of the actual models proposed by these researchers. We refer to these articles to show that valid proposals can be made from each of these computational frameworks.

tences. In this paper, we investigated whether or not scrambled word order is associated with any cost for on-line comprehension of Japanese. Using two questionnaires, an eye-movement monitoring experiment, and a self-paced reading experiment, simple and complex sentences with scrambled word order were tested. We found that even the simplest scrambled sentence is indeed associated with psycholinguistically measurable processing costs.

In the sections below, we will first describe how scrambling is treated in Japanese syntax. We will then discuss why scrambling is critical for a model of Japanese sentence processing. We will also review previous psycholinguistic studies of scrambled sentences in Japanese. Data will be presented from the two questionnaires, the eye-movement monitoring experiment, and the self-paced reading experiment. We will discuss the results of our study in relation to various models of Japanese sentence processing.

1.1 Syntax of Scrambling

The basic word order of Japanese is S(ubject) O(bject) and V(erb). However, except for the verb, which is strictly clause-final, the order of arguments is relatively free. So, both (1a) and (1b) are grammatical in Japanese.

(1) a. Yoko-ga   Hiroshi-o   mita.
       -Nom   -Acc   saw
    'Yoko saw Hiroshi.'

   b. Hiroshi-o   Yoko-ga   mita.
      -Acc   -Nom   saw
    'Yoko saw Hiroshi.'

During the 1980's, the presence of scrambling was used to argue for a flat structure of Japanese. For example, Farmer (1980, 1984) and Hale (1980, 1981) argued that Japanese allows scrambling because Japanese does not have a verb phrase, and the subject and object are in equal position in relation to the verb, as in (2a). In this interpretation, sentences with a canonical word order as in (1a), and with a scrambled word order as in (1b), have essentially the same structure as in (2a) and (2b), respectively.

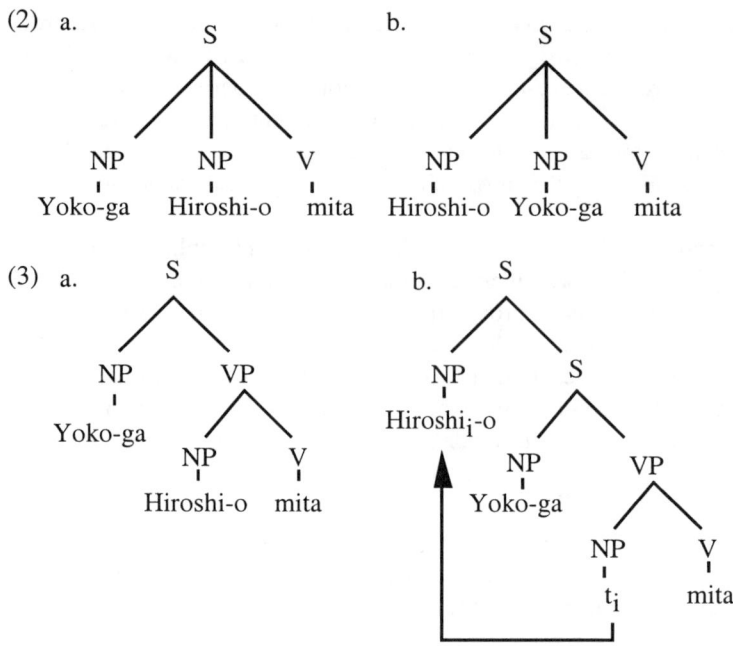

In the ensuing years, however, a number of linguists presented a range of syntactic evidence to demonstrate that Japanese does have a verb phrase as in (3a). This evidence included syntactic phenomena such as pronominal co-reference, weak cross-over, and numeral quantifiers (cf. Saito and Hoji 1983, Saito 1985, Whitman 1987, Miyagawa 1988, 1989; see also Nemoto, 1999 for an overview). In this analysis, a scrambled sentence is considered to be generated by a movement of the object NP. Thus, a scrambled sentence such as (1b) above has a structure such as (3b).

More recently, Tonoike (1997) has proposed that a scrambled sentence such as (1b) is base-generated. Thus, the structure of a scrambled sentence such as (1b) above is similar to (3b), but in Tonoike's analysis, the verb's object position is occupied by *pro*, rather than a trace, which is coindexed with the scrambled argument.

1.2 Psycholinguistic Studies of Scrambled Sentences

As discussed above, the challenge of processing Japanese is that a sentence is highly ambiguous at the onset. The critical question is what kind of parsing decisions are made as a sentence is processed incrementally from left to right. If a sentence is scrambled, the marked order of NPs is detectable with the overt case marker before the verb is reached. How do speakers of Japanese utilize this word order information in on-line comprehension of a scrambled sentence? Depending on which syntactic representation one assumes, and what types of parsing decisions are assumed to be made at what point, different predictions emerge. Let us examine each of these predictions in turn.

Suppose a pair of sentences such as 1a and 1b are to be processed. If one supposes a hierarchical representation of Japanese sentences, such as those in (3), the structure that needs to be recovered to process a scrambled sentence would be (3b). This is significantly more complex than the one for a canonical sentence as in (3a). Assuming that computing the syntactic representation is a critical part of sentence comprehension, and that such computation is associated with some measurable cost, a scrambled sentence as a whole should be more costly than a canonical sentence to some measurable degree.

When the first NP is received in (1b), the accusative marker signals that the sentence needs an empty category somewhere, even though, at this point it is not clear whether it is a scrambled sentence or some other construction -- e.g., a simple clause with an empty subject, or a part of a relative clause, etc. If sentence processing in Japanese is truly incremental, there might be a difference between sentences (1a) and (1b) already at this point.

When the second NP is received, different predictions will be made depending on the processing model. In an incremental model, where a node may be created without waiting for the grammatical head, a VP should be built, and it should be attached to S with the arrival of an accusative marked NP in (1a). In (1b), an additional S node must be built with the arrival of a nominative-marked NP. It has been found that a clause is a critical unit for processing, and an extra clause is considered to add additional cost in processing (cf., Frazier and Rayner 1988, Bock and Cutting 1992, Mazuka and Itoh 1995). Thus, compared to (1a), the scrambled sentence 1b is predicted to have increased processing load at this position. In addition, a VP with an empty object (either a trace or a pro) needs to be built either at this point or when the verb is received.

Alternatively, if one assumes that the attachment of arguments takes place when the head (i.e., verb) is received, the two NPs should be held unattached in 1a or 1b. There ought to be no difference between the two types of sentences at this point. In a delay model as well, there is no motivation to make a pre-head attachment decision at this point.

When the verb is received, it needs to be attached to the VP node. Both the head-driven model and the delay model predict that attachment decisions are made at this point. Thus, the scrambled sentence should show an increased processing cost at this point. In the incremental model, however, all that needs to be done for either sentence is to attach the verb to the VP node that is already built. Thus, no difference is predicted at this point.

In contrast, if one assumes a flat structure for Japanese, as shown in (2) above, there is little reason to predict an increased processing load for a scrambled sentence, either on-line or off-line, in terms of processing the structure of the sentence per se.

Note however that a very similar prediction could be made, simply by considering the frequency of the scrambled sentences. It has been repeatedly noted that scrambled word order is marked in Japanese, and it does not occur very frequently in natural corpora. For example, Yamashita (in press) gathered various types of written texts and found that only less than 1% of the sentences she analyzed had scrambled word order. Previous studies in English have demonstrated that the frequency of a given syntactic structure significantly influences the processing of that structure (e.g. MacDonald 1994, MacDonald, Perlmutter, and Seidenberg 1994). Therefore, we may predict an increased processing cost associated with scrambled sentences on the basis of frequency alone. Depending on how quickly such a frequency information is assumed to interact with the on-line processing, a model will predict an increased processing cost at different point on the sentence. This is independent of whether one adopts a flat structure of a Japanese sentence as shown in (2) above, or a hierarchical structure as shown in (3).

Therefore, we must be careful to note that simply because we find an increased processing cost for a scrambled sentence, it does not necessarily support one version of syntactic analysis over the other. There would be strong ramifications, however, if we did not find any costs associated with scrambled word order at any position. If we adopt an assumption that the processor computes the syntactic structure of the sentence, no-difference would be most consistent with the flat structure analysis of scrambled sentences. One must also conclude that the frequency of occurrence also has no impact on the processing of scrambled sentences in Japanese.

If, on the other hand, we adopt the assumption that scrambled sentences have a syntactically more complex structure than canonical sentences, then we would reason that such syntactic structures are either not computed while comprehending a scrambled sentence, or that computing such structures involves no psycholinguistically measurable cost. Either of these is a very strong claim with regard to how a Japanese sentence may be processed.

The first experimental study to investigate on-line processing of scrambled sentences in Japanese was conducted by Nakayama (1995). Nakayama tested whether or not a trace of the scrambled object reactivated its antecedents such that the recognition of a probe word related to the antecedent would be facilitated. Using a probe recognition task, he tested pairs of sentences such as (4) below. (4a) is a canonical word-order sentence, while

(4b) is a scrambled sentence. In both of these sentences, a word from the subject phrase, *shujutu* (operation), or a word from an object phrase, *byooki* (disease) was used as a probe word. Sentences were presented phrase by phrase in a self-paced reading paradigm. At the end of each sentence, participants were presented with a probe word (shown here with an underline in the stimuli), and were asked to decide whether or not the word had appeared in the sentence they had just read.

(4) a. Byooin-de   shujutsu-o   okonatta isha-ga
       hospital at   operation-Acc   did   doctor-Nom

   byooki-o   shinpaishita kanja-o   hagemashita.
   disease-Acc   worried   patient-Acc   encouraged

   'The doctor who did the operation encouraged the patient who worried about his disease at the hospital.'

   b. Byooin-de   byooki-o   shinpaisita kanja-o
      hospital at   disease-Acc   worried   patient-Acc

   shujutu-o   okonatta isha-ga   hagemashita.
   operation-Acc   did   doctor-Nom   encouraged

   'The doctor who did the operation encouraged the patient who worried about his disease at the hospital.'

Nakayama found that the reaction times for the object probe in the canonical sentence, and for the subject probe in the scrambled sentences, were shorter than the subject probe of the canonical sentence or the object probe of the scrambled sentences. In other words, the probes that were more recent had significantly shorter reaction time. However, the reaction times to the probes in the scrambled sentence (4b) were not different from those in the canonical sentence (4)a.

Nakayama's experiment was based on previous studies in English (cf. Bever and McElree 1988) as well as his own studies with unergative and unaccusative sentences in Japanese (Nakayama 1990, 1991). In these studies, faster reaction times to the probe word were found when the sentences involved movement which left a trace and the probe word was part of the antecedent of the trace, compared to sentences that did not contain a trace. If the scrambled sentence (4b) has a structure such as (3b) above, there should be a trace between the subject and the matrix verb. Thus, the latency for the object probe *byooki* for (4b) should have been faster than the subject probe in the canonical sentence *shujutsu* in (4a).

Nakayama was attempting to test the accessibility of the trace, rather than directly assessing the processing cost of the scrambled sentence. Thus, he was not arguing that scrambling in Japanese is not associated with processing costs. He interpreted the results as possibly showing that optional movement such as scrambling may not leave a trace. For our discussion, however, the study did not find positive evidence to show that scrambled word order is associated with psychologically measurable consequences.

Yamashita (1997) tested the effects of scrambling using two self-paced reading experiments and a lexical decision task. She found no effect of word order in her experiments. She used sentences with ditransitive verbs, such as (5). In a self-paced reading experiment, she found no difference in reading times between the canonical word order sentence and any of the scrambled sentences shown in (5b) to (5d).

(5) a. Canonical [NP-ga NP-ni NP-o v]
Wakai zimuin-ga   mukuchi-na syatyoo-ni omosiroi hon-o
young secretary-Nom quiet   president-Dat fun   book-Acc

ageta.
gave

'A young secretary gave the quiet company president a fun book.'

b. Scrambled Indirect Object [NP-ni [NP-ga t NP-o V]]
c. Scrambled Direct Object [NP-o [NP-ga NP-ni V]]
d. Scrambled Indirect and Direct Objects [NP-ni NP-o [NP-ga V]]

In another self-paced reading experiment, she tested sentential complement structures with scrambled word orders as shown in (6). She found that the reading times for the second nominative NP in the canonical word order sentence in (6a) was significantly longer than the other two sentences. Yet, the two scrambled sentences did not produce any increase in the reading time at any of the positions.

(6) a. Canonical word order [NP-ga NP-ni [NP-ga NP-o V] V]
[Denwa-de hansamuna gakusee-ga sensee-ni
phone-on handsome student-Nom teacher-Dat

[tsumetai koibito-ga nagai tegami-o yabutta-to] itta.]
cold girlfriend-Nom long letter-Acc tore-Comp said

'On the phone, a handsome student told the teacher that the cold-hearted girlfriend ha torn the long letter.'

b. [NP-ga NP-ni [NP-o NP-ga V] V]
c. [NP-ni NP-ga [NP-o NP-ga V] V]

Yamashita discusses various possibilities why she did not find a significant effect of scrambled word order, but concludes that given her results, she may have to assume the possibility that the Japanese parser does not compute a hierarchical structure of the phrases, as in (3) above, during on-line processing.

In contrast to Japanese studies, however, studies using other languages have found significant effects of scrambled word order. In German, for example, Clahsen and Featherston (1998) found a significant priming effect for the trace of scrambled arguments using a cross-modal priming method. In Dutch, many studies have shown that in a variety of sentence comprehension experiments, subject-object word order is strongly preferred over object-subject word order in a wh-clause, relative clauses, and main clauses when either of these orders are permissible (cf. Frazier 1987, Frazier and Flores d'Arcais 1989, Kaan 1997, among others).

In summary, the two experimental studies that have tested the scrambled sentences in Japanese did not find a positive effect of scrambled word order. As discussed before, if scrambling does not leave any measurable costs in Japanese, this will have very strong implications -- viz., we will have to entertain possibilities such as: (i) Syntactic structure computed during on-line processing (i.e., flat structure, or no trace for the movement) is different from those assumed to be more appropriate in syntactic analyses (i.e., hierarchical, with a trace for the movement); or (ii) the syntactic structure for a scrambled sentence (an extra S node, and a trace) which needs to be computed during on-line processing has no psychological consequences. In addition, as scrambling in other languages such as German and Dutch have been found to be associated with experimentally measurable processing consequences, we will also have to assume that the scrambling operation in Japanese is somehow different from those in the other languages.

However, not finding a statistically significant difference could be due to many factors. For example, both of the previous studies used the self-paced reading method. It has been well established by now that self-paced reading experiments can be very sensitive to many processing phenomena. Yet, it is quite unnatural to read a sentence that is presented phrase by phrase on a screen. Especially, with very complicated sentences such as (5) and (6) above, the unnaturalness of the phrase by phrase presentation, and the difficulty of not being able to look back, might overwhelm the subtle processing costs associated with scrambled word order. If we use an eye-movement monitoring technique, which can present an entire sentence at one time, we might be able to detect a subtle cost of scrambling.

It is also possible that the use of ditransitive verbs obscured the effect of word order change in Yamashita's study. The unmarked order of nominative and accusative argument is very clear in Japanese. However, once a noun phrase with *ni* is introduced, it becomes less clear. As shown in Sadakane and Koizumi (1995), *ni* in Japanese has multiple syntactic roles, and the noun phrases in many of those syntactic roles do not have a particular position in a sentence that is clearly unmarked. Even when it is a dative case marker, it has sometimes been claimed that both *ga-ni-o* order as well as *ga-o-ni* order are canonical in Japanese (Miyagawa 1997). If the default word order is not clear, then the effect of changing that order cannot be clear either. Therefore, if we used transitive verbs, with only a nominative and an accusative marked NPs, the effect of word-order change from *ga-o* to *o-ga* might be more readily observable.

In the present study, therefore, we investigated whether or not there is an experimentally measurable cost associated with scrambled sentences. We tested two types of scrambled sentences -- simple transitive sentences and sentences with center embedding -- with two questionnaires, an eye-movement monitoring experiment, and a self-paced experiment.

More recently, Miyamoto and Takahashi (2001) also found a significant processing cost for scrambled sentences with ditransitive verbs using a self-paced reading paradigm. Since our studies were conducted independently, we were not able to take their study into consideration in designing our study. But we will try to incorporate their results in the discussion.

2 Experiments

2.1 Material

We tested five types of sentences as shown in (7a) to (7e). All of the sentences had a nominative-marked NP, an accusative-marked NP and a transitive verb. Both arguments in the sentence refer to humans, who can be either the agent or the patient of the transitive action. (7a) and (7b) are simple sentences with only three *bunsetsu* each.[2] (7a) has a canonical word order, while (7b) has a scrambled word order. (7c) and (7d) are sentences with center embedding, i.e., a long modifier phrase is added to the second NP of each sentence. These sentences are included in the study because it is possible that the effect of scrambling may be too subtle to detect in a simple scrambled sentence such as (7a) or (7b). It has been well established that center-embedding adds processing difficulty to a sentence (cf., Miller and Chomsky 1963, Kuno 1973, Abney and Johnson 1991, Gibson 1991, Mazuka et al. 1989, Lewis, 1996). Thus, if it is the case that the effect of scrambling becomes detectable only when there is additional processing complexity, we should be able to find the effect when we compare (7c) and (7d).

(7) a. Canonical Simple Sentence [NP-ga NP-o V]
    Mariko-ga   otooto-o   yonda.
       -Nom   brother-Acc   called
    'Mariko called the younger brother.'

b. Scrambled Simple Sentence [NP-o NP-ga V]
    Otooto-o   Mariko-ga   yonda.
    brother-Acc   o-Nom   called

c. Canonical sentence with a center-embedding
       NP-ga [Modifier Phrase] NP-o V
    Mariko-ga   [soto-de buranko-ni notte-ita]   otooto-o   yonda.
       -Nom outside swinging on a swing   brother-Acc called
    'Mariko called the younger brother who was swinging on a swing outside.'

d. Scrambled sentence with a center-embedding
       NP-o [Modifier Phrase] NP-ga V
    Mariko-o   [soto-de buranko-ni notte-ita]   otooto-ga   yonda.
       -Acc outside swinging on a swing   brother-Nom called
    'The younger brother, who was swinging on a swing outside called Mariko.'

---

[2] A *bunsetsu* in Japanese is a content word plus a function word, or a content word plus its inflection. For example, a noun plus a case particle, or a verb plus its inflection are examples of *bunsetsu*.

e. Scrambled sentence with a modifier phrase on the scrambled NP
   [Modifier Phrase] NP-o NP-ga V
   [soto-de buranko-ni notte-ita] otooto-o   Mariko-ga   yonda.
   outside swinging on a swing   brother-Acc   -Nom called
   'Mariko called the younger brother who was swinging on a swing outside.'

(7e) is a scrambled sentence. However, (7e) contrasts to (7d) in that the modifier phrase in this sentence modifies the first NP. It has been argued that one of the motivations for producing a scrambled word order in Japanese is to avoid center-embedding (cf., Kuno 1973, Yamashita in press, Yamashita and Chen 2001), which may be similar to a heavy NP shift in English. Though Yamashita considered primarily the efficiency of production, it is quite likely that the comprehension of scrambled sentences also becomes easier when the heavy NP is scrambled to the left of the nominative NP. If this is the case, a sentence such as (7e) may be generated to avoid the center embedding of a sentence such as (7c), which is a canonical center-embedded sentence. Note, however, this argument assumes that the cost of the center embedding is greater than that of scrambling. As it is likely that the cost of a given center-embedded structure depends on the specific structure of the sentence, it is not automatically clear whether left-branching scrambled sentences (7e) are easier than the canonical center-embedded sentences (7c) of the present study.

There were ten original sentences, each of which had five versions as discussed above. Five sets of stimuli were created using a Latin Square method such that each original sentence appeared once in each of the five sets, and each set had the two exemplars for each of the five types.

As discussed above, scrambled word order occurred in only 1% of the sentences in Yamashita's corpus analysis. In the present study, the ten test sentences were mixed with fifty filler sentences of various types, some of which were simple sentences while the others were complex sentences of various types. However, none of the filler sentences had a scrambled word order. A given participant saw six scrambled sentences out of sixty sentences in total, i.e. 10% of the sentences.[3]

Sentences were written with standard Japanese orthography that mixes historically Chinese characters (*kanji*) with two types of syllabary, called *katakana* and *hiragana*. A sentence was always presented in a single line. See Appendix A for the list of the sentences.

---

[3] As discussed below in the results section, we found a reliable effect of scrambling in our results. The subject analyses and item analyses in most tests were comparable. Thus, it appears that the small number of sentences we used in this study was appropriate.

2.2 Questionnaire Studies

First, in order to measure Japanese native speakers' intuitive judgments about the scrambled sentences, we tested our stimuli sentences in two kinds of questionnaire studies.[4]

2.2.1 Difficulty Rating

In one of the questionnaires, we asked Japanese native speakers to rate how easy or difficult each sentence was to comprehend, using a five point scale from very easy to very difficult. The motivation for this study is that one's subjective judgment of comprehension difficulty is probably the most obvious processing difficulty a reader/hearer could experience. Sixty sentences were written on a two-page long questionnaire, and the participants were asked to circle the appropriate number for each sentence.

2.2.2 Misleadingness Rating

In a different questionnaire, we asked participants to judge whether or not they felt the sentence was misleading. The motivation for this questionnaire was that the cost of scrambled sentences may be experienced by a reader in other ways than difficulty in comprehension. For example, a reader may feel the scrambled sentence as initially misleading, yet it could be easily comprehended. Subjects in this experiment were asked to rate whether or not they felt that the sentence was misleading, using a five-point scale from very unlikely to be misled to very likely to be misled.

2.2.3 Participants

Participants for the difficulty questionnaire were 103 undergraduate students at a university in the Tokyo area. They participated in this experiment as a part of a psychology class. Participants for the misleadingness questionnaire were 102 undergraduate students at another university also in the Tokyo area. They participated in this experiment as a part of a linguistics class.

2.2.4 Results

Table 1 summarizes the results of the two questionnaire studies. The results were analyzed using one way ANOVA, with Version (five versions in (7a) to (7e) above) as the independent variable. In both questionnaires, the Version was highly significant. $F1(4, 408) = 80.59$, $p < .001$; $F2 (4, 36)=41.46$, $p <.001$ for Difficulty Rating, and $F1 (4, 404) = 50.16$, $p < .001$; $F2 (4, 36)$

---

[4] The stimuli sentences were also tested for comprehension in a off-line 'who did what' questionnaire (cf. Mazuka, Itoh, and Kondo 1997). All of the test sentences had over 95% response accuracy.

= 30.45, p < .001 for Misleadingness Rating.[5] Post hoc analysis revealed that canonical simple sentences (Version A) were rated easier to comprehend and less likely to be misleading than all other versions (Versions B, C, D, and E). Scrambled center-embedded sentences (Version D) were rated more difficult and more misleading than all other versions. Canonical center-embedded sentences (Version C) were rated more difficult than scrambled simple sentences (Version B) in subject analyses, but this difference was not significant in item analyses.

	Difficulty	Misleadingness
A Canonical Simple	1.03	1.36
B Scrambled Simple	1.38	1.82
C Canonical Center-Embedding	1.63	1.76
D Scrambled Center-Embedding	2.21	2.71
E Scrambled Left-Branching	1.49	2.87

Table 1. Average of the difficulty rating and the misleadingness rating

The results of the questionnaire studies showed that the native speakers of Japanese judged that scrambled sentences were more difficult and more misleading than their canonical counterpart. This was true either when the sentences were simple (Version A vs. Version B) or when the sentences involved center embedding (Version C vs. D). The scrambled left-branching sentences (Version E) were significantly easier than their center-embedded counterparts (Version D). But it was not significantly different from the canonical center-embedded sentences (Version C).

In general, the results from the difficulty rating and misleadingness ratings were similar. The only difference was that in the difficulty rating, canonical center-embedded sentences (Version C) had a tendency to be more difficult than simple scrambled sentences (Version B), while in the misleadingness rating, we found no such difference.

---

[5] In all statistical analyses reported in this paper, two separate analyses of variances were performed; once using subjects as a random variable, reported as F1, and another using sentences as a random variable reported as F2. Unless otherwise stated, the results were reported as significant when both of the analyses were significant at a minimum 5% level. All post hoc analyses reported in this paper used a Bonferroni-Dunn T test. Unless otherwise stated, results were reported to be significant when both subject analyses and item analyses were significant at 5% Type I experiment wise error rate.

2.3 Eye-movement Experiment

The questionnaire studies showed that the scrambled sentences were judged more difficult to comprehend in the readers' subjective judgment. However, the off-line nature of the questionnaire method does now allow us to investigate exactly at what point such difficulties were experienced by the readers. Thus, the same sentences were tested using an eye-movement monitoring technique.

2.3.1 Method

2.3.1.1 Material

The sentences used in the eye-movement monitoring experiment were the same as the questionnaire studies.

2.3.1.2 Apparatus

Stimulus sentences were presented on a graphic display monitor (348 mm x 278 mm). The eye camera (Nac Eyemark Recorder, Type V; using infrared light reflection on the retina) was located 57cm away from the display screen. The sampling frequency of this apparatus is 60Hz (every 33 msec). Subjects rested their chins on a chin rest, and their head movements were restrained by a head band. The eye-movement was monitored from the right eye but the viewing was binocular.

2.3.1.3 Participants

Participants for the eye-movement experiment were forty-nine undergraduate students of a university in the Tokyo area. They were paid for their participation.

2.3.1.4 Procedure

The initial calibration usually took five to ten minutes. At the beginning of each session, a circular pattern appeared at the four corners of the screen, in the middle of each side, and at the center of the screen at 1.5 second intervals, in random order. Subjects were asked to follow the movement of the circle. Before each sentence, a cross appeared on the screen and subjects were told to focus on it. The position of the cross corresponded to the beginning of a sentence. Subjects were told to read the sentences on the screen normally as though they were reading a book, or newspaper. They were told to read the sentences as quickly as they normally do without sacrificing comprehension. The subjects would press a key on the keyboard when they finished reading each sentence, and the sentence would disappear from the screen.

In order to ascertain that subjects were paying attention to the sentences, approximately one-third of the stimulus sentences were followed by comprehension questions. Subjects were asked to answer it yes or no by pressing the designated key. The sentences were presented in ten separate sessions, and their eye movement was calibrated at the onset of each session.

2.3.2 Results

For some subjects, data from some of the sessions were not available due to experimenter error, apparatus failure, or failure to calibrate their eye movement properly at the onset of a session. For these subjects, the data from successful sessions were included in the analyses while the data from the failed sessions were treated as missing values. Gaze times that were larger than two standard deviations from the mean for each subject were treated as missing values.[6] If the gaze time was zero for a *bunsetsu*, it was also treated as a missing value.

We analyzed the results using four measures: the first-pass gaze time; the presence or absence of regressive eye movements originating from the given region during the first pass; the total gaze time; and the total number of regressive eye-movements originating from that region (Rayner, Carlson, and Frazier 1983, Ferreira and Clifton 1986). The first-pass gaze time was defined as the sum of fixation time on each *bunsetsu* from the first fixation on that *bunsetsu* until there was a fixation on another *bunsetsu*, either before or after the current *bunsetsu*. The total gaze time is defined as the sum of all fixations on each *bunsetsu*. In addition, it was recorded whether or not there was regressive eye movement originating from any of the *bunsetsu*.

In analyzing the eye movement data, it was necessary to adjust the raw data for the length of the sentence or the phrase. Some studies using eye movement data in English have used a linear or quadratic regression to adjust their data for length in terms of the number of letters (Trueswell, Tanenhaus, and Garnsey 1994). As mentioned above, the Japanese orthography mixes Chinese characters and *kana* (syllabary). A single Chinese character could correspond to several morae while some characters correspond to only a single mora. For example, a character that means 'head' could be read as *atama*, *too*, or *zu* depending on context, corresponding to three, two and one mora respectively. The regression analyses of eye-movement and self-paced reading data indicated that both the number of characters and the

---

[6] In computing the cutting point, the data were ranked within each subject for each variable using Blom Approximation (SAS 1990).

number of morae contribute to the reading times (Mazuka, Itoh, Kondo, and Brown 1999, 2000). Thus, the gaze time data presented in this paper used a linear regression using both the number of morae and the number of characters in calculating the expected value of the data. For each subject, the value of coefficients a, b and c were determined using (8).

(8) Y(expected) = a + b*(number of mora) + c*(number of character)
     Y (residual) = Y(raw) - Y(expected)

The expected value for each region was calculated using this formula. The data reported here are the differences between the raw data and the expected value for that region.[7] The regressive eye movement data were analyzed without these adjustments.

We also analyzed the overall reading time. This was calculated on the basis of the time from the onset of the sentence presentation until the participant pressed the key to end the sentence presentation. The total reading times were also adjusted for the length of each sentence using the formula discussed above.

Figure 1 shows the residual overall reading time for the five types of sentences. The effect of Version was significant (F1 (4, 188) = 20.49, p < .001, F2 (4, 36) = 15.27). The post hoc comparison of means showed that the difference between canonical simple sentence (Version A) and scrambled simple sentence (Version B) did not reach significance. But scrambled center-embedded sentences were read significantly more slowly than canonical center-embedded sentences. Scrambled left-branching sentences were read significantly faster than scrambled center-embedded sentences or scrambled simple sentences.

The sentences were divided into four regions: The first argument, the second argument, the verb, and the modifier phrases. Of primary interest for our discussion are the positions of first argument, second argument and the verb. However, the arguments of the simple sentences and those in the complex sentences differ in length and position in the whole sentence. Thus, it is not clear whether or not they should be directly comparable. For our discussion, we are interested in comparing the canonical and scrambled versions of the same type of sentences, not between simple versus complex sentences. For this reason, we analyzed the simple sentences (A and B) separately from the complex sentences (Versions C, D, and E).

---

[7] We thank Charles Clifton Jr. for his help on how to use the regression analysis for adjusting the length of the phrases.

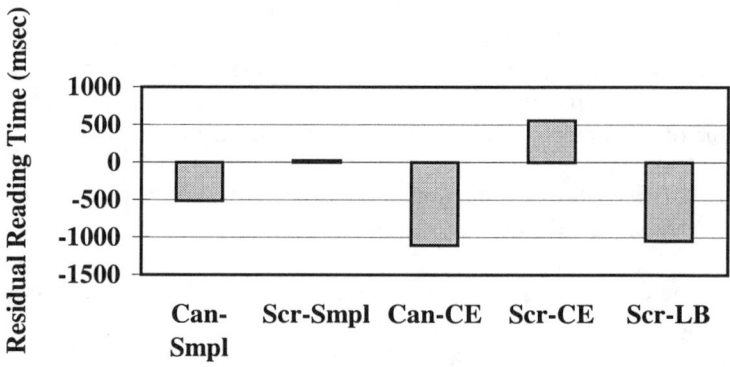

Figure 1. Residual overall reading time in the eye-movement experiment

We first discuss the results for the simple sentences. Figure 2 shows the residual first pass gaze and the residual number of first pass regressive eye movement for these sentences. No difference was significant at the first argument position. At the second argument position, first pass gaze time (FGT) approached significance in subject analysis (F1 (1, 42) = 3.79, p = .058), but did not reach significance in item analysis (F2 (1, 9) = 3.13, p= .11) [8]. The number of first pass regressive eye-movements (FRN), however, was significantly larger for scrambled sentences than canonical sentences (F1 (1, 44) =9.55, p < .01, F2 (1, 9) =8.42, p < .05). Neither FGT or FRN was significant at the verb position.

Figure 3 shows the total gaze time (TGT) and total number of regressive eye-movements (TRN) for each position. TGT was not significantly different at the first argument position. At the second argument position, TGT was significantly longer (F1 (1, 43) = 8.22, p < .01, F2 (1, 9) = 23.62, p < .001) and TRN was significantly larger (F1 (1, 44) =7.32, p < .05, F2 (1, 9) = 16.71, p < .001) for scrambled sentences than for canonical sentences. Neither TGT nor TRN was significant at the verb position.

---

[8] Note that the degree of freedom for each analysis varies because of missing data. As described above, it was not possible to include all data from all of the subjects. Since there were a variety of reasons why a particular data may be missing -- e.g. equipment failure, zero gaze time in a given phrase, data beyond two standard deviations, etc. -- we decided not to replace missing data with some other value, such as an average for the condition. The missing data was left as missing, and the ANOVA was carried out with an unbalanced size data, using SAS GLM procedure (SAS 1990).

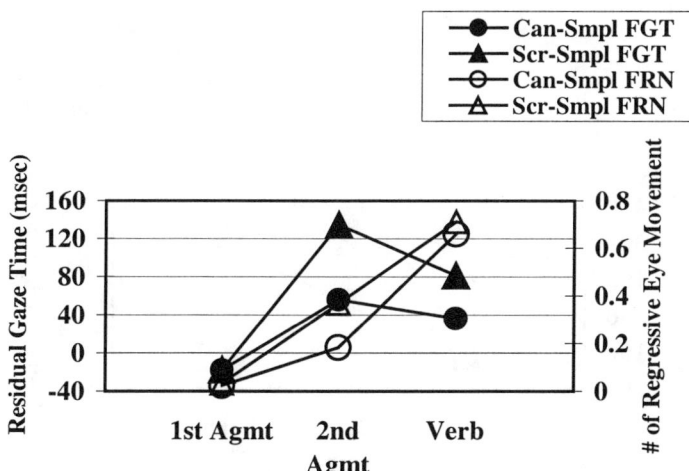

Figure 2. Residual first pass gaze time, and the number of first pass regressive eye-movement for canonical simple and scrambled simple sentences

When we compared the two nominative-marked NPs -- i.e. the first argument of the canonical sentence, and the second argument of the scrambled sentence -- the nominative-marked NP in the scrambled sentence had significantly longer FGT and TGT (F1 (1, 35) = 8.36, p < .01, F2 (1, 9) = 13.57, p < .01, for FGT; F1 (1, 38) = 15.56, p < .001, F2 (1, 9) = 66.26, p < .001, for TGT). When we compared the two accusative-marked NPs -- the second argument of the canonical sentence and the first argument of the scrambled sentence -- FGT was not significantly different between them. But TGT was significantly longer for canonical sentences than the scrambled sentences (F1 (1, 41) = 5.64, p < .05, F2 (1, 9) = 7.03, p < .05).

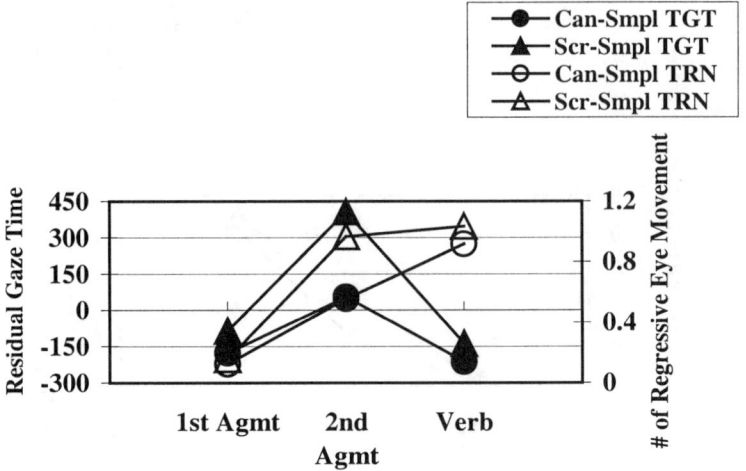

Figure 3. Residual total gaze time, and regressive eye-movement for canonical simple and scrambled simple sentences

In summary, the data from the simple sentences showed that the scrambled sentences do have increased processing cost. During the first pass reading, the readers tended to gaze longer and make more regressive eye-movements in the scrambled sentences at the second argument position. In total gaze time and total number of regressive movements, the second argument of the scrambled sentences was more costly to process. When we compared the two nominative-marked NPs and two accusative-marked NPs, it seemed that the one in the second argument position was more difficult than the first one. But the nominative-marked NP of the scrambled sentence was particularly difficult. The accusative-marked NP that was fronted in the scrambled sentence did not appear to take longer time to read.

Let us now turn to the complex sentences. The second argument of the center-embedded sentences and the first argument of the left-branching sentences had sentential modifiers. Thus, the two argument positions for the three versions of the sentences are not straightforwardly comparable. We analyzed the data in two different ways, i.e., argument NPs alone without the modifier phrases, and with modifier phrases combined with the head nouns.

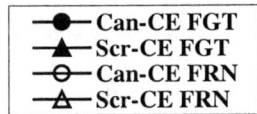
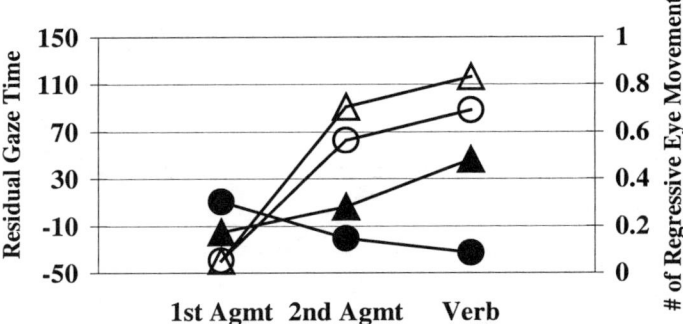

*The figures in the graph represent the average for the region that combines argument NPs and the modifier phrases.

Figure 4. Residual first pass gaze time, and regressive eye-movement for canonical center-embedded sentences (ga-[ ] o) and scrambled center-embedded sentences (o-[ ] ga)

First, we compared the argument NPs without the modifier phrases. At the first argument position, neither the first pass gaze time (FGT) nor total gaze time (TGT) was significant. At the second argument position, FGT was significant (F1 (2, 92) = 84.17, p < .05; F2 (2, 18) = 3.56, p < .05). FGT for scrambled center-embedded sentences were significantly longer than the other two versions of the sentences. TGT was also significant (F1 (2, 92) = 7.12, p < .001; F2 (2, 18) = 5.73, p < .05). Post hoc comparison of means showed that TGTs for scrambled center-embedded sentences were significantly longer than for canonical center-embedded sentences. First pass regressive eye movement (FRN) was not significant at this position. But the total number of regressive eye movement (TRN) was significant (F1 (2, 96) = 6.35, p < .001; F2 (2, 18) = 5.94, p < .05). It was significantly larger for scrambled center-embedded sentences than canonical center-embedded sentences. At the verb position, FGT, TGT, and FRN were significant in subject analysis, but not in item analysis (F1 (2, 86) = 3.11, p < .05; F2 (2, 18) = 2.10, p = .15 for FGT; F1 (2, 88) = 3.93, p < .05; F2 (2, 18) = 1.49, p =

.25 for TGT, (F1 (2, 96) = 3.10, p < .05; F2 (2, 18) = 2.48, p = .11 for FRN.) TRN was significant in both analyses (F1 (2, 96) = 9.88, p < .001; F2 (2, 18) = 4.11, p < .05). TRN for scrambled center-embedded sentences were significantly larger than for canonical center-embedded sentences.

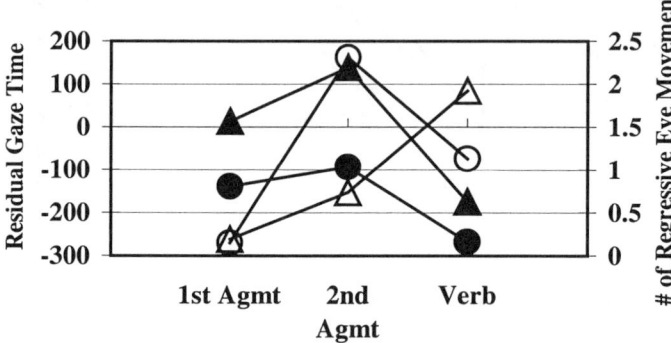

*The figures in the graph represent the average for the region that combines argument NPs and the modifier phrases.

Figure 5. Residual total gaze time, and regressive eye-movement for canonical center-embedded sentences (ga-[ ] o) and scrambled center-embedded sentences (o-[ ] ga)

We also analyzed the arguments combined with the sentential modifiers. When we compared the second arguments of the canonical center-embedded sentences and scrambled center-embedded sentences, FGT and FRN were not significantly different between the two. But TGT, and TRN were significantly higher for scrambled center-embedded sentences than canonical center-embedded sentences (F1 (1, 40) = 10.59, p < .01; F2 (1, 9) = 41.73, p < .001 for TGT; F1 (1, 48) = 21.92, p < .001; F2 (1, 9) = 36.04, p < .001, for TRN). Among the three NPs with the sentential modifiers, FGT was significant in subject analysis, and it approached significance in item analysis (F1 (2, 45) = 5.37, p < .01; F2 (1, 9) = 3.18, p = .07). FGT for the second argument for scrambled center-embedded sentence tended to be longer than the first argument of scrambled left branching sentences. TGT, FRN, and TRN for the second argument of scrambled center-embedded sentences were significantly larger than the second argument of canonical center-embedded sentences or the first argument of scrambled left-branching sentences (F1 (2, 61) = 17.56, p < .001; F2 (2, 17) = 17.56, p < .001 for TGT; F1 (2, 96) = 6.16, p < .01; F2 (2, 18) = 4.7, p < .05 for FRN; F1 (2, 96) = 29.31, p < .001; F2 (2, 18) = 35.99, p < .001 for TRN).

The critical contrast is between the canonical center-embedded sentences and scrambled center-embedded sentences. At the first argument position, where neither of the NPs had sentential modifiers, these two sentences did not differ in any of the measures. At the second argument position, however, scrambled center-embedded sentences had larger TGT and TRN when we compared just the head nouns alone. When we analyzed the NPs with their sentential modifiers, scrambled center-embedded sentences had significantly larger TGT and TRN. At the verb position, only TRN was significantly larger for scrambled center-embedded sentences compared to canonical center-embedded sentences. In summary, then, the pattern of results for complex sentences is similar to that for the simple sentences.

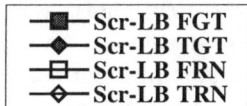

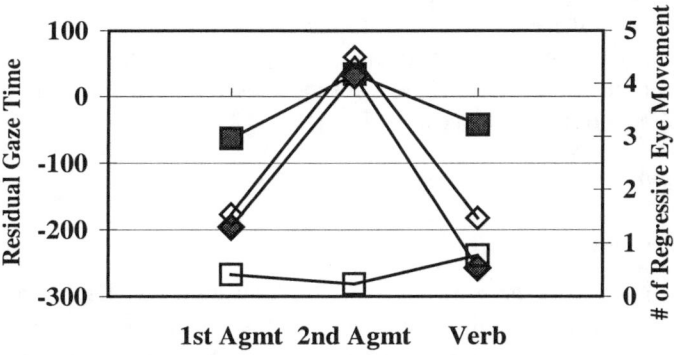

*The figures in the graph represent the average for the region that combines argument NPs and the modifier phrases.

Figure 6. Residual first pass and total gaze time, and first pass and total regressive eye-movement for scrambled left-branching sentences

That is, at the second argument position, the scrambled sentences had increased processing cost, as measured by FRN, TGT, and TRN.

Scrambled left-branching sentences in general were not more difficult than canonical center-embedded sentences. The only exception was that the second argument of scrambled left-branching sentences had longer FGT than the canonical center-embedded or scrambled center-embedded sentences. But the difference was no longer significant in TGT. In several places, scrambled left branching sentences were significantly easier than scrambled center-embedded sentences.

2.4 Self-Paced Reading Experiment

We tested the same set of sentences in a self-paced reading experiment as well. The goal of this study is to examine whether or not the effect of scrambling could be detectable under strictly cumulative presentation conditions -- i.e., the reader having no opportunity to go back to earlier parts of sentences, nor having any idea how long a sentence would be. To this end, there were two modifications we made from a typical self-paced reading method. First, in a typical moving-window self-paced reading experiment, only the current phrase was visible to the reader. Other parts of the sentences are shown with '-', or 'x'. In our study, a sentence was presented one *bunsetsu* at a time, but nothing else was presented for the other parts of the sentence. Thus, a participant in our experiment could not predict how long a sentence would be before reaching its end.

In addition, approximately one-third of the sentences in our study were terminated before the end. This was to encourage the reader to read each phrase carefully as it came, rather than quickly pass it, and think about them at a later point in the sentence. The test sentences were presented up to the second argument of the sentences.

2.4.1 Method

2.4.1.1 Material

The same sentences as the previous experiments were used. Each sentence was followed by a sentence that tested the participants' comprehension. The comprehension sentences were declarative sentences, a half of which were consistent with the content of the test sentences, and the other half were not. In this experiment, approximately one-third of all sentences were terminated before the end. The test sentences were presented up to the second arguments. Half of the comprehension sentences for the test sentences were simple sentences with the same nominative- and accusative-marked NP as the test sentence plus the verbs that were deleted from the original sentences. The other half were simple sentences with a dative-marked NP, with a verb taking the dative-marked argument. The nouns in these sentences were, however, identical to the other comprehension sentences.

2.4.1.2 Participants

Participants for this experiment were 103 undergraduate students at a university in the Tokyo area. They were paid for their participation.

2.4.1.3 Procedure

Participants were told that they would see sentences on a screen, one *bunsetsu* at a time. When they pressed a space key, the present *bunsetsu* disappeared and the next *bunsetsu* would appear. They were to read the sentence for comprehension as though reading a book. After each sentence, a comprehension sentence appeared, and the participants were told to answer 'yes' or 'no' by pressing the pre-designated keys. They were also told that some sentences would terminate before the end. When that happened, they were to decide if the comprehension sentence was likely to be consistent with the sentence, had it continued to the end.

2.4.2 Results

The overall rate of correct answers to the comprehension questions was approximately 82%, while it was about 74% for the test sentences. Strictly speaking, there were no 'incorrect' answers for the test sentences, since the test sentences were presented only up to the second argument. Preliminary analysis showed that the pattern of results was almost identical when we analyzed all of the sentences together or only those with "correct" answers to the comprehension sentences. Thus, we only report the results from the sentences with "correct" answers.

The reading times for each *bunsetsu* are adjusted for length using the same formula as (8) above. We first compare the canonical simple sentences and scrambled simple sentences.

The residual reading time for the canonical simple sentences and scrambled simple sentences were not significantly different from each other either at the first argument position. At the second argument position, it approached significance in subject analysis, but not in item analysis ($F1 (1, 86) = 2.96$, $p = .09$; $F2 (1, 9) < 1$). Neither the nominative marked NPs in the two sentences, nor the accusative marked NPs differed from each other.

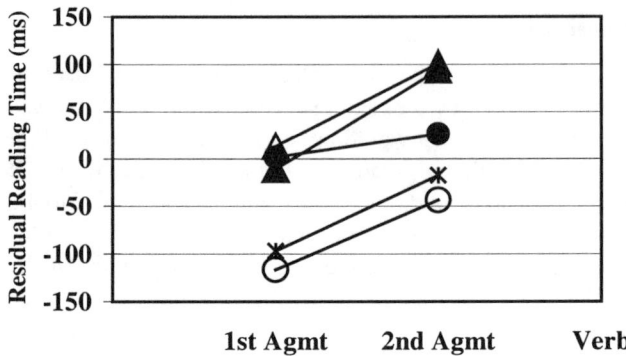

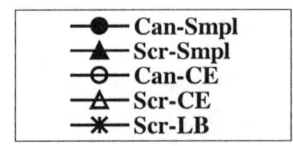

*The figures in the graph represent the average for the region that combines argument NPs and the modifier phrases.

Figure 7. Residual reading time for the first argument and second argument position from the self-paced reading experiment

When we compared just the head nouns of the complex sentences, the residual reading time for the first argument was significant in subject analysis, but not in item analysis (F1 (2, 157) = 4.37, p < .05; F2 (2, 18) = 2.29, p = .13). At the second argument position, the residual reading time was significantly longer for scrambled center-embedded sentences than either canonical center-embedded sentences or scrambled left-branching sentences (F1 (2, 157) = 12.71, p < .001; F2 (2, 18) = 46.68, p < .001).

As in the eye-movement experiment, we also analyzed the whole region that combines the head nouns with the modifier phrases. When we compared the second argument position of the canonical center-embedded sentences and scrambled center-embedded sentences, the residual reading time for scrambled center-embedded sentences were significantly longer than those for canonical center-embedded sentences (F1 (1, 68) = 22.93, p < .001; F2 (1, 9) = 28.83, p < .001). When we compared the three phrases with modifier phrases, the residual reading times for scrambled center-embedded sentences were significantly longer than for canonical center-embedded sentences or scrambled left-branching sentences (F1 (2, 152) = 17.96, p < .001; F2 (2, 18) = 16.07, p < .001).

In summary, few differences between canonical and scrambled sentences were found in simple sentences. But when the complex sentences were compared, a pattern of results similar to the eye-movement experiment emerged. At the second argument position, the reading times for the scrambled sentences were significantly longer than those of canonical sentences. The scrambled left-branching sentences were more similar to the canonical center-embedded sentences, than the scrambled left-branching sentences.

3 Discussion

In all of the experiments, we found that scrambled sentences cost more processing resources than canonical sentences. In three methods of testing - subjective rating of sentences, an eye-movement monitoring method, and a self-paced reading method - scrambled sentences were shown to be more costly than their canonical counterparts. As discussed below, the experiments diverged as to where we found the differences between scrambled and canonical sentences. But taken together, the data clearly showed that scrambled word order information in Japanese is processed on-line, and it incurs a psycholinguistically measurable cost.

3.1 Flat versus Hierarchical Structure for Japanese

In the introduction, we observed that there are alternative proposals for syntactic representation of scrambled sentences in Japanese - i.e. the flat structure of (2) and the hierarchical structure of (3). As discussed above, psycholinguistic evidence such as ours alone cannot determine which one is more appropriate for a scrambled sentence in Japanese. However, in the current linguistic literature, the predominant view is to assume that Japanese phrases have hierarchical structures as in (3). If we assume a hierarchical structure of Japanese phrases -- following Nakayama (1995) and Yamashita (1997), whose experimental results did not show any difference between canonical and scrambled sentences -- we are forced to postulate a syntactic representation that is not well motivated (e.g., a movement that does not leave a trace), or else we must entertain the possibility that a syntactic structure which is computed during on-line processing is different from one which is appropriate at other times. This violates the transparency between the parser and the grammar (Sakamoto 1995, Pritchett 1992, among others). The fact that our experiments found an increased processing cost for scrambled sentences allows us to avoid this dilemma.

3.2 Frequency of Occurrence

In interpreting our results, we must consider the possibility that the frequency of occurrence for scrambled and canonical sentences caused increased processing costs. It has been well established for English that frequency of occurrence of a particular construction can influence sentence comprehension (cf. MacDonald 1994, MacDonald, Perlmutter, and Seidenberg 1994). Thus, it could be the frequency of scrambled sentences, which occur much less frequently than canonical sentences, that causes their difficulty. As discussed above, this is independent of what syntactic structure a Japanese sentence may have. The data from our experiments cannot rule out this possibility entirely.

As noted by others before (cf. Miyamoto and Takahashi 2001), the frequency of occurrence *per se* is not an explanation for why a given construction is difficult for people. If a given construction does not occur frequently, we must find an explanation why people do not produce such a construction to begin with. A study such as Yamashita (in press) is a first step towards that direction. But even when we constrain our discussion to sentence comprehension, frequency of occurrence alone cannot account for increased processing cost at a particular position, or with a different measurement. Considering the fact that frequency does influence many aspects of language processing, it is not likely that it has no effect to the processing of scrambled sentences in Japanese. However, if we are to account for the entire range of data found in our study, we will have to have a specific model of how the frequency information may interact with left-to-right incremental processing.

3.3 The Locus of Difficulty

In our study, we found that the locus of the increased processing load is at the second argument of the scrambled sentences. We found no measurable increase of processing cost for the accusative-marked NP at the first argument position. At the second argument position, in contrast, we found a significant increase in regressive eye-movement in the eye-movement experiment, and an increased reading time in the scrambled center-embedded sentences in the self-paced reading experiment. These data show that readers found the second argument of the scrambled sentence more difficult to process even before they reached the verb. This was true even when the sentence was a simple OSV sentence in the eye-movement experiment. In our self-paced reading experiment, where we did not even present the verb at all, an increased reading time was found at the second argument position of the scrambled center-embedded sentences.

If we are to adopt a hierarchical structure of Japanese sentences, our results are most consistent with an incremental model that allows pre-head parsing decisions (cf. Kamide and Mitchell 1997, 1999). As discussed in the introduction, if parsing decisions are delayed until the head, we do not predict an increased processing cost at the second argument position. Our data showed an increased processing cost before the verb was reached. A model that assumes that a parser simply accumulates the arguments until the verb is reached (e.g., a head-driven parser such as Pritchett's) is not compatible with our data.

However, our data alone will not allow us to determine exactly how detailed a structure a parser would build with the information from the two arguments alone. In a fully incremental model, without any delay (cf. Inoue and Fodor 1995, Fodor and Inoue 1998), a full structure except for the verb itself might be built. In this case, building of the extra structure in the scrambled sentences could be the cause of the increased processing load. In our stimuli, however, the scrambled sentences have not only an additional S node, but also a trace. Therefore, it could be either the additional S node that needs to be created, the presence of the trace, or the combination of the two, that is the source of the increased processing cost in our study. Miyamoto and Takahashi (2001) tested the clause-internal scrambling of dative and accusative arguments, and found an increased processing cost for a scrambled word order. They argue, therefore, that scrambled word order, even without an additional clause node, adds processing difficulty. Still, the results of our study could be the combination of the effect of trace and an additional clause.

Alternatively, one may hypothesize that a nominative-marked NP triggers an extra clause node, since the preceding NP with an accusative case marker would indicate scrambling. In this case, no other details may be built at this point. Then, a model that allows building of an additional clause when necessary, though they would not build further details, is also compatible with the current data. (e.g. Mazuka and Itoh 1995, Mazuka 1998).

Miyamoto and Takahashi (2001) consider the possibility that a nominative marker is inherently more difficult to process than other case markers. A nominative-marked NP has been associated with increased processing cost when encountered out of its ordinary position (Yamashita 1997, Miyamoto 1999, Mazuka, Itoh, and Kondo 2000). Our data do not show a particular difficulty for a nominative-marked NP *per se*. In our analysis, we compared the nominative marked NPs of the scrambled and the canonical sentences. It was only when it appeared in the second argument position of the scrambled sentences that had an increased processing cost. However, as our study does not allow us to analyze the difficulty of case markers independent of their position in a sentence, further study is necessary to evaluate this possibility (cf. Uehara 1997).

3.4 Scrambled Left-Branching Sentences

We included scrambled left-branching sentences in our study. The results showed that these sentences are significantly easier to comprehend than their center-embedded counterparts. As discussed above, it has sometimes been argued that one of the motivations for using scrambled word-order is to avoid center-embedding (cf. Kuno 1973, 1974, Hawkins 1994). Our data show that not only in production, but also in sentence comprehension as well, having a heavy modifier on the first argument is easier than having the same modifier in a center-embedded position. However, the difference we found was between scrambled left-branching sentences and scrambled center-embedded sentences, not between scrambled left-branching sentences and canonical center-embedded sentences. If one were to argue that the scrambled word order would be chosen to avoid center-embedding, the scrambled left-branching sentences should be easier than canonical center-embedded sentences. With the sentences we used, the canonical center-embedded sentences were not much different from scrambled center-embedded sentences in terms of difficulty of processing. It appears as though the cost of center-embedding in our stimuli was approximately equivalent to the cost of scrambling. The canonical center-embedded sentences in our study do not become easier to comprehend by scrambling the heavy NP to the left.

4 Concluding Remarks

In this paper, we presented data from two questionnaire studies and two on-line reading experiments that showed that scrambled sentences are indeed more costly to comprehend than canonical sentences. As earlier experimental studies have failed to find experimentally measurable costs associated with scrambled sentences, it has begun to be discussed as though it were an established fact (e.g. Nakayama 1999). The present paper provides valuable evidence to counter that view. As discussed earlier, given the far-reaching implications if scrambling were cost-free, this is a significant step towards our understanding of Japanese scrambling. The next step in the inquiry should be exactly what causes the difficulty for scrambled sentences. As discussed above, there are several possibilities. Further experiments with additional experimental controls are necessary to disentangle these factors. More recent studies, such as that by Miyamoto and Takahashi (2001), already show a promising direction.

References

Abney, S. P. & M. Johnson. 1991. Memory Requirements and Local Ambiguities of Parsing Strategies. *Journal of Psycholinguistic Research* 20:233-250.

Bever, T. & B. McElree. 1988. Empty Categories Access their Antecedents during Comprehension. *Linguistic Inquiry* 19:35-43.

Berwick, R. C. & S. Fong. 1995. Madama Butterfly Redux: Parsing English and Japanese with a Principles and Parameters Approach. *Japanese Sentence Processing*, eds. R. Mazuka & N. Nagai, 177-208. Hilsdale, NJ: Lawrence Erlbaum.

Bock, J. K. & J. C. Cutting. 1992. Regulating Mental Energy: Performance Units in Language Production. *Journal of Memory & Language* 31:99-127.

Chomsky, N. 1981. *Lectures on Government and Binding*. Dordrecht: Foris.

Clahsen, H. & S. Featherston. 1998. Attachment Priming at Trace Positions: Evidence from German Scrambling. Unpublished manuscript, University of Essex, Colchester, U.K.

Farmer, A. K. 1980. On the Interaction of Morphology and Syntax. Doctoral dissertation, MIT.

Farmer, A. K. 1984. *Modularity in Syntax: A Study of Japanese and Syntax*. Cambridge, MA: MIT Press.

Ferreira, F. & C. Clifton Jr. 1986. The Independence of Syntactic Processing. *Journal of Memory & Language* 25:348-368.

Fodor, J. D. & A. Inoue. 1997. Attach Anyway. *Reanalysis in Sentence Processing*, eds. J. D. Fodor & F. Fernanda. Dordrecht: Kluwer Academic Publisher.

Frazier, L. 1987. Processing Syntactic Structures: *Evidence from Dutch. Natural Language & Linguistic Theory* 23:407-434.

Frazier, L. & G. Flores d'Arcais. 1989. Filler-driven Parsing: A Study of Gap-filling in Dutch. *Journal of Memory & Language* 28:331-344.

Frazier, L. & K. Rayner. 1988. Parameterizing the Language Processing System: Left-branching vs. Right-branching within and across Languages. *Explaining Language Universals*, ed. J. Hawkins, 247-279. Oxford: Blackwell.

Gibson, E. 1991. A Computational Theory of Human Linguistic Processing: Memory Limitations and Processing Breakdown. Doctoral dissertation. Carnegie Mellon University. CMU-CMT-91-125.

Gorrell, P. 1995. *Syntax and Parsing*. Cambridge: Cambridge University Press.

Hale, K. 1980. Remarks on Japanese Phrase Structure: Comments on the Papers on Japanese Syntax. *MIT Working Papers in Linguistics* 2, 185-203.

Hale, K. 1981. *On the Position of Warlpiri in a Typology of the Base*. Bloomington, IN: IULC.

Hawkins, J. 1994. *A Performance Theory of Order and Constituency*. Cambridge: Cambridge University Press.

Inoue, A. & J. D. Fodor. 1995. Information-paced Parsing of Japanese. *Japanese Sentence Processing*, eds. R. Mazuka & N. Nagai, 9-63. Hilsdale, NJ: Lawrence Erlbaum.

Kaan, E. 1997. Processing Subject-object Ambiguities in Dutch. Doctoral dissertation, University of Groningen.

Kamide, Y. & D. C. Mitchell. 1997. Relative Clause Attachment: Nondeterminism in Japanese Parsing. *Journal of Psycholinguistic Research* 26:247-254.

Kamide, Y. & D. C. Mitchell. 1999. Incremental Pre-head Attachment in Japanese Parsing. *Language & Cognitive Processes* 14:631-662.

Kuno, S. 1973. *The Structure of Japanese Language*. Cambridge, MA: MIT Press.

Kuno, S. 1974. The Position of Relative Clauses and Conjunctions. *Linguistic Inquiry* 5:117-136.

Lewis, R. L. 1996. Interference in Short-term Memory: The Magical Number Two (or Three) in Sentence Processing. *Journal of Psycholinguistic Research* 25:93-115.

MacDonald, M. C. 1994. Probabilistic Constraints and Syntactic Ambiguity Resolution. *Language & Cognitive Processes* 9:35-56.

MacDonald, M. C., N. J. Perlmutter, & M. S. Seidenberg. 1994. The Lexical Nature of Syntactic Ambiguity Resolution. *Psychological Review* 101:676-703.

Mazuka, R. 1998. *The Development of Language Processing Strategies: A Cross-Linguistic Study between Japanese and English*. Marwah, NJ: LEA.

Mazuka, R. & K. Itoh. 1995. Can Japanese Speakers be Lead down the Garden Path? *Japanese Sentence Processing*, eds. R. Mazuka & N. Nagai, 295-329. Hilsdale, NJ: Lawrence Erlbaum.

Mazuka , R. & N. Nagai. eds. 1995. *Japanese Sentence Processing*. Hilsdale, NJ: Lawrence Erlbaum.

Mazuka, R., K. Itoh, & T. Kondo. 2000. Costs of Avoiding Misanalysis versus Costs of Recovering from Misanalysis of Japanese Relative Clauses. A paper presented at 13th annual CUNY sentence processing conference, University of California at San Diego.

Mazuka, R., K. Itoh, T. Kondo, & J. S. Brown. 1999. Relative Contributions of Morae and Characters in Reading Japanese Sentences. A paper presented at International East Asian Psycholinguistics Workshop, The Ohio State University, Columbus, OH.

Mazuka, R., K. Itoh, S. Kiritani, S. Niwa, K. Ikejiri, & K. Naitoh. 1989. Processing of Japanese Garden Path, Center-embedded, and Multiply-left-ebmedded Sentences: Reading Time Data from an Eye Movement Study. *Annual Bulletin, The Research Institute of Logopedics and Phoniatrics* 23:187-212. University of Tokyo.

Miller, G. A. 1956. The Magical Number Seven plus or minus Two, or some Limits on our Capacity for Processing Information. *Psychological Review* 93:81-96.

Miller, G. A. & N. Chomsky. 1963. Finittary Models of Language Users. In, eds., *Handbook of Mathematical Psychology* Vol. 2, eds. R. D. Luce, R. Bush, & E. Galanter, 419-491. New York: Wiley.

Miyagawa, S. 1988. Predication and Numeral Quantifier. *Paper from the Second International Workshop on Japanese Syntax*, ed. W. Poser. Stanford CA: CSLI.

Miyagawa, S. 1989. *Structure and Case Marking in Japanese. Syntax and Semantics Vol. 22*. San Diego: Academic Press.

Miyagawa, S. 1997. Against Optional Scrambling. *Linguistic Inquiry* 28:1-26.

Miyamoto, E. T. 1999. Relative Clause Processing in Brazilian Portuguese and Japanese. Doctoral dissertation, MIT.

Miyamoto, E. T. & S. Takahashi. 2001. Source of Difficulty in the Processing Scrambling in Japanese. *Sentence Processing in East Asian Languages*, ed. M. Nakayama. Stanford, CA: CSLI.

Nakayama, M. 1990. Accessibility to the Antecedents in Japanese Sentence Processing. Unpublished manuscript, Ohio State University.

Nakayama, M. 1991. Japanese Motion Verbs and Probe Recognition. Unpublished manuscript, Ohio State University.

Nakayama, M. 1995. Scrambling and Probe Recognition. *Japanese Sentence Processing*, R. Mazuka & N. Nagai, 257-273. Hilsdale, NJ: Lawrence Erlbaum.

Nakayama, M. 1999. Sentence Processing. *The Handbook of Japanese Linguistics*, ed. N. Tsujimura, 398-424. Malden, MA: Blackwell.

Nemoto, N. 1999. Scrambling. *The Handbook of Japanese Linguistics*, ed. N. Tsujimura, 121-153. Malden, MA: Blackwell..

Pritchett, B. L. 1988. Garden Path Phenomena and the Grammatical Basis of Language Processing. *Language* 64.3:539-576.

Pritchett, B. L. 1992. *Grammatical Competence and Parsing Performance.* University of Chicago Press, Chicago, IL.

Rayner, K., G. N. Carlson, & L. Frazier. 1983. The Interaction of Syntax and Semantics during Sentence Processing: Eye Movements in the Analysis of Semantically Biased Sentences. *Journal of Verbal Learning & Verbal Behavior* 22:358-374.

Sadakane, K. & M. Koizumi 1995. On the Nature of the 'Dative' Particle *ni* in Japanese. *Linguistics* 33:5-33.

Saito, M. 1985. Some Asymmetries in Japanese and Their Theoretical Implications. Doctoral Dissertation, MIT.

Saito, M. & H. Hoji. 1983. Weak Cross-over and Move α in Japanese. *Natural Language & Linguistic Theory* 1:245-259.

Sakamoto, T. 1995. Transparency between Parser and Grammar: On the Processing of Empty Subjects in Japanese. In eds., *Japanese Sentence Processing*, eds. R. Mazuka & N. Nagai, 275-294. Hilsdale, NJ: Lawrence Erlbaum.

Tonoike, S. 1997. On scrambling -- Scrambling as a Base-generated Scopal Construction. *Scrambling*, S. Tonoike, 125-159. Tokyo: Kurosio Publishers.

Trueswell, J., M. Tanenhaus, & S. Garnsey. 1994. Semantic Influences on Parsing: Use of Thematic Role Information in Syntactic Ambiguity Resolution. *Journal of Memory & Language* 33.3:285-318.

Uehara, K. 1997. Judgements on Processig Load in Japanese: The Effect of NP-ga Sequences. *Journal of Psycholinguistic Research* 26:255-263.

Weinberg, A. 1993. Parameters in the Theory of Sentence Processing: Minimal Commitment Theory Goes East. *Journal of Psycholinguistic Research* 22.3:339-364.

Whitmann, J. 1987. Configurationality Parameters. *Issues in Japanese Linguistics*, eds. T. Imai and Mamoru Saito. Dordrecht: Foris.

Yamashita, H. 1997. The Effects of Word-order and Case Marking Information on the Processing of Japanese. *Journal of Psycholinguistic Research* 26:163-188.

Yamashita, H. in press. Scrambled Sentences in Japanese: Linguistic Properties and Motivations for Production. *Text*.

Appendix A

The following are the sentences used in the study. The slashes indicate the breaks between *bunsetsu* that were used for the regression analyses discussed in (8) above. These were also the breaks used for presenting the stimuli in the self-paced reading experiment. Note, however, the sentences were presented only up to the second argument in the self-paced reading experiment.

All five versions of the sentences were shown for Sentence 1. For all remaining sentences, only versions (a) and (c) were shown.

(1) a. Obaasan-ga/otokonoko-o/kooen-ni/tsuretekita.
 b. Otokonoko-o/obaasan-ga/kooen-ni/tsuretekita.
 c. Obaasan-ga/ame-o/nakushite/oogoe-de/naiteiru/otokonoko-o/
   grandmother-Nom/candy-Acc/lost/loudly/crying/boy-Acc/
   kooen-ni/tsuretekita.
   park-to/brought.
   'Grandmother brought a boy who lost a candy and was crying loudly to the park.'
 d. Obaasan-o/ame-o/nakushite/oogoe-de/naiteiru/otokonoko-ga/kooen-ni/
   tsuretekita.
   'The boy, who lost a candy and was crying loudly, brought grandmother to the park.'

(2) a. Mariko-ga/otooto-o/oogoe-de/yonda.
 c. Mariko-ga/soto-de/branko-ni/notteita/otooto-o/
   Mariko-Nom/outside/swing/swinging/younger brother-Acc/

oogoe-de/yonda.
with a loud voice/ called
'Mariko loudly called her younger brother, who was swinging on a swing outside.'

(3) a. Noriko-ga/yuujin-o/tazuneta.
  c. Noriko-ga/ onaji/daigaku-o/jukensuru/yakusoku-no/yuujin-o/tazuneta.
     Noriko-Nom/same/university-Acc/apply/promiss-Gen/friend-Acc/
     visited.
     'Noriko visited a friend who promised to apply to the same university as her.'

(4) a. Yasuhiro-ga/otooto-o/nagutta.
  c. Yasuhiro-ga/oyatsu-no/toriai-de/kenka-ni/natta/
     Yasuhiro-Nom/snack-Gen/sharing/fight-to/became/
     otooto-o/nagutta.
     younger brother-Acc/hit.
     'Yasuhiro hit his younger brother with whom he got into a fight over sharing a snack.'

(5) a. Yuuko-ga/Noriaki-o/kissaten-de/matta.
  c. Yuuko-ga/kyuuna/shutchoo-de/Kyuushuu-ni/iku/koto-ni/natta/
     Yuko-Nom/sudden/business trip-on/Kyushu-to/go/that/became/
     Noriaki-o/ kissaten-de/matta.
     Noriaki-Acc/coffee shop-at/ waited.
     'Yuko waited for Noriaki, who has togo to Kyushu on a sudden business trip.'

(6) a. Hitomi-ga/Maiko-o/eiga-ni/sasotta.
  c. Hitomi-ga/onaji/kenkyuushitsu-no/daigakuinsei-no/
     Hitomi-Nom/same/lab-Gen/graduate student-Gen/
     Maiko-o/eiga-ni/sasotta.
     Maiko-Acc/movie-to/asked out
     'Hitomi asked Maiko, who is a graduate student in the same lab, to a movie.'

(7) a. Naganuma-ga/Shimazaki-o/Ginza-de/mikaketa.
  c. Naganuma-ga/sotsugyoo/irai/onshinhutsuu-no/
     Naganuma-Nom/graduation/since/lost touch
     Shimazaki-o/Ginza-de/mikaketa.
     Shimazaki-Acc/Ginza-at/saw.
     'Naganuma saw Shimazaki, with whom he had lost touch since graduation, on the Ginza.'

(8) a. Fujimura-ga/Noguchi-o/yobidashita.
  c. Fujimura-ga/nen-ni/ichido-no/gakkai-de/
     Fujimura-Nom/a year/once/conference-because of/
     Tokyo-ni/detekita/Noguchi-o/yobidashita.

Tokyo-to/came/Noguchi-Acc/paged
'Fujimura paged Noguchi, who came to Tokyo for an annual conference.'

(9) a. Fumiko-ga/Horiguchi-o/isshookenmei/sagashita.
  c. Fumiko-ga/rasshuji-no/Yaesuguchi-de/hagurete/
     shimatta/Horiguchi-o/isshookenmiei/sagashita.
     Fumiko-Nom/rush hour during/Yaesu entrance-at/lost/
     became/Horiguchi-Acc/very hard/looked for
     'Fumiko looked hard for Horiguchi, who got lost at the Yaesu Entrance (of Tokyo Station) during the rush hour.'

(10) a. Sugiura-ga/Rie-o/tetsudatta.
   c. Sugiura-ga/saigomade/nokotte/zangyoositeita/Rie-o/tetsudatta.
      Sugiura-Nom/until the last/remained/doing over time/Rie-Acc/helped.
      'Sugiura helped Rie, who remained until the very end working overtime.'

7

Sources of Difficulty in Processing Scrambling in Japanese*

EDSON T. MIYAMOTO AND SHOICHI TAKAHASHI

1 Introduction

Word order flexibility in Japanese has generated a vast literature in theoretical linguistics (Bošković and D. Takahashi 1998, Hale 1980, Hoji 1985, Miyagawa 1997, Saito 1985, Takano 1996, inter alia). However, there have been few studies investigating the processing of non-canonical word orders in this language, and their results have often yielded conflicting results. In particular, behavioral studies do not agree as to whether non-canonical word orders are more difficult to process than their canonical counterparts (Mazuka, Itoh, and Kondo 1998, 2001; Yamashita 1997).

---

* We would like to thank the audiences at the Keio Minimalist Syntax group (Keio University) and at Tsujii Laboratory (University of Tokyo) for helpful comments on earlier presentations of this work. We would also like to thank Reiko Mazuka and Kenji Itoh for discussions clarifying various points in their experiment and in the present work, and Mineharu Nakayama for comments on an earlier version of the manuscript. All remaining errors are our own. Experiment I was funded by the JST/MIT joint international research project 'Mind/Articulation' while the first author was a graduate student at MIT. Experiment II was supported by a Grant-in-Aid for COE Research (08CE1001) from the Japanese Ministry of Education. CD-ROMs of the Mainichi Shinbun and Nippon Keizai Shinbun were used in order to obtain the sentences for Experiment III. Address correspondence to the first author.

Sentence Processing in East Asian Languages.
Mineharu Nakayama (ed.).
Copyright ©2002, CSLI Publications.

We report a self-paced reading experiment (Experiment I) that taken together with a previous result (Mazuka, Itoh, and Kondo 1998, 2001) supports the view that the processing of non-canonical word orders requires longer reading times. In the second part of the paper, we discuss the possible sources of this difficulty. We propose that the processing of non-canonical word orders involves searching for the gap required by a displaced element. Positing such a gap leads to longer reading times especially when readers have limited memory resources available (e.g. when the gap is far away from its antecedent; following Gibson 1998, Just and Carpenter 1992). It will not be relevant for the present discussion whether the gap is encoded as a phonologically null constituent (*pro* or a trace left behind by movement, Chomsky 1981) or as a slash feature (Gazdar, Klein, Pullum and Sag 1985).

However, in all experiments reported thus far in the literature, including Experiment I below, a number of alternative factors may have been responsible for the slow-down observed, rather than the proposed filler-gap association process. For example, the slow-down may have been detected because NPs with different case markers were compared; or perhaps because non-canonical word orders are less frequently encountered than their canonical counterparts; or because there is a preference for accusative NPs to be immediately followed by their subcategorizing verb. A second type of experiment designed to rule out these alternative factors is described. Preliminary results of a self-paced reading experiment support the gap hypothesis, and a corpus count indicates that the behavioral data collected are not easily explained by frequency factors.

2 Scrambling in Japanese

The canonical word order in Japanese is SOV (subject-object-verb). However, constituents can be scrambled (i.e. moved leftward in the sentence) as long as the verb is the last element in the clause. For example, consider the following sentences (from Mazuka, Itoh and Kondo 2001).

(1) a. Scrambled accusative NP
        Otooto$_i$-o   Mariko-ga   gap$_i$ mita.
        brother-Acc   -Nom   saw
        'Mariko saw her brother.'

   b.   Canonical word order
        Mariko-ga   otooto-o   mita.
        -Nom   brother-Acc   saw
        'Mariko saw her brother.'

In (1a), the constituent *brother*-Acc was scrambled to the beginning of the sentence and gap$_i$ indicates its original position according to generative linguistics proposals. The canonical word order is shown in (1b) (see, for example, Hoji 1985, for syntactic tests to determine which order is canonical).

In processing terms, two questions are particularly relevant. The first question is whether scrambled word orders are more difficult to process than their canonical versions. The second question is whether a more complex structure is computed for scrambled sentences. The two questions are often assumed to be related in that difficulty is taken to be a sign of more complex structure building. In the first part of this paper, we will concentrate on the first question and will not concern ourselves with the possible factors that could lead to such a difficulty.

An earlier study did not observe any significant slow-downs in the processing of scrambled word orders (Yamashita 1997). More recently, however, Mazuka, Itoh, and Kondo (1998, 2001) detected longer reading times at *Mariko*-Nom in the scrambled sentence (1a) above when it was compared to *brother*-Acc in the canonical (1b). Thus, these authors concluded that scrambled sentences involve some extra processing cost.

One objection that may be raised, however, is that NPs with nominative case may signal a clause boundary in Japanese (Inoue 1991, Miyamoto 2001), and their occurrences are particularly marked. Consequently, the slow-down observed by Mazuka and colleagues may be related to properties of the *ga* marker and not necessarily to extra costs incurred by the scrambling of the accusative NP. The use of nominative NPs as clause boundary markers may be necessary because Japanese does not provide any other indicator to signal the beginning of an embedded clause; in particular, a complementizer when present comes at the left end of the clause. Nominative subjects are good candidate markers because they cannot be scrambled (Saito 1985 and references therein); hence, their position is fixed in the initial segment of the clause. The result by Mazuka and colleagues, although suggestive, cannot be unambiguously interpreted without further investigation of the role of nominative NPs in parsing.

3 Experiment I: Scrambling and Memory Load

In this section, we provide further evidence that scrambling requires some extra effort to be processed. It is possible that previous studies (e.g. Yamashita 1997) did not detect any significant differences in the reading times of scrambled sentences in relation to their canonical versions because the items used were rather simple and may have been read rapidly in all conditions.[1] Mazuka and colleagues provide evidence in this direction as the slow-down in their experiment was more pronounced when center-embedded sentences were used (Mazuka, Itoh, and Kondo 2001).

We conducted an experiment in which the memory load of the task was increased by using complex sentences, which required close attention from the participants. The basic construction used involves ditransitive verbs such as *ageru* 'give' and *shookai-suru* 'introduce'. The canonical order is shown in (2a) below. In (2b), the accusative argument was scrambled to the position prior to the dative argument.

(2) a. Canonical: Subject NP-Dat NP-Acc ditransitive-verb
    b. Scrambled: Subject NP_i-Acc NP-Dat gap_i ditransitive-verb

This particular construction was chosen because its scrambled version is commonly used by native speakers; therefore, familiarity issues are less likely to be a concern (see Experiment III below for further discussion on frequency factors). Moreover, it has been suggested that both word orders in (2) are canonical (Miyagawa 1997), despite the fact that (2b) has been traditionally assumed to involve scrambling (Hoji 1985, Takano 1996, inter alia). Therefore, processing results may be helpful in resolving the controversy at the syntactic level. Another advantage of this construction is that scrambling occurs inside the VP; thus, reading time differences cannot be caused by the detection of clause boundaries. Both clauses in (2) were further embedded as indicated below.

(3) a. Canonical: [Subject [$_{RC}$ ec_j NP-Dat <u>NP-Acc</u>   ditransitive-verb]
           NP_j-Acc verb-Comp] NP-Nom report-verb
    b. Scrambled: [Subject [$_{RC}$ ec_j NP_i-Acc <u>NP-Dat</u> gap_i ditransitive-verb]
           NP_j-Acc verb-Comp] NP-Nom report-verb

The ditransitive clause is a relative clause modifying an accusative NP (relative clauses precede the modified head in Japanese), which in turn is part of a sentential complement. The empty category ec_j indicates that the subject position inside the ditransitive clause was relativized. The main clause is headed by a report-verb (see the Materials section for an example sentence). Fillers of comparable complexity were included. Complex items were used

---

[1] Another possible reason for the lack of significant differences is that the study did not control for the number of characters in the regions compared, and the statistical analyses did not compensate for the differences (Yamashita, personal communication).

in order to force participants to read carefully, and intently store words in working memory.

We adopt an incremental processing model in which case-marked NPs are associated within a partial representation of the sentence before the subcategorizing verb is read (see Miyamoto 2001, for experimental evidence on the use of case markers in this process). Thus, readers may detect a non-canonical word order before a verb is processed. As a consequence, the crucial region for comparison in (3) is the underlined object NP. In (3b), the NP-Dat is the first word that indicates that the accusative NP was scrambled. Before that point, readers could assume that the sequence *Subject NP-Acc* is the initial fragment of a simple transitive sentence that does not involve scrambling and only requires a transitive verb to be completed. The underlined NP-Acc in (3a) provides the baseline reading time.

3.1 Method

3.1.1 Participants

Thirty-eight native speakers of Japanese participated for $20 each. They had gone to the U.S. as adults and were residents of the Boston area at the time of the experiment.

3.1.2 Materials

Twenty-five sentence pairs like the following were constructed (see Appendix A for the complete list of items used).

(4) a. Ofisu-de   shokuin-ga   kakarichoo-ni ocha-o   dasita
     office-Loc employee-Nom manager-Dat   tea-Acc served

     josei-o   teineini hometa-to   Aiharasan-ga hanasiteita.
     woman-Acc politely praised-Comp Aihara-Nom   said

     'At the office, Aihara said that the employee politely praised the woman who had served tea to the manager.'

   b. Ofisu-de   shokuin-ga   ocha-o   kakarichoo-ni dasita
      office-Loc employee-Nom tea-Acc manager-Dat   served

      josei-o   teineini hometa-to   Aiharasan-ga hanasiteita.
      woman-Acc politely praised-Comp Aihara-Nom   said

'At the office, Aihara said that the employee politely praised the woman who had served tea to the manager.'

As previously observed, the regions of interest are the underlined NPs. In (4b), *manager*-Dat is the earliest point in which it is clear that the NP *tea*-Acc was scrambled. The experiment included three more conditions, which were unrelated to the present claims. Five lists were created by distributing the twenty-five stimuli in a Latin Square design. Each participant saw exactly one of the lists intermixed with 53 unrelated foil items in pseudo-random order.

3.1.3 Procedure

The experiment was conducted on a Power Macintosh 7500/100 running PsyScope (Cohen, MacWhinney, Flatt, and Provost 1993) with a button-box. Participants were timed in a phrase-by-phrase self-paced non-cumulative moving-window reading task (Just, Carpenter, and Woolley 1982). Each phrase was constituted of a content word plus functional particles such as a case marker, a postposition, or a complementizer. The segmentation in the sentences in (4) (represented by intervening spaces) was the actual segmentation used in the self-paced reading presentation. Sentences were shown using Japanese characters (as in Appendix A) with the uniform-width font Osaka Toohaba 14. Stimuli initially appeared as dots, and participants pressed the leftmost button of the button-box to reveal each subsequent region of the sentence and cause all other regions to revert to dots. All sentences were presented on a single line. At the end of each sentence, a yes/no question appeared on a new screen, which participants answered by pressing one of the two rightmost buttons. No feedback was given. Corresponding data points were eliminated from further analyses if the participant did not answer the comprehension question correctly.

The experimental trials were preceded by one screen of instructions and eight practice trials. The experiment took participants approximately 20 minutes.

3.1.4 Analysis

We analyzed comprehension question response accuracy and reading times. Analyses were conducted on residual reading times per region (Ferreira and Clifton 1986), derived by subtracting from raw reading times each participant's predicted time to read regions of the same length (measured in number of characters), which in turn was calculated from a linear regression equation across all of a participant's sentences in the experiment. The residual reading times were trimmed so that data points beyond three standard deviations from the relevant condition x region cell mean were discarded, corresponding to less than 2.5% of the total data. The means and analyses presented below are based on the trimmed residual reading times. Analyses conducted on raw reading times yielded a similar pattern of results as the residual reading times analyses reported. We report the residual reading times because the number of characters was not controlled for in the critical region.

3.2 Results

3.2.1 Comprehension Question Accuracy

Comprehension question accuracy was low with participants providing correct answers for 61% of the canonical word order items and 65% of the scrambled items. The difference was not statistically significant (Fs < 1).

3.2.2 Reading Times

At the critical region, the argument prior to the ditransitive verb, the scrambled condition was significantly slower than the canonical condition (185.10 msec and -207.2 msec respectively in the residual reading time analysis; 1588.68 msec and 1215.29 msec in the raw reading time analysis) in the analysis by subjects ($F(1,37) = 7.48$; $P < 0.05$) as well as by items ($F(1,23) = 5.41$; $P < 0.05$).[2] The two conditions did not differ significantly at the ditransitive verb (Fs < 1). No significant differences were observed at any of the other regions.

Because of the low comprehension performance, a further analysis was conducted in which the data from the ten participants with the worst comprehension performance were eliminated. In this analysis, the correct response rates for the scrambled condition (73%) and for the canonical condition (69%) were not statistically different (Fs < 1). The scrambled condition was marginally slower than the canonical condition at the region prior to the ditransitive verb (analysis by subjects: $F(1,27) = 3.79$, $P = 0.062$; analysis by items: $F(1,22) = 3.34$, $P = 0.081$). There was no significant difference at the ditransitive verb (Fs < 1.8) or at any of the other regions.

3.3 Discussion

The present result provides evidence that scrambling leads to longer reading times as previously observed by Mazuka, Itoh, and Kondo (1998, 2001).

---

[2] One item was eliminated in the analysis by items because it had no data points for the canonical condition as participants answered the comprehension question incorrectly.

Because scrambling in the present case occurs inside the VP, the slow-down observed cannot be related to clause boundary ambiguities.

However, there are a number of factors that could be used to explain the slow-down in this experiment. In the next section, we discuss some possible alternatives.

Of particular interest in Experiment I is the fact that the slow-down occurs at the NP preceding the ditransitive verb, but not at the verb itself (see Mazuka, Itoh, and Kondo 2001, for a similar pattern of results; and the discussion below on the "direct association hypothesis", Pickering and Barry 1991).

4 Sources of Difficulty in Scrambling

Although Experiment I provides evidence that scrambled word orders involve more processing difficulty than their respective canonical word orders, the source of such a difficulty is not entirely clear. In this section, we argue that the difficulty can be explained based on the assumptions below.

(I) Readers compute gaps for scrambled constituents in sentences with non-canonical word order.

(II) The positing of a gap leads to processing slow-downs.

According to these assumptions, readers should slow down whenever it is necessary for a gap to be posited in a scrambled sentence. Furthermore, given proposals in the language processing literature related to working memory constraints (Gibson 1998, Just and Carpenter 1992), we also adopt the following.

(III) The slow-down in (II) is affected by the amount of working memory that readers have available during parsing and, consequently, by the distance between the gap and its antecedent.

The processing of a gap necessarily requires maintaining and eventually finding a discourse entity (the antecedent for the gap) in working memory. Therefore, the less working memory available the harder the retrieval of the relevant entity, and slower processing times arise as a consequence. Because constituents intervening between the gap and its antecedent occupy space in working memory, they should contribute to the slow-down in (II). Related evidence comes from a self-paced reading experiment using the following sentences in English (Gibson and Warren 1998).

(5) a. The victim [who$_i$ the counselor concluded [$_{CP}$ gap$_i$ that the critical comment had annoyed gap$_i$]] has switched to another psychoanalyst.
   b. The victim [who$_i$ the counselor's conclusion about the critical comment had annoyed gap$_i$] has switched to another psychoanalyst.

According to Gibson and Warren, the verb *annoyed* was read faster in (5a) than in (5b) because the intermediate trace (after *concluded*) in the former sentence facilitated the processing of the trace being posited at *annoyed*. Under one possible interpretation, the trace at *annoyed* was processed faster in (5a) because its antecedent had been reactivated more recently at the intermediate trace.

The adoption of (I) to (III) above provides an account of Japanese scrambling which is compatible not only with prevailing theoretical linguistics proposals for the phenomenon (e.g. Hoji 1985), but also with previous behavioral literature that suggests that the processing of gaps in English have a number of observable effects in on-line processing (Bever and McElree 1988, Gibson and Warren 1998, MacDonald 1989, inter alia).

4.1 The Incremental Processing of Scrambling

In the following, we discuss how assumptions (I) to (III) above apply to the processing of scrambled ditransitive constructions in Japanese such as the one schematically represented below.

(6) NP-Nom NP-Acc NP-Dat ...

In the incremental parsing model adopted here, Japanese speakers create a partial representation for NPs based on various sources of information such as plausibility, animacy and, in particular, case marking. Initially, when reading the sequence in (6), there is a preference to associate the first two NPs in a simple transitive construction (Miyamoto 2001). However, as the dative NP is read, there is a preference for a ditransitive clause to be built (Yamashita 1997). Moreover, it is also clear at this point that the accusative NP was scrambled within the ditransitive clause, and its gap can be posited immediately after the dative NP. In this respect, we follow previous findings in the processing of filler-gap dependencies in assuming that gaps are inserted as early as possible in the input string (e.g. Frazier and Clifton 1989, and references therein). In short, even before the verb is read, there is enough information for a gap to be inserted after the dative NP in (6).

In the processing of fronted wh-phrases in English, filler-gap dependencies involve two separate processes: detecting a filler (e.g. a wh-phrase) which signals the requirement for a gap, and at a later point, positing the gap. In contrast, in Japanese scrambling, the two processes often occur simultaneously because it is not immediately apparent that a constituent was displaced and requires a gap. Thus, in (6) the fact that NP-Acc was scrambled only becomes clear when NP-Dat is read, at which point the gap is also posited.

According to assumption (II), there should be a slow-down at the indirect object NP-Dat in order for the gap to be inserted. Moreover, following (III), such a delay should be longer if the distance between the accusative NP and the position of the gap is larger.

In what follows, we discuss three alternative factors that could also explain the slow-down observed in Experiment I. As should be clear from the discussion, the inability to determine the source of the difficulty more precisely is not a problem exclusive to Experiment I, but rather it may be unavoidable whenever a scrambled sentence is directly compared to its corresponding canonical version.

4.2 A Case Marker Processing Hierarchy

In experiments comparing canonical and scrambled word orders directly (such as Experiment I; as well as Mazuka, Itoh, and Kondo 2001; Yamashita 1997), one unavoidable design restriction is that NPs with different case markers have to be compared. Consequently, it could be suggested that the reading time differences at those points result from intrinsic properties of the case markers being processed, and not from scrambling itself.

In more general terms, there may be a hierarchy according to which some case markers may require longer processing time than others. The nominative *ga* seems particularly marked in a number of ways as it involves complex discourse settings (see Kuno 1973, for the exhaustive reading of the *ga* marker) and idiosyncratic syntactic properties (nominative subjects cannot be scrambled, Saito 1985). Consequently, among the various case markers, the nominative *ga* may take the longest to be processed.

The difference between the dative *ni* and the accusative *o* markers is more subtle, without one being necessarily more salient than the other. But if importance of a constituent for the interpretation of a clause correlates with processing slow-down, then an accusative marked NP should require longer reading times than a dative NP (see Sadakane and Koizumi 1995, for a hierarchy based on "affectedness"; also Chomsky 1981, for differences between structural and inherent case).

If confirmed by empirical evidence, such a case marker hierarchy may pose problems to scrambling experiment in which NPs with distinct case markers are compared. For example, in Mazuka and colleagues' experiment, the slow-down observed at the nominative NP in the scrambled condition (in comparison to an accusative NP in the canonical condition) may have been caused by the processing of the nominative marker and not by scrambling.

In Experiment I above, the dative NP in the scrambled condition was read more slowly than the accusative NP in the canonical condition, whereas the case marking hierarchy would predict the opposite result. Thus, case marking differences may be less of an issue in this experiment. However, independent results investigating the processing time of the various case markers would be desirable.

4.3 Frequency

A second factor that requires consideration is the relative frequency of the constructions compared. If less frequent constructions require longer reading times to be processed, then any slow-down observed in scrambled sentences can be readily explained because these constructions are less common than their respective canonical versions (see the corpus count in Experiment III confirming this tendency).

But even if the correlation between frequency and reading time turns out to be empirically supported, frequency in itself is not an explanation. It would be desirable to provide independent motivation (e.g. cognitive or historical factors) that led such frequency patterns to emerge in the first place. Moreover, there is evidence suggesting that frequency in corpora do not always match behavioral preferences in Dutch (Mitchell and Brysbaert 1998) and in English (Gibson, Schütze, and Salomon 1996).

Nevertheless, considering the importance of frequency in lexical access and recent models integrating it to sentence-level processing (e.g. Elman 1991, MacDonald, Pearlmutter, and Seidenberg 1994), frequency factors should be carefully considered when interpreting experiments investigating alternative word orders.

4.4 The Adjacency Constraint on Direct Objects

A third factor that cannot be easily dismissed in scrambling experiments is a preference for direct objects to be placed adjacent to their subcategorizing verbs. This preference is strictly observed in English as the following sentences suggest (from Stowell 1981).

(7) a. Paul quickly opened the door.
    b. * Paul opened quickly the door.

Sentence (7b) is ungrammatical because the adverb *quickly* intervenes between the verb and the direct object. In Japanese, the adjacency constraint is also observed, but less directly because of word order flexibility. For example, in informal conversations, the accusative marker can be omitted from direct objects, but grammaticality is degraded if the direct object without case marker is not immediately followed by the verb (Saito 1985).

If the adjacency constraint is also a factor during parsing (as intuitive judgments suggest), then it should not be surprising that a slow-down is observed immediately after a scrambled accusative NP because the following constituent is not going to be the expected transitive verb.

In the next section, we describe a different experimental design which avoids the confounding factors discussed above, with the added advantage of testing a proposed property of gaps, namely, that they take longer to process when far away from their antecedents.

5 Distance between Gap and Antecedent

In order to rule out the alternative factors that could explain the result of Experiment I, we devised the experimental design in (8). The basic construction is the simple ditransitive construction in (2). In the present case, however, a long intervening phrase (an XP for short) is included before the two object NPs (as schematically shown in (8a, b)) or between them as in (8c, d). In (8a, c), the accusative NP is in its canonical position; whereas in (8b, d), it was scrambled over the dative NP (the gaps indicate the original position of the accusative NP).

(8) a. Canonical (preposed XP):
Subject XP NP-Dat NP-Acc ditransitive-verb

b. Short scrambling (preposed XP):
Subject XP NP_i-Acc NP-Dat gap_i ditransitive-verb

c. Canonical (intervening XP):
Subject NP-Dat XP NP-Acc ditransitive-verb

d. Long scrambling (intervening XP):
Subject NP_i-Acc XP NP-Dat gap_i ditransitive-verb

As in Experiment 1, the region of interest is the argument prior to the ditransitive verb because this is where readers may be positing a gap for the accusative NP in the scrambled conditions. If assumption (II) above is correct, there should be a slow-down in this region in (8b) when compared to the same region in (8a). However, because (8a, b) are relatively simple sentences, the memory load may be small and the positing of the gap in (8b) may be easily overridden by other factors. For example, given that the case markers are different, they could potentially wash out any differences related to the positing of the gap.

Instead, consider (8d) in relation to (8b). Participants should be positing a gap in both sentences. But if the distance between the gap to its antecedent is a factor, the slow-down should be more pronounced in (8d) than in (8b). One advantage in this procedure is that the NPs compared have the same dative case marker. Hence, one of the issues raised in the previous section is addressed.

One problem in that comparison is that, intuitively, an XP is more awkward when it intervenes between the two object NPs, independent of scrambling. Thus, (8d) may be more difficult than (8b) not only because of the distance between gap and antecedent, but also because of the intervening XP. In order to obtain a baseline for the intervening-XP effect, we included the canonical conditions with a preposed XP (8a) and with an intervening XP (8c). In this type of experiment, we would like to find out whether there is an interaction between the position of the XP (preceding or intervening between the two object NPs) and the position of the accusative NP (scrambled or canonical).

The adjacency constraint, which posed a problem in Experiment I, becomes less of an issue in the present design. Because the accusative NP is not immediately followed by the verb in either of (8b) or (8d), the processing of the dative NPs in these two conditions should be equally affected by the adjacency constraint.

Another advantage of the present design is that it may resolve the frequency bias discussed in the previous section as well. An intervening XP is awkward regardless of the order in which the object NPs appear. Thus, the frequency of canonical sentences with intervening XP such as (8c) should be low; in which case, a frequency-based model would be less likely to account for an interaction in reading times (see Experiment III for further discussion and relevant corpus counts).

As in Experiment I, the positing of a gap in the present construction occurs before the relevant predicate is read; thus, we should also be able to investigate processing proposals in which gaps are not adopted. According to the "direct association hypothesis", gaps are not computed by readers, and any effects should only be detectable when a constituent (an argument NP, for example) and its predicate are associated (Pickering and Barry 1991). Thus, in the present case, the model predicts no differences when the argument NPs are read, but only at the ditransitive verbs. In contrast, if the positing of gaps does lead to slow-downs as we have proposed, the delay should be observed before the verb is read.

5.1 Experiment II: Intervening Adverbials - A Preliminary Report

We are in the process of conducting a series of experiments using the basic paradigm depicted in (8) with various types of intervening XPs. Among the alternatives considered are adverbials (e.g. locatives) and relative clauses. Preliminary analyses of an experiment using long adverbial phrases (locatives and temporals) as XPs have yielded promising results. The self-paced reading set-up was the same as the one used in Experiment I. Thirty-two native speakers of Japanese, who were students or staff members at Kanda University of International Studies, participated in the experiment. The comprehension performance in the four conditions (between 87.5% and 91.9%) did not differ significantly. In the reading time analyses, the predicted interaction was observed at the object NP preceding the ditransitive verb ($F(1,31) = 7.95$, $P < 0.01$ in the analysis by subjects; $F(1,19) = 5.03$, $P < 0.05$ in the analysis by items). The two canonical conditions did not differ significantly in this region ($Ps > 0.2$); whereas the long scrambling condition was significantly slower than the short scrambling condition ($Ps < 0.05$). The four conditions did not differ significantly at the ditransitive verb ($Fs < 1$).

6 Experiment III: Corpus Frequency

A well-known property of scrambled word orders is that in general they are used less often than their corresponding canonical versions (see, for example, Yamashita 1997, and references therein). Thus, any effects associated to scrambling may be a result of its low incidence. In the previous section, however, we suggested that constructions such as (8c, d) with intervening adverbial phrases (AdvPs for short) are equally rare.

Consider a model according to which frequent constructions are read faster than similar but less frequent constructions. For a study involving constructions such as the ones in Experiment II, a natural prediction of such a frequency model would be that an interaction effect observed in the behavioral data should also be observable in the frequency of the constructions in an appropriate corpus. In the preliminary results of Experiment II, the scrambled condition with intervening AdvP ((8d); condition D for short) was shown to be harder to process than the scrambled condition with pre-posed AdvP (condition B). On the other hand, the canonical conditions with pre-posed AdvP (condition A) and with intervening AdvP (condition C) did not differ significantly. Therefore, frequency counts should yield a similar pattern of results such that freq(B)/freq(D) > freq(A)/freq(C), where freq(X) is the frequency of construction X in a given corpus.

A corpus count was conducted in order to determine the frequency of the relevant constructions.

6.1 Procedure

A frequency count was conducted on sentences from the Mainichi Shinbun (a general daily newspaper) between 1991 and 1995, and from the Nippon Keizai Shinbun (a daily financial newspaper) between 1990 and 1996. The sentences were automatically parsed using SLUNG (Mitsuishi, Torisawa, and Tsujii 1998).[3] Only sentences with 50 or less Japanese characters were included because of accuracy constraints of the parser.

From the partially bracketed constituents produced by SLUNG, we obtained 215,999 sentences that contained both a *ni* marked NP and an *o* marked NP in the same clause. Next, sentences containing the verbs used in Experiment II were extracted (see Appendix B for the complete list of verbs used), resulting in 5,102 sentences. These sentences were manually checked by a native speaker to remove irrelevant cases (e.g. collocations, temporals marked with the *ni* postposition, constituents other than an AdvP intervening between the two object NPs). The remaining 1,834 sentences were counted and classified according to whether the accusative NP was scrambled and whether an AdvP intervened between the two object NPs.

6.2 Results

We obtained 1,834 sentences which contained two arguments (a dative NP and an accusative NP) and a ditransitive verb in the same clause. Among those sentences, 1202 (65.5%) were sentences with adjacent object NPs in canonical order (condition A). In 565 sentences (30.8%), the accusative NP was scrambled to the position immediately before the dative NP (condition B). In 46 sentences (2.5%), the object NPs were in canonical word order with an intervening AdvP (condition C). In the remaining 21 sentences (1.2%), the accusative NP was scrambled with an intervening AdvP between the two object NPs (condition D).

The frequency of condition A is approximately 26 times the frequency of condition C. A similar proportion is observed between the other two conditions as the frequency of condition B is approximately 27 times the frequency of condition D.

---

[3] We would like to thank Hiroshi Kanayama for providing the bracketed sentences.

6.3 Discussion

The results confirm the generalization that canonical word orders are used more often than scrambled word orders. Even for a common sequence such as *NP-Acc NP-Dat* (in condition B), its canonical version *NP-Dat NP-Acc* (in condition A) is approximately twice as frequent.

As expected, very few sentences (3.7% overall) presented an intervening AdvP between the two object NPs. Moreover, given that the frequency counts of the adjacent and non-adjacent object NPs do not interact with scrambling, it suggests that frequency cannot easily explain the interaction observed in the behavioral study. As suggested earlier, a direct conversion from reading time patterns onto frequency counts, should have yielded a larger ratio between conditions B and D when compared to conditions A and C.

7 General Discussion

Experiment I provides evidence that scrambled word orders lead to longer reading times when compared to canonical word orders. Contrary to previous studies, a structure was used in which scrambling occurs inside the VP; therefore, the slow-down observed cannot be reduced to ambiguities introduced by potential clause boundaries. Moreover, because the case markers on the NPs compared are not as salient as the nominative marker, the comparison may have avoided confounds at the case marking level as well. In addition, because the scrambled construction (the accusative-dative order) is commonly used by native speakers, familiarity issues may have been minimized (although Experiment III suggests that even in this case the canonical dative-accusative order can be twice as frequent). Based on Experiment I and the results reported by Mazuka, Itoh, and Kondo (1998, 2001), the first part of the paper concluded that scrambling in Japanese involves extra difficulty (contra Yamashita 1997).

This conclusion naturally raises the question as to what leads to the extra difficulty in scrambled word orders. We argued that the kind of experimental design used thus far, in which the canonical sentence and the scrambled sentence are directly compared, involve several confounding factors and is consequently ill-suited to provide an answer. We then proposed a different experimental design based on the assumption that the processing of a gap for a scrambled constituent is responsible for the slow-down observed in Experiment I. The design of Experiment II has several advantages over the traditional experiments in this area. One of them is illustrated in Experiment III, in which corpus count results suggest that frequency factors are less of an issue.

The results obtained suggest that readers slow down as soon as it is clear that a constituent was scrambled. We have suggested that this is because a gap must be posited at this point and that the slow-down is more noticeable when the task requires close attention and, presumably, more working memory, or when the gap being posited is far away from its antecedent. The results are compatible with studies in English showing that there is reactivation of an entity when a related gap is processed (Bever and McElree 1988, MacDonald 1989). It is also compatible with results in English in which the distance to the antecedent influences the time necessary to process the gap (Gibson and Warren 1998). The result also favors syntactic proposals according to which the *NP-Acc NP-Dat* order involves scrambling of the accusative NP (Hoji 1985, Takano 1996), and it is not easily explained if this word order is assumed to be canonical (Miyagawa 1997).

7.1 Probe Recognition Experiments

Contrary to our conclusions, Sakamoto (2001) detected no measurable effects of scrambling in a series of experiments using a probe recognition task. In this type of experiment, an antecedent that was reactivated more recently (e.g. at a related pronoun or gap) is predicted to be recognized faster (see Bever and McElree 1988, for discussion and experimental results with gaps in English sentences). However, in Sakamoto's experiments, no such advantage should be expected in the first place because the antecedent is reactivated equally recently - at the *PRO* - in all sentences.

In related work, Nakayama (1995) found that recognition of a probe was significantly slower when its antecedent was part of a scrambled constituent. This is the opposite of the expected result if gap processing in scrambling leads to antecedent reactivation. However, when independent factors such as linear position of the probed word in the sentences are controlled for, recognition turns out to be faster after the scrambled sentence in comparison to its canonical version, thus supporting the gap processing hypothesis (Miyamoto and Takahashi 2000; see Nakano, Felser, and Clahsen 2000, for a similar conclusion for long-distance scrambling).

7.2 Alternatives to Gap Processing: The Direct Association Hypothesis

The discussion above was based on linguistics approaches that encode gaps (as traces or as slash features); but it should be noted that syntactic proposals which do not assume gaps (e.g. categorical grammars, Ades and Steedman 1982) cannot be ruled out without more careful scrutiny. It is necessary to consider how those theories explain syntactic phenomena related to scrambling and how the corresponding mechanisms (that are posited instead of gaps) can be translated into a model of on-line processing. We mentioned in passing one such a model, which attempts to provide an account of behavioral phenomena using categorial grammars (Pickering and Barry 1991, Pickering 1993, and for criticisms of their model see Gibson and Hickok 1993, Gorrell 1993). Pickering and Barry correctly observe that most behavioral experiments in English use sentences in which the gap occurs soon after the verb. Therefore, they argue that those results do not require gaps in order to be explained and can be accounted for if one assumes that the association of a verb to a phrase requires the reactivation of the entire phrase. In this case, the processes that were claimed to occur at the gap take place at the verb itself. Although this proposal can account for various aspects of the English results, it requires further assumptions in order to explain the results in Japanese scrambling, where we have observed that the slow-down occurs at an NP, even before the verb is processed. However, the fact that Pickering and Barry's model cannot readily account for the behavioral data in Japanese scrambling, is not necessarily an argument against categorial grammars.

8 Conclusion

The present paper reported the results of a self-paced reading experiment as evidence for difficulty in the processing of scrambling in Japanese. It also discussed ways of further investigating the sources of this difficulty and suggested that the preliminary results of a self-paced reading experiment and a corpus count support the view that gaps for displaced constituents are posited during the on-line processing of scrambled sentences.

References

Ades, A. E., & M. Steedman. 1982. On the Order of Words. *Linguistics & Philosophy* 4:517-558.

Bever, T. G., & B. McElree. 1988. Empty Categories Access their Antecedents during Comprehension. *Linguistic Inquiry* 19:35-43.

Bošković, Ž., & D. Takahashi. 1998. Scrambling and Last Resort. *Linguistic Inquiry* 29:347-366.

Chomsky, N. 1981. *Lectures on Government and Binding*. Dordrecht: Foris.

Cohen, J. D., B. MacWhinney, M. Flatt, & J. Provost. 1993. PsyScope: An Interactive Graphic System for Designing and Controlling Experiments in the Psychology Laboratory using Macintosh Computers. *Behavior Research Methods, Instruments & Computers* 25:257-271.

Elman, J. L. 1991. Distributed Representations, Simple Recurrent Networks, and Grammatical Structure. *Machine Learning* 7:195-225.

Ferreira, F., & C. Clifton Jr. 1986. The Independence of Syntactic Processing. *Journal of Memory & Language* 25:348-368.

Frazier, L., and C. Clifton Jr. 1989. Successive Cyclicity in the Grammar and the Parser. *Language and Cognitive Processes* 4:93-126.

Gazdar, G., Klein, E., Pullum, G., & Sag, I. (1985). *Generalized Phrase Structure Grammar*. Cambridge, MA: Harvard University Press.

Gibson, E. 1998. Linguistic Complexity: Locality of Syntactic Dependencies. *Cognition* 68:1-76.

Gibson, E., & G. Hickock. 1993. Sentence Processing with Empty Categories. *Language & Cognitive Processes* 8:147-161.

Gibson, E., C. T. Schütze, & A. Salomon. 1996. The Relationship between the Frequency and the Processing Complexity of Linguistic Structure. *Journal of Psycholinguistic Research* 25:59-92.

Gibson, E., & T. Warren. 1998. The Psychological Reality of Intermediate Linguistic Structure in Long-distance Extractions. Talk presented at the 11th Annual CUNY Conference on Human Sentence Processing, New Brunswick, NJ.

Gorrell, P. 1993. Evaluating the Direct Association Hypothesis: A Reply to Pickering and Barry (1991). *Language & Cognitive Processes* 8:129-146.

Hale, K. 1980. Remarks on Japanese Phrase Structure: Comments on the Papers on Japanese Syntax. *MIT Working Papers in Linguistics* 2, eds. Y. Otsu, & A. Farmer, 185-203. Cambridge, MA: MITWPL.

Hoji, H. 1985. Logical Form Constraints and Configurational Structures in Japanese. Doctoral dissertation, University of Washington.

Inoue, A. 1991. A Comparative Study of Parsing in English and Japanese. Doctoral dissertation, University of Connecticut.

Just, M. A., & P. A. Carpenter. 1992. A capacity theory of comprehension: Individual differences in working memory. *Psychological Review* 99:122.149.

Just, M. A., P. A. Carpenter, & J. D. Woolley. 1982. Paradigms and Processes in Reading Comprehension. *Journal of Experimental Psychology: General* 3:228-238.

Kuno, S. 1973. *The Structure of the Japanese Language*. Cambridge, MA: MIT Press.

MacDonald, M. C. 1989. Priming Effects from Gaps to Antecedents. *Language & Cognitive Processes* 4:35-56.

MacDonald, M. C., N. J. Pearlmutter, & M. S. Seidenberg. 1994. The Lexical Nature of Syntactic Ambiguity Resolution. *Psychological Review* 101:676-703.

Mazuka, R., K. Itoh, & T. Kondo. 1998. Cost of Scrambling in Japanese Sentence Processing. Poster presented at the 11th Annual CUNY Conference on Human Sentence Processing, New Brunswick, NJ.

Mazuka, R., K. Itoh, & T. Kondo. 2001. Cost of Scrambling in Japanese Sentence Processing. *Sentence Processing in East Asian Languages*, ed. M. Nakayama. Stanford: CSLI.

Mitchell, D. C., & M. Brysbaert. 1998. Challenges to Recent Theories of Crosslinguistic Variation in Parsing: Evidence from Dutch. In *Sentence Processing: A Crosslinguistic Perspective, ed.* D. Hillert. San Diego, CA: Academic Press.

Mitsuishi, Y., K. Torisawa, & J. Tsujii. 1998. HPSG-style Underspecified Japanese Grammar with Wide Coverage. *Proceedings of COLING-ACL'98*, 876-880.

Miyagawa, S. 1997. Against Optional Scrambling. *Linguistic Inquiry* 28:1-25.

Miyamoto, E. T. 2001. Case Markers as Clause Boundary Inducers in Japanese. Under review.

Miyamoto, E. T., & S. Takahashi. 2000. The Processing of VP-Internal Scrambling in Japanese. Talk presented at the Japanese Language Processing Workshop. Makuhari, Chiba, Japan.

Nakano, Y., C. Felser, & H. Clahsen. 2000. Antecedent Priming at Trace Positions in Japanese Long-distance Scrambling. *Essex Research Reports in Linguistics* 31:45-76. University of Essex.

Nakayama, M. 1995. Scrambling and Probe Recognition. *Japanese Sentence Processing*, eds. R. Mazuka & N. Nagai. Mahwah: Lawrence Erlbaum.

Pickering, M. 1993. Direct Association and Sentence Processing: A Reply to Gorrell and to Gibson and Hickock. *Language & Cognitive Processes* 8:163-196.

Pickering, M., & G. Barry. 1991. Sentence Processing without Empty Categories. *Language & Cognitive Processes* 6:229-259.

Sadakane, K., & M. Koizumi. 1995. On the Nature of the 'Dative' Particle *ni* in Japanese. *Linguistics* 33:5-33.

Saito, M. 1985. Some Asymmetries in Japanese and Their Theoretical Implications. Doctoral dissertation, MIT.

Sakamoto, T. 2001. Processing Filler-Gap Constructions in Japanese: The Case of Empty Subject Sentences, in *Sentence Processing in East-Asian Languages, ed. M. Nakayama.* Stanford, CA: CSLI.

Stowell, T. A. 1981. Origins of Phrase Structure. Doctoral dissertation, MIT.

Takano, Y. 1996. Movement and Parametric Variation in Syntax. Doctoral dissertation, University of California at Irvine.

Yamashita, H. 1997. The Effects of Word-order and Case Marking Information on the Processing of Japanese. *Journal of Psycholinguistic Research* 26:163-188.

Appendix A

The following were the items used in Experiment I. The slashes indicate the regions used in the self-paced reading presentation. Both conditions are presented for item 1. For all remaining items, the scrambled condition (B) can be obtained from the canonical condition (A) by exchanging the order of the third and fourth regions.

1A. Canonical:
オフィスで/ 職員が/ 係長に/ お茶を/ 出した/ 女性を/ 丁寧に/ 誉めたと/ 相原さんが/ 話していた。
1B. Scrambled:
オフィスで/ 職員が/ お茶を/ 係長に/ 出した/ 女性を/ 丁寧に/ 誉めたと/ 相原さんが/ 話していた。
2A. バーで/ 訪問客が/ やくざに/ 花びんを/ 見せた/ ホステスを/ ひそかに/ 殺したと/ 井原さんが/ しゃべった。
3A. 教室で/ 先生が/ 大学生に/ 公式を/ 説明した/ 研究者を/ 簡単に/ 招待したと/ 上野さんが/ 言った。
4A. 喫茶店で/ 不良が/ 友人に/ 後輩を/ 紹介した/ オーナーを/ 思いきり/ なぐったと/ 入江さんが/ 漏らした。
5A. 京都駅で/ 少年が/ 係員に/ 荷物を/ 渡した/ 駅員を/ 徹底的に/ 捜していたと/ 大島さんが/ 聞いた。
6A. 食堂で/ 運転手が/ おばさんに/ 定食を/ 注文した/ 若者たちを/ すぐ/ 告訴したと/ 川村さんが/ しゃべっていた。
7A. 田舎で/ 作家が/ アシスタントに/ カメラを/ 譲った/ 写真家を/ すぐに/ 首にしたと/ 川野さんが/ つぶやいた。
8A. 駐車場で/ 主人が/ マネージャーに/ 車を/ まかせた/ 有名人を/ 堂々と/ 説得したと/ 木村さんが/ おっしゃった。
9A. 自宅で/ お兄さんが/ 友人に/ ビデオを/ 貸した/ 仲間を/ ためらいがちに/ だましたと/ けい子さんが/ 漏らした。
10A. 下町で/ おばあさんが/ 米屋に/ 借金を/ 払った/ 酒屋を/ 簡単に/ 追い出したと/ 阪本さんが/ 叫んだ。
11A. カラオケで/ 歌手が/ オーナーに/ 歌を/ 捧げた/ お客を/ 優しく/ 座らせたと/ 田中さんが/ 言った。
12A. 大阪で/ 女優が/ 監督に/ 手袋を/ 投げた/ 観客を/ 一生懸命/ 思い出していたと/ 中村さんが/ 聞いた。
13A. 駅で/ 婦人が/ 長男に/ かばんを/ 預けた/ 友達を/ 静かに/ 眺めていたと/ 平野さんが/ 話していた。
14A. 会議で/ 社長が/ 部長に/ 新製品を/ 披露した/ 副部長を/ 怒って/ やめさしたと/ 森さんが/ つぶやいた。
15A. 農家で/ 老人が/ 一人娘に/ 土地を/ 残した/ 親戚を/ すぐに/ 呼び出したと/ 松本さんが/ しゃべった。

16A. デパートで/ 店員が/ 女の子に/ 洋服を/ 見せていた/ 高校生を/ 長い間/ 見はったと/ 篠原さんが/ おっしゃった。
17A. 運動会で/ 役員が/ お母さん達に/ お菓子を/ 焼いた/ 子供達を/ 大声で/ 呼んだと/ 村上さんが/ 言っていた。
18A. 広島で/ 政治家が/ 校長に/ ピアノを/ 届けた/ 市長を/ 無理に/ 推薦したと/ 山上君が/ 漏らした。
19A. バーで/ 音楽家が/ 踊子に/ 花束を/ あげた/ 知人を/ さりげなく/ 呼んだと/ 長谷川さんが/ 聞いた。
20A. 長崎で/ 少女が/ お姉さんに/ おみやげを/ 頼んだ/ 級友を/ 楽し気に/ からかったと/ 木村君が/ 叫んでいた。
21A. レストランで/ 男性が/ 恋人に/ 指輪を/ おくった/ 売り子を/ すばやく/ 誘拐したと/ レポーターが/ 聞いた。
22A. 公園で/ 男の子が/ 両親に/ キャンデイを/ ねだった/ 仲良しを/ 元気よく/ 呼び出したと/ 山下君が/ 言った。
23A. 研究室で/ 教授が/ 先輩に/ 壺を/ 作った/ 後輩を/ 周到に/ おとし入れたと/ 秘書が/ 漏らした。
24A. 横浜で/ 女優が/ 母親に/ 車を/ 買った/ 男性を/ 親切に/ 世話したと/ 宮田さんが/ 話した。
25A. 大学で/ 教授が/ 学生に/ 古文書を/ 貸した/ 図書館司書を/ 急いで/ 呼び出したと/ 植田さんが/ しゃべった。

Appendix B

The following are the ditransitive verbs used in Experiments II and III.

推薦する 'recommend'
渡す 'hand over'
紹介する 'introduce'
注文する 'order' (e.g. at a restaurant)
預ける 'entrust'
届ける 'deliver'
貢ぐ 'give' (as a tribute)
説明する 'explain'
貸す 'lend'
残す 'leave/hand down'
あげる/ 上げる 'give'
差し上げる 'give' (respectfully)
押し付ける 'force upon'
出す 'put out/serve'
勧める 'suggest'

8

Processing Filler-gap Constructions in Japanese: The Case of Empty Subject Sentences*

TSUTOMU SAKAMOTO

1 Introduction

In English, there are a number of syntactic constructions known as 'control sentences.' Some examples are shown below:

(1) John promised Mary to go to Tokyo.
(2) John persuaded Mary to go to Tokyo.

In (1) *John* is supposed to go to Tokyo, while in (2) the person going to Tokyo is *Mary*. An 'empty subject' is assumed to exist in these infinitival clauses. This empty subject is 'controlled' by the main clause subject in (1) while it is controlled by the main clause object in (2); therefore, in linguistic

---

* This work could not have been completed without the cooperation of the members of "Empty Subject Project": Jiro Gyoba, Yuri Ninose, Junri Oda, and Yuko Sakaki. I would like to thank the participants of the International East Asian Psycholinguistics Workshop held in the summer of 1999 at The Ohio State University where the first draft of this paper was presented. I would also like to thank Mineharu Nakayama for helpful discussions. All remaining errors, however, are my own. This work was supported in part by a Grant-in-Aid for Scientific Research No. 09610538 and No. 10610517 from the Japanese Ministry of Education.

Sentence Processing in East Asian Languages.
Mineharu Nakayama (ed.).
Copyright ©2002, CSLI Publications.

literature, (1) would be called a 'subject-control' (henceforth, S-control) sentence and (2) would be called an 'object-control' (henceforth, O-control) sentence. In the framework of the generative grammar called GB theory (or the principles and parameters approach, see Chomsky 1981), it is a common practice to postulate an empty element (represented as PRO) in the subject position of infinitival (and gerundive) clauses. Thus, (1) and (2) would be represented as follows:[1]

(3) John$_1$ <u>promised</u> Mary$_2$ [PRO$_1$ to go to Tokyo].
(4) John$_1$ <u>persuaded</u> Mary$_2$ [PRO$_2$ to go to Tokyo].

The main clause verb carries information that indicates whether the antecedent for the empty subject will be the main clause's subject or object. In English, thus, one can make use of this verb information before encountering the empty subject in the embedded infinitival clause. In Japanese, however, the verb information is not readily available, since the main clause verb is located at the end of a sentence. Consider the following sentences:[2]

(5) Taro$_1$-ga Hanako$_2$-ni [PRO$_1$ Tokyo iki]-o   <u>hakuzyoosita</u>.
     -Nom   -Dat   going-Acc confessed
     'Taro confessed to Hanako that *he* would go to Tokyo.'

(6) Taro$_1$-ga Hanako$_2$-ni [PRO$_2$ Tokyo iki]-o   <u>meireisita</u>.
     -Nom   -Dat   going-Acc ordered
     'Taro ordered Hanako, (saying) *she* would go to Tokyo.'

The existence of an empty subject is also assumed in the above Japanese examples. This theoretical construct (i.e., empty subject) may or may not be a syntactic entity. Note that the term 'subject' is used in a broader sense, which includes not only 'true arguments' but also 'default arguments' in the sense of Pustejovsky (1998).[3] The important point is that the interpretation of the sentence depends on identifying the Agent of the embedded event, namely identifying *who it is that goes to Tokyo* in the above examples. The

---

[1] Identical numbers in subscript indicate a co-indexation relation.

[2] Nom=Nominative, Dat=Dative, Acc=Accusative, *Taro* is a male first name, and *Hanako* is a female first name.

[3] See also the discussions about an implicit argument (Williams, 1985; Roeper, 1987; Abney, 1987).

detailed characterization of this empty subject is a matter of theoretical concern.[4]

Summarizing the above observations, the surface order of the relevant elements in English is 'Subject - <u>Verb</u> - Object – PRO' (S-V-O-P), while in Japanese the order is 'Subject - Object - PRO – <u>Verb</u>' (S-O-P-V). The crucial point is the position of the main clause verb that carries the control information. It is important to note that the above two Japanese sentences are completely equivalent until the main clause verbs. In other words, these two sentences construct a 'minimal pair' in the sense that the only one element, the main verb, produces the different interpretations. In this situation, how should the human parser process these sentences? Should one 'wait and see' the final verb before parsing? Alternatively, does one make some decision regarding the interpretation before the final verb? If so, what kind of information does one utilize?

2 Multi-level Parsing Model

Examining the results of four experiments to be reported later, I claim that there are at least two distinct levels of sentence processing in Japanese. One level involves rather automatic and shallow mode of processing, in which the human parser uses Case information to perform the given task of comprehension. The other level involves rather conscious and deep mode of processing, in which the parser relies on Theta-role information to perform the given task of comprehension. In this 'Multi-level Parsing Model,' these two levels may correspond to the syntactic and semantic levels respectively, because Case and Theta-role are considered to be relevant to these two levels. However, I do not deny other possibilities, such that both are syntactic and/or semantic. It would be a matter of controversy whether the distinction of Case and Theta-role directly reflect the distinction of the syntactic and semantic level of sentence processing.

The basic idea of this multi-level parsing model is essentially the same as what Frazier and Fodor (1978) call 'Two Stage Parsing Model' that postulates two levels of sentence processing. Employing the Cross Modal Lexical Priming method, Hickok et al. (1992) claim that there is positive evidence to support this dichotomy of processing levels. Hahne and Friederici (1999) also argue that they have found neurolinguistic evidence for the two levels of sentence processing by conducting experiments with Event-related brain potentials. Our experiments with Japanese data also support the claim that two different levels are involved in sentence processing. If the same

---

[4] See Sakamoto (1996) for a more detailed discussion.

property is observed in the processing of two fairly different languages, it suggests that the observed property is a universal characteristic of the human sentence-processing mechanism.

There is, however, an important difference between these previous studies and the present study. Most of the previous studies assume a sequential ordering between the two stages (or steps) of the processing. The 'Principle of Processing' proposed by Kimball (1973) claims that "When a phrase is closed, it is pushed down into a syntactic (possibly semantic) processing stage and cleared from short-term memory". Frazier and Fodor (1978) claim that there are two steps of syntactic operation called 'Preliminary Phrase Packager (PPP)' and 'Sentence Structure Supervisor (SSS),' and that PPP always precedes SSS. However, the present study neither support nor deny this kind of step-wise process of parsing. Although the experimental findings do support the claim that there exist (at least) two distinct levels of processing, the results do not allow us the commitment to the sequential ordering of these levels. This is simply because the experiments were not designed to examine the ordering of the two levels, but designed to clarify the difference of the two levels of parsing. We need another experimental setting to investigate the sequential ordering of these levels (see Hahne and Friederici 1999; Hickok et al. 1992).

Needless to say, it is necessary to integrate all kinds of linguistic information in order to comprehend a sentence: phonetic perception, phonological segmentation, lexical meaning, syntactic construction, semantic interpretation, and pragmatic consideration. Furthermore, the final understanding of any utterance requires not only linguistic information but also world knowledge, memory, inference, etc. However, the present study suggests that the 'comprehension' itself is not restricted to a single (or, final) level, but there are some levels of understanding. Although these levels may not represent the full-fledged (or, final) comprehension, they do represent some level of comprehension. Even in our everyday life, shallow understanding could be enough for some routine work such as greetings. On the other hand, deep understanding would be required in reading instructions for entrance examinations. The point is that the level of comprehension is not uni-level but multi-level. The fundamental claim drawn from our experiments is that there are (at least) two distinct levels of parsing, in which the human parser makes use of different types of information in performing different tasks.

3 Filler-gap Dependency

As in (5) and (6) above, the sentences examined in the following experiments contain an antecedent as a possible filler and an empty subject as a possible gap. Before going on to the discussion of the experiments, let us briefly consider some general aspects of filler-gap dependencies. Such dependencies can be divided into three types.

(7) Three Types of Filler-gap Dependency
   A: antecedent - trace
       Who does John love *trace*? / John seems *trace* to be rich.

   B: antecedent - PRO
       John promised Mary [PRO to leave].

   C: antecedent - trace - PRO
       John loved the girl who the boy forced *trace* [PRO to sing this song].

Type A represents the relationship between a Wh-element and its trace. This kind of 'antecedent-trace' relationship is also shown by a moved NP and its trace, a so-called 'raising' structure. Fodor (1989) argues that the antecedent is recognized at the trace position. On the other hand, Pickering and Barry (1991) propose the 'Direct Access Hypothesis,' claiming that a trace does not play a role in the gap-filling process. They argue that the antecedent is accessed directly at the position of the main verb.

Type B exhibits the relationship between the antecedent and the base-generated empty subject: PRO.[5] Nicol and Swinney (1989) claim that the identification of the antecedent for PRO is delayed. On the other hand, Boland et al. (1990) argue that the antecedent for PRO is determined immediately.

Type C is a combination of Types A and B. Frazier et al. (1983) claim that the parser does not recognize a trace as a possible antecedent for a PRO. That is, the parser chooses the lexical antecedent as the only filler for a PRO. Their claim does not agree with Fodor (1989), who says that the antecedent is recognized at the trace position. On the other hand, Frazier et al.'s argument may support the claim by Pickering & Barry (1991) that a trace does not play a role in identifying the antecedent. Furthermore, the claim by Frazier et al. may not be in line with the claim that the identification of a PRO is delayed (Nicol and Swinney 1989), but may support the claim that a PRO is accessed by the parser without delay (Boland et al. 1990).

---

[5] Here, for the sake of simplicity, we do not deal with *pro*, which is assumed to be base-generated at a governed position.

As this section has shown, the findings accumulated through English data exhibit the complexity of the issue of filler-gap dependencies. The current study provides an opportunity to consider the issue from a different viewpoint by presenting some experimental findings from Japanese data. The experimental sentences examined in Experiments 1 and 3 correspond to Type B, and the sentences in Experiments 2 and 4 correspond to Type C. The main focus of the discussion is not on the linguistic characterization of trace and PRO (see Sakamoto (1996) for the related discussion). The principal issue of the present study is to examine the relationship between the experimental tasks and the levels of processing in filler-gap constructions.

4 Experiments

This section presents the results of four experiments conducted by various researchers. The first experiment was originally reported in Oda et al. (1997) and the second in Ninose et al. (1998). From these two experiments, however, I have extracted relevant results to our discussion. The detail is to be explained later. The third and fourth experiments were reported in Sakamoto (1995, 1996). Because these findings were reported separately, they have not been examined in a unified fashion. In this paper, I will present an integrated interpretation of the results of these four experiments and reexamine their theoretical implications.

4.1 Experiment 1

In the following experimental setting, to begin with, we tested whether the participants were able to identify the correct antecedent of the empty subject in filler-gap constructions.[6] And then, the purpose of this experiment was to examine whether there was any difference of preference between the two types of control sentences: Subject-control and Object-control sentences. If there is a detectable difference concerning a response time and/or a percentage of correct answer, which of them would be preferred? Then, what is the reason why one of them is preferred?

4.1.1 Materials

The stimuli were twelve S-control sentences and twelve O-control sentences. Below are examples of these two types of control sentences (*Kooiti* is a male first name, and *Tamae* is a female first name. In total, six names

---

[6] The term "subject" refers to both a "subject for an experiment" and a "grammatical subject" and may cause confusion. When it is necessary, thus, I use the term "participant" instead of "subject."

were used.) Both types of sentences have the same construction: [NP$_1$-*ga* Locative-PP NP$_2$-*ni* [(PRO$_{1/2}$) *Tokyo iki*]-*o* Adverb Verb]. Sentence (8) is called a Subject-control (S-control) sentence because the person going to Tokyo is the subject referent. Sentence (9) is called an Object-control (O-control) sentence because the person going to Tokyo is the object.

(8) Subject-Control Sentence
Kooiti-ga kaisya-de Tamae-ni Tokyo iki-o wazato   moosideta.
    -Nom company-at   -Dat going-Acc purposely offered
'Kooiti, at the company, purposely offered Tamae that *he* would go to Tokyo.'

(9) Object-Control Sentence
Kooiti-ga kaisya-de Tamae-ni Tokyo iki-o wazato   saisokusita.
    -Nom company-at   -Dat going-Acc purposely urged
'Kooiti, at the company, purposely urged Tamae that *she* would go to Tokyo.'

The experimental sentences were made-up in the following way. Fifty-two phrases (called *bunsetsu* in Japanese) were randomly read by a woman and recorded by a computer. She was totally unaware of the sentential construction of the experimental sentences. The sentences were produced through combining these phrases, which had been recorded separately. Each phrase has only a phrasal contour, and a 100 msec interval was automatically inserted between phrases. This means that the sentences did not have a normal sentential intonation. Thus, all the experimental sentences were 'synthesized sentences' in the sense that the combination of phrases created each sentence. The purpose of synthesizing sentences in this way was to examine the syntactic and/or semantic aspects of sentence processing by eliminating the effect of phonological information on sentential constructions.

In the original experiment by Oda et al. (1997), there were six test points from the end of the sentence with 300msec intervals: 0msec, 300msec, 600msec, 900msec, and 1500msec. Here, we concentrate on the comparison between the RTs of the S-control and O-control sentences in the case of 'Yes' response at 0msec. In this paper, thus, I selectively report the response times at the end of the sentence among six different points. There were so many test points in the original experiment that distracting sentences were not affordable in considering the heavy burden of the participants. Also, a Latin Square design was adopted with the counterbalance concerning sentence types and test points. See Oda et al. (1997) for more detail.

4.1.2 Participants and Procedure

Eight native speakers of Japanese participated in this experiment. They were undergraduate students, aged nineteen to twenty two, at Kyushu University. The experiment took about fifty minutes, including a five-minute break. Note that the time was for six test points, among which I selectively reported only one test point. They were paid nominal fees for their participation.

Through a headphone, the participants heard a sentence in one ear. Right after the end of each sentence, the participants heard a possible antecedent for the empty subject, either the subject or the object of the main clause, in the other ear. The task was to decide whether the given antecedent was really the person who would go to Tokyo. The participant responded by pressing Yes-key or No-key as quickly as possible. This experiment is therefore a 'recognition' experiment in which the participants have to decide whether the given answer is correct or not. The time was measured how long the participants took to press the Yes-key for both S-control and O-control sentences when the correct answer was given right after the end of the sentence. Note that the response time includes the time for presenting the possible antecedent, since the timer starts at the end of each sentence.

4.1.3 Results and Discussion

The time was measured from the onset (not the end) of the stimulus (the name of the possible antecedent) to the point that the participant pressed the key. The mean reaction time (RT) and the mean percentage of Consistency Score (CS) were computed. CS indicates the percentage of agreement among the participants concerning the classification of S-control and O-control sentences. For example, there are 8 (participants) x 12 (sentences) = 96 cases that should be classified as S-control sentences. When all 96 cases were classified as S-control, the CS of S-control sentences came to 100 %.

The data was submitted to an analysis of variance (ANOVA) to determine statistical significance. F_1 represents the analysis by subjects (across items), and F_2 represents the analysis by items (across subjects). In calculating RTs, missing data points were replaced by the grand mean RT. In calculating CS, the angular (or inverse sine) transformation was used to adjust the percentage.[7] The results are shown in Table 1.

The mean RT of the S-control sentences is significantly faster than that of the O-control sentences in both the subject analysis (F_1) and item analysis

---

[7] ANOVA assumes that the population exhibits "normal distribution". However, the distribution of the data represented by the percentage is not 'normal' because the variance of the data becomes smaller as the data departs from 50%. Thus, we need to adjust the data so that it follows normal distribution.

(F_2). This suggests that there is a significant time difference in responding that the given answer is correct, even if the correct answer is given equally to both types of sentences.

	Sentence Type		Difference
	S-control	O-control	
RT (msec)	752	835	-83[a]
CS (%)	95.8	85.4	10.4[b]

a: $F_1(1, 7) = 9.16$, $p < .05$, $F_2(1, 11) = 5.07$, $p < .05$
b: $F_1(1, 7) = 1.56$, $p < .26$, $F_2(1, 11) = 2.46$, $p < .15$

Table 1. Results of Experiment 1 (Recognition task with S-O order)

As for the percentage of Consistency Score (CS), the S-control sentences have a higher CS than the O-control sentences, although the difference is not big enough to reach a statistically significant level. Thus, the S-control sentences have a significantly faster RT and a (slightly) higher CS than the O-control sentences. It is therefore plausible to conclude that the results show a 'subject preference' phenomenon: the grammatical subject is preferred as the candidate for the empty subject.

This may suggest a parsing strategy that favors the subject as a possible antecedent. The subject might be the preferred antecedent because it has the grammatical function of 'subject.' However, this may not be the only possible way to explain the results because the subject is the first NP at the beginning of a sentence. It is plausible that the parser prefers the first mentioned NP as a possible antecedent for the empty subject. This preference may be explained by the very general cognitive phenomenon called the 'primacy effect.' In other words, a so-called 'first-in-first-out' strategy may be at work. In conclusion, one cannot determine whether the preference is due to some grammatical reason (i.e., 'subject' preference) or some general cognitive effect (i.e., 'primacy' effect). Since Experiment 1 alone cannot resolve this issue, the following section will consider the data of Experiment 2.

4.2 Experiment 2

The purpose of this experiment was to examine what would happen when the surface positions of the two antecedents were reversed. The 'scrambling' of NPs should directly affect the application of the primacy strategy, because the sentence initial NP is changed. If the primacy strategy applies, the parser will have to assign a different antecedent to the gap according to what the sentence initial NP is.

4.2.1 Materials

In Experiment 2, the only difference from Experiment 1 is the word order of the subject and object NPs. Sample sentences are presented below (*Tamae* is a female first name, and *Kooiti* is a male first name).

(10) Subject-Control Sentence
 Tamae-ni kaisya-de Kooiti-ga Tokyo iki-o wazato moosideta.
 -Dat company-at -Nom going-Acc purposely offered
 'To Tamae, at the company, Kooiti purposely offered that *he* would go to Tokyo.'

(11) Object-Control Sentence
 Tamae-ni kaisya-de Kooiti-ga Tokyo iki-o wazato saisokusita.
 -Dat company-at -Nom going-Acc purposely urged
 'To Tamae, at the company, Kooiti purposely urged that *she* would go to Tokyo.'

Both types of sentences have the same construction: [NP_2-*ni* Locative-PP NP_1-*ga* (*trace*$_2$) [($PRO_{1/2}$) *Tokyo iki*]-*o* Adverb Verb]. Sentences (10) and (11) are called Subject-control (S-control) and Object-control (O-control) sentences because the person who goes to Tokyo is the subject and object referent respectively. Despite the permutation of the subject and object NPs, the interpretation of the empty subject is the same as in (8) and (9).

4.2.2 Participants and Procedure

Eight native speakers of Japanese participated in this experiment. They were undergraduate students, aged nineteen to twenty two, at Kyushu University. They consisted of a different group of participants from those that participated in Experiment 1. The experiment took about fifty minutes, including a five-minute break(Note again that the time was for all the six test points.). They were all paid nominal fees for participation.

4.2.3 Results and Discussion

The results have been submitted to the same statistical analysis as in Experiment 1. Table 2 shows the summary of the results, which revealed that the RT for the S-control sentences was significantly faster than that for the O-control sentences. In addition, the difference of CS percentages between the two types of sentences increased in Experiment 2 when compared to Experiment 1, and the S-control sentences have a significantly higher CS than the O-control sentences.

	Sentence Type		
	S-control	O-control	Difference
RT (msec)	639	714	-75[a]
CS (%)	100	79.2	20.8[b]

a: $F_1(1, 7) = 21.41$, $p < .005$, $F_2(1, 11) = 13.32$, $p < .005$
b: $F_1(1, 7) = 6.34$, $p < .05$, $F_2(1, 11) = 7.36$, $p < .05$

Table 2. Results of Experiment 2 (Recognition task with O-S order)

Experiment 2 produced the results similar to Experiment 1. The findings showed that the 'subject preference' remained even if the order of the subject and object in the main clause was scrambled. Thus, the results of these two recognition experiments indicate that, regardless of the scrambling in word order, the participants tend to prefer the main clause subject as a possible antecedent for the empty subject. The findings from Experiments 1 and 2, then, suggest that not the 'primacy' but the 'subject' affects the preference in parsing these Japanese control sentences.

4.3 Comparison of Experiments 1 and 2

Now, let us consider the filler-gap relations in the examples of Experiments 1 and 2. The schematic representation for them would be as in Table 3 below (X=subject, Y=object, S-cont.V=subject control verb, O-cont.V=object control verb):

		stimuli	response
(A=8)	X_1-ga Y_2-ni [PRO$_1$ Tokyo iki]-o S-cont.V	X	Yes (fast)
(B=9)	X_1-ga Y_2-ni [PRO$_2$ Tokyo iki]-o O-cont.V	Y	Yes (slow)
(C=10)	Y_2-ni X_1-ga t_2 [PRO$_1$ Tokyo iki]-o S-cont.V	X	Yes (fast)
(D=11)	Y_2-ni X_1-ga t_2 [PRO$_2$ Tokyo iki]-o O-cont.V	Y	Yes (slow)

Table 3. Schematic representation of materials in Experiments 1 and 2

Reexamining the RTs in these two experiments, we notice that the RTs of Experiment 1 (Subject-Object word order) are slower than those of Experiment 2 (Object-Subject word order) in both the S-control and O-control sentences. Consider Table 4 and Figure 1 below.

The two-way ANOVA (2 x 2) revealed that there was a main effect of sentence type [$F_1(1, 14) = 24.714$, $p < .001$, $F_2(1, 22) = 14.103$, $p < .005$]. There was also a main effect of word order [$F_1(1, 14) = 6.155$, $p < .01$, $F_2(1, 22) = 22.9$, $p < .001$]. The interaction between sentence type and word order was not significant [$F_1 (1, 14) = .052$, $p < .83$, $F_2(1, 22) = .031$, $p < .87$].

	Sentence Type		
	S-control	O-control	Effect of sentence type
Exp.1(S-O)	<u>752</u>	835	-83
Exp.2(O-S)	<u>639</u>	714	-75
Effect of word order	113	121	

Table 4. Mean RTs in Experiments 1 and 2 (Recognition task with S-O and O-S order)

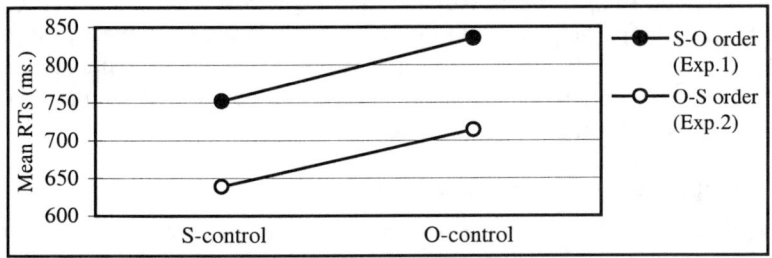

Figure 1. Comparison of Experiments 1 and 2

The results revealed that the RTs of S-control sentences were significantly faster that those of O-control sentences. The results also showed that the RTs of 'Object-Subject' word order (Experiment 2) are significantly faster than those obtained in the 'Subject-Object' word order (Experiment 1). Thus, the permutation of word order shortened response times. It could be possible that the 'recency' of the subject NP in Object-Subject order decreased the RTs of S-control sentences (752 msec → 639 msec). In O-control sentences, on the contrary, the 'primacy' of the object NP in the reversed word order could have decreased the RTs (835 msec → 714 msec). Therefore, neither the recency nor the primacy can account for the decrease of RTs across the board. Other than the distance of NPs, there must be some other, unknown reason ('synthesized prosody' could be the one) for the decrease of RTs.

This result is very interesting in comparing the experimental results reported by other researchers. Nakayama (1995) and Yamashita (1997) showed that the scrambling of word order does not affect the response times. On the other hand, Mazuka et al. (2001) and Miyamoto and Takahashi

(2001) reported the experimental results that exhibited the *increase* of response times owing to the scrambling. In our experiment, the changing word order invited the *decrease* of RTs. I will return this issue later.

4.4 Experiment 3

The results of both Experiments 1 and 2 showed the same 'subject preference' in spite of the difference in word order. In these two recognition experiments, the participants were instructed to decide whether the given answer was correct or not. In the following experiments, we will investigate whether this preference holds for a different experimental paradigm. If the same results can be reproduced in a different setting, this attests to the significance of the subject in processing Japanese empty subject sentences. If not, it is necessary to further scrutinize the factors that affect the processing of empty subject sentences. Here, we are interested in whether this subject preference is prevailing at any level of parsing or whether it is a reflection of some limited aspect of parsing.

In the following sections, we examine the results of two 'retrieval' experiments, namely Experiments 3 and 4. The task in these experiments was to orally answer the correct filler (antecedent) for the gap (empty subject). The experimental sentences were read out by the experimenter, and then tape-recorded to present them to the participants. Thus, the task and the way of constructing sentences were altered so that we can test whether the different experimental settings affect the results.

4.4.1 Materials

Twenty-four S-control sentences, twenty-four O-control sentences, and forty-eight nontarget sentences were given to the participants. Four exercise and four warm-up sentences were also inserted at the beginning of the experiment. The total number of sentences given to each participants was 104. The experimenter tape-recorded the sentences that were read out with normal intonation and pauses; therefore, all the experimental sentences were 'read-out sentences' that had normal sentential contours. Examples of the two types of control sentence are the same as (8) and (9) in Experiment 1 which are repeated below as (12) and (13).

(12) Subject-Control Sentence
    Kooiti-ga kaisya-de Tamae-ni Tokyo iki-o wazato moosideta.
      -Nom company-at -Dat going-Acc purposely offered
    'Kooiti, at the company, purposely offered Tamae that *he* would go to Tokyo.'

(13) Object-Control Sentence
Kooiti-ga kaisya-de Tamae-ni Tokyo iki-o wazato <u>saisokusita</u>.
-Nom company-at -Dat going-Acc purposely urged
'Kooiti, at the company, purposely urged Tamae that *she* would go to Tokyo.'

Both types of sentences have the same construction as those in Experiment 1: [NP$_1$-*ga* Locative-PP NP$_2$-*ni* [(PRO$_{1/2}$) Tokyo iki]-*o* Adverb Verb]. Sentence (12) is a Subject-control (S-control) sentence because the person who is supposed to go to Tokyo is the subject. Sentence (13) is an Object-control (O-control) sentence because 'the person who is to go to Tokyo' is the object.

4.4.2 Participants and Procedure

Twenty-three native speakers of Japanese participated in this experiment. They were undergraduate students, aged nineteen to twenty three, at Kyoto University. The experiment took about half an hour including a five-minute break. They were paid nominal fees for their participation.

The task was for the participants to state orally 'who is supposed to go to Tokyo', i.e., the Agent of the embedded event, after listening to each sentences. That is, the participants were to 'retrieve' the correct filler for the empty subject. The time was measured from the end of the sentence to the beginning of the response utterance. Here, note that it was possible for the participants to start to respond slightly before the end of the sentence. The morphological ending of verb conjugation is fairly simple in Japanese. For example, *yakusokusita* can be analyzed as *yakusoku* 'promise' and *sita* 'did.' Thus, the participants could start responding before the ending such as *sita*. Therefore, the RTs for this retrieval task might have been shortened.

4.4.3 Results and Discussion

The results are summarized in Table 5 below. The findings showed that the O-control sentences had significantly faster RT and slightly higher CS (although not reached the significant level) than S-control sentences. This may suggest a parsing strategy that favors the 'object' as a possible antecedent. The object might be preferred because of its grammatical function.

However, the object could be preferred because it is the most 'recent' antecedent, given that it is closer to the end of a sentence than the subject. It is possible that the parser employed a very general strategy such as 'last-in-first-out.' In other words, the 'recency effect' might have played a role. Thus, it is not possible to determine whether the preference is caused by the grammatical object or by the recency effect. This issue can be resolved by examining the data from Experiment 4.

	Sentence Type		Difference
	S-control	O-control	
RT (msec)	666	607	59[a]
CS (%)	88.9	90.2	1.3[b]

a: $F_1(1, 22) = 6.23$, $p < .05$, $F_2(1, 23) = 6.87$, $p < .05$
b: $F_1(1, 22) = .491$, $p < .5$, $F_2(1, 23) = .183$, $p < .68$

Table 5. Results of Experiment 3 (Retrieval task with S-O order)

4.5 Experiment 4

This experiment was designed to examine whether the object preference detected in Experiment 3 arose for some grammatical reason or due to the recency effect. For this purpose, the order of the subject and object NPs was scrambled so that the most recent NP changed.

4.5.1 Materials and Methods

Examples of the two types of control sentence are the same as (10) and (11) in Experiment 2 which are repeated below as (14) and (15).

(14) Subject-Control Sentence
    Tamae-ni kaisya-de Kooiti-ga Tokyo iki-o   wazato   moosideta.
        -Dat company-at   -Nom going-Acc purposely offered
    'To Tamae, at the company, Kooiti purposely offered that *he* would go to Tokyo.'

(15)   Object-Control Sentence
    Tamae-ni kaisya-de Kooiti-ga Tokyo iki-o   wazato   saisokusita.
        -Dat company-at   -Nom going-Acc purposely urged
    'To Tamae, at the company, Kooiti purposely urged that *she* would go to Tokyo.'

Both types of sentences have the same construction: [NP$_2$-*ni* Locative-PP NP$_1$-*ga* (*trace*$_2$) [(PRO$_{1/2}$) *Tokyo iki-o* Adverb Verb]. Except for the word order, the stimulus sentences and the procedures were the same as those in Experiment 3. The participants were seventeen native speakers of Japanese. They were undergraduate students, aged nineteen to twenty three, at Kyoto University. They consisted of a different group of participants from those that participated in Experiment 3. The experiment took about half an hour with a five-minute break. They were paid a nominal sum for their participation.

4.5.2 Results and Discussion

The data was analyzed in the same way as in Experiment 3. If there was a recency effect (i.e., a word-order effect or a scrambling effect) affecting the parsing process, then the results would be opposite to those obtained in Experiment 3. On the other hand, if the object was preferred because of its grammatical function, then the results would be the same as those in Experiment 3. Table 6 shows the summary of the results.

	Sentence Type		
	S-control	O-control	Difference
RT (msec)	749	648	101[a]
CS (%)	84.4	90.8	6.4[b]

a: $F_1(1, 16) = 7.93$, $p < .05$, $F_2(1, 23) = 14.23$, $p < .001$
b: $F_1(1, 16) = 3.01$, $p < .11$, $F_2(1, 23) = 6.13$, $p < .05$

Table 6. Results of Experiment 4 (Retrieval task with O-S order)

The RT of the O-control sentences is significantly faster than that of the S-control sentences in both the subject analysis (F_1) and item analysis (F_2). The CS of the O-control sentences is higher than that of the S-control sentences. This difference is significant in the item analysis (F_2), although the difference did not reach a statistically significant level in the subject analysis (F_1).

The results of Experiment 4, in which the experimental sentences had 'object-subject' order, also showed that the object was preferred as a controller, even when the word order is reversed. Regardless of the change of word order, Experiment 4 exhibited the same 'object preference' effect observed in Experiment 3. The findings of Experiments 3 and 4 thus indicate that not the recency but the grammatical function of the object affects the preference in processing these sentences.

4.6 Comparison of Experiments 3 and 4

Now, let us consider the filler-gap relations in the examples of Experiments 3 and 4. The schematic representation for them would be as follows (X=subject, Y=object, S-cont.V=subject control verb, O-cont.V=object control verb):

			response	
(A=12)	X_1-ga Y_2-ni [PRO_1 Tokyo iki]-o S-cont.V	X	(slow)
(B=13)	X_1-ga $\boxed{Y_2\text{-ni}}$ [PRO_2 Tokyo iki]-o O-cont.V	Y	(fast)
(C=14)	Y_2-ni X_1-ga t_2 [PRO_1 Tokyo iki]-o S-cont.V	X	(slow)
(D=15)	$\boxed{Y_2\text{-ni}}$ X_1-ga t_2 [PRO_2 Tokyo iki]-o O-cont.V	Y	(fast)

Table 7. Schematic representation of materials in Experiments 3 and 4

Comparing these two experiments, it should be noticed that the RTs in Experiment 4 were slower than those in Experiment 3. Consider Table 8 and Figure 2 below. The two-way ANOVA (2 x 2) revealed that there was a main effect of sentence type [F_1 (1, 38) = 15.016, $p < .001$, F_2 (1, 46) = 20.919, $p < .001$]. On the other hand, there was no main effect of word order [F_1 (1, 38) = 1.184, $p < .29$, F_2 (1, 46) = 4.015, $p < .051$]. The interaction between word order and sentence type was not significant [F_1 (1, 38) = 1.009, $p < .33$, F_2 (1, 46) = 1.412, $p < .25$].

	Sentence Type		
	S-control	O-control	Effect of sentence type
Exp.3(S-O)	666	607	59
Exp.4(O-S)	749	648	101
Effect of word order	-83	-41	

Table 8. Mean RTs in Experiments 3 and 4 (Retrieval task with S-O and O-S order)

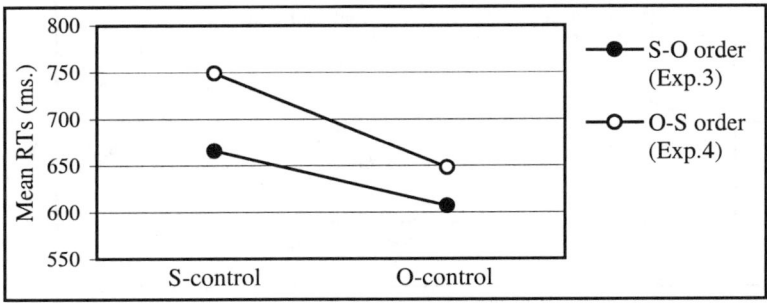

Figure 2. Comparison of Experiments 3 and 4

The results clearly showed that O-control sentences had faster RTs than S-control sentences. Although the difference did not reach a statistically significant level, as Table 8 and Figure 2 show, the permutation of the word order has increased response times. This finding is surprising when we reconsider the comparison between Experiments 1 and 2 in which the permutation of word order brought about a decrease in RTs. Interestingly, the change in experimental tasks invited the opposite effect. The scrambling of word order *decreased* RTs in the 'recognition' experiments while it *increased* RTs in the 'retrieval' experiments.

4.7 Summary of the Four Experiments

Experiments 1 and 2 utilized a 'recognition task' with a Yes/No decision, whereas Experiments 3 and 4 employed a 'retrieval task' that required the participants to answer orally with the proper antecedent. The findings of Experiments 1 and 2 indicated a 'subject preference' despite different word-orders. The results of Experiments 3 and 4 exhibited a constant 'object preference' regardless of word order. We can summarize the experimental findings in Table 9 and Figure 3 below.

	Task			
	Recognition		Retrieval	
	S-control	O-control	S-control	O-control
S-O	<u>752</u>	835	666	<u>607</u>
O-S	<u>639</u>	714	749	<u>648</u>

Table 9. Mean RTs in the four experiments

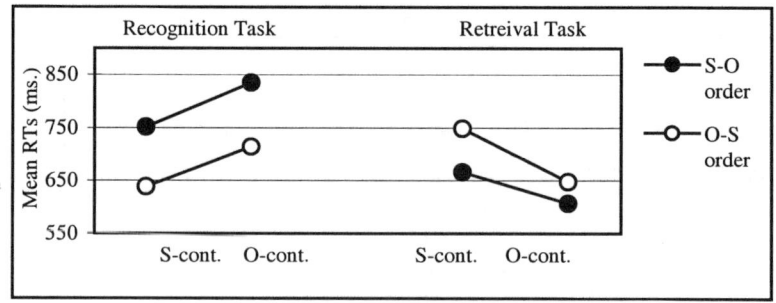

Figure 3. Comparison of the four experiments

At a glance, RTs in the recognition task (Experiments 1 and 2) are slower than those in the retrieval task (Experiments 3 and 4). However, we need the following proviso. In the recognition task, the stimulus (one of six different names) was given right after the end of each sentence. Since the timer starts at the end of sentence, the time for presenting the stimulus was included in the RTs. In other words, the participants had to press the Yes-No key after they had recognized the stimulus at the end of each sentence. In the retrieval task, on the other hand, the participants were able to respond without any extra time for recognizing the stimulus of names. In Retrieval task, furthermore, it was possible to start to respond before the end of the sentence. The morphological ending of verb conjugation is fairly simple in Japanese. For example, *yakusokusita* can be analyzed as *yakusoku* 'promise' and *sita* 'did.' Thus, the participants could neglect the ending such as *sita*. Therefore, the RTs for recognition task were prolonged, and the RTs for retrieval task were shortened. So, it is impossible to compare directly the RTs between these two tasks.

With the above proviso in mind, let us examine the three-way ANOVA (2 x 2 x 2), which revealed that there was a significant effect of interaction between the tasks and sentence types [F_1 (1, 52) = 21.705, $p < .001$, F_2(1, 68) = 30.345, $p < .001$]. No other interaction was significant. The mean RTs for this interaction is shown in Table 10 and Figure 4 below.

| | Sentence Type | | |
	S-control	O-control	Effect of sentence type
Recognition	695	774	-79
Retrieval	707	627	80
Effect of task	-12	147	

Table 10. Mean RTs in interaction between Task and Sentence Type

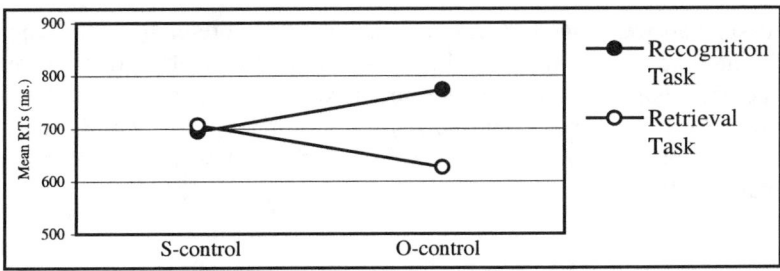

Figure 4. Comparison of RTs in the interaction between Task and Sentence Type

The simple main effect of task was not significant at S-control [F_1 (1, 104) = .054, $p < .82$, F_2 (1, 136) = .183, $p < .67$], but was significant at O-control [F_1 (1, 104) = 8.458, $p < .005$, F_2 (1, 136) = 28.169, $p < .001$]. That is, the effect of task clearly showed up at O-control construction. The simple main effect of sentence type was significant at both the recognition task [F_1 (1, 52) = 10.757, $p < .005$, F_2 (1, 68) = 15.077, $p < .001$], and the retrieval task [F_1 (1, 52) = 10.948, $p < .005$, F_2 (1, 68) = 15.268, $p < .001$]. Namely, the effect of sentence type clearly showed up in both the recognition and retrieval tasks. Here, note that the direction of effect is different: the RTs for O-control was <u>slower</u> in the recognition task, and the RTs for O-control was <u>faster</u> in the retrieval task.

There are two important findings that can be read form this preference pattern (see Figure 3). One is that the surface word order of the subject and object does not affect the preference pattern of the possible antecedent for the empty subject. That is, the preference pattern is stable between the two different word orders. The other important finding is that the preference pattern is reversed between the two different tasks. In short, there is a Subject-Object asymmetry of preference between the tasks but no such asymmetry between the word orders.

5 General Discussion

The findings from the four experiments lead to the following two questions: (i) Why does the scrambled word order fail to invite the reversed preference? (ii) Why do the different tasks cause the different preferences? Note that the scrambling of word orders is the change that affects the experimental materials. On the other hand, the alternation of tasks is the change of the instructions given to the participants.

5.1 Stable Preference Between Different Word Orders

A possible answer to the first question (i.e., the same preference between the different word orders) may be rather simple. Information about distance may not be important in constructing the structure of a sentence. It is not the *linear order* of the elements but the *relationship* among the elements that is crucial for processing a sentence. Consider the following examples from Yamashita (1997).

(16) a. (NP-*ga* NP-*ni* NP-*o* order: Canonical word order)
Wakai zimuin-*ga*   mukuti-na syatyoo-*ni*   omosiroi hon-*o*
young secretary-Nom quiet   president-Dat fun   book-Acc

ageta.
gave

'A young secretary gave the quiet president a fun book.'

b. (NP-*ni* NP-*ga* NP-*o* order: Scrambled word order)
Mukuti-na syatyoo-*ni*   wakai zimuin-*ga*   omosiroi hon-*o*
quiet   president-Dat young secretary-Nom fun   book-Acc

ageta.
gave

'To the quiet president, a young secretary gave a fun book.'

(16b) is a scrambled version of (16a). The word order is the only point of difference between the above two sentences. Yamashita (1997) gave a self-paced reading task to the participants in order to investigate whether this difference in word order caused any difference in parsing time. In these two conditions (Canonical vs. Scrambled), the reading times of each phrase were computed.[8] Since there are seven phrases, there were seven positions at which the times were measured. The results revealed "no significant differences across the conditions at any position" (p. 171). That is, Yamashita detected no word-order effect in parsing these sentences.

Therefore, it seems that there is neither primacy nor recency effect in processing Japanese sentences. This fundamental principle of sentence comprehension is reflected in the stability of preference between the different word orders in the four experiments reported here. As was mentioned in Section 4.3, the change of word order (i.e., scrambling) may affect the response times. However, the important point is that the response <u>pattern</u> is not affected by the scrambling. Of course, it is necessary to accumulate more experimental studies to support this claim. See also Nakayama (1995), Mazuka et al. (2001), and Miyamoto and Takahashi (2001) for the issue of scrambling effect in Japanese.

---

[8] The original data by Yamashita includes two more conditions for a total of four conditions. Although we reduced the number of conditions to two in order to save a space, the essence of the argument does not change.

5.2 Reversed Preference Between Different Tasks

A plausible answer to the second question (i.e., the reversed preference between the two tasks) is rather complicated. There seems to be at least four points of difference between the recognition experiment (Experiments 1 and 2) and the retrieval experiment (Experiments 3 and 4). The first point concerns the number of participants and items. The number of participants and items in the recognition experiments (16 participants and 24 items) is less than that of the retrieval experiments (40 participants and 48 items). It has sometimes been observed that significant factors do not show up statistically when there are not enough number of participants and items for inspection; however, it would not make sense to say the experiment produces completely *opposite* results only because the number of participants and items is different.

The second point concerns the non-target sentences used to disguise the purpose of the experiments. Because non-target sentences were not used in the recognition experiments, there is a possibility that the participants may have created some specific strategy in responding to the sentences; however, it would not make sense to argue that the participants used completely *opposite* strategies simply because of the presence of non-target sentences.

The third point is related to the way of constructing the experimental sentences. Studies have pointed out that intonational information like pitch, loudness, and duration play an important role in sentence comprehension (Misono et al. 1997, Venditti and Yamashita 1994). In the recognition experiments, experimental sentences were synthesized by combining phrases that had been recorded separately, and therefore, the sentences did not have a normal sentential intonation. In the retrieval experiments, on the other hand, the experimenter read out the complete sentences with a normal sentential contour. This difference in the way of constructing experimental sentences may have caused preference patterns to differ. In order to examine this possibility, another experiment, the likes of which are discussed in the final section, would be necessary.

The fourth point has to do with the difference in the experimental tasks given to the participants. It is known that language processing is sensitive to the task involved. For example, Kamide and Mitchell (1997) report the different results between off-line and on-line tasks. Nagata (1993) also reports different results between probe recognition tasks and antecedent identification tasks. In the following two subsections, therefore, I will try to account for the difference of preference patterns in terms of the difference in the tasks.

5.3 Subject Preference and Case Hierarchy

In the experimental sentences, there were two possible candidates for the correct antecedent: *NP-ga* or *NP-ni*. The findings indicated that *NP-ga* was preferred in the recognition task, while *NP-ni* was selected in the retrieval task. In short, observation shows that the different tasks cause different preferences, and therefore, one must plausibly account for the relationship between the tasks and the preferences. It is natural to assume the human parser selects the most suitable strategy to accomplish the given task. The selection of a strategy requires relevant information. The preference pattern seems to be determined by what kind of information is utilized; that is, we assume that the participants pursue the following path:

(17)   [task] ⟶ [strategy] ⟶ [preference]
                         ↑
                 <information>

Note that the proposed process is not a sequence of logical steps, but a practical procedure that the participants might have adopted for solving the given task. In Experiments 1 and 2, the participants were given a recognition task that required them to decide whether the given name was the correct antecedent for the empty subject then to press the Yes-key or No-key. Because the question required the parser to answer simply Yes or No, the task was relatively easy to perform. In performing the task, thus, the parser could have relied on a strategy that works at rather automatic and shallow level of parsing. As is discussed below, we assume that the parser makes use of Case information in applying the strategy.

If the human parser ignores information available from the Case-marking particle or delays utilization of this information, the parser must wait until the final verb appears. With this 'wait-and-see' strategy, the parser should have made no mistake in determining which lexical unit was the controlling one. This means that the RTs of the S-control and O-control sentences should not have been different. This contradicts the findings of our experiments. Thus, it is reasonable to assume that the parser uses information from the Case markers before the final verb appears.

Yamashita (1997) presents positive evidence that indicate the parser constructs a tentative structure relying on Case-marker information. Consider the following examples:

(18) a. Kawaii onnanoko-*ga* wakai sensei-*ni*   oisii otya-*o*   *dasita.*
         cute   girl-Nom   young teacher-Dat good tea-Acc served
         'The cute girl served the young teacher good tea.'

b. Kawaii onnanoko-*ga* wakai sensei-*ni*   oisii otya-*o*   *nonda*
   cute   girl-Nom   young teacher-Dat good tea-Acc drank

(to itta).
(that said)

'The cute girl (told) the young teacher (that she) drank good tea.'

At the point of each verb (*dasita* 'served' vs. *nonda* 'drank'), the participants were asked to decide whether the given word was a correct Japanese word or not (some nonwords are also included). The results of this lexical decision task revealed that the response time of the ditransitive verb (*dasita*) was significantly faster than that of the transitive verb (*nonda*). If the parser did not make any predictions regarding the coming verb, there would not have been any difference in lexical decision time. Furthermore, the same results were obtained when the word order was scrambled (Wakai sensei-*ni* kawaii onnanoko-*ga* oisii otya-*o dasita/nonda*). Yamashita (1997), therefore, claims that "the parser appears to have utilized case information independently of word order when it made a decision on the syntactic computation prior to the verb" (p. 176).

So far, we have argued that the parser utilizes Case information in performing the recognition task. Then, why was the 'subject' preference detected in Experiments 1 and 2? To explain this, I propose a 'Case Filling Strategy,' which I will define as "filling the empty subject (PRO) with an NP carrying Nominative Case." The 'Case Hierarchy' explains why the parser selects the Nominative Case. Shibatani (1978) proposes the following Case Hierarchy:

(19) Nominative > Accusative > Dative > Other Cases

He presents four reasons to support this proposal: (i) The Nominative Case is indispensable at some level of derivation; (ii) Only the Nominative and Accusative Cases allow quantifier floating; (iii) When topicalized, the Dative marker (-*ni*) can be deleted very often compared to other Case markers except Nominative and Accusative; (iv) The topic marker (-*wa*) cannot co-occur with the Nominative and Accusative Cases. As this is not the place to discuss these points extensively, I will discuss only the final point. Take the following examples (Top=Topic marker).

(20) *Taro-<u>ga-wa</u>   wakai.
         -Nom-Top young
    (lit.) 'As for Taro, he is young.'

(21) *Taro-ga   <u>Jiro-o-wa</u>   nagutta.
         -Nom   -Acc-Top   hit
    (lit.) 'As for Jiro, Taro hit him.'

(22) Taro-ga   <u>Jiro-ni-wa</u>   atta.
         -Nom   -Dat-Top   met
    'As for Jiro, Taro met him.'

(23) Taro-ga   <u>Jiro-kara-wa</u>   tegami-o moratta.
         -Nom   -from-Top   letter-Acc received
    'As for Jiro, Taro received a letter from him.'

The topic marker (-*wa*) cannot co-occur with the Nominative nor Accusative Cases as in (20) and (21), but it can co-occur with the Dative and Oblique Cases as in (22) and (23). Taking other conditions into consideration, Shibatani (1978) claims in (19) that the Nominative Case is located at the highest position in the Case Hierarchy.

The Nominative Case tends to correspond to the grammatical function of the 'subject' (although, as I will discuss below, this is not necessarily true). Thus, the human parser may assume this correspondence so that it regards a NP with the Nominative Case marker as a subject NP. Considering our experimental sentences, we notice that the preferred NP is marked with the Nominative marker (-*ga*). This means that this NP is in the highest position of the Case Hierarchy represented in (19). The subject preference in the recognition experiments appears to reflect the mental representation of this Case Hierarchy within the participants.

Here, one should notice that the syntactic category 'Subject' does not uniquely correspond to the 'Nominative' Case category. Take the following examples in (24) below (Gen = Genitive).

(24) a. Watasi-no otooto-wa Yamada sensei-ga   sukida.
         I-Gen   brother-Top   professor-Nom love
         'My brother loves Professor Yamada.'

    b. *Watasi-no otooto wa Yamada sensei-ga o-sukida.
        (honorific form of (24a))

If the NP marked with the Nominative (*Yamada sensei-ga*) is really the subject, (24b) should be acceptable because the honorification rule applies to the referent of this NP who is worthy deference. The fact that (24b) is unacceptable indicates that this is not the subject. There are two types of *-ga*: one is 'Nominative subject' as in (22) and the other is 'Nominative object' as in (24a). Nonetheless, it is important to notice that the Nominative object is restricted to cases in which the predicate is a specific stative such as *sukida* 'like', *hosii* 'want', *wakaru* 'understandable', and *Verb + tai* 'want to do', etc.

Thus, it might be suitable to call the preference detected in our experiments a 'Nominative preference' instead of a 'subject preference,' even though the two terms are not distinguishable as long as the parser regards the Nominative as being equivalent to the subject. Thus, I will continue to use the term subject preference for the sake of simplicity. This hypothesis of Case Hierarchy accounts for the subject preference observed in Experiments 1 and 2. In what follows, I will present a hypothesis to explain the object preference detected in Experiments 3 and 4.

5.4 Object Preference and Theta-role Hierarchy

In Experiments 3 and 4, the participants were given the retrieval task that required them to identify the antecedent verbally. Because the task was to answer a 'who-did-what' question, the task was more difficult to perform than the task required in Experiments 1 and 2. (Although the RTs of Experiments 3 and 4 were faster than those of Experiments 1 and 2, this does not mean that Experiments 3 and 4 were easier to perform than Experiments 1 and 2. As was mentioned in Section 4.7, the direct comparison of RTs is meaningless because the measuring method is different.) The retrieval task does not allow to say just Yes or No, but it demands to select only one name among possible six names used in the experiments (two names were used in each sentence). To perform the task in Experiments 3 and 4, thus, the parser seemed to employ a strategy that works at rather conscious and deep level of processing. The parser appears to utilize Theta-role information in applying this strategy. Many studies have pointed out that Theta-roles play important roles in language processing (Ahrens and Swinney 1995, Boland et al. 1995, Carlson and Tanenhaus 1988, Tanenhaus et al. 1993).

Here, we argue that the 'Theta-checking Strategy' of Sakamoto and Walenski (1998) applies in performing the retrieval task for Japanese control constructions. This strategy says, "Assign a tentative Theta-role using information available from Case markers, and check it using verb information". We assume that Case markers (e.g., *-ga*, *-ni*, *-o*, etc.) are sources of two different levels of information: one for Case information (e.g., Nominative, Accusative, Dative, etc.), and the other for Theta-role (i.e., Agent, Theme, Goal, etc.). The human parser appears to make a top-down prediction using Theta-role information available from a noun with a Case marker. To begin with, take the following English examples in order to consider how this top-down prediction works.

(25) a. John gave [$_{NP}$ the boy] [$_{NP}$ the dog] bit a bandage?? : Garden path
 b. John gave [$_{NP}$ the boy$_1$ [$_S$ the dog bit e_1]] a bandage. : Reanalyzed

In (25a), when the parser gets to the verb *gave*, it expects that two NPs will follow: one for Goal and another for Theme. This expectation is tentatively satisfied at the point where *the dog* is attached to a parse tree, but ultimately, this expectation is disappointed when the parser gets to the verb *bit*, because this verb requires an Agent and a Patient NP. (25a) results in a garden-path effect and must be reanalyzed as in (25b). Now, take the following examples from Japanese.

(26) a. [$_{NP}$ Taro-ga] [$_{NP}$ Hanako-ni] [$_{NP}$ ringo-o] tabeta inu-o   ageta.
                -Nom   -Dat   apple-Acc ate   dog-Acc gave
    'Taro ate an apple to Hanako gave a dog??': (mild) Garden path

 b. [$_{NP}$ Taro-ga] [$_{NP}$ Hanako-ni] [$_{NP}$ [$_S$ e_1 ringo-o tabeta] inu$_1$]-o
                -Nom   -Dat   apple-Acc ate   dog-Acc

ageta.
gave

'Taro gave Hanako the dog that ate the apple.': Reanalyzed

In (26a), when the parser encounters three NPs in succession, it expects to find a three-place predicate such as *ageta* 'gave,' which can take Agent, Goal, and Theme Theta-roles. This expectation is not satisfied because *tabeta* 'ate' is a two-place predicate that does not subcategorize three NPs. This verb takes only Agent and Theme Theta-roles. In other words, the tentative construction expected from the three successive NPs (NP$_1$-*ga* NP$_2$-*ni* NP$_3$-*o*) is checked against this verb information. On encountering the following noun *inu* 'dog,' the parser has to reanalyze (26a) as (26b), resulting in a mild garden-path effect (or 'surprise effect' See Mazuka and Itoh 1995). This line of discussion is supported by Yamashita (1997) mentioned in Section 5.3, which indicates that the human parser makes prediction based on the sequence of NPs.[9]

I argue that in both a head-initial language (e.g., English) and a head-final language (e.g., Japanese), the parser utilizes Theta-role information. The only difference is the way in which the parser gets this information. In English, the parser relies on Theta-role information available from a verb. In Japanese, on the other hand, the parser uses Theta-role information available from a noun with a Case-marking particle. Here, we assume a very simple process is in operation. When the human parser gets to a verb that assigns a certain Theta-role, it expects to encounter a noun with the pertinent Theta-role. By the same token (but the opposite direction), when the parser gets to a noun with a certain Case marker, it assumes that there must be some appropriate Theta-role associated with that Case marker. And then, the parser anticipates a verb that can assign the expected Theta-role.

Here, it is assumed that such-and-such Case marker corresponds uniquely to such-and-such Theta-role. For example, a NP marked with the Nominative particle (-*ga*) usually represents the Agent. An NP with the Dative particle (-*ni*) usually represents the Goal. An NP with the Accusative particle (-*o*) usually represents the Theme. Thus, it is assumed a sentence has (at least) two levels of representation: one for Case and the other for Theta-role as is shown in (27) below.

(27) Taro-ga Hanako-ni Jiro-o syookaisita.
     -Nom   -Dat   -Acc introduced   ← [Case level]
   [Agent]   [Goal] [Theme]   ← [Theta-role level]
   'Taro introduced Jiro to Hanako.'

Note that we are not claiming that there is *always* a unique correspondence between Case and Theta-role. In (24a), for example, the NP marked with the Nominative (*Yamada sensei-ga*) is not the Agent but the Theme. The point is that the human parser *assumes* that there is a one-to-one correlation between Case and Theta-role. Since it is costly to prepare for all possibilities, the parser seems to construct a tentative parse tree using this simple assumption.

If Theta-role information is consulted in performing the retrieval task, which Theta-role is to be selected as the preferred one? Sakamoto (1996) and Sakamoto and Walenski (1998) claim that the Goal role is preferred as a possible candidate for an empty subject because the Goal role is the highest in the 'Theta-role Hierarchy' proposed by Nishigauchi (1983). He claims

---

[9] See also Inoue and Fodor (1995) and Mazuka and Itoh (1995).

that the Goal is chosen as the controller in the control constructions. Consider the following examples:

(28) a. Bill bought for Susan$_1$ a large flashy car [PRO$_1$ to drive].
   b. John$_1$ received from Susan a book [PRO$_1$ to read].

Nishigauchi (1985) claims that the indirect object (*Susan*) denotes the Goal in (28a), since the Theme (*a large flashy car*) moves to this indirect object. On the other hand, the subject (*John*) is assumed to be the Goal in (28b) because the movement of the Theme (*a book*) is directed toward this subject. This difference of control behavior is explained by the difference of predicate (*buy* vs. *receive*) that governs the control relation. Regardless of the difference of the grammatical function (i.e., subject or object), the NP with the Goal role is always chosen as the controller.

However, there are cases in which no Goal is specified in a sentence. Consider the following examples (29) and (30). Nishigauchi (1985) argues that the subject of verbs such as *own*, *retain*, etc. is associated with the thematic relation of Location to which the Theme (e.g., *a car* in (29)) belongs. On the other hand, the object of verbs like *deprive*, *cure*, etc. is assumed to bear the thematic relation of Source from which the Theme (e.g., *the money* in (30)) is transferred.

(29) John$_1$ owns a car [PRO$_1$ to carry his own belongings in].
(30) They deprived Mary$_1$ of the money [PRO$_1$ to pay her rent with].

If the Goal is specified in a sentence, it is always chosen as the controller. When only the Location or Source is specified, it serves as the controller. Nishigauchi (1985) claims that there is a hierarchical relation among Theta-roles and this hierarchy determines which Theta-role is chosen as the controller:[10]

(31) The Primary Location Hierarchy
   1. Goal > 2. Location, Source

---

[10] See Ladusaw and Dowty (1988) for a different view which claims that "principles of control of subjectless infinitives are ultimately determined by entailments of verbs together with principles of human action that exist quit apart from language." This claim seems to be too strong, since some aspects of the control phenomenon should be explained in terms of linguistic properties. See Sakamoto (1996) for more discussion on this issue.

Note that the proposed hierarchy is to account for the construal of the control constructions. It is not intended to apply for <u>any type of sentences</u>. Returning to Experiments 3 and 4, I claim that the parser is ready to assign the Goal role to an NP that is marked with the Dative (-*ni*). At this point, the parser commits to a decision about the thematic structure of the sentence. This tentative commitment is either confirmed by subsequent information provided by a final Object-control verb or not confirmed by a subsequent Subject-control verb. The failure of this confirmation seems to result in a slower processing time for S-control sentences.

6 Concluding Remarks

So far, I have argued that different tasks require the parser to employ different strategies, which in turn use different sources of information. Then, it is assumed that these different levels of information affected the strategy to invite the different patterns of preference observed in our experiments. Except lexical information, Case markers are very informative cues for the parser when information about the sentence final predicate is not available (see Section 7 below about the importance of prosodic information). In both the recognition and retrieval experiments, the parser is supposed to construct a tentative sentence structure by making use of the available information provided by Case markers. The issue at hand is how the parser uses this information. I claim that the parser utilizes it in two different ways. In the recognition task, the parser selects a NP with Nominative as a possible antecedent because of the Case Hierarchy represented in (19). In the recognition task, on the other hand, the parser selects a NP with Dative because of the Theta-role Hierarchy in (31).

However, note that I do not claim that the human parser uses these two types of information in this sequential order. Nothing is said about the timing to use the relevant information. Actually, it is not so easy to design an experiment to testify this kind of sequential ordering of sentence processing (see Hahne and Friederici 1999, Hickok et al. 1992). Since, in most experiments, participants are required to perform some task, what we can investigate is inevitably the process of task-oriented performance. The important point in our experiments is that there are (at least) two distinct levels of sentence processing. By altering the experimental tasks, one can find out which level is activated by the human parser.

7 Remaining Problems

In this paper, I have concentrated on the difference between the tasks performed by the participants: *recognition* and *retrieval*. However, when we closely observe the tasks and the experimental materials, we notice that Experiments 1 and 2 exhibit a 'Recognition Task + Synthesized Sentence' pattern while Experiments 3 and 4 exhibit a 'Retrieval Task + Read-out Sentence' pattern. We can summarize the situation in Table 11.

There are two factors (i.e., task and material) that could cause the difference in the response pattern, and there is a confounding between the task and the material. It is therefore necessary to fix one factor before examining the effect of the other factor. In other words, we need to examine the combinations 'Retrieval Task + Synthesized Sentence' and 'Recognition Task + Read-out Sentence'. As mentioned earlier, phonological information plays an important role in parsing. The proposed experiments should tell us more about the interaction of phonological, syntactic, and semantic information in sentence processing.

Task Material	Recognition	Retrieval
Synthesized	Experiment 1 (S-O order) Experiment 2 (O-S order)	Not yet done
Read-out	Not yet done	Experiment 3 (S-O order) Experiment 4 (O-S order)

Table 11. Combination of Tasks and Sentences

References

Abney, S. 1987. The English Noun Phrase in its Sentential Aspect. Doctoral dissertation, MIT.

Ahrens, K. & D. Swinney. 1995. Participant Roles and the Processing of Verbs During Sentence Comprehension. *Journal of Psycholinguistic Research* 24.6:533-547.

Boland, J., M. Tanenhaus & S. Garnsey. 1990. Evidence for the Immediate Use of Verb Control Information in Sentence Processing. *Journal of Memory & Language* 29:413-432.

Boland, J., M. Tanenhaus, S. Garnsey, & G. Carlson. 1995. Verb Argument Structure in Parsing and Interpretation: Evidence from Wh-questions. *Journal of Memory & Language* 34:774-806.

Carlson, G. & M. Tanenhaus. 1988. Thematic Roles and Language Comprehension. *Syntax and Semantics* 21, ed. W. Wilkins, 263-288. New York: Academic Press.
Chomsky, N. 1981. *Lectures on Government and Binding*. Dordrecht: Foris.
Fodor, J. D. 1989. Empty Categories in Sentence Processing. *Language & Cognitive Processes* 4:155-209.
Frazier, L., C. Clifton, & J. Randall. 1983. Filling Gaps: Decision Principles and Structure in Sentence Comprehension. *Cognition* 13:187-222.
Frazier, L. & J. D. Fodor. 1978. The Sausage Machine: A New Two-stage Parsing Model. *Cognition* 6:291-325.
Hahne, A. & A. Friederici. 1999. Electrophysiological Evidence for Two Steps in Syntactic Analysis: Early Automatic and Late Controlled Processes. *Journal of Cognitive Neuroscience* 11.2:194-205.
Hickok, G., E. Canseco-Gonzalez, E. Zurif, & J. Grimshaw. 1992. Modularity in Locating Wh-gaps. *Journal of Psycholinguistic Research* 21:545-561.
Inoue, A. & J. D. Fodor. 1995. Information-Paced Parsing of Japanese. *Japanese Sentence Processing*, eds. R. Mazuka & N. Nagai, 9-63. Hillsdale, NJ: Lawrence Erlbaum Associates.
Kamide, Y. & D. Mitchell. 1997. Relative Clause Attachment: Nondeterminism in Japanese Parsing. *Journal of Psycholinguistic Research* 26:247-254.
Kimball, J. 1973. Seven Principles of Surface Structure Parsing in Natural Language. *Cognition* 2:15-47.
Ladusaw, W. & D. Dowty. 1988. Toward a Nongrammatical Account of Thematic Roles. *Syntax and Semantics* 21, ed. W. Wilkins, 61-73. New York: Academic Press.
Mazuka, R., K. Itoh, & T. Kondo. 2001. Costs of scrambling in Japanese sentence processing. in this Volume
Mazuka, R. & K. Itoh. 1995. Can Japanese Speakers be Led Down to the Garden Path? *Japanese Sentence Processing*, eds. R. Mazuka & N. Nagai, 295-329. Hillsdale, NJ: Lawrence Erlbaum Associates.
Misono, Y., R. Mazuka, T. Kondo, & S. Kiritani. 1997. Effects and Limitations of Prosodic and Semantic Biases on Syntactic Disambiguation. *Journal of Psycholinguistic Research* 26.2:229-245.
Miyamoto, E. & S. Takahashi. 2001. Sources of Difficulty in Processing Scrambling in Japanese. in this Volume
Nakayama, M. 1995. Scrambling and Probe Recognition. *Japanese Sentence Processing*, eds. R. Mazuka & N. Nagai, 257-273. Hillsdale, NJ: Lawrence Erlbaum Associates.
Nagata, H. 1993. Unimmediate Construction of Syntactic Structure for Garden Path Sentences in Japanese. *Journal of Psycholinguistic Research* 22:365-381.

Nicol, J. & D. Swinney. 1989. The Role of Structure in Coreference Assignment During Sentence Comprehension. *Journal of Psycholinguistic Research* 18:5-20.
Ninose, Y., J. Oda, Y. Sakaki, T. Sakamoto, & J. Gyoba. 1998. Ryooji-bunri-choohoo Niyoru Kuushugo Hantei Purosesu-no Bunseki (2): Gojun-no Kooka. [On the Real-time Processing of Empty Subjects in Japanese Using a Dichotic-listening Method (2): The Word Order Effect]. *Ninchi Kagaku [Cognitive Science]* 5.1:82-88.
Nishigauchi, T. 1984. Control and the Thematic Domain. *Language* 60:215-250.
Oda, J., Y. Ninose, Y. Sakaki, J. Gyoba, & T. Sakamoto. 1997. Ryooji-bunri-choohoo Niyoru Kuushugo Hantei Purosesu-no Bunseki. [On the Real-time Processing of Empty Subjects in Japanese Using a Dichotic-listening Method]. *Ninchi Kagaku [Cognitive Science]* 4.2:58-63.
Pickering, M. & G. Barry. 1991. Sentence Processing without Empty Categories. *Language & Cognitive Processes* 6:229-259.
Roeper, T. 1987. Implicit Arguments and the Head-Complement Relation. *Linguistic Inquiry* 18:267-310.
Pustejovsky, J. 1998. *The Generative Lexicon*. Cambridge, MA: MIT Press
Sakamoto, T. 1995. Transparency between Parser and Grammar: On the Processing of Empty Subjects in Japanese. *Japanese Sentence Processing*, eds. R. Mazuka & N. Nagai, 275-294. Hillsdale, NJ: Lawrence Erlbaum Associates.
Sakamoto, T. 1996. *Processing Empty Subjects in Japanese: Implications for the Transparency Hypothesis*. Fukuoka: Kyushu University Press.
Sakamoto, T. & M. Walenski. 1998. The Processing of Empty Subject in English and Japanese. *Syntax and Semantics 31, Sentence Processing: A Crosslinguistic Perspective*, ed. D. Hillert, 95-111. San Diego: Academic Press.
Shibatani, M. 1978. *Nihongo-no Bunseki [Analysis of Japanese]*. Tokyo: Taishukan.
Tanenhaus, M, J. Boland, G. Mauner, & G. Carlson. 1993. More on Combinatory Lexical Information: Thematic Structure in Parsing and Interpretation. *Cognitive Models of Speech Processing: The Second Sperlonga Meeting*, eds. G. Altman & R. Shillcock, 297-319. Hillsdale, NJ: Lawrence Erlbaum Associates.
Venditti, J. & H. Yamashita. 1994. Prosodic Information and Processing of Complex NPs in Japanese. *MIT Working Papers in Linguistics* 24, 375-391.
Williams, E. 1985. PRO and Subject of NP. *Natural Language & Linguistic Theory* 3:297-315.
Yamashita, H. 1997. The Effects of Word-order and Case Marking Information on the Processing of Japanese. *Journal of Psycholinguistic Research* 26:163-188.

9

Effects of Accentual Phrasing on Adjective Interpretation in Korean[*]

AMY J. SCHAFER AND SUN-AH JUN

1 Introduction

Several studies of prosody and sentence processing have now demonstrated that prosodic phrasing can exhibit strong effects on processing decisions in English (e.g. Warren, Grabe, and Nolan 1995, Schafer 1997, Kjelgaard and Speer 1999). However, very little work on prosodic effects on parsing has been done with other languages. Given that there is variability in prosodic structure and its relationship to syntactic or semantic form across languages (e.g. Beckman and Pierrehumbert 1986, Venditti, Jun, and Beckman 1996), it could be the case that prosody has very different effects on processing across languages. Thus, just as syntactic processing models can be better evaluated by testing syntactically diverse languages, experimentation on prosodically diverse languages should further our understanding of both the universal and the language-specific relationships between prosodic form and sentence processing decisions.

---

[*] Address correspondence to Amy Schafer, Department of Linguistics, 3125 Campbell Hall, UCLA, Los Angeles, CA 90095-1543 or schafer@ucla.edu. This research was supported by NIH grant DC00029 to UCLA and a UCLA faculty research grant to S.-A. Jun. We thank Chuck Clifton, Lyn Frazier, and Shari Speer for their many helpful comments on this work; Hyuck-Joon Lee for his assistance with acoustic analyses; and Hyunjoo Koo and Sun-ju Oh for their assistance in conducting the experiments.

Sentence Processing in East Asian Languages.
Mineharu Nakayama (ed.).
Copyright ©2002, CSLI Publications.

The research described in this paper had two primary goals. The first goal was to determine if Korean sentence comprehension could be affected by the accentual phrasing pattern of the sentence. Korean accentual phrases are similar to intermediate phrases in English in that they are the level of prosodic structure which is intermediate between phonological words and intonation phrases. A small set of studies on English have provided evidence that intermediate phrase boundaries can affect comprehension (Kjelgaard 1995, Schafer 1997, Kjelgaard and Speer 1999). However, Korean accentual phrases are arguably less phonetically salient than English intermediate phrases, as described further in Section 2. They also tend to differ in span. Korean accentual phrases generally contain fewer syllables and fewer content words than English intermediate phrases. In an analysis of the prosody produced by reading a standard passage, Jun and Fougeron (Jun 1999, Jun and Fougeron 2000) found that Korean accentual phrases contained an average of 3.2 syllables and 1.2 content words, and thus generally contained a single phonological word. In contrast, with an English version of the passage, Ueyama (1998) found that English intermediate phrases contained an average of 5.3 syllables. Using a different reading text, Ayers (1994) found that English intermediate phrases contained over 3.9 content words on average.

Accentual phrases may therefore show smaller effects on comprehension than intermediate phrases for either of two reasons. First, if they are less acoustically salient, they might be less reliably detected during sentence comprehension. Second, if syntactic disambiguation depends on grouping syntactic units into prosodic units, the small size of Korean accentual phrases may mean that they are less commonly associated with disambiguated syntactic structures than English intermediate phrases. Thus, Korean accentual phrases could be a less reliable source of information about syntactic structure than English intermediate phrases.

Nevertheless, Jun (1993, 1994) showed that correspondences exist between accentual phrasing and syntactic phrasing in Korean. She found that speakers produced different accentual phrasings for the Korean equivalent of *black cat's ankle* depending on whether *black* modified *ankle* or *cat*. Speakers grouped *black* with *cat's* to show that *black* modified *cat*, and grouped *cat's* and *ankle* to indicate the other interpretation. We therefore expected there to be some effect of accentual phrasing on sentence comprehension, and so our second goal was to compare and contrast the effects of prosodic phrasing in Korean and English.

In both languages, prosodic phrases can group together material which is closely related syntactically or semantically. This "chunking" aspect of prosodic phrasing has been captured explicitly in some models of sentence processing to explain prosodic disambiguation effects. For example, on the basis of observations about English and Japanese, Marcus and Hindle (1990) proposed that material in separate prosodic phrases can be freely combined at later stages of processing, but material within a single prosodic phrase cannot be separated. Such a view of prosodic phrasing effects would most likely predict very similar effects of accentual phrasing in Korean and intermediate phrasing in English.

However, the structure of the prosodic system and its relationship to syntactic and semantic structure differs for Korean and English in several important respects. As mentioned above, accentual phrases and intermediate phrases tend to contain different amounts of phonological and morphological material. The two languages also differ in how their prosodic systems encode information structure. English has a large number of pitch accents, and marks information structure primarily through the type and placement of these pitch accents. Korean has no pitch accents, and marks information structure primarily by manipulating accentual phrasing. Thus, English is prominence-driven, while Korean is boundary-driven (Beckman 1995, Jun 1999). Korean might therefore show different prosodic phrasing effects from English because of such differences between the two languages in the grammatical constraints on prosodic form.

Here, we briefly report on two experiments on prosody and sentence processing in Korean, a production experiment and a comprehension experiment, which are part of an on-going research project on prosodic effects on sentence processing in Korean. The production study served to confirm our expectations about prosodic patterns in Korean under various syntactic, semantic, and discourse conditions. It also allowed us to elicit materials for our comprehension experiment from native speakers. The comprehension experiment then tested a syntactically ambiguous structure under four conditions of accentual phrasing. On the basis of the results, we will argue that sentence comprehension in Korean, like in English, shows effects of acoustically subtle prosodic phrase boundaries. Yet the two languages can differ in how prosodic phrasing effects are realized. We will claim that these apparent differences in prosodic effects stem from differences between the two languages in the grammatical constraints governing prosody and the mappings between prosodic structure and syntactic and semantic structures. In the next section, we review the intonational structure of Seoul Korean. We then turn to the description of the experiments.

2 Description of Seoul Korean Intonation

Korean has two prosodic units which are marked by intonation. These are called the "intonation phrase" and the "accentual phrase" by Jun (1993,

1998), adopting the intonation framework developed by Pierrehumbert and her colleagues (Pierrehumbert 1980, Beckman and Pierrehumbert 1986, Pierrehumbert and Beckman 1988; see Ladd (1996) for extensive review). A schematic representation of the intonational structure of Seoul Korean is shown in Figure 1. The intonation phrase (IPh) consists of one or more accentual phrases, and is demarcated by a boundary tone. An IPh boundary tone can be a simple high or low tone (H%, L%) or a combination of high and low tones (e.g. HL%, LHL%, LH%). It is realized on the phrase-final syllable and delivers pragmatic information about the sentence. An IPh-final syllable is subject to final lengthening—such syllables are about 1.8 times longer than IPh-medial syllables (Korea Telecom 1996)—and is optionally followed by a pause.

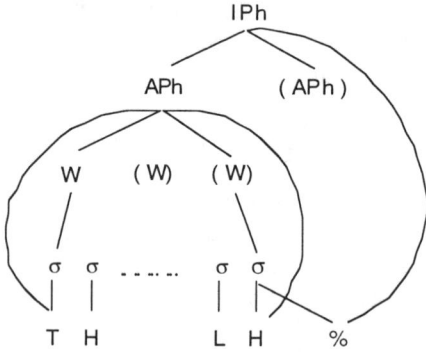

Notes: Elements in parentheses are optional. Accentual phrase tones are realized on the first, second, penultimate, and ultimate syllable of the accentual phrase, regardless of how those syllables are parsed into phonological words. (IPh = intonation phrase; APh = accentual phrase; w = phonological word; σ = syllable; T = tone, realized as H when the initial segment is aspirated/tense, L otherwise; H = high tone; L = low tone; % = intonation phrase boundary tone.)

Figure 1. Intonational structure of Seoul Korean (Jun 1993)

An accentual phrase (APh) in Korean consists of one or more phonological words (a lexical item followed by case markers or postpositions; written as "w" in Figure 1), and is defined by phrasal tones demarcating the beginning and the end of the phrase. The underlying tonal pattern of an accentual phrase in Seoul Korean is either Low-High-Low-High (LHLH) or High-High-Low-High (HHLH): thus, THLH in Figure 1. The APh-initial tone is determined by the laryngeal feature of the phrase-initial segment. When the phrase-initial segment is either aspirated or tense, having [+stiff vocal cords] (Halle and Stevens 1971), an APh begins with an H tone; otherwise it carries an L tone. For details about this tonal difference, see Jun (1996, 2000).

The surface pattern of tones for an APh depends on the underlying APh contour, the length of the APh, and whether the APh is final in the IPh or not. All four underlying tones are realized on the surface when an APh has four or more syllables and is not IPh-final. The initial two tones of the underlying APh contour are associated with the initial two syllables of the APh and the final two tones of the underlying contour are associated with the final two syllables. If the APh is longer than four syllables, the tones on the syllables between the second syllable and the penult are determined by interpolation from the H tone on the second syllable to the L tone on the penult.

When an APh has fewer than four syllables, several additional surface tonal patterns can be observed, as a result of undershoot (i.e., missing the pitch target) of the medial H or the following L tone. When an APh has three syllables, both the medial H and the following L tone can be undershot, resulting in LH (or HH for the HHLH pattern); just the medial H can be undershot, resulting in LLH (or HLH); or just the following L can be undershot, resulting in LHH (or HHH).[1] When an APh has one or two syllables, only a LH (or HH) pattern is observed.

Finally, when an APh is final to an IPh, the final syllable of the APh and IPh is associated at the underlying level with both an APh-final tone and an IPh boundary tone. In this case, the boundary tone of the IPh preempts the tonal specification that would otherwise be realized on an APh-final syllable. For example, when the IPh has a L% boundary tone, the final H tone of the last APh is not realized; thus when the last APh has four syllables, its tonal pattern is LHLL% (or HHLL%).

Unlike the case for IPhs, an APh-final syllable is not consistently lengthened. In those cases when it is lengthened, the degree of lengthening is substantially smaller than for IPh-final lengthening. The final syllable of an APh is only followed by a pause when it is also the last syllable of an IPh. However, APh-initial segments have been shown to be "strengthened" (Jun 1995, Fougeron and Keating 1997, Keating et al. 1999, Cho and Keating 1999). That is, the first segment of an APh is realized with a longer duration and more extreme articulation (e.g., a greater degree of contact between articulators) than segments internal to an APh.

---

[1] The conditions triggering undershoot of the medial H or the following L are not clear. Informal observation of data shows that the choice of tones varies across speakers and across different pragmatic contexts. Furthermore, different tonal realizations do not seem to have contrastive meaning (Jun 2000).

An example of Seoul Korean intonation is shown in the pitch track in Figure 2. The sentence means 'Hyungmin's family hates Younga'. It has three phonological words, which correspond to 'Hyungmin's family' 'Younga', and 'hates'. The utterance consists of three APhs, with each phonological word forming a single APh: ((Hyungmin's family-Top)_APh (Younga-Acc)_APh (hates)_APh)_IPh.

The first APh shows a HHLH pattern since the phrase is five syllables long and begins with [h], [+stiff vocal folds]. The second APh shows a LH pattern since the phrase is three syllables long and begins with [j], [-stiff vocal folds]. The last APh shows a LHLL pattern because it is four syllables long, begins with [m], and is the final APh of an IPh which marks a declarative with a L% boundary tone. The underlying tonal pattern of the utterance is given in (1a) and the surface tonal pattern is given in (1b) and Figure 2. The symbol 'a' following a tone (e.g. 'LHa') marks the end of an accentual phrase in (1) and the 'tones' transcription in Figure 2.

(1) a. Underlying tones: (HHLHa) (LHLHa) (LHLHa L%)
    b. Surface tones: (HHLHa) (LHa)   (LHLL%)

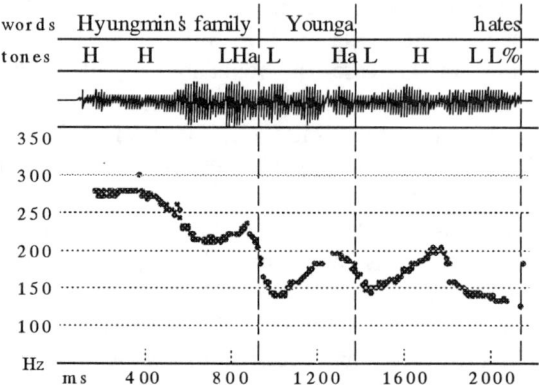

Figure 2. An example pitch track of an utterance consisting of three accentual phrases, (hjəŋmininenɨn 'Hyungmin's family') (jəŋalil 'Younga') (miwəhejo 'hates'), where each phrase includes one phonological word

Based on reading data, Kim et al. (1997), Korea Telecom (1996), Jun (2001) and Jun and Fougeron (2000) show that an APh generally contains two to four syllables; thus, an APh generally contains one phonological word. We will call the pattern of producing each phonological word in a separate APh the "default" phrasing pattern. This seems to be the most common phrasing pattern for reading and spontaneous speech, particularly in wide-focus or "out of the blue" situations. We note, however, that further research is needed on the relative frequency of different phrasing patterns in Korean, particularly for spontaneous speech, and on the grammatical constraints that determine which prosodic structures are well-formed in various situations.

The default phrasing can be altered for adjacent words that are closely related to each other syntactically or semantically. In this case, these adjacent words often form a single APh (Jun 1993, 1998). In addition, the default phrasing pattern is often overridden when a word is contrastively focused. The focused word initiates a new APh and the following words are often dephrased, forming one large APh together with the focused word (Jun 1993; see Jun and Lee (1998) for discussion of inter-speaker variation in the realization of focused phrases).

Our experimental studies focused on these distinct accentual phrasing patterns—default phrasing, focus phrasing, and phrasings which indicate relationships among words. In the production study, we elicited these patterns from naïve speakers. In the comprehension study, we then tested whether these different patterns of accentual phrasing would have discriminable effects on the comprehension of an ambiguous structure.

3 Experimental Studies

Both our production experiment and our comprehension experiment employed an ambiguity of the sort shown in (2), in which a single adjective is followed by a complex noun phrase. The adjective in such a phrase can readily be interpreted as modifying either the entire complex NP or only the first noun. This ambiguity is not resolved by syntactic information, although it can be influenced by pragmatic information and prosodic information. (2) is given in Korean Hangul orthography, followed by a phonetic transcription, a word-by-word gloss, and the English translation. The diacritic '*' is used in transcriptions throughout this paper to indicate tense or fortis stops.

(2) 현명한   아기의   아빠
 hjənmjənhan akiɰi   ap*a
 wise   baby-Gen   daddy
 'the [wise baby]'s daddy' *or*
 'the wise [baby's daddy]'

We expected that listeners who encountered constructions such as (2) would show an initial syntactic preference for the structure associated with N1 modification. This expectation is consistent with the classic 'Garden Path' depth-first model of sentence comprehension, in which a single structure is built as quickly as possible in all cases of structural ambiguity (e.g. Frazier 1987), with minimal revisions when necessary (Frazier 1990, Frazier and Clifton 1998). It also fits the predictions of Constraint-Based models (e.g. MacDonald, Pearlmutter, and Seidenberg 1994), under the assumption that N1 modification is more frequent in such constructions than N2 modification. We believe this is a reasonable assumption, given that speakers have another, unambiguous option for producing sentences with N2 modification: They can re-order the items as N1-Adj-N2. Frazier and Clifton (1996) have proposed that non-primary phrases such as our adjectives are associated less rapidly and less deterministically into the partial phrase structure, with influence from non-structural information. Under the assumption that there is a bias to associate a non-primary phrase which precedes the material it modifies with the first site encountered by the parser (cf. Frazier and Clifton 1996, Chapters 3 and 5), an initial preference for the N1-modification structure is also consistent with their proposal. Further, previous psycholinguistic work on Japanese has suggested an initial N1-modification preference for similar structures (Inoue and Fodor 1995, Kamide and Mitchell 1997).

We constructed two sets of materials, a Main set and a Control set, which were always compatible, initially, with this assumed syntactic preference for the N1-modification structure. These materials were employed in both the production study (which used complete sentences) and in the comprehension study (which used only the initial portion of each sentence). Because we know of no research on Korean that has tested the assumed N1 bias, the Control set was designed to test the strength of this potential syntactic bias in sentence comprehension (see Section 3.2). The differences between the Main and Control sets are not relevant for the central research questions in the production study.

Both the Main set and the Control set contained two lexically distinct versions for each item (when realized as a full sentence), an N1-bias version and an N2-bias version. In the Main set, modification of N2 by the adjective was implausible in the N1-bias version. In the N2-bias version, modification of N2 by the adjective was far more plausible than N1 modification. The adjective and N1 never varied across versions for the Main set; only N2 changed. A sample item is given in (3).

(3) Example of a Main Item
    a. ...hjənmjəŋhan akiɯi   akki...   N1-bias
       ...wise   baby's   musical instrument...

    b. ...hjənmjəŋhan akiɯi   ap*a...   N2-bias
       ...wise   baby's   daddy...

The two N2 words were matched for number of syllables, within each item, to avoid any effects of syllable count on the accentual phrasing pattern produced. Because these items would later be used in our comprehension study as fragments truncated between N1 and N2, the initial segments of the N2 pairs were also matched as closely as was practicable for manner and place of articulation, to minimize coarticulation differences between the two conditions. A full list of the experimental items used in the production and comprehension studies is given in the Appendix.

In the Control set, N2 modification was possible in the N1-bias version, although less likely than N1 modification. In the N2-bias version, modification of N2 by the adjective was far more plausible than N1 modification, as in the Main set. The Control items were created by varying N1 between versions while keeping the adjective and N2 constant. The number of syllables in N1 was matched, within items, for the two conditions. A sample item is given in (4).

(4) Example of a Control Item
    a. ...seljəntwen motelɯi   titʃainə...   N1-bias
       ...stylish   model's   designer...

    b. ...seljəntwen kjohwaŋɯi titʃainə...   N2-bias
       ...stylish   Pope's   designer...

These biases were tested with a written questionnaire study. Sixteen subjects, all native speakers of Korean from the UCLA community, participated in the experiment. Subjects read full sentences containing the Adj-N1-N2 strings, presented in standard Korean orthography. For each sentence, the subject rated both the plausibility of interpreting the adjective as modifying N1 and the plausibility of it modifying N2, on a scale which ranged from 1 (very unnatural) to 5 (very natural). Each subject rated both lexical versions of each item. Subjects rated 33 Main items and 17 Control items. From these, the 24 Main and 12 Control items that best fit the intended pragmatic biases were selected. The mean ratings for the selected items are given in (5).

(5) Mean ratings of the naturalness of the adjective modifying N1/N2
   Main Set: N1-Bias: N1: 4.27, N2: 1.73
                N2-Bias: N1: 2.45, N2: 4.38

   Control Set: N1-Bias: N1: 3.58, N2: 3.42[2]
                N2-Bias: N1: 2.03, N2: 4.44

Phrases like the ones in (3) and (4) can be grammatically produced with multiple prosodic patterns, as described in Section 2. We were particularly interested in the four patterns indicated in (6).[3] The first pattern, in (6a), is the default prosodic pattern. As noted above, this pattern appears to be quite frequent in Korean, particularly in wide focus ('out of the blue') situations. It commonly occurs with both the interpretation in which the adjective modifies only the first noun and the interpretation in which the adjective modifies the entire complex NP. Patterns (6b) and (6c) are used for purposeful disambiguations toward N1 modification and complex-NP (or N2) modification, respectively; they reflect the 'semantic closeness' factor described in Section 2. Pattern (6d) occurs when contrastive focus is placed on the adjective, for either interpretation, following Korean's general pattern of dephrasing after a focused constituent that was described above. Henceforth, we will refer to the pattern in (6a) as the default prosody, to the patterns in (6b) and (6c) as N1-modification prosody and N2-modification prosody, respectively, and to the pattern in (6d) as Adj-focus prosody.

(6) a. (hjənmjəŋhan)$_{APh}$ (akiɥi)$_{APh}$ (ap*a)$_{APh}$ **Default Prosody**
       (wise)$_{APh}$ (baby's)$_{APh}$ (daddy)$_{APh}$ (Adj)$_{APh}$ (N1)$_{APh}$ (N2)$_{APh}$

    b. (hjənmjəŋhan akiɥi)$_{APh}$ (ap*a)$_{APh}$ **N1-mod. Prosody**
       (wise baby's)$_{APh}$ (daddy)$_{APh}$ (Adj N1)$_{APh}$ (N2)$_{APh}$

    c. (hjənmjəŋhan)$_{APh}$ (akiɥi ap*a)$_{APh}$ **N2-mod. Prosody**
       (wise)$_{APh}$ (baby's daddy)$_{APh}$ (Adj)$_{APh}$ (N1 N2)$_{APh}$

    d. (hjənmjəŋhan akiɥi ap*a)$_{APh}$ **Adj-focus Prosody**
       (wise baby's daddy)$_{APh}$ (Adj N1 N2)$_{APh}$

---

[2] The N1-Bias condition shows a weaker lexical bias than the N2-Bias condition. As discussed below, this allows a stronger test of whether there is an initial bias for the N1-modification structure.

[3] Other prosodic patterns which are possible for this string include productions with an intonation phrase boundary at one or more of the accentual phrase boundary positions and productions in which the phonetic indications for a prosodic boundary are ambiguous.

3.1 Production Study

3.1.1 Introduction

The production experiment was designed to confirm that native speakers of Korean would reliably produce the four prosodic structures of interest (see (6) above) under the expected conditions. The production study also allowed us to collect a set of utterances produced by naïve speakers for use in the comprehension study. The differences between Main and Control items will not be relevant for the brief discussion of the production study presented here, so the distinction will not be noted below.[4]

3.1.2 Methods

The experimental items were produced under three sets of instructions, which were intended to elicit productions appropriate for three different discourse situations. Four native speakers of Seoul Korean first produced the sentences in Set 1, followed in order by Sets 2 and 3.

Set 1 was designed to elicit the default prosody. For this set, subjects were simply instructed to read a list of printed sentences out loud in a natural manner. To discourage them from inserting intonation phrase boundaries into the sentences, they were told to utter each sentence in one breath group, without pausing between words. With Set 2, subjects were instructed to read the sentences with contrastive focus on the adjective. The adjective was underlined and in boldface, and the subject was instructed to imagine that it contrasted with another adjective. With Set 3, subjects were informed of the ambiguity and instructed to prosodically disambiguate the sentences. As with Set 1, they were told to produce each sentence in one breath group, without pausing between words, to discourage them from inserting intonation phrase boundaries into the sentences.

Utterances were digitized at 16 kHz and $F_\emptyset$ tracks of each utterance were created using Entropic's xwaves (v. 5.3). The phrasing of each utterance was determined on the basis of the pitch contour, amplitude, and segment realizations in critical regions and the perception of one of the authors (Jun). For example, the existence of an APh boundary was confirmed by high $F_\emptyset$ at the end of a phonological word followed by low $F_\emptyset$ when the initial segment of the next word was not aspirated nor tensed.

---

[4] The Main and Control sets have the same syntactic structure, and so were expected to elicit the same range of prosodic structures in the production study. In the comprehension study, the Control items will be used to test the syntactic bias of the ambiguous structure, and the Main items will be used to test for effects of prosodic structure.

3.1.3 Results

The results largely confirmed our expectations. For the sentences in Set 1, over 90% of the target noun phrases were produced with the default prosody, for both N1- and N2-bias sentences. For Sets 2 and 3, the expected phrasing pattern was always the most frequent pattern, although other patterns, particularly the default phrasing pattern, were also common. The distribution of phrasing patterns across the three sets can be seen in Figures 3 through 6. In Figures 5 and 6, "Other" phrasing patterns include productions with intonation phrase boundaries and productions with prosodic boundaries that were ambiguous between levels of phrasing.

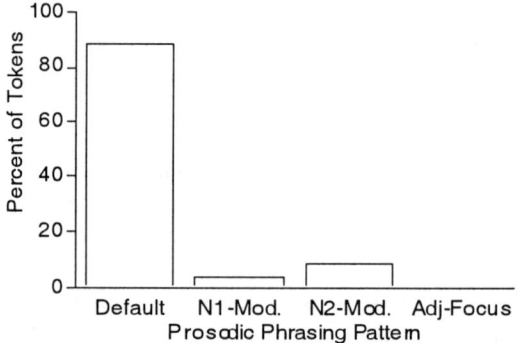

Figure 3. Percentage of each phrasing pattern for Set 1: Default reading style

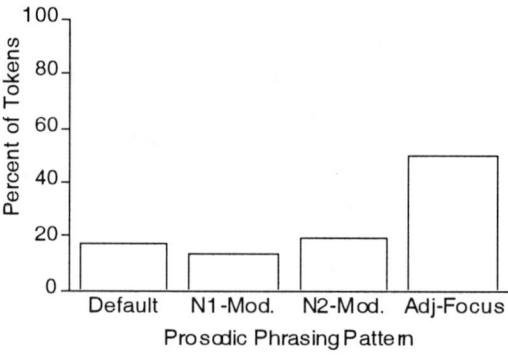

Figure 4. Percentage of each phrasing pattern for Set 2: Adjective focus

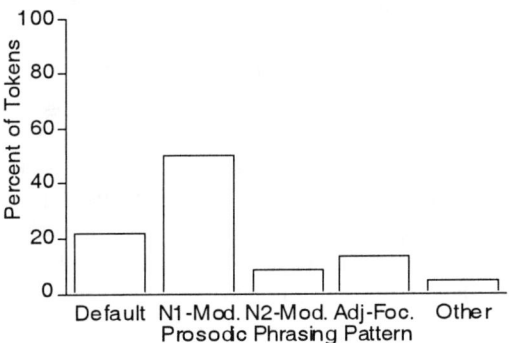

Figure 5. Percentage of each phrasing pattern for Set 3: Intentional disambiguation, N1-modification bias sentences

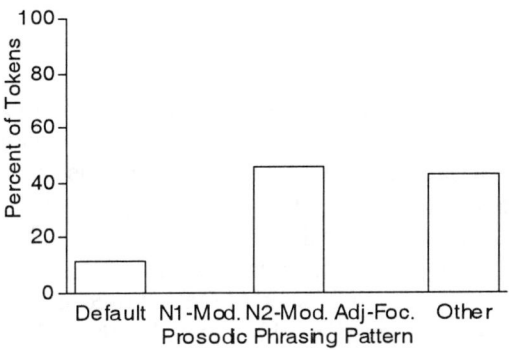

Figure 6. Percentage of each phrasing pattern for Set 3: Intentional disambiguation, N2-modification bias sentences[5]

Thus, when speakers read the sentences without being told to disambiguate or use a particular focal structure, they generally uttered each

---

[5] A substantial majority of the "Other" phrasing patterns for these items employed a prosodic structure that somehow indicated a stronger prosodic boundary between the adjective and N1 than between N1 and N2. However, because these did not follow the specific pattern of accentual phrasing that we were interested in, we have coded them separately.

phonological word in a separate accentual phrase, using the default pattern.[6] When speakers were told to contrastively focus the adjective, they tended to produce the adjective, N1, and N2 together in a single prosodic phrase, following the Adj-focus pattern. When speakers were instructed to prosodically disambiguate the sentences, they tended to combine the adjective and N1 into a single accentual phrase for items pragmatically biased toward N1 modification, and tended to combine N1 and N2 into a single accentual phrase for items pragmatically biased toward N2 modification.

The production study succeeded in eliciting the four prosodic patterns that we planned to test in the comprehension study. It also supported our assumption that the default prosody and the Adj-focus prosody are both ambiguous, and that the other two prosodic patterns are disambiguating. As expected, we found that the default prosody and the Adj-focus prosody were produced for both interpretations of the Adj-N1-N2 string, and that each disambiguating prosody was produced most frequently with sentences in which the pragmatic bias matched the assumed prosodic bias. We now turn to discussion of the effects of these four prosodic structures on comprehension.

3.2 Comprehension Study

3.2.1 Introduction

The comprehension study tested a subset of the materials collected in the production study in a cross-modal naming task. This task was designed to test whether accentual phrasing could have early effects on the interpretation of the ambiguous phrase. Subjects heard auditory fragments that consisted of the beginning of the sentence through N1, and then named N2, as indicated in (7) and (8). It is at N2 that the phrase becomes pragmatically disambiguated. Thus, collecting naming times for N2 allowed us to evaluate whether accentual phrasing information which preceded the point of prag-

---

[6] The low percentages of N1-modification and N2-modification prosodies for Set 1 could be taken to suggest that prosodic disambiguation of syntax is somewhat uncommon in Korean. However, we believe that such a conclusion is premature. Studies of English have found differences in prosodic phrasing between spontaneous and read speech (Lehiste 1975, Brown, Currie, and Kenworthy 1980, French and Local 1986, Ayers 1994), so the frequency of the default pattern with sentences read aloud in the laboratory may not generalize well to spontaneous speech styles. In addition, studies of prosodic disambiguation of syntax have found higher percentages of disambiguation in quasi-spontaneous speech than in speech produced through oral reading tasks (Speer, Warren, Schafer, White, and Kneale 1999, Schafer, Speer, Warren, and White 2000). Thus, while we believe that it is safe to conclude that the default pattern is very common in Korean, we cannot predict on the basis of these results whether ambiguous prosodies are more common in Korean than disambiguating ones.

matic disambiguation could influence initial processing decisions for the ambiguous string. A finding that accentual phrasing affects cross-modal naming times for such structures would suggest that the processor makes use of accentual phrasing information incrementally, and early in the course of processing, as it is first building the appropriate syntactic and semantic structures.[7]

We tested both Main and Control items. The Control items provided an explicit test of the syntactic bias for N1-modification structures that we have assumed for these sentences. Two lexically distinct conditions were tested, as shown in (7). In the N1-bias condition, N1 modification was pragmatically supported; in the N2-bias condition, N2 modification was supported. All Control items were presented with default prosody; the prosody does not differ across conditions. We predicted that an N1-modification structure would be constructed initially for both versions, but that reanalysis would often occur for the condition pragmatically biased toward N2 modification. Naming times were therefore predicted to be shorter in the N1-biased condition than in the N2-biased condition. Note, however, that both conditions are ambiguous: N2-modification is possible, although unlikely, in the N1-bias condition, and N1-modification is possible, but again unlikely, in the N2-modification condition.

(7) Example of Control item, Comprehension Experiment

Auditory Fragment:	Visual Target:	Condition:
a. (seljəntwen) $_{APh}$ (moteluɥi) $_{APh}$ ...(stylish) $_{APh}$ (model's) $_{APh}$	디자이너도 DESIGNER-ALSO	N1-bias
b. (seljəntwen) $_{APh}$ (kjohwaŋuɥi) $_{APh}$ (stylish) $_{APh}$ (Pope's) $_{APh}$	디자이너도 DESIGNER-ALSO	N2-bias

For the Main items, we tested only the lexical version of each item that was pragmatically resolved toward N2 modification. These 24 sentences were tested under four prosodic conditions, using the four accentual phrasing patterns described above and repeated in (8). Recall that patterns (8b) and (8c) are disambiguating prosodies, but that patterns (8a) and (8d) are ambiguous. Note that the lexical content of the auditory fragment and the visual target never varies across conditions for Main items. Only the prosody differs across conditions.

---

[7] Note that alternative tasks such as paraphrase selection require that all of the complex NP be presented, and thus are less useful in assessing whether there are early and incremental effects of prosody on parsing.

(8) Example of Main item, Comprehension Experiment

Auditory Fragment:	Visual Target:	Condition:
a. ...(hjənmjəŋhan) $_{APh}$ (akiɯi) $_{APh}$ ...(wise) $_{APh}$ (baby's) $_{APh}$	아빠 DADDY	Default Prosody
b. ...(hjənmjəŋhan akiɯi) $_{APh}$ ...(wise baby's) $_{APh}$	아빠 DADDY	N1-mod. Pros.
c. ...(hjənmjəŋhan) $_{APh}$ (akiɯi ...(wise) $_{APh}$ (baby's	아빠 DADDY	N2-mod. Pros.
d. ...(hjənmjəŋhan akiɯi ...(wise baby's	아빠 DADDY	Adj-focus Pros.

We predicted that, first, accentual phrasing would be salient enough to listeners to affect the processing of the ambiguous structure. Assuming that it would be, there are several tenable hypotheses about how prosodic phrasing might affect processing decisions, and thus how these four phrasing patterns should affect interpretation. We briefly describe three possibilities. In all cases, we assume that there is the initial syntactic preference for N1 modification discussed above, possibly modulated by the accentual phrasing, and reanalysis (if necessary) at the point that the disambiguating pragmatic information in N2 is interpreted.

One reasonable hypothesis is that disambiguating prosody should strongly support the relevant interpretation, but ambiguous prosody should have little effect on the parsing process (Warren, Grabe, and Nolan 1995, Kjelgaard and Speer 1999). This hypothesis can be viewed as predicting a relationship between the whole contour (for the critical region) and the syntactic and semantic structures that are built. For our materials, this would predict that the syntactic N1 bias would be followed initially for the default prosody, Adj-focus prosody, and N1-modification prosody, but the N2-modification prosody would block the otherwise preferred N1-modification structure. Thus, no reanalysis would be required for the N2-modification prosody, and naming times for it should be quite short. Reanalysis would be required in the remaining conditions, and would presumably be harder for the N1-modification prosody, in which the prosodic information conflicts with the pragmatic information. Naming times for the two ambiguous prosody conditions would thus be similar to each other, but longer than for the N2-modification prosody and shorter than for the N1-modification prosody. These predictions are summarized in (10), along with the predictions of the two other hypotheses we consider.

A second possibility is that only the "local" prosodic boundary matters: Processing is influenced only by prosodic information that occurs at the point where the parser must choose between attachment sites (for further discussion of this idea, and a review of its occurrence in the psycholinguistic literature, see Schafer (1997)). For our study, the critical processing point is when the parser encounters N2. Thus, the presence of an accentual phrase boundary between N1 and N2 would be predicted to support N1 modification, and the absence of an accentual phrase boundary in that position would support N2 modification, but no prosodic information that occurs earlier in the sentence would be relevant to the ambiguity resolution. Naming times would therefore be predicted to be similar for the two prosodies which contain an APh boundary between N1 and N2 and similar for the two prosodies which lack that boundary. They would also be expected to be longer in the former two prosodies, in which the prosody conflicts with the pragmatic information, than in the latter two prosodies, in which the prosodic and pragmatic information both support the same interpretation.

We predicted a third possibility: Prosodic information would have an incremental effect on interpretation. Specifically, we predicted that Korean accentual phrases would cause the effects proposed by Schafer (1997) for English intermediate phrases, since the two kinds of phrases are found at the same level of the prosodic hierarchy (i.e. above the phonological word but below the intonation phrase level). Schafer's hypothesis, adapted for Korean accentual phrases, is given in (9).[8]

(9) Prosodic Visibility (adapted from Schafer (1997))
 a. The accentual phrasing of an utterance determines the *visibility* of syntactic nodes.

 b. Nodes projected by material within the accentual phrase currently being processed are more visible than nodes associated with material outside of that accentual phrase; visibility is gradient across multiple accentual phrases.

 c. In first analysis and reanalysis, attachment to a node with high visibility is less costly in terms of processing/attentional resources than attachment to a node with lower visibility.

---

[8] Prosodic Visibility is closely related to Frazier and Clifton's more general Visibility Hypothesis (Frazier and Clifton, 1998). However, because Prosodic Visibility claims that visibility is graded across prosodic phrases, it makes slightly different predictions from their proposal.

According to the Prosodic Visibility hypothesis, the presence of an accentual phrase boundary between the adjective and N1 should impede construction of the initially preferred N1-modification structure, since the adjective and all nodes it has projected would be less visible to the parser at the point that it is processing N1. Assuming a depth-first processor, a structure which supports N1 modification would nevertheless be constructed at N1 for all four prosodies, but this syntactic structure should be built more quickly, and thus undergo further interpretive processing, when no APh boundary intervenes between the adjective and N1 than when one is present. Similarly, the presence of an APh boundary between N1 and N2 should impede construction of the N2-modification structure (or reanalysis to this structure), since N1 and all nodes it has projected would be less visible at the point that N2 is being processed when that boundary is present than when it is not.

The N1-modification prosody and the Adj-focus prosody both lack an APh boundary between the adjective and N1. Therefore, both of them should support at least partial semantic interpretation with N1 modification before the pragmatic information in N2 is interpreted. Following the Minimal Revisions principle (Frazier 1990, Frazier and Clifton 1998), when N2 is first encountered and identified as a noun, it should initially be integrated into the N1-modification structure. Reanalysis should be initiated for both prosodies when N2 is interpreted. This reanalysis should be easier with Adj-focus prosody than with N1-modification prosody, because the former has no APh boundary between N1 and N2 while the latter contains one. Naming times for N2 should thus be longer for the N1-modification prosody than for the Adj-focus prosody.

For the remaining two contours, the processor should be less strongly committed to N1 modification at the point it encounters N2, because the presence of the early APh boundary has decreased the likelihood of semantic interpretation of the initial N1-modification structure. When N2 is received in the N2-modification prosody condition, the absence of an APh boundary between N1 and N2 should allow relatively easy reanalysis, because of the high visibility of N1. The N2-modification condition should thus show the shortest naming times. Reanalysis should be harder with default prosody than with N2-modification prosody, because of the additional APh boundary in the default contour between N1 and N2. However, reanalysis should be easier with the default prosody than with the Adj-focus prosody, because the presence of the early APh boundary in the default conditions should mean that less interpretive processing of the ultimately incorrect structure will have taken place with the default prosody than with the Adj-focus prosody. To summarize, the N2-modification prosody should show the shortest naming times, followed in order by the default prosody, the Adj-focus prosody, and the N1-modification prosody.

(10) Summary of Predictions
    Hypothesis: Pattern of Naming Times:
    Hyp 1: Whole contour effects   N2-mod < Def, Adj-foc < N1-mod
    Hyp 2: Local boundary effects   N2-mod, Adj-foc < Def, N1-mod
    Hyp 3: Prosodic Visibility   N2-mod < Def < Adj-foc < N1-mod

As can be seen in the summary in (10), all three hypotheses predict a difference in naming times for the two disambiguating prosodies. The hypotheses differ in their predictions for the ambiguous prosodies.

3.2.2 Methods

Productions from one of the four speakers who participated in the production experiment were selected for use in the comprehension experiment, and the phrasing of each token was confirmed to match the planned prosodic condition.[9] The 24 Main items and 12 Control items were mixed with an additional 24 filler sentences. Half of the fillers contained a prenominal adjective followed by a simplex NP; half contained an adjective followed by a complex NP. In all cases, the materials were pragmatically biased toward N1 modification (if a choice existed). Thus, the material set as a whole contained equal numbers of items pragmatically biased for N1 modification and items pragmatically biased for N2 modification. Each experimental sentence was truncated with a digital waveform editor just before the second noun in the ambiguous string. The truncation point in the filler sentences varied across a range of structural points, and included points that were early, medial, and late in the original sentence.

The four prosodic conditions for each Main item and the two lexical conditions for each Control item were distributed across four experimental lists, following a Latin-square design. These lists were then presented to thirty-six native speakers of Seoul Korean from the UCLA community. None of the subjects had previously participated in the production experiment or the pretest of the materials. All could comprehend, speak, and read Korean fluently, and all had lived in the U.S. for at most 10 years.

Subjects were tested individually in a sound-attenuated booth equipped with a computer monitor, headphones, a hand-held microphone, and a

---

[9] A small number of the items produced by this speaker in the production study failed to meet our segmental and prosodic criteria. These items were re-recorded by the speaker for the comprehension experiment, following a similar procedure to the one used in the production experiment.

CMU button box with a voice-operated relay for millisecond timing. Subjects were seated next to an experimenter and in front of the computer monitor. On each trial, there was a visual prompt, and then subjects heard a sentence fragment over the headphones. Immediately following the offset of the auditory stimulus, a word appeared on the monitor in standard Korean orthography. Subjects named the visual target out loud as quickly as possible and then completed the sentence, using the visual target as the first word in the completion. For the Main and Control set items, the visual target was N2. For the filler items, the visual target was whatever word had originally occurred next in the full sentence; a range of syntactic categories were instantiated in these targets. Naming times appeared on the monitor after each response. If a subject did not name the visual target within 2000 ms, a reminder to respond quickly appeared instead of the response time.

The accuracy of the naming response was noted by the experimenter. Trials in which the subject failed to name the correct word, mispronounced the word, or failed to set off the voice relay at the beginning of the word were noted and subsequently excluded from analysis. The fragment completions were recorded in writing by the experimenter and the entire session was recorded onto audiotape. Completions which indicated that the subject had not understood the sentence fragment were noted and excluded from analysis.

Following the complete set of experimental naming trials, subjects completed a second block of control naming trials. These trials consisted of a neutral carrier phrase followed by a visual target. Each visual target from the experimental set (for both Main and Control items) was presented three times in a pseudorandomized order. These trials served to measure lexical effects on naming times, such as effects of word frequency, orthography, or the initial phonetic segment. Individual reaction times for the experimental items were corrected for lexical variability by subtracting the difference between the mean of the three neutral context tokens for each item and the grand mean of the neutral-context trials from each item for each subject.

3.2.3 Results

The results are shown in Figures 7 and 8. As predicted, the Control items exhibited shorter naming times in the N1-bias condition than the N2-bias condition. This result was significant by subjects ($F1(1,35) = 4.2$, $p < .05$), although not by items ($F2(1,10) = 2.4$, $p = .15$).[10] The pattern of naming times supports the prediction that there was an initial syntactic preference for the N1 modification structure. Presumably, this preference could be

---

[10] One item was eliminated from the analysis because of experimenter error in truncating the stimuli.

maintained for the N1-bias condition, but could not always be maintained for the N2-bias condition, resulting in reanalysis and longer naming times.[11]

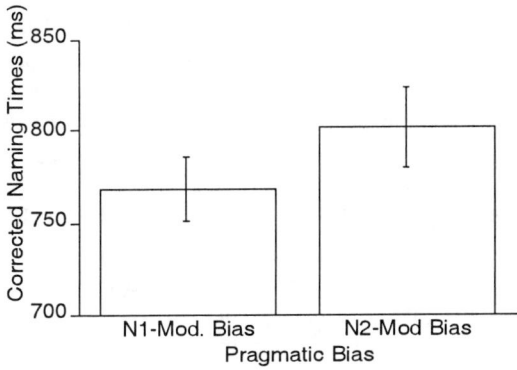

Figure 7. Corrected naming times for Control items

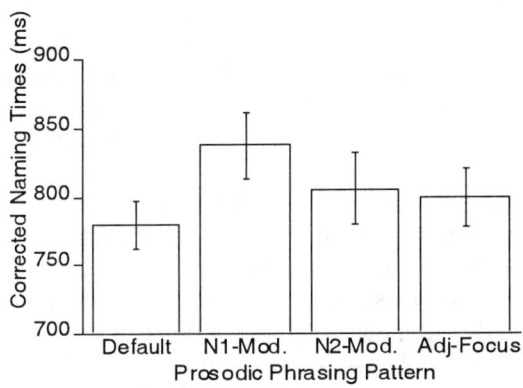

Figure 8: Corrected naming times for Main items

---

[11] Note that the pattern of results does not follow from an assumption that naming times would be longer for the condition in which the two interpretations were more equally balanced in their pragmatic bias. According to the results of the written questionnaire, the difference in bias for the Control items between the two interpretations was actually stronger in the N2-bias condition (2.03 vs. 4.44) than in the N1-bias condition (3.58 vs. 3.42).

For the Main items, as predicted by two of the three prosodic hypotheses, naming times were significantly longer for the N1-modification prosody, which conflicted with the ultimate interpretation of the ambiguous phrase, than for the default prosody ($F1(1,35) = 7.9$, $p < .01$; $F2(1,23) = 4.2$, $p < .05$). This is consistent with the first hypothesis, which posits differences between ambiguous and disambiguating contours. It is also consistent with the Prosodic Visibility hypothesis, which posits an incremental effect from each prosodic boundary in the string. However, the difference between the default and N1-modification conditions disconfirms the second hypothesis, which predicted that processing would be affected only by a prosodic cue which occurred at the point of a clear syntactic attachment ambiguity. Thus, these data support the claim of Schafer (1997) that a complete prosodic representation is constructed during the early stages of sentence comprehension, and that all information encoded in this structure is available to influence subsequent processing decisions.

Contrary to the predictions of all three hypotheses, naming times for the remaining two conditions were intermediate between the times for the N1-modification and default prosodies, and not significantly different from either of them. Most strikingly, naming times were not significantly different for the two disambiguating conditions, although they did show a trend in the predicted direction. In addition, the disambiguating N2-modification prosody condition did not show significantly shorter naming times than the ambiguous default and Adj-focus prosody conditions, and the default condition was numerically shorter than the N2-modification condition. This suggests that processing was just as easy with ambiguous prosody as with disambiguating prosody.

The pattern of relatively short naming times for the default prosody condition cannot be attributed to an effect of additional processing time due to its additional APh boundaries. The duration of the adjective was not significantly different across prosodic conditions. The duration of N1 was significantly longer in the N2-modification condition than in the other three conditions, which did not differ significantly from each other. Thus, the duration of the Adj-N1 region was not longer in the default condition than in other conditions, nor was the region shorter in the N2-modification condition than in the other conditions. Therefore, the unexpectedly long naming times for the N2-modification condition relative to the times for the default and Adj-focus conditions cannot be explained by a lack of sufficient processing time in the critical region. However, it is conceivable that the longer duration N1 for the N2-modification condition allowed further time for interpretation of the ultimately incorrect N1-modification structure. If so, this could lead to longer reanalysis times than expected for this condition.

3.2.4 Discussion

The results confirm that the subtle acoustic information which demarcates accentual phrase boundaries in Korean was salient enough to be exploited by listeners during sentence comprehension. In this respect the Korean results are similar to results for English that show effects of acoustically subtle intermediate phrase boundaries on comprehension. The Korean results are also similar to English results in showing that the processor is sensitive not just to prosodic information that occurs at a syntactic choice point, but to the larger contour. The one significant difference that emerged in the Main items was between conditions that were identical at the point that a choice had to be made between attachment sites: Both the default condition and the N1-modification condition contain an APh boundary between N1 and N2. However, the overall pattern of naming times failed to show contrasts predicted by each of the hypotheses we considered, and was very different from what might be expected on the basis of English results.

Prosodic experiments on English have shown that a sentence with an ambiguous prosodic structure can be processed as easily as a sentence with a disambiguating prosodic structure when an ambiguous phrase is resolved to what is arguably the preferred syntactic structure (Slowiaczek 1981, Speer, Kjelgaard, and Dobroth 1996, Kjelgaard and Speer 1999). However, these studies have found that when an ambiguity is resolved toward an initially dispreferred syntactic structure, as in our Main items, a prosodic contour that is associated with the ultimately correct syntactic structure results in significantly faster processing than an ambiguous contour. In other words, a 'cooperating' prosody might not facilitate processing relative to an ambiguous prosody for the preferred syntactic structure, but it will facilitate the processing of a dispreferred syntactic structure. We believe several factors may account for why our N2-modification prosody did not appear to facilitate processing of the syntactically dispreferred N2-modification structure.

First, the nature of the default prosody in Korean may have significantly facilitated processing in the default prosody condition at the lexical level. Recall that the default prosody places each phonological word into a separate accentual phrase. This may have made the identification of phonological word boundaries, and thus lexical access, significantly easier in the default condition than in the other three conditions. We hope to explore this possibility further in future research.

Second, the Korean structure we tested differs from the English cases that have been studied in the relative timing of key syntactic and prosodic information. In studies of English, the crucial disambiguating prosodic information has been the presence of a prosodic boundary preceding an ambiguously attached phrase, such as an NP that could be the direct object of a subordinate clause or the subject of a matrix clause. Arguably, the presence of the prosodic boundary could prevent or delay the parser from building the otherwise preferred attachment during the first stage of syntactic analysis and, crucially, no structural revisions were required for material which preceded the disambiguating boundary.

In the Korean case, it is the absence of an APh boundary between N1 and N2 which distinguishes the N2-modification contour from the default contour. However, by the time the parser reaches this point, it has presumably already attached N1 to the partial phrase structure.[12] Unlike the cases tested in English, where no other attachments must be modified to incorporate the material which follows the disambiguating prosodic break, the Korean case requires some revision of the previously built structure to support the N2-modification interpretation. N1 must be lowered, so a new node can be inserted to attach N1 and N2, and any semantic interpretation of the adjective-N1 relation must be undone. Thus, in Korean, the most critical prosodic information in the N2-modification contour arguably arrives too late to influence all of the initial attachment decisions, and is limited to having effects on semantic interpretation and reanalysis. It is therefore not surprising that the disambiguating contour might show relatively weak effects in Korean.[13]

Finally, although what we have been calling the N2-modification prosody is indeed the prosodic structure that speakers used to indicate N2-modification in our production study, it is possible that this is not the parser's preferred interpretation of this prosodic structure. Recall from Section 2 that Korean marks focus by grouping the words which follow a contrastively focused word into an accentual phrase that begins with the focused word. Thus, the N2-modification prosody may have occasionally been interpreted as indicating contrastive focus on N1 instead of the N2-modification structure. This strikes us as a somewhat unlikely interpretation given that there were no other indications of focus on N1, such as an expanded pitch range or greater amplitude (Jun and Oh 1996, Jun and Lee 1998), but it is not one that we can currently rule out.

---

[12] Note that Prosodic Visibility predicts that this attachment is delayed for the default prosody and N2-modification prosody relative to contours without a boundary between the adjective and N1, but the attachment has not been completely prevented.

[13] We assume that it is easy for the processor to recover from the short-duration misanalysis that we are postulating for this prosodic-syntactic structure. We also believe that this structure may have a relatively low frequency in Korean, either because speakers tend to use a stronger prosodic boundary between the adjective and the complex NP (see Figure 6 above) or because they tend to adopt an N1-Adj-N2 word order for N2 modification.

More generally, we cannot say with certainty which interpretation of the ambiguous structure was ultimately chosen for any item or condition. Although the cross-modal naming task we employed was useful in indicating early effects of accentual phrasing, it has limitations: It does not directly show whether the adjective was taken to modify N1 or N2. Thus, it is possible that the percentage of items that were reanalyzed varied across conditions. For example, the presence of focus on the adjective may have licensed the less plausible N1-modification interpretation in the Adj-focus condition, and an interpretation of the N2-modification prosody as an indication of focus on N1 could conceivably have led to more interpretations of the adjective modifying N1 (cf. Schafer, Carter, Clifton, & Frazier, 1996). We are presently conducting further research on these structures to address this issue.

Each of these possible explanations for why the N2-modification prosody did not appear to facilitate processing rests on differences in the linguistic structures of Korean and English. We thus conclude that prosodic phrasing likely has, at an abstract level, very similar effects on sentence comprehension across languages, but that the specific effects of prosody on the interpretation of particular structures must be interpreted with respect to the grammatical patterns of the language. Such a conclusion challenges psycholinguistic models of prosody which have effectively treated prosodic boundaries as cues from outside of the grammatical system (e.g. Marcus & Hindle, 1990). It is unsurprising, though, from a linguistic perspective that predicts that the processor is sensitive to all grammatical structure, including phonetic and phonological structure, and to the relationships between phonological structure and other levels of linguistic structure.

4 Conclusion

We have presented findings on how accentual phrasing is used during sentence production and comprehension in Korean. Our production study showed that Korean speakers use distinct patterns of accentual phrasing in a systematic fashion, at least for sentences read aloud in a laboratory setting. We found that in wide focus, "out of the blue" situations, speakers show a very strong tendency to produce each phonological word in a separate accentual phrase, while in contrastive focus situations speakers tend to produce multiple phonological words in a single accentual phrase. In addition, speakers can disambiguate syntactically or semantically ambiguous structures by grouping related phrases into a single accentual phrase. These findings are consistent with previous reports of the Korean prosodic structures produced in reading tasks. Further work remains, though, to determine whether the patterns found in reading tasks generalize well to spontaneous speech.

We also found that differences in the accentual phrasing pattern of a sentence affect listener's comprehension of the sentence. This result provides further evidence that subtle phonetic differences can ultimately influence higher-level linguistic processing. Intriguingly, we discovered that, at least at a superficial level, the pattern of prosodic effects on sentence comprehension differs for Korean and English. Nevertheless, we believe these differences stem from grammatical contrasts between the two languages, and not from highly variable use of prosodic information by the processing system across languages.

The experiments presented here are in keeping with an ever-increasing set of studies which demonstrate prosodic influences on sentence comprehension. Yet they also highlight how little we currently know about how prosody's effects should be modeled. Most of the experimental results in the literature are consistent with multiple hypotheses of how the processor treats prosodic information. In addition, the grammatical constraints on prosody, and particularly those governing the relationships between prosodic structure and syntactic, semantic, and discourse structure, are far from being fully understood. It is our hope that continued cross-linguistic psycholinguistic research on prosody will be particularly helpful in specifying more precisely how and when the processor makes use of critical prosodic, syntactic, and semantic information. We also hope that continued work on the connections between production patterns and comprehension patterns will help illuminate such matters as how default contours or frequent contours might have significant effects on comprehension even when the contours do not disambiguate syntactic or semantic structures.

References

Ayers, G. 1994. Discourse Functions of Pitch Range in Spontaneous and Read Speech. *Ohio State University Working Papers in Linguistics* 44, 1-49.

Beckman, M. 1995. On Blending and the Mora: Comments on Kubozono. *Papers in Laboratory Phonology* IV, eds. B. Connell & A. Arvaniti, 157-167. Cambridge: Cambridge University Press..

Beckman, M. & J. Pierrehumbert. 1986. Intonational Structure in Japanese and English. *Phonology Yearbook* 3, 255-309.

Brown, G., K.L. Currie, & J. Kenworthy. 1980. *Questions of Intonation*. London: Croom Helm.

Cho, T. & P. Keating. 1999. Articulatory and Acoustic Studies of Domain-initial Strengthening in Korean. To appear in *Journal of Phonetics*.

Frazier, L. 1987. Sentence Processing: A Tutorial Review. *Attention and Performance*, ed. M. Coltheart, 559-586. Hillsdale, NJ: Lawrence Erlbaum.
Frazier, L. 1990. Identifying Structure under X0. *Yearbook of Morphology* 3, eds. A. Jongman & A. Lahiri, 87-109.
Frazier, L. & C. Clifton. 1996. *Construal*. Cambridge, MA: MIT Press.
Frazier, L. & C. Clifton. 1998. Sentence Reanalysis, and Visibility. *Reanalysis in Sentence Processing*, eds. J.D. Fodor & F. Ferreir, 143-176. Dordrecht: Kluwer.
French, P. & J. Local. 1986. Prosodic Features and the Management of Interruptions. *Intonation in Discourse*, ed. C. Johns-Lewis, 157-180. San Diego, CA: College-Hill Press.
Halle, M. & K. Stevens. 1971. A Note on Laryngeal Features. *MIT Quarterly Progress Report* 101, 198-212.
Inoue, A. & J.D. Fodor. 1995. Information-paced Parsing of Japanese. *Japanese Sentence Processing*, eds. R. Mazuka & N. Nagai, 9-64. Hillsdale, NJ: Lawrence Erlbaum.
Jun, S.-A. 1993. The Phonetics and Phonology of Korean Prosody. Doctoral dissertation, The Ohio State University.
Jun, S.-A. 1994. The Domain of Laryngeal Feature Lenition Effects in Chonnam Korean. *OSU Working Papers in Linguistics* 43, 15-29. Department of Linguistics, The Ohio State University.
Jun, S.-A. 1995. Asymmetrical Prosodic Effects on the Laryngeal Gesture in Korea. *Papers in Laboratory Phonology* IV, eds. B. Connell and A. Arvaniti, 235-253. Cambridge: Cambridge University Press.
Jun, S.-A. 1996. Influence of Microprosody on Macroprosody: A Case of Phrase Initial Strengthening. *UCLA Working Papers in Phonetics* 92, 97-116.
Jun, S.-A. 1998. The Accentual Phrase in the Korean Prosodic Hierarchy. *Phonology* 15, 189-226.
Jun, S.-A. 1999. Prosodic Typology. To appear in *Prosodic Models and Transcription: Toward Prosodic Typology* (temporary title), ed. S.-A. Jun. Oxford: Oxford University Press.
Jun, S.-A. 2000. K-ToBI (Korean ToBI) Labelling Conventions, Version 3. *The Korean Journal of Speech Sciences* 7:143-169.
Jun, S.-A. & C. Fougeron. 2000. A Phonological Model of French Intonation. *Intonation: Analysis, Modelling and Technology*, ed. A. Botinis, 209-242. Dordrecht: Kluwer.
Jun, S.-A. & H.J. Lee. 1998. Phonetic and Phonological Markers of Contrastive Focus in Korean. *Proceedings of the 5th International Conference on Spoken Language Processing*, 1295-1298. Sydney, Australia, November 30 - December 4 1998.
Jun, S.-A. & M. Oh. 1996. A Prosodic Analysis of Three Types of Wh-phrases in Korean. *Language & Speech* 39:37-61.

Kamide, Y. & D.C. Mitchell. 1997. Relative Clause Attachment: Nondeterminism in Japanese Parsing. *Journal of Psycholinguistic Research* 26:247-254.

Keating, P., T. Cho, C. Fougeron, & C.-S. Hsu. 1999. Domain-initial Articulatory Strengthening in Four Languages. To appear in *Laboratory Phonology* VI. Cambridge: Cambridge University Press.

Kjelgaard, M.M. 1995. *The Role of Prosodic Structure in the Resolution of Phrase-Level and Lexical Syntactic Ambiguity.* Doctoral dissertation, Northeastern University.

Kjelgaard, M.M. & S.R. Speer. 1999. Prosodic Facilitation and Interference in the Resolution of Temporary Syntactic Closure Ambiguity. *Journal of Memory & Language* 40:153-194.

Kim, J.-J., S.-H. Lee, H.-J. Ko, Y.-J. Lee, S.-H. Kim, & J.-C. Lee. 1997. An Analysis of Some Prosodic Aspects of Korean Utterances Using K-ToBI Labeling System. *Proceedings of the International Conference on Speech Processing.* Seoul.

Korea Telecom Research & Development Group Report. 1996. *A Study of Korean Prosody and Discourse for the Development of Speech Synthesis/Recognition System in Korean.*

Ladd, D.R. 1996. *Intonational Phonology.* Cambridge: Cambridge University Press.

Lehiste, I. 1975. The Phonetic Structure of Paragraphs. *Structure and Process in Speech Perception,* eds. A. Cohen & S. G. Nooteboom, 195-203. Springer-Verlag.

MacDonald, M.C., N.J. Pearlmutter, & M.S. Seidenberg. 1994. The Lexical Nature of Syntactic Ambiguity Resolution. *Psychological Review* 101:676-703.

Marcus, M. & D. Hindle. 1990. Description Theory and Intonation Boundaries. *Cognitive Models of Speech Processing: Computational and Psycholinguistic Perspectives,* ed. G. Altmann, 483-531. Cambridge, MA: MIT Press.

Pierrehumbert, J. 1980. The Phonetics and Phonology of English Intonation. Doctoral dissertation, MIT.

Pierrehumbert, J.B. & M.E. Beckman. 1988. *Japanese Tone Structure.* Cambridge, MA: MIT Press.

Schafer, A.J. 1997. Prosodic Parsing: The Role of Prosody in Sentence Comprehension. Doctoral dissertation, University of Massachusetts.

Schafer, A.J., J. Carter, C. Clifton, & L. Frazier. 1996. Focus in Relative Clause Construal. *Language & Cognitive Processes* 11:135-163.

Schafer, A.J., S.R. Speer, P. Warren, & S.D. White. 2000. Intonational Disambiguation in Sentence Production and Comprehension. *Journal of Psycholinguistic Research* 29:169-182.

Slowiaczek, M. 1981. Prosodic Units as Language Processing Units. Doctoral dissertation, University of Massachusetts.

Speer, S.R., M.M. Kjelgaard, & K.M. Dobroth. 1996. The Influence of Prosodic Structure on the Resolution of Temporary Syntactic Closure Ambiguities. *Journal of Psycholinguistic Research* 25:247-268.

Speer, S.R., P. Warren, A.J. Schafer, S.D. White, & J. Kneale. 1999. Situational Constraints on the Prosodic Resolution of Syntactic Ambiguity. *Proceedings of the Fourteenth International Congress of Phonetic Sciences*, 1301-1304. San Francisco, 1-7 August 1999.

Venditti, J.J., S.-A. Jun, & M.E. Beckman. 1996. Prosodic Cues to Syntactic and Other Linguistic Structures in Japanese, Korean, and English. *Signal to Syntax: Bootstrapping from Speech to Grammar in Early Acquisition*, eds. J. Morgan & K. Demuth, 287-311. Mahwah, NJ: Lawrence Erlbaum.

Warren, P., E. Grabe, & F. Nolan. 1995. Prosody, Phonology and Parsing in Closure Ambiguities. *Language & Cognitive Processes* 10:457-486.

Ueyama, M. & S.-A. Jun. 1998. Focus Realization in Japanese English and Korean English Intonation. *Japanese and Korean Linguistics* 7, 629-645. Stanford: CSLI.

Ueyama, M. 1998. Speech Rate Effects on Phrasing in English and Japanese. Unpublished manuscript, University of California, Los Angeles.

Appendix: Experimental Materials

Full pairs of sentences, used in the production study, are shown. In the comprehension study all materials were truncated at the onset of N2. The two words in parentheses are the alternate N2s (for the Main set) and alternate N1s (for the Control set). The first of the pair in parentheses supports an N2-modification interpretation; the second supports an N1-modification interpretation. Each Korean sentence is given in its phonemic representation below, using the International Phonetic Alphabet, and followed by a word-by-word gloss and an English translation. Case markers and postpositions are indicated only for the parenthesized words.

Main Set:
1. ulinɨn hjənmjəŋhan akiɰi (ap*a-e/akki-e)   tehesə malhes*ta
   we wise   baby's   (daddy/muscial instrument)-about talked
   'We talked about wise baby's (daddy/musical instrument)'
2. ulinɨn kopaltwen pekkomɰi (milsupəm-i*l*/moktəlmi-l*i*l) poas*ta
   we reported   white bear's(smuggler/nape)-Acc   saw
   'We saw the reported white bear's (smuggler/nape)'
3. tʃʰepʰotwen tʃokʰaɰi   (jukwepəm-i/ilkitʃaŋ-i) sinmune nawas*ta
   arrested   niece's/nephew's (kidnapper/diary)-Nom newspaper appeared
   'The arrested niece/nephew's (kidnapper/diary) was in the newspaper.'

4. haksentilin kwijəun toŋmulwənɰi (tʰok*i-e/tʰoŋpʰuŋ-e) tehesə koŋpuhes*ta
   students cute zoo's   (rabbit/ventilation)-about about studied
   'The students studied about the cute zoo's (rabbit/ventilation)'.
5. nanin tʃʰaŋpekhan sonjəɰi (əlkul-i/usim-i) itʃʰjətʃitʃika anhas*ta
   I   pale   girl's (face/smile)-Nom forget   could not
   'I could not forget the pale girl's (face/smile)'.
6. isaŋhaketo kiltʃ*ukhan namhaksenɰi (tali-ka/tesa-ka) nune t*iəs*ta
   strangely longish   male-student's(leg/line)-Nom eye outstanded
   'Stangely, the longish student's (leg/line) came into (my) sight'.
7. jutʃʰaŋhan sitʃaŋɰi (tʰonjəkkwan-i/tʰutʃiljək-i) hwatʃeka t*weəs*ta
   fluent   mayor's (translator/clairvoyance)-Nom issue became
   'The fluent mayor's (translator/clairvoyance) became an issue.'
8. onil tʃənjəkenin palkin pamkəliɰi (kalotiŋ-i/kukjəŋk*un-i) manhi pojəs*ta
   today evening bright night-street's (lamp/spectator)-Nom many could see
   'Tonight, there were many bright night-street's (lamp/spectator).'
9. nanin jumaŋhan tʃənlatoɰi (totʃisa-ka/tankjəlljək-i) tʰikhi maime tinta
   I   promising Cholla-do's(governor/unity)-Nom especially mind entered
   'I especially like the promising Cholla-do's (governor/unity).'
10. ulinin posutʃəkin k*omaɰi (ap*a-lil/inhjəŋ-il) pokilohes*ta
    we conservative child's (daddy/doll)-Acc meet-decide
    'We decided to meet the conservative child's (daddy/doll).'
11. uli ənninin pʰjənanhan kəsilɰi (anlakɯitʃa-lil/juli inhjəŋ-il) tʃeil tʃoahanta
    my sister comfortable living room's (armchair/glass doll)-Acc best likes
    'My sister likes the comfortable living room's (armchair/glass doll) the best.'
12. sinkihaketo nals*inhan k*omaɰi (imo-ka/ilim-i) tʃənhjə natʃʰsəltʃika anhas*ta
    marvelously slim   child's (aunt/name)-Nom not at all unfamiliar was not
    'Marvelously, the slim child's (aunt/name) was nothing unfamiliar.'
13. sinkihaketo tʃalseŋkin kanhowənɰi (nampʰjən-i/nole-ka) tʃeil p*alli nawas*ta
    marvelously handsome nurse' (husband/song)-Nom the best fast came out
    'Marvelously, the handsome nurse's (husband/song) came out the fastest.'
14. salamtilin silmaŋhan pəminɰi (pumo-ka/punno-ka) ki sakənɰi wəninilako seŋkakhes*ta thought
    people disappointed criminal's (parents/rage)-Nom that event's cause
    'People thought that disappointed criminal's (parents/rage) was the cause of that event.'

15. manhɨn salamtɨli putʃilənhan tesauɨi (pʰatʃʰulpu-e/pʰjotʃʰantʃaŋ-e) tehesə
    many people diligent ambassador's (housekeeper/award)-about
    malɨlhakois*əs*ta
    were talking
    'Many people were talking about the diligent ambassador's (housekeeper/award).'
16. kɨ pjənhosanɨn sukamtwen toseŋuɨi (salintʃa-lɨl/satʃintʃʰəp-ɨl) tʃasehi
    that lawyer arrested yngr-brother's (assassin/album)-Acc attentively
    salpʰjəpoas*ta
    observed
    'That lawyer attentively observed the arrested younger brother's (assassin/album).'
17. ipən tʃumalenɨn pit*ulətʃin temunuɨi (munpʰe-lɨl/munuɨi-lɨl) pak*ul
    this weekend crooked front door's (nameplate/pattern)-Acc change
    kjehwekita
    plan to
    'This weekend, (I) plan to change the crooked front door's (nameplate/pattern).'
18. sənseŋnimk*esə kansahan waŋuɨi (nesi-etehe/neljək-etehe) tʃasehi
    teacher sly king's (eunuch/history)-about explicitly
    səlmjəŋhasjəs*ta
    explained
    'The teacher explained explicitly about the sly king's (eunuch/history).'
19. sənsentɨlɨn sutasɨlən kjotʃaŋuɨi (puin-ɨl/pimil-ɨl) tʃʰəim manas*ta/alas*ta
    teachers talkative principal's (wife/secret)-Acc first time met/knew
    'The teachers met/knew the talkative principal's (wife/secret) for the first time.'
20. salamtɨlɨn kopunkopunhan jəŋsauɨi (pisə-lɨl/pinso-lɨl) silhəhes*ta
    people obedient consul's (secretary/coffin room)-Acc dislike
    'People did not like the obedient consul's (secretary/coffin room).'
21. amuto sutʃupɨn kuninuɨi (t*al-ɨl/t*ɨs-ɨl) mollas*ta
    no one timid soldier's (daughter/will)-Acc knew not
    'No one knew the timid soldier's (daughter/will).'
22. əsekhan tʃʰinkuuɨi (usɨm-i/ilɨm-i) kaptʃaki seŋkaknas*ta
    awkward friend's (smile/name)-Nom suddenly remembered
    '(I) suddenly remembered the awkward friend's (smile/name).'
23. kotʃaŋnan kapaŋuɨi (tʃipʰə-lɨl/tʃoŋlju-lɨl) tʃʰatʃninte sikani k*we tɨləs*ta
    broken purse's (zipper/kind)-Acc find time quite spent
    'It took (me) quite a lot of time to fine the broken purse's (zipper/kind).'
24. salamtɨlɨn k*ank*anhan pəminuɨi (pʰansa-etehe/pʰankjəl-etehe) malhes*ta
    people tenacious criminal's (judge /judgment)-about talked
    'People talked about the tenacious criminal's (judge/judgment).'

Control Set:
1. salamtɨlɨn pantʃ*akinɨn (kʰapale-ɯi/neonpitʃʰ-ɯi) kanpʰanɨl tʃoahanɨn kət
   people   shiny   (cabaret's/neon light's)   sign-Acc   like
   katʰta
   seem
   'People seem to like the shiny (cabaret's/neon light's) sign.'
2. ipəneto pujuhan (kohaksen-ɯi/salipte-ɯi)   huwəntʃanɨn
   this time wealthy (self-supporting-student's/private univ.'s) sponsor
   palkhjətʃitʃi anas*ta
   revealed   not
   'This time too, the wealthy (self supporting student's/private univ.'s) sponsor was not revealed'
3. uli motunɨn saljəkipʰɨn (k*aŋpʰe-ɯi/sunjə-ɯi) kʰaunsɨllə-etehe
   we all   thoughtful   (gangster's/nun's)   counselor-about
   kuŋkɨmhehes*ta
   wondered
   'We all wandered about the thoughtful (gangster's/nun's) counselor.'
4. nanɨn uahan (pʰjəntʃiptʃaŋ-ɯi/pʰatʰipok-ɯi) puinkwa tehwalɨl nanuəs*ta
   I   elegant (editor's/party-dress's)   wife/lady-with conversation shared
   'I had a conversation with the elegant (editor's/party-dress's) wife/lady.'
5. nanɨn silljəkis*nɨn (toŋsen-ɯi/tʃipan-ɯi)   katʃəŋkjosalɨl manas*ta
   I   competent   (younger-brother's/family's) private tutor met
   'I met the competent/powerful (younger-brother's/family's) private tutor.'
6. kwijəun (kjotʃaŋ-ɯi/pisə-ɯi) jətoŋseŋi   mikukɨlo juhakkantako tɨləs*ta
   cute   (principal's/secretary's) younger-sister US-to study abroad (I) heard
   '(I) heard that the cute (principal's/secretary's) younger sister was going to America to study'
7. ipənenɨn seljəntwen (kjohwaŋ-ɯi/motel-ɯi) titʃainəto   pʰatʰi-e
   this time stylish   (Pope's/model's)   designer-also party-at
   tʃʰamsəkhes*ta
   attended
   'This time, the stylish (Pope's/model's) designer attended the party too.'
8. imsinhan (k*oma-ɯi/jətʃa-ɯi) əmənɨnɨn miinisjəs*ta
   pregnant (child's/woman's)   mother   beauty was
   'The pregnant (child's/woman's) mother was a beauty.'
9. onɨl sinmune tʰɨksuhan (jənkusil-ɯi/tʃʰiljojak-ɯi) silhəmtʃaŋtʃʰika
   today newspaper special   (laboratory's/medicine's)   exp. equipment
   tʃʰəimɨlo pototweəs*ta
   first time reported
   'In today's newspaper, a special (laboratory's/medicine's) experimental equipment was reported for the first time.'

10. nanɨn joŋkamhan (motel-ɰi/tʃaŋkjo-ɰi) kjəŋhowəni nukuintʃi alko
    I   brave   (model's/officer's)   bodyguard who is know
    sipʰəs*ta
    wanted
    'I wanted to know who the brave (model's/officer's) bodyguard was.'
11. kɨ jətʃanɨn tʰoŋtʰoŋhan (pallelina-ɰi/atʃumәni-ɰi) akilɨl
    that woman chubby   (ballerina's/lady's)   baby
    pwatʃukois*tako hajəs*ta
    caring   said
    'That woman said that she's taking care of the chubby (ballerina's/lady's) baby.'
12. kapspis*an (supʰəmakʰes-ɰi/suipkake-ɰi) tʃaŋmik*otʃʰɨn siŋsiŋhatʃiman
    expensive (supermarket's/import store's) rose-Top   fresh-but
    hjaŋkika əpəs*ta
    fragrance no
    'The expensive (supermarket's/import store's) rose was fresh but had no fragrance.'

10

Center-embedding Problem and the Contribution of Nominative Case Repetition

KEIKO UEHARA AND DIANNE C. BRADLEY

1 Introduction

Processing difficulty associated with doubly center-embedded sentences is one of the long-standing problems in psycholinguistic research. It is standardly observed that processability degrades suddenly with the step from single to double center-embedding. An appropriate account for this phenomenon is still being called for in theories of the human sentence processing mechanism. The English examples in (1) and the Japanese examples in (2) below illustrate this problem.

(1) a. The student the girl likes met the teacher.
  b. #The teacher the student the girl likes met knew the boy.

(2) a. Gakusei-**ga** onnanoko-**ga** shoonen-o mikaketa-to hanasita.
    student-Nom girl-Nom   boy-Acc saw-that spoke
    'The student said that the girl saw the boy.'

Sentence Processing in East Asian Languages.
Mineharu Nakayama (ed.).
Copyright © 2002, CSLI Publications.

b. #Sensei-**ga** gakusei-**ga** onnanoko-**ga** shoonen-o mikaketa-to
teacher-Nom student-Nom girl-Nom boy-Acc saw-that

hanasita-to itta.
spoke-that said

'The teacher said that the student said that the girl saw the boy.'

Since English is an SVO language, verb-initial, and complementizer-initial, the structure involves object relatives. Singly center-embedded (1a) is not difficult to understand, while doubly center-embedded (1b) suddenly becomes unprocessable (the symbol # represents unprocessability). Since Japanese is an SOV language, verb-final, and complementizer-final, the corresponding center-embedded structure to the one in English has sentential complements. Despite the difference of the structure involved, the parser for Japanese experiences the same phenomenon as that for English. There is a negative jump in processability from singly embedded (2a) to doubly embedded (2b). Examining processability of four kinds of English center-embedded sentences, Eady and Fodor (1981) pointed out that the parser has particular difficulty with sequences of more than two consecutive NPs when they are isolated from the rest of their clauses in the surface structure. Doubly center-embedded (1b) and (2b) share a common feature, in having a sequence of three consecutive NPs sentence-initially, separated from the remainder of their clauses.

Japanese has overt case-markers. By examining the effect of such markers, we may be able to know more about the problem that the parser experiences. In the NP sequence in (2b) shown again as (3) below for convenience, the nominative case-marker -*ga* is repetitively used three times.

(3) #Sensei-**ga** gakusei-**ga** onnanoko-**ga** shoonen-o mikaketa-to
teacher-Nom student-Nom girl-Nom boy-Acc saw that

hanasita-to itta.
spoke that said

'The teacher said that the student said that the girl saw the boy.'

Interestingly, when -*ga* marking the first NP in (3) is replaced by the topic-marker -*wa*, as shown in (4) below, the sentence immediately becomes much easier to process.

(4) #?Sensei-**wa** gakusei-**ga** onnanoko-**ga** shoonen-o mikaketa-to
teacher-Nom student-Nom girl-Nom   boy-Acc   saw that

hanasita-to itta.
spoke that said

'As for the teacher, he said that the student said that the girl saw the boy.'

That is, although the level of embedding does not change, processability clearly improves when the degree of -*ga* repetition is reduced from three times to twice. Repetitive sequences of similar kind are regularly predicted as problematic for the parser in sentence processing theories (e.g. Stabler 1994, Lewis 1993, 1996, 1998, Lewis and Nakayama 1999). The contrast between (3) and (4) illustrates a possibility that repetitive use of nominative case-marker impairs processability of Japanese doubly center-embedded sentences.

The above two observations, the commonality between (1b) and (2b) and the contrast between (3) and (4), suggest an interesting point. That is, the first and second NPs both in (3) and (4) are separated from the rest of their clauses in the surface structure, and the only difference between the two sentences is whether the nominative case is used three times or twice. It seems, therefore, that there are two components of the source of processing difficulty associated with Japanese doubly center-embedded sentences such as (3): double center-embedding *per se*, on the one hand, and the degree of repetition of the same nominative case-marker, on the other.

Of these two components, this paper explores the effect of nominative case repetition, particularly the contrast between three times and twice, drawing on the findings of three off-line experiments (Uehara 1996, 1997a, b, c, d, 1999, Uehara and Bradley 1996). Experiment 1 (Uehara 1996, 1997a) investigates the effect of repeated nominative case-marker -*ga* on Japanese doubly center-embedded sentences, using an off-line processability rating task (Section 2). Three kinds of devices were employed to allow pair-wise comparisons of processability between sentences in which -*ga* is used three times and those in which -*ga* is used twice. Experiment 2 (Uehara and Bradley 1996) examines the phonological repetition effect of the nominative case-marker on processing doubly center-embedded sentences (Section 3). A processability rating task was performed, using Korean sentences, since Japanese does not have phonologically-conditioned nominative case-markers, but Korean does (-*ga* is the only nominative case-marker in Japanese). Finally, Experiment 3 (Uehara 1997b, c, d, 1999, Uehara and Bradley 1998) employs the sentence completion technique, and investigates the ambiguity effect of multiple syntactic functions associated with -*ga* on processing (Section 4). If multiply ambiguous -*ga* is repeatedly used, it may be very difficult for the parser to build structural hypotheses. For this reason, it is of particular interest to investigate the syntactic ambiguity effect of -*ga*. Based on the findings of the three experiments, we will discuss the effect of nominative case repetition on processing center-embedded sentences in Japanese, and consider what are possible sources of the processing difficulty associated with double center-embedding (Section 5).

2 Experiment 1: -*ga* Repetition Cost in Double Embedding

2.1 Procedure

Thirty-two native speakers of Japanese (average age 31 years) living in New York City participated in the experiment. They had received B.A. degrees from Japanese colleges, and the average length of their stay in the U.S. was 3;6 years.

In order to investigate the effect of -*ga* repetition on processability of doubly center-embedded sentences, five basic sentence structures each in which -*ga* was repeated three times were first created. Then, without changing either basic sentential meaning or structural complexity, those structures were adapted to reduce the degree of -*ga* repetition from three to two (hereafter, REP3 and REP2, respectively), employing one of the following three kinds of devices (see Table 1): (a) -*ga*/-*no* substitution, (b) -*ga*/-*wa* substitution, and (c) adverb placement. Device (a) replaced an NP-*ga* with an NP marked with the genitive marker, -*no*. In Japanese, -*no* can mark not only a possessor noun but also the subject of a relative clause or the head of a noun-complement clause (see Miyagawa 1994). Device (b) substituted a topicalized NP-*wa* for the first NP-*ga* of an NP-*ga* sequence. Device (c) split up repeated -*ga*'s by relocating an adverb modifying the verb of the middle clause from the preverbal position to the beginning of the same clause. One basic sentence structure was adapted with Device (a). Three basic structures (two REP3 and one REP4 structures) were adapted with Device (b) because topicalization involves few restrictions. Finally, one basic structure was adapted with Device (c).

Each of the five basic structures was used to create two sentences that differed from each other only in lexical content. Then, these 10 sentences were adapted in the way described above, to make two each for (a) and (c), and six for (b). Finally, the 20 experimental sentences were distributed to form two counterbalanced versions of a questionnaire, so that no subjects saw any REP3 (or REP4) sentence and its adapted counterpart simultaneously. The sentences in (5) are an example pair of an REP3 sentence and its counterpart which was created with Device (b).

(5) REP3 Tanaka-san-**ga** Suzuki-san-**ga** kachoo-**ga**
-Mr.-Nom -Mr.-Nom section chief-Nom

Yamada-san-o suisensuru-to itta-to omotta.
-Mr.-Acc recommend-that said-that thought

REP2 Tanaka-san-wa Suzuki-san-**ga** kachoo-**ga**
-Mr.-Top -Mr.-Nom section chief-Nom

Yamada-san-o suisensuru-to itta-to omotta.
-Mr.-Acc recommend-that said-that thought

'Mr.Tanaka thought that Mr. Suzuki said that the section chief would recommend Mr. Yamada.'

The questionnaire presented sentences singly, and asked for processability ratings on a 6-point scale, from 'very easy to understand' to 'impossible to understand'. The six points were represented by symbols frequently used in the Japanese culture, and were converted later to numerical values ('very easy to understand' = 1 and 'impossible to understand' = 6) for parametric analyses. It was assumed that subjects treated the rating scale as at least quasi-interval.

2.2 Results

Table 1 presents the summary data and analyses for Experiment 1's processability ratings. The numbers in the column labeled as REP represent degrees of *-ga* repetition, e.g., REP3 means that the basic structure contained three NP-*ga*'s in a row. For each comparison, the REP3 (or REP4) versions of sentences were rated significantly less processable than their REP2 (or REP3) counterparts. Furthermore, an overall analysis (Manipulation x Comparison) showed no reliable difference in the magnitude of the REP3 cost among the instances tested ($F < 1$). Overall, the existence of a REP3 sequence resulted in a negative shift in processability, 0.86 units on the 6-point scale.

The middle value of the 6-point scale used for ratings (i.e., 3.5) indicates roughly the difference between a sentence that was understandable and one that had led to processing difficulty. Ratings for REP3 sentences were all larger than the middle value, suggesting that there is a processing cost associated with REP3. This in turn means that a doubly center-embedded sentence becomes difficult to process whenever the nominative case-marker is repeated three times.

Manipulation	REP	Basic Test Sentence Structures	Mean Rating	F Value[a]
-ga/-no substitution	3	[-ga [NP[IP -ga [NP[IP -ga V]] V]] V]	3.88	8.75**
	2	[-ga [NP[IP -ga [NP[IP -no V]] V]] V]	3.09	
-ga/-wa substitution # 1	3	[-ga [NP[IP -ga [NP[IP -ga V]] V]] V]	3.59	4.87*
	2	[-wa [NP[IP -ga [NP[IP -ga V]] V]] V]	2.84	
-ga/-wa substitution # 2	3	[-ga [IP -ga [IP -ga -o V] V] V]	4.31	20.07***
	2	[-wa [IP -ga [IP -ga -o V] V] V]	3.16	
-ga/-wa substitution # 3	4	[-ga [IP -ga -ga [IP -ga V] V] V]	4.72	8.66**
	3	[-wa [IP -ga -ga [IP -ga V] V] V]	4.03	
ADV placement	3	[-ga [IP -ga [IP -ga -o V] Adv V] V]	4.53	16.19***
	2	[-ga [IP -ga Adv [IP -ga -o V] V] V]	3.63	

a. Degrees of freedom (1,30) for all comparisons
* $p < .05$ ** $p < .01$ *** $p < .0001$

Table 1. Processability ratings, Experiment 1

2.3 Discussion

Experiment 1's results show that repeating the same nominative case-marker -*ga* three times adds more burden to the processing difficulty associated with double center-embedding *per se*. This suggests that there is a processing cost associated with such uses of -*ga*.

Why does that degree of repetition of form lead to processing difficulty? There seems to be at least two possible kinds of explanation: One is based on discourse functions associated with -*ga*. For example, one of -*ga*'s discourse functions discussed in the literature (e.g., Kuno 1973a, b, 1978) is that -*ga* is used to signal new information. If so, the parser may be overwhelmed by three NP-*ga*'s in a row, with too much information that is introduced into discourse as new. Also, -*ga* is considered to function as "exhaustive listing" (Kuno 1973a), which, out of the current universe of discourse, picks out the specific entity represented by an NP that it marks, to mean 'NP and *only* NP'. When such NP-*ga* is repeated three times, there is unlikely to be a context for each to be picked out naturally.

Another kind of explanation is more directly parser-oriented. That is, repeating -*ga* makes it very difficult for the parser to construct structural hypotheses. Under this view are two types of assumptions as to why the difficulty arises: One assumption is that -*ga* repetition impairs discrimin ability among NPs which are to be incorporated into the parser's structure building. For example, Rosenbaum and Kim (1976) discuss their observation about a problem with repetitive use of the nominative case-marker in

Korean center-embedding in terms of a phonological/morphological cue effect. Also, Lewis (1993) attributes processing difficulties to syntactic interference due to human short-term memory limitations, and remarks on a phonological discriminability effect. Another assumption is that *-ga per se* is structurally ambiguous since it has more than one syntactic function. It might be this ambiguity that confronts the parser, and ambiguity increases when NP-*ga* is repeated. The nominative *-ga* predominantly marks the subject of a sentence, but can also mark the object of stative predicates as well as external possessors (see Section 4). With this background, opinions vary as to the parser's preference in structural assignment of the second NP-*ga* of an [NP-*ga* NP-*ga*] sequence. While some (e.g., Nagai 1995) consider that the parser tends to minimally attach a second NP-*ga* to the same clause as the first NP-*ga*, others (e.g., Inoue 1991) argue that the parser takes it as a signal to open a new clause.

In the remainder of this study, we will focus on the more directly parser-oriented view, and attempt to narrow down the range of possible explanations for the processing difficulty associated with repetitive use of the nominative case-marker in double embedding. We will consider the two assumptions discussed above in the following two sections: Section 3 focuses on the question of whether there is a phonological effect of nominative case repetition on processing doubly center-embedded sentences. Section 4 examines whether NP-*ga* is syntactically ambiguous for the parser.

3 Experiment 2: Phonological Repetition Effect

One possible explanation for *-ga* repetition difficulty we speculated in the previous section is that it may make subject NPs of a center-embedded sentence indiscriminable from each other, and so confront the parser's structure building. Experiment 2 focuses particularly on the problem of phonological discriminability (see Lewis 1993), i.e., whether repetition of the nominative marker of the same phonological form impairs processability of center-embedded sentences. Experiment 2 is performed in Korean, which is syntactically similar to Japanese and has phonologically-conditioned nominative case-markers that Japanese does not have.

Particularly relevant here is a study by Rosenbaum and Kim (1976), who observed that there is a clear contrast in processability between the Korean doubly center-embedded sentences in (6a-b).

(6) a. #ku ay-tul-**i** wuli hyeng-**i** sensayng-**i** olh-ko-lul
that child-Pl-Nom we brother-Nom teacher-Nom right-that-Acc

palanta-nun kes-ul alkoissta.
Wish-AdNom that-Acc knows

'The children know that my brother wishes that the teacher is right.'

(Rosenbaum and Kim 1976: 54)

b. ku ay-tul-**i** wuli apenim-**kkeyse** nal ssi-**ka**
that child-Pl-Nom we father-Nom (Hon) weather-Nom

kay-ko-lul palako-keysita-nun-kes-ul alkoissta.
clear-that-Acc wish-AdNom that-Acc knows

'The children know that our father wishes that the weather clears up.'

(Rosenbaum and Kim 1976: 47)

Notice that the structure of the sentence in (6a) is identified with a Japanese REP3 sentence. According to Rosenbaum and Kim, (6a) is much more difficult than identically structured (6b) because the former lacks the "structural aiding cues" which altogether facilitate comprehension of (6b). The cues which Rosenbaum and Kim observed appear to be classified into two different types: The first type provides information that is useful in discriminating among the three subject NPs. While those in (6a) are marked with the same nominative case-markers, -*i*, those in (6b) are marked with three different ones, -*i*, -*kkeyse*, and -*ka*. The second type provides helpful information in associating the subjects with their predicates. That is, in the easier sentence (6b), honorific agreement cues *father* and *wish* to be associated with each other, and lexical/conceptual content helps *children* and *weather* be linked with *know* and *clear up*, respectively. In (6a), by contrast, two of the three subject NPs (*child* and *brother*) can freely be associated with any of the predicates (*know*, *wish*, and *be right*). To investigate the effect of phonological discriminability among subject NPs' case-markers, only the first type is relevant. Thus, Experiment 2 (Uehara and Bradley 1996) employs two phonologically-conditioned nominative case-markers, -*i* and -*ka*. The former marks consonant-final NPs whereas the latter marks vowel-final NPs (Note that the honorific nominative case-marker, -*kkeyse*, is not relevant because it is not phonologically conditioned).

3.1 Procedure

Forty native speakers of Korean living in New York City participated in the experiment. Their average age was 27 years, and their average length of stay in the U.S. was nine months. All subjects held B.A. degrees from colleges in Korea, and were attending a summer ESL session at a college in New York City.

In order to create critical materials, basic structures containing double center-embedding were first constructed, using a phonological substitution device with *-i* and *-ka*. Basic structures for *i*-REP3 sentences specified consonant-final NPs in all three subject positions, whereas those for *ka*-REP3 sentences specified vowel-final NPs. The innermost clause of *i*-REP3 and *ka*-REP3 structures specified a vowel-final object NP marked with *-lul* (Acc) and a consonant-final object NP marked with *-ul* (Acc), respectively. To create REP2 counterparts, phonological substitution devices altered the specification of the third NP from consonant-final to vowel-final in the *i*-REP3 structure and from vowel-final to consonant-final in the *ka*-REP3 structure. Lexical items for these positions were carefully chosen so that the phonological substitution would alter overall plausibility of sentence meanings as little as possible between the *i*-REP3/*ka*-REP3 sentences and their adapted counterparts. Also, NP types used in the REP3 and REP2 sentences were consistent (i.e., proper names were replaced by proper names, kinship terms by kinship terms, and content NPs by content NPs). This basic design was expanded to include a complexity factor (double versus single embedding), and singly-embedded sentences were made by eliminating the middle clauses (see Table 2). The final design thus combined two factors, Phonological Substitution and Complexity.

For each of the *i*-REP3 and *ka*-REP3 structures, four sentences differing only in lexical content were created to make eight basic sentences. These eight sentences were then adapted with the phonological substitution device described above, to make 16 sentences. Finally, each of the 16 sentences was further adapted to decrease complexity, resulting in a materials set of 32 experimental sentences, i.e., eight sets of quadruples. Test sentences were distributed in four counter-balanced versions of a questionnaire with 40 filler sentences per version. The sentences in (7) are an example of *i*-REP quadruple, where *i*-REP2' and *i*-REP1' are singly embedded sentences.

(7) *i*-REP3　Sachon-**i**　　Kyengchal-**i**　Kiyeong-**i**　　wuncensa-lul
　　　　　　cousin-Nom　police-Nom　　　　-Nom　driver-Acc

　　　　　　ttayliessta-ko　cwucanghanta-ko　cenhay cwuessta.
　　　　　　hit-that　　　　insisted-that　　　　report gave

　　i-REP2　Sachon-**i**　　Kyengchal-**i**　Yengswu-**ka**　wuncensa-lul
　　　　　　cousin-Nom　police-Nom　　　　-Nom　driver-Acc

　　　　　　ttayliessta-ko　cwucanghanta-ko　cenhay cwuessta.
　　　　　　hit-that　　　　insisted-that　　　　report gave

　　　　　　'My cousin told (me) that the police insisted that
　　　　　　Kiyeong/Yengswu hit the driver.'

　　i-REP2'　Sachon-**i**　　Kiyeong-**i**　　wuncensa-lul
　　　　　　cousin-Nom　　　-Nom　driver-Acc

　　　　　　ttayliessta-ko　cenhay cwuessta.
　　　　　　hit-that　　　　report gave

　　i-REP1'　Sachon-**i**　　Yengswu-**ka**　wuncensa-lul
　　　　　　cousin-Nom　　　-Nom　driver-Acc

　　　　　　ttayliessta-ko　cenhay cwuessta.
　　　　　　hit-that　　　　report gave

　　　　　　'My cousin told (me) that Kiyeong/Yengswu hit the driver.'

As in Experiment 1, the questionnaire presented sentences singly, and asked subjects for absolute processability ratings on a 6-point scale from 'very easy to understand' to 'impossible to understand'. The six points were represented by symbols frequently used in the Korean culture and were converted later to numerical values ('very easy to understand' = 1 and 'impossible to understand' = 6). The data were treated parametrically.

Manipulation	REP	Basic Test Sentence Structures					
-i/-ka Phonological	3	[-i	[IP –i	[IP -i -lul V]	V]	V]	
Substitution	2	[-i	[IP –i	[IP -ka -lul V]	V]	V]	
	2'	[-i		[IP -i -lul V]	V]		
	1'	[-i		[IP -ka -lul V]	V]		
-ka/-i Phonological	3	[-ka	[IP –ka	[IP -ka -lul V]	V]	V]	
Substitution	2	[-ka	[IP –ka	[IP -i -lul V]	V]	V]	
	2'	[-ka		[IP -ka -lul V]		V]	
	1'	[-ka		[IP -i -lul V]		V]	

-i/-ka = Nom; -ul/-lul = Acc; REP2'/REP1' = single embedding

Table 2. Phonological manipulation with Korean nominative case-markers, Experiment 2

3.2 Results and Discussion

Table 3 presents mean processability ratings at two levels of complexity (double embedding and single embedding) for *i*-REP3/*ka*-REP3 sentences and for their adapted counterparts, *i*-REP2/*ka*-REP2 sentences. Table 3 collapses the data over *i*- and *ka*-sentences because there was neither an effect of case-marker type, $F(1, 36) = 1.22$, $p>.25$, nor an interaction of case-marker with other factors, $p>.25$, for all terms.

	Phonological Conversion	
	i-REP3/ka-REP3	i-REP2/ka-REP2
Complexity		
Double embedding	3.28	3.30
Single embedding	2.04	1.79

Table 3. Processability ratings, Experiment 2

Processability ratings did not show, overall, any difference between *i*-REP3/*ka*-REP3 sentences and their adapted counterparts. For the former, mean rating was 2.66 on the 6-point scale, and for the latter, 2.54, $F(1, 36) = 2.07$, $p>.10$. There was no interaction between Phonological Substitution and Complexity, $F(1, 36) = 2.31$, $p>.10$. Doubly embedded sentences, however, were rated much less favorably (mean rating 3.29) for processability than singly embedded-sentences (mean rating 1.91), $F(1, 36) = 97.71$, $p<.001$. This shows that the failure to detect any effect of a variation in phonological form of nominative markers is not because of any insensitivity in participants' use of the rating scale. The one-level difference in embeddedness reflected in processability ratings as a shift of 1.38 units on the rating scale.

Experiment 2's outcomes did not indicate that the processing cost associated with repeating NP-Nom's three times is reduced even though there is a variation in phonological form of the nominative case-markers. The processing cost associated with three NP-Nom's in Korean is identified as the REP3 cost for Japanese -*ga*, but phonological substitution appears to function quite differently from the substitution devices employed in Experiment 1. That is, the phonologically-converted counterparts are not detectably less problematic at all than *i*-REP3/*ka*-REP3 sentences. If we assume that the above finding in Korean applies cross-linguistically, then it seems to suggest that the processing difficulty associated with repeating -*ga* three times is not due to impaired phonological discriminability in nominative-case repetition. That is, the difficulty arises not because of repetition of particular phonological forms, but rather because of repetition of nominative case *per se*.

4 Experiment 3: Structural Ambiguity Effect

As we discussed in Section 2.3, a second possible explanation for -*ga* repetition difficulty under a directly processor-oriented view is that the parser may suffer ambiguity problems in its structure building because -*ga* has multiple syntactic functions. Using sentence completion tasks, Experiment 3 (Uehara 1997b, c, d, 1999, Uehara and Bradley 1998) explores the question of whether -*ga* is of itself ambiguous in sentence processing.

Some of -*ga*'s syntactic functions that are relevant to our interest are the following: (a) the most prototypical use, marking the single subject of a clause in the Single Subject Construction (hereafter, SSC); (b) a special use, marking two or more parallel subjects of a clause in the Parallel Subject Construction (hereafter, PSC); (c) a second special use, marking the object of a stative predicate in the Nominative Object Construction (hereafter, NOC); (d) a third special use, marking the external possessor of a *ga*-marked (mostly) subject NP in the External Possession Construction (hereafter, EPC). Examples of (a) to (d) are given in (8), (9), (10), and (11a) below, respectively.

(8) [$_{IP}$ Taro-ga [$_{IP}$ tomodachi-ga okotta]-to   itta]
     -Nom   friend-Nom   got mad-that said
     'Taro said that his friend got mad'

(9)   [$_{IP}$ Taro-ga   tomodachi-ga sorezore utatta]
         -Nom   friend-Nom   each   sang
      '(lit.) Taro and his friend each sang.'

(10) [$_{IP}$ Taro-ga   tomodachi-ga daisuki-da]
         -Nom   friend-Nom   much fond-is
      '(lit.) Taro likes his friend very much.'

(11) a. [$_{IP}$ Taro-ga   tomodachi-ga totemo sinsetu-da]
            -Nom   friend-Nom   very   kind-is
         '(lit.) Taro's friend is very kind.'

    b.   [$_{IP}$ Taro-no   tomodachi-ga totemo sinsetu-da]
            -Nom   friend-Nom   very   kind-is
         '(lit.) Taro's friend is very kind.'

Among the four functions listed above, the PSC has rarely been taken up in the literature to the authors' knowledge, perhaps due to its emphatic and poetic nature, its typical use being in literary contexts. Two or more entities represented by NPs in the PSC must be in the equivalent status to each other because they share the same predicate and receive an exotic 'NP1, NP2, ... NPn (each)' interpretation. The EPC is also known as the genitive-driven (not locative-driven) multiple subject construction. An EPC in Japanese must consist of two NP-*ga*'s, the first being a possessor and the second its possessum. Thus, the two NPs must lexically support a possessor-possessum relationship, and the possessor NP in the EPC is focused (cf. the internal possession construction in (11b) in which the possessor NP is marked with the genitive marker, -*no*). As for the NOC, Japanese allows *ga*-marked objects with stative predicates, including some transitive verbs, all transitive adjectives, and all transitive nominal adjectives (see Kuno 1973a). Note that the English translations for (9) to (11) do not attempt to express focus effects.

Given the variety of -*ga*'s syntactic functions, a question arises as to whether the -*ga* repetition problem occurs in processing because ambiguity associated with -*ga* combinatorially multiplies as the parser encounters NP-*ga*'s one after another. That is, since each -*ga* in an REP3 sequence is four-way ambiguous, there are logically 64 ways for the parser to make a structural hypothesis, if lexically permitted. For example, if there is a sentence-beginning with an REP3 sequence like the one in (12), it can be continued as in any of (13a-c), or in many other ways. If each of the three NP-*ga*'s is the subject of three separate clauses (i.e., three SSCs), the remainder of the sentence will become a sentence such as (13a), containing a doubly center-embedding. Alternatively, if *Taro* is the single subject of a matrix clause, and *friend* and *younger brother* are the subject and object of a singly-embedded clause, respectively (two SSCs and one NOC), then the sentence will be continued as in (13b). Or, if *Taro* is the possessor of *friend* which is the possessor of *younger brother* (i.e., two EPCs), the sentence will be completed in a single clause, as in (13c). The English translations given in (13a-c) are for the entire sentences, combining the sentence-beginning given in (12) in bold with the parts continued in (13a-c).

(12)   **Taro-ga   tomodachi-ga otooto-ga   ...**
       -Nom   friend-Nom   younger brother-Nom

(13) a.   ... naiteiru]-to   osieta]-to   itta]
          crying-is-that taught-that said
          '**Taro** said that **his friend** said that **his younger brother** was crying.'

     b.   ... kirai-da]-to omotte-iru]
          dislike-that thinking-is
          '**Taro** thinks that **his friend** does not like **his younger brother**.'

     c.   ... monosugoku   ijiwaru-da]
          extraordinally mean-is
          '(lit.) **Taro's friend's younger brother** is very mean.'

One of the most interesting consequences here is that an REP3 sequence encountered in an input can end up bearing the extremely difficult double center-embedding structure that we saw in Experiment 1, such as (13a). The structures such as those in (13a-c) and all other possible ones are in a way rivals with each other in the parser's structure building. Experiment 3 presents two types of sentence completion database and explores what the parser's structural preference is most likely to be when it faces syntactically ambiguous nominative case-marker, *-ga*.

4.1 Procedure

Eighteen native speakers of Japanese at a university in Japan (average age 32 years) participated in data extraction for Database 1, and 23 native speakers of Japanese at an English conversation school in New York City (average age 32 years), for Database 2. Subjects were asked to complete natural and well-formed sentences, using given sentence-beginnings in paper-and-pencil questionnaires. They could add whatever they wanted in order to complete sentences, but were disallowed to add anything either to the front or to the middle of the sentence-beginnings.

The sentence completion task employed in Experiment 3 is a production task, but it is very useful to explore the probable ranking among competing structural analyses of an ambiguous input (see Forster 1968). In this task, sentence-beginnings are presented to ask for completion of a natural and well-formed sentence for each of them. Response analyses run the steps underlying performance in the task in reverse, and examine completion responses to determine the structure imposed on the stimulus fragment. Behind this is an assumption that the way a stimulus has been processed constrains what is added. Since Japanese is an SOV language, head-final, and complementizer-final, it is very common to begin a sentence with a sequence of NPs each of which is marked with a case-marker. If a stimulus sentence-beginning includes an ambiguously case-marked NP (or NPs), what has been added in its completion response will provide us with information about how that ambiguous part was interpreted. In other words, for a sentence to be completed, the ambiguous part must have been processed first, so that the added part fits a given sentence-beginning. By analyzing structures of completed sentences, we will be able to find out patterns of preferred structural hypotheses. Thus, if there is any systematicity in the patterns of many responses collected with a variety of fragment types, it will tell us the parser's preference in its structure building.

For Experiment 3, fragments with three or four case-marked NPs were created to form Questionnaires 1 and 2: Questionnaire 1 included 24 fragments, all possible orderings of {NP-*ga*, NP-*ni*, NP-*o*}, all distinguishable orderings of {{NP-*ga*, NP-*ga*} plus one of {NP-*ni*, NP-*o*}}, and all distinguishable orderings of {NP-*ga*, NP-*ga*, NP-*ni*, NP-*o*}, as shown in Table 4. NP content in any REP2 sequence of -*ga* in these fragments was designed not to support possessor-possessum relation, i.e., to rule out EPC interpretations. NP content in the fragments of Questionnaire 1 was all human, such as role terms, kinship terms, and proper nouns.

Questionnaire 2 consisted of eight fragments, each of which contained a REP2 sequence of -*ga*, as shown in Table 5. Unlike Questionnaire 1, NP content in any REP2 sequence of NP-*ga*'s in Questionnaire 2 supported a possessor-possessum relationship, so that an EPC interpretation would be possible if it was preferred over other possible structural hypotheses. An important point here is that possibilities for EPC interpretations were not obligatory. While the fragments in (1a-d) had only human nouns, those in (2a-d) were designed to contain a human NP and an inanimate NP, each marked with -*ga*, to avoid PSC interpretations.

# of NPs		Ordering of Case Markers		
3	All possible orderings of {NP-ga, NP-ni, NP-o}	(1) -ga -ni -o (2) -ga -o -ni	(3) -o -ga -ni (4) -o -ni -ga	(5) -ni -ga -o (6) -ni -o -ga
	All distinguishable orderings of {{NP-ga, NP-ga} plus one of {NP-ni, NP-o}}	(7) -ga -ga -o (8) -ga -o -ga (9) -o -ga -ga	(10) -ga -ga -ni (11) -ga -ni -ga (12) -ni -ga -ga	
4	All distinguishable orderings of {NP-ga, NP-ga, NP-ni, NP-o}	(13) -ga -ga -ni -o (14) -ga -ga -o -ni (15) -ga -ni -ga -o (16) -ga -o -ga -ni (17) -ga -ni -o -ga (18) -ga -o -ni -ga	(19) -o -ga -ga -ni (20) -o -ga -ni -ga (21) -o -ni -ga -ga	(22) -ni -ga -ga -o (23) -ni -ga -o -ga (24) -ni -o -ga -ga

NP-*ga*= Nom; NP-*ni* = Dat; NP-*o* = Acc

Table 4. Ordering of case-markers in sentence fragments, Questionnaire 1

	Ordering of Case Markers	
(1a)	H-ga H-ga	(2a) H-ga I-ga
(1b)	H-ga H-ga H-o	(2b) H-ga I-ga I-o
(1c)	H-ga H-ga H-ni	(2c) H-ga I-ga H-ni
(1d)	H-ga H-ga H-ni H-o	(2d) H-ga I-ga H-ni I-o

H = human noun; I = inanimate noun

Table 5. Ordering of case markers in sentence fragments, Questionnaire 2

4.2 Results and Discussion

To obtain Database 1, 432 responses to Questionnaire 1 (24 fragments x 18 subjects) were analyzed to determine what kind of structures were imposed on the stimulus fragments, examining clause boundary placements, in particular. Of those 432 sentences, incomplete, ambiguous, or uninterpretable responses (approximately 16%) were discarded, and thus Database 1 resulted in 361 sentences. A strongly preferred processing strategy observed in the pattern of this database is generalized as "Assign NP-*ga*'s to separate clauses". There were some violations of this generalization (approximately 11% of all possible occasions) by assigning two NP-*ga*'s in the same clause. All these violations were PSCs, and not NOCs. Recall that noun content blocked EPC interpretations by discouraging possessive relationships between any two adjacent NP-*ga*'s in fragment stimuli. In the absence of possibilities for EPC interpretations, the PSC and the NOC were rivals for each other if two NP-*ga*'s were to be assigned in the same clause. The fragments originally containing NP-*o* ruled out NOC interpretations, but even though the fragments in (10) to (12) did not contain NP-*o* and had NP-*ga*'s as possibilities for NOC interpretations, hardly any responses exhibited this interpretation. Interestingly, the PSC is emphatic and poetic, and not used in daily conversation, whereas the NOC is very common. This suggests that frequency considerations do not explain the pattern in responses. As the generalization states, the majority of responses took NP-*ga* as the SSC. Violation responses of the generalization preferred the PSC over the NOC, despite the very special characteristics of the PSC. This appears to suggest that the nominative case-marker, -*ga*, is unambiguously taken as the subject marker for the parser.

Table 6 presents the summary of outcomes in Database 2, which consists of 182 sentences. Originally, there were 184 responses to Questionnaire 2 (8 fragments x 23 subjects), but two incomprehensible responses were discarded. The column labeled as EPC/PSC includes responses that are ambiguous between EPC and PSC interpretations. Interestingly, there was a strong structural preference that assigned two NP-*ga*'s to separate clauses, each NP-*ga* being interpreted as an SSC, even though the resulting structure involved a single embedding. This was 88% of analyzable responses for the fragments in (1a-d) and (2a-d) taken together, and 83% and 94% for these two separate fragment subgroups, respectively. A probable reason for the higher preference for double embedding in (2a-d)'s responses is the effect of blocking PSCs by the non-equivalent combination of human and inanimate NPs.

A minority of responses assigned two NP-*ga*'s in the same clause. Although single-EPC interpretations were possible for all fragments, there was only one response that unambiguously showed a single-EPC interpretation. This contrasts with 10 responses that unambiguously imposed PSC interpretations, and they were all for the fragments in (1a-d). Recall that the fragments in (1a-d) had no lexical constraints that blocked either EPC or PSC interpretations, while those in (2a-d) discouraged PSC interpretations by specifying NP content in 2*ga* strings as a human-inanimate combination which made NPs' status non-equivalent to each other. The effect of ruling out PSCs in (2a-d) only increased the frequency of SSC interpretation. There were a small number of ambiguous responses in the data (9 responses), and all but one such instance were ambiguous between EPC and PSC interpretations. With the very unlikely assumption that all those ambiguous responses were intended as EPCs, the structural preference for the EPC would be estimated as 5.5%, *at maximum*. Since the fragments in (1b-d) and (2b-d) contained NP-*o*'s, NOC interpretations were in effect ruled out. By contrast, NOCs were possible in (1a) and (2a), but no responses contained such interpretations. The results of analyses show that the SSC was overwhelmingly preferred over the EPC, PSC, and NOC, even though the resulting structure involved single embedding. The fact that discouraging the PSC did not increase EPC interpretations seems to suggest that the EPC is structurally less preferred than the PSC, even though the PSC has very exotic characteristics.

	Separate clause	Same clause			Total
		EPC	EPC/PSC	PSC	Other	
(1a) H-ga H-ga	17	0	2	4	0	23
(1b) H-ga H-ga H-o	21	0	1	1	0	23
(1c) H-ga H-ga H-ni	20	0	1	2	0	23
(1d) H-ga H-ga H-ni H-o	18	0	2	3	0	23
	76	0	6	10	0	92
(2a) H-ga I-ga	22	0	0	0	1[a]	23
(2b) H-ga I-ga I-o	20	0	2	0	0	22[b]
(2c) H-ga I-ga H-ni	23	0	0	0	0	23
(2d) H-ga I-ga H-ni I-o	20	1	0	0	1	22[b]
	85	1	2	0	2	90

[a] Response ambiguous between EPC and NOC
[b] N=1 response incomprehensible

Table 6. Completion response frequency, as a function of structural interpretation, Database 2 in Experiment 3

Overall, Experiment 3's outcomes appear to indicate that -*ga* is unambiguously taken as the single subject of a clause. (This supports Inoue's observation, see Section 2.3.) This suggests that it is not the ambiguity associated with the multiplicity of -*ga*'s syntactic functions that makes -*ga* repetition problematic for the parser in processing doubly center-embedded sentences.

5 General Discussion

Experiment 1 investigated the effect of repetitive use of nominative case-marker, -*ga*, on processability ratings of Japanese multiply center-embedded sentences. Outcomes show that when NP-*ga* is repeated three times, sentences are rated as substantially less comprehensible than their counterparts in which NP-*ga* is repeated twice. This suggests that there is a processing cost associated with repetitive use of NP-*ga*, above and beyond the processing cost associated with multiple center-embedding *per se*. This finding supports Lewis's (1993, 1996, 1998) similarity-based interference theory.

Two possibilities were explored under a directly parser-oriented view as explanations for the substantial negative effect of nominative case repetition on processing center-embedded sentences: Experiment 2 tested the repetition effect of the nominative case-marker with the same phonological form. In order to create phonologically-controlled critical pairs that were not possible in Japanese, Korean sentences were used. Results of analysis did not show any difference between the sentences in which the nominative marker of the same phonological form was repeated three times and their counterparts in which the repetition was one degree fewer by exchanging one nominative marker with its phonological alternative. With the assumption that this finding applies cross-linguistically, it was concluded that phonological repetition of the nominative marker does not detectably contribute to processing difficulty associated with doubly center-embedded sentences. Experiment 3 examined the effect of ambiguity associated with the variety of *-ga*'s syntactic functions. Outcomes suggest that *-ga* is unambiguously taken to signal the single subject of a clause.

The above findings taken altogether suggest that the problem with nominative case repetition in double center-embedding occurs neither because of phonological indiscriminability in repetitive use of the same nominative case, nor of syntactic ambiguity of the nominative marker. Rather, the problem appears to be more structural.[1] It seems to be repeated subjectness that is problematic (see also Miyamoto and Takahashi both in this volume). This is consistent with Lewis and Nakayama (1999), who investigated the semantic and syntactic similarity effect on processing Japanese multiply center-embedded sentences, and concluded that it is not semantic indiscriminability that is problematic, but rather syntactic and positional similarity.

It is not certain, however, whether it is only for the nominative case or for any other case that its repetition is problematic for the parser. Cowper (1976) observed that there is a clear processability difference between REP3 sentences in which NP-*ga* is repeated three times and those in which NP-*wa* is repeated three times, the latter being much easier to process. It seems to be difficult to perform systematic studies on repeating *-wa* three times because embedded *wa*-phrases receive contrastive readings (see Kuno 1973a, among others) which require special contexts. However, more research is necessary on this problem. It is also quite difficult to test effects of repetition of other case-markers in Japanese, such as *-o* (Acc) and *-ni* (Dat) because of unavoidable syntactic complications, e.g., occurrences of *pro*.

---

[1] Here, "structural" is in a broad sense, and does not strictly distinguish between syntactic and semantic factors.

More research is needed in other languages that allow direct examination of the repetition effect of case-markers other than the nominative marker.

There was a strong preference to take NP-*ga* as the subject of a clause in Experiment 3. Even in responses that assigned two NP-*ga*'s in the same clause, the PSC was preferred over the EPC and the NOC. Although external possessors and nominative objects are nominatively marked, they are associated with genitive- and accusative-like meaning, respectively. That is, the use of -*ga* is not transparent, and it might be that non-transparent use of -*ga* is costly for processing. If the parser prefers to build 'compact structure' (Fodor 1995), it should stay in the same clause as long as possible, minimally attaching arguments to the preceding constituents. Given this principle, the parser should prefer a single-clause structure involving the PSC, EPC, or NOC over a singly-embedded structure, all other things being equal. However, the current data suggest that there is something *not equal* that makes the parser disprefer those constructions. Further research is needed in this area.

Although this study focused on some possible explanations under directly parser-oriented consideration, it is necessary to investigate contextual and focus effects on processing NP-*ga*, in general. For example, the NOC occurs with a stative predicate, and if the subject of a sentence containing an NOC (i.e., containing a stative predicate) is also marked with -*ga*, it is likely to be interpreted as exhaustive-listing, which requires special contexts. It is of interest to systematically investigate how NP-*ga*'s are processed without such special contexts. Moreover, -*ga* can be associated with focus, and the effect of focus on processing NP-*ga* sentences needs to be studied in more detail as well.

Finally, we have discussed the effect of -*ga* repetition only in double center-embedding contexts, but a question arises as to whether it is problematic only in double embedding or in single-embedding, as well. More research is necessary in this area (see Uehara in preparation).

6 Concluding Remarks

This study focused the effect of nominative case repetition on processing doubly center-embedded sentences, and considered two possible explanations under a directly parser-oriented view. Findings of the study can be summarized as follows: (a) When nominative case is repeated three times, there is a substantial cost associated with it in processing Japanese doubly center-embedded sentences, above and beyond the processing cost associated with double center-embedding itself; (b) There is no phonological effect of nominative-case repetition; (c) Although -*ga* has various syntactic functions, it is not ambiguous for the parser's structure building; the parser prefers to take NP-*ga* as the single subject of a clause. These findings together suggest that it is repeated subjectness that is problematic.

References

Chomsky, N. & G. Miller. 1963. Introduction to the Formal Analysis of Natural Languages. *Handbook of Mathematical Psychology II*, eds. R. D. Luce, R. R. Bush, & E. Galanter. New York: John Wiley and Sons.

Cowper, E. 1976. Constraints on Sentence Complexity: A Model for Syntactic Processing. Doctoral dissertation, Brown University.

De Vincenzi, M. 1991. *Syntactic Parsing Strategies in Italian*. Dordrecht: Kluwer.

De Vincenzi, M. 1994. Syntactic Analysis in Sentence Comprehension: Evidence form Italian. *Sentence Processing and the Nature of the Human Syntactic Parser, Special Issue of Folia Linguistica, XXVIII/1-2*:139-173.

Eady, S. & J. D. Fodor. 1981. Is Center-embedding a Source of Processing Difficulty? Paper presented at the Annual Meeting of the Linguistic Society of America, New York.

Fodor, J. D. 1979. Superstrategy. *Sentence Processing*, eds. W. Cooper & E. Walker. Hillsdale: Erlbaum.

Fodor, J. D. 1995. Comprehending Sentence Structure. *An Invitation to Cognitive Science, Volume 1: Language (Second Edition)*, eds. L. R. Gleitman & M. Liberman. Cambridge: MIT Press.

Forster, K. I. 1968. Sentence Completion in Left- and Right-branching Languages. *Journal of Verbal Learning & Behavior* 7:296-299

Frazier, L. 1990. Identifying Structure under X^0. *Yearbook of Morphology* 3, eds. A. Jongman and A. Lahili, 87-109.

Frazier, L. & J. D. Fodor. 1978. The Sausage Machine: A New Two-stage Parsing Model. *Cognition* 6:417-459.

Gibson, E. 1991. Memory Limitations and Linguistic Processing Breakdown. Doctoral dissertation, Carnegie Mellon University.

Hoji, H. 1985. Logical Form Constraints and Configurational Structures in Japanese. Doctoral dissertation, University of Washington.

Inoue, A. 1991. A Comparative Study of Parsing in English and Japanese. Doctoral dissertation, University of Connecticut.

Kimball, J. 1975. Predictive Analysis and Over-the-top Parsing. *Syntax and Semantics Vol.4*, ed. J. Kimball. New York: Academic Press.

Kuno, S. 1973a. *The Structure of the Japanese Language*. Cambridge: MIT Press.

Kuno, S. 1973b. *Nihon Bonpoo Kenkyuu*. Tokyo: Taishukan.

Kuno, S. 1978. *Danwa-no Bonpoo*. Tokyo: Taishukan.

Lewis, R. 1993. An Architecturally-Based Theory of Human Sentence Comprehension. Doctoral dissertation, Carnegie Mellon University.

Lewis, R. 1996. Interference in Short-term Memory: The Magical Number Two (or Three) in Sentence Processing. *Journal of Psycholinguistic Research* 25:93-115.

Lewis, R. 1998. Interference in Working Memory: Retroactive and Proactive Interference in Parsing. Paper presented at the 11th Annual CUNY Conference on Human Sentence Processing, New York.

Lewis, R. & M. Nakayama. 1999. Determinants of Processing Complexity in Japanese Embeddings: New Theory and Data. Paper presented at International East Asian Psycholinguistics Workshop. Columbus, Ohio.

Miller, G. & N. Chomsky. 1963. Finitary Models of Language Users. *Handbook of Mathematical Psychology II*, eds. R. D. Luce, R. R. Bush, & E. Galanter. New York: John Wiley and Sons.

Miller, G. & S. Isard. 1965. Free Recall of Self-embedded English Sentences. *Information & Control* 7:202-303.

Miyagawa, S. 1993. Case, Agreement, and *ga/no* Conversion. *Japanese/Korean Linguistics* 3, ed. S. Choi. Stanford: CSLI.

Nagai, N. 1995. Constraints on Topics and Their Gaps: From a Parsing Perspective. *Japanese Sentence Processing*, eds. R. Mazuka and N. Nagai. Hillsdale: Lawrence Erlbaum Associates.

Rosenbaum, H. & K. Kim. 1976. Factors Affecting Comprehension in Korean and English Self-embedded Structures. *Working Papers on Language Universals* 20:43-57.

Stabler, E. 1994. The Finite Connectivity of Linguistic Structure. *Perspectives on Sentence Processing*, eds. C. Clifton, Jr., L. Frazier, & K. Rayner. Hillsdale: Lawrence Erlbaum Associates.

Takahashi, C. 1996. Multiplicity, Optimality, and Constraints on the Distribution of Nominative Case in Japanese. Doctoral dissertation, Cornell University.

Tateishi, K. 1991. The Syntax of 'Subjects'. Doctoral dissertation, University of Massachusetts.

Uehara, K. 1996. The Effect of *-ga* Sequences on Judged Processing Load in Japanese. Poster presented at The 9th Annual CUNY Conference on Human Sentence Processing, New York.

Uehara, K. 1997a. Judgments of Processing Load: The Effect of NP-*ga* Sequences. *Journal of Psycholinguistics Research* 26:255-263.

Uehara, K. 1997b. Structuring Japanese Argument Sequences: A Sentence-completion Study. Poster presented at The 10th Annual CUNY Conference on Human Sentence Processing, Santa Monica.

Uehara, K. 1997c. Clause Segmentation Strategies in Japanese. Paper presented at The Annual Student/Faculty Conference, Ph.D. Program in Linguistics, The Graduate Center of The City University of New York.

Uehara, K. 1997d. Processing and Non-transparent Interpretation of Case: External Possessors in Japanese. Paper presented at Psycholinguistic Research Club, Ph.D. Program in Linguistics, The Graduate Center of The City University of New York, New York.

Uehara, K. 1999a. Center-embedding Difficulty in Japanese: The Contribution of Nominative Case Repetition. Paper presented at International East Asian Psycholinguistic Workshop. Columbus, Ohio.

Uehara, K. 1999b. External Possession Constructions in Japanese: A Psycholinguistic Perspective. *External Possession*, eds. D. Payne & I. Barshi. Amsterdam: John Benjamins.

Uehara, K. in preparation. Sentence Processing and Nominative Case Repetition. Doctoral dissertation, The City University of New York.

Uehara, K. & D. C. Bradley. 1996. The Effect of *-ga* Sequences on Processing Japanese Multiply Center-embedded Sentences. *Language, Information and Computation*, eds. B.-S. Park & J.-B. Kim. Seoul: Kyung Hee University.

Uehara, K. & D. C. Bradley. 1998. Processing Scrambled Argument Structures in Japanese. Paper presented at the 72nd Annual Meeting of The Linguistic Society of America, New York.

Appendix A: Materials of Experiment 1

(a) -ga/-no substitution

REP3   Keiichi-ga   otooto-ga   ryoosin-**ga**   dekaketa toki kaettekita no-ni
        -Nom   brother-Nom parents-**Nom**   went-out time came-home fact-at
      tomadotta.
      embarrassed

REP2   Keiichi-ga otooto-ga ryoosin-**no** dekaketa toki kaettekita no-ni tomadotta.
                                   -Gen
      'Keiichi was embarrassed at the fact that his brother came home when their parents went out.'

REP3   Sobo-ga   Takasi-ga ane-**ga**   utaidasita   toki nakidasita no-ni
      grandmother-Nom   -Nom sister-**Nom** singing-started time crying-started fact-that
      kizuita.
      noticed

REP2   Sobo-ga Takasi-ga ane-**no** utaidasita toki nakidasita no-ni kizuita.
                           -Gen
      'My grandmother noticed the fact that Takashi started crying when my sister started singing.'

(b) -ga/-wa substitution #1
REP3   Satoo-san-**ga** Takahashi-san-ga sono hito-ga Yamane-san-o kokusosita to
            -**Nom**   -Nom that person-Nom   -Acc sued   that
       omotta to itta.
       thought that said
REP2   Satoo-san-**wa** Takahashi-san-ga sono hito-ga Yamane-san-o kokusosita to
            -**Top**
       omotta to itta.
       'Mr. Sato said that Mr. Takahashi thought that the person sued Mr. Yamane.'

REP3   Tanaka-san-**ga** Suzuki-san-ga kachoo-ga Yamada-san-o suisensuru to itta
                -**Nom**   -Nom section-chief-Nom   -Acc recommend that said
       to omotta.
       that thought
REP2   Tanaka-san-**wa** Suzuki-san-ga kachoo-ga Yamada-san-o suisensuru to itta
                 -**Top**
       to omotta.
       'Mr. Tanaka thought that Mr. Suzuki said that the section chief would recommend Mr. Yamada.'

(c) -ga/-wa substitution #2
REP3   Hahaoya-**ga** Michiko-ga tomodati-ga asondeita toki benkyoositeita no-ni
       mother-**Nom**   -Nom friends-Nom playing-were time studying-was fact-by
       kandoosita.
       impressed
REP2   Hahaoya-**wa** Michiko-ga tomodati-ga asondeita toki benkyoositeita no-ni
                -**Top**
       kandoosita.
       'Mother was impressed by the fact that Michiko was studying when her friends were playing.'

REP3   Sekiya-san-**ga** Yoshida-san-ga dooryoo-ga   atumatta toki
                  -**Nom**   -Nom co-workers-Nom got-together time
       byooki-datta no-ni doojoosita.
       sick-was fact-with   sympathized
REP2   Sekiya-san-**wa** Yoshida-san-ga dooryoo-ga atumatta toki
                  -**Top**
       byooki-datta no-ni doojoosita.
       'Mr. Sekiya sympathized with the fact that Mr. Yoshida was sick when their co-workers got together.'

(d) -ga/-wa substitution #3
REP4 Kiyosi-**ga** titi-ga Midori-ga imooto-ga dekaketa to itta to   settoku
      -**Nom** father-Nom -Nom sister-Nom went-out that said that persuade
      dekinakatta.
      could-not
REP3 Kiyosi-**wa** titi-ga Midori-ga imooto-ga dekaketa to itta to settoku
            -**Top**
      dekinakatta.
      'Kiyosi could not persuade my father that Midori said that (my) sister went out.'

REP4 Haha-**ga** ani-ga   sono hito-ga Hayashi-san-ga nakunatta to   itta
      mother-**Nom** brother-Nom that person-Nom   -Nom passed-away that said
      to settoku dekinakatta.
      that persuade could-not
REP3 Haha-**wa** ani-ga sono hito-ga Hayashi-san-ga nakunatta to itta to settoku
            -**Top**
      dekinakatta.
      'My mother could not persuade my brother that the person said that Mr. Hayashi passed away.'

(e) ADV placement
REP3 Keiko-ga Tadashi-ga sensei-ga Kenji-o kiraida to **kesa** itta to omotteiru.
              -Nom   -Nom teacher-Nom -Acc hates that **this morning** said that thinks
REP2 Keiko-ga Tadashi-ga **kesa** sensei-ga Kenji-o kiraida to itta to omotteiru.
      'Keiko thinks that Tadashi said this morning that the teacher hates Kenji.'

REP3 Oji-ga Yoko-ga Keiji-ga sono seito-o sukida to **yuube** itta to omotta.
      uncle-Nom   -Nom -Nom that student-Acc likes that **last night** said that thought
REP2 Oji-ga Yoko-ga **yuube** Keiji-ga sono seito-o sukida to itta to omotta.
      'My uncle thought that Yoko said last night that Keiji likes the student.'

Appendix B: Materials of Experiment 2

(a) -i/-ka phonological substitution
i-REP3 Sachon-i   kyengchal-i **Kiyeong-i**   wuncensa-lul ttayliessta ko
        cousin-Nom police-Nom   -**Nom**   driver-Acc   hit   that
        cwucanghanta ko   cenhay cwuessta.
        insisted   that report   gave

i-REP2 Sachon-i   kyengchal-i **Yengswu-ka** wuncensa-lul ttayliessta ko
                                 -Nom
        cwucanghanta ko cenhay cwuessta.
        'My cousin told (me) that the police insisted that **Kiyeong/Yengswu** hit the driver.'

i-REP2 Sachon-i   **Kiyeong-i**   wuncensa-lul ttayliessta ko cenhay cwuessta.
        cousin-Nom **-Nom** driver-Acc hit   that report gave
i-REP1 Sachon-i   **Yengswu-ka** wuncensa-lul ttayliessta ko cenhay cwuessta.
                    -Nom
        'My cousin told (me) that **Kiyeong/Yengswu** hit the driver.'

i-REP3 Myeng Hwan-i kyengchal-i   **pesuchancang-i**   nwuna-lul
                    -Nom younger brother-Nom bus conductor-**Nom** elder sister-Acc
        ttemilessta ko   pulphyenghayssta ko hayssta.
        pushed   that complained   that said
i-REP2 Myeng Hwan-i kyengchal-i **kacengbu-ka** nwuna-lul ttemilessta ko
                                 housewife-**Nom**
        pulphyenghayssta ko hayssta.
        'Myeng Hwan said that his younger brother complained that a **bus conductor/ housewife** pushed his older sister.'

i-REP2 Myeng Hwan-i **pesuchancang-i**   nwuna-lul   ttemilessta ko hayssta.
                     -Nom bus conductor-**Nom** elder sister-Acc pushed that said
i-REP1 Myeng Hwan-i **kacengbu-ka** nwuna-lul   ttemilessta ko hayssta.
                     housewife-**Nom**
        'Myeng Hwan said that a **bus conductor / housewife** pushed his older sister.'

i-REP3 Han cunghaksayng-i   apenim-i **Hyey Yeng-i**   halmeni-lul
        junior highschool student -Nom father -Nom   **-Nom** grandmother -Acc
        cal posalphye tulyessta mye   kkippeha-si-essta ko allye cwuessta.
        well care   gave   since was happy(Hon) that inform gave
i-REP2 Han cunghaksayng-i apenim-i **Mili-ka** halmeni-lul cal posalphye
                                    -Nom
        tulyessta mye kkippeha-si-essta ko allye cwuessta.
        'A junior high school student informed (me) that his father was happy that **Hyey Yeng/Mili** took good care of her grandmother.'

i-REP2 Han cunghaksayng-i   **Hyey Yeng-i**   halmeni-lul
        junior highschool student -Nom   **-Nom** grandmother -Acc
        cal posalphye tulyessta ko allye cwuessta.
        well care   gave   that inform gave

i-REP1   Han cunghaksayng-i **Mili-ka** halmeni-lul cal posalphye tulyessta ko
                                    -Nom
         allye cwuessta.
         'A junior high school student informed (me) that **Hyey Yeng/Mili** took good care of her grandmother.'

i-REP3   Namtongsayng-i   Kichel-i   **ku yesensayng-i**   Sanghuy-lul
         younger brother-Nom   -Nom   that woman teacher-**Nom**   -Acc
         talmassta ko   mitko issta   ko   malhay cwuessta.
         resembled that believing was that say gave

i-REP2   Namtongsayng-i Kichel-i **yeca chinkwu-ka** Sanghuy-lul talmassta   ko
                                  woman friend-**Nom**
         mitko issta   ko   malhay cwuessta.
         'My younger brother said (to me) that Kichel believed that **that woman teacher/his girlfriend** resembled Sanghuy.'

i-REP2   Namtongsayng-i   **ku yesensayng-i**   Sanghuy-lul talmassta   ko
         younger brother-Nom that woman teacher-**Nom**   -Acc resembled   that
         malhay cwuessta.
         say   gave

i-REP1   Namtongsayng-i **yeca chinkwu-ka** Sanghuy-lul talmassta ko
                         woman friend-**Nom**
         malhay cwuessta.
         'My younger brother said (to me) that **that woman teacher/his girlfriend** resembled Sanghuy.'

(a) -ka/-i phonological substitution

ka-REP3 Yenghuy-ka   cito kyoswu-ka   **enni-ka**   yuhaksyng-ul
              -Nom   advisor -Nom   older sister-**Nom**   foreign student-Acc
         mannayahanta   ko   seltukhako issta ko   kangcohayssta.
         meet-must   that insisting was that emphasized

ka-REP2 Yenghuy-ka cito kyoswu-ka **tongsayng-i** yuhaksyng-ul mannayahanta ko
                                    younger brother-**Nom**
         seltukhako issta ko kangcohayssta.
         'Yenghuy emphasized that her advisor was insisting that her **older sister/younger brother** should meet the foreign student.'

ka-REP2 Yenghuy-ka **enni-ka**   yuhaksyng-ul mannayahanta ko kangcohayssta.
                 -Nom older sister-**Nom** foreign student-Acc meet-must that emphasized

ka-REP1 Yenghuy-ka **tongsayng-i** yuhaksyng-ul mannayahanta ko kangcohayssta.
                    younger brother-**Nom**

'Yenghuy emphasized that her **older sister/younger brother** should meet the foreign student.'

ka-REP3 Yuchiwen kyosa-ka   Mira-ka **oppa-ka**   Selak-ul   kassta
    kindergarden teacher-Nom   -Nom older brother-**Nom** Mt.Sōrak-Acc went
    ko kekcenghako issta ko malssumhay cwu-si-essta.
    that worrying was   that said gave(Hon)
ka-REP2 Yuchiwen kyosa-ka Mira-ka **samchon-i** Selak-ul kassta ko
            uncle-**Nom**
    kekcenghako issta ko malssumhay cwu-si-essta.
'The kindergarden teacher said (to me) that Mira was worrying that her **older brother / uncle** had gone to Mt. Sōrak.'

ka-REP2 Yuchiwen kyosa-ka   **oppa-ka**   Selak-ul   kassta ko
    kindergarden teacher-Nom older brother-**Nom**   Mt.Sōrak-Acc went   that
    malssumhay cwu-si-essta.
    said gave(Hon)
ka-REP1 Yuchiwen kyosa-ka **samchon-i** Selak-ul kassta ko malssumhay
         uncle-**Nom**
    cwu-si-essta.
'The kindergarden teacher said (to me) that her **older brother / uncle** had gone to Mt. Sōrak.'

ka-REP3 Emeni-ka   kyohoy moksa-ka **Yanghuy-ka** yakhonca-ul cal kollassta
    mother-Nom church pastor -Nom   -**Nom** fiancé -Acc   well chose
    ko chingchanha-si-essta ko   calangha-si-essta.
    that praised(Hon)   that was proud(Hon)
ka-REP2 Emeni-ka kyohoy moksa-ka **Swuhyeng-i** yakhonca-ul cal kollassta ko
             -**Nom**
    chingchanha-si-essta ko   calangha-si-essta.
'Mother was proud that the pastor had expressed admiration (for the fact) that **Yanghuy/Swuhyeng** had chosen her fiancé well.'

ka-REP2 Emeni-ka **Yanghuy-ka** yakhonca-ul cal kollassta ko calangha-si-essta.
    mother-Nom   -**Nom** fiancé -Acc   well chose   that was proud(Hon)
ka-REP1 Emeni-ka **Swuhyeng-i** yakhonca-ul cal kollassta ko   calangha-si-essta.
       -**Nom**
'Mother was proud that **Yanghuy/Swuhyeng** had chosen her fiancé well.'

ka-REP3 Minsu-ka apeci-ka **minpangwiacessi-ka** ttal-ul colonghayssta
-Nom father -Nom national guardsman-**Nom** daughter-Acc inveigled
ko noyeweha-si-ko-issta ko kwittumhay cwuessta.
that resenting was(Hon) that hint gave
ka-REP2 Minsu-ka apeci-ka **ku hoysa sacangi-nim-i** ttal-ul colonghayssta ko
that company president-**Nom**
noyeweha-si-ko-issta ko kwittumhay cwuessta.
'Minsu gave a hint that the father resented that the **national guardsman/ company president** had inveigled (his) daughter.'

ka-REP2 Minsu-ka **minpangwiacessi-ka** ttal-ul colonghayssta ko
-Nom national guardsman-**Nom** daughter-Acc inveigled that
kwittumhay cwuessta.
hint gave
ka-REP1 Minsu-ka **ku hoysa sacangi-nim-I** ttal-ul colonghayssta ko
that company president-**Nom**
kwittumhay cwuessta.
'Minsu gave a hint that the **national guardsman/ company president** had inveigled (his) daughter.'

APPENDIX C: Materials of Experiment 3, Questionnaire 1

Example numbers correspond to those in the text.

(1) shoogakusei-ga ane-ni Sugita-sensei-o
 elementary school student-Nom my older sister-Dat Teacher Sugita-Acc
(2) Taro-ga sinseki-o sensei-ni
 -Nom relative-Acc teacher-Dat
(3) koibito-o Miki-ga ryoosin-ni
 lover-Acc -Nom parents-Dat
(4) imooto-ga ueitaa-ni Yumiko-ga
 younger sister -Acc waiter-Dat -Nom
(5) Ogawa-san-ni koochoo-ga raikyaku-o
 Mr. -Dat principal-Nom guest-Acc
(6) hudoosan'ya-ni mei-o Jiroo-ga
 realtor-Dat niece-Acc -Nom
(7) kangohu-ga ani-ga Kenji-o
 nurse-Nom my older brother-Nom -Acc
(8) otooto-ga Keiichi-o yopparai-ga
 younger brother-Nom -Acc drunk-Nom

(9) Yokoyama-san-o titi-ga   untenshu-ga
         Mr. -Acc my father-Nom (bus/train)conductor-Nom
(10) otetudaisan-ga Takashi-ga sobo-ni
     house keeper-Nom   -Nom my grand mother-Dat
(11) itoko-ga Yoshio-ni ryuugakusei-ga
     cousin-Nom   -Dat foreign student-Nom
(12) Watanabe-san-ni haha-ga   kenji-ga
         Mr. -Dat my mother-Nom prosecutor-Nom
(13) Masaaki-ga roojin-ga   ani-ni   bengosi-o
         -Nom old man -Nom my older brother-Dat lawyer-Acc
(14) dookyuusei-ga Sachiko-ga Mariko-o kyoodai-ni
     classmate-Nom   -Nom   -Acc brother-Dat
(15) Yukio-ga koohai-ni   otooto-ga   buin-o
         -Nom junior (student/worker)-Dat younger brother-Nom club member-Acc
(16) roohujn-ga   Hirai-san-o siriai-ga   omawarisan-ni
     old woman-Nom   Mr. -Acc acquaintance-Nom cop-Dat
(17) oji-ga   kachoo-ni   Sato-san-o   roosinsi-ga
     my uncle-Nom section chief-Dat   Mr. -Acc old gentleman-Nom
(18) buchoo-ga   Kanai-san-o   sinrui-ni   tokuisaki-ga
     managing director-Nom   Mr. -Acc relative-Dat client-Nom
(19) biyoosi-o   musume-ga   Kawada-san-ga Saito-san-ni
     hair cutter-Acc daughter-Nom   Mr. -Nom   Mr. -Dat
(20) hisho-o   Naito-san-ga   kakarichoo-ni   kodomo-ga
     secretary-Acc   Mr. -Nom section chief-Dat child-Nom
(21) hahoya-o Michiko-ni tomodati-ga seerusuman-ga
     mother-Acc   -Dat friend-Nom salesperson-Nom
(22) imooto-ni   Hiroshi-ga hannin-ga Mamoru-o
     younger sister-Dat   -Nom criminal-Nom   -Acc
(23) Yamada-san-ni gakusei-ga eigahaiyuu-o   senpai-ga
         Mr. -Dat student-Nom movie actor-Acc senior (student/worker)-Nom
(24) Tanaka-san-ni yuujin-o   dooryoo-ga   Keiko-ga
         Mr. -Dat friend-Acc co-worker-Nom   -Nom

APPENDIX D: Materials of Experiment 3, Questionnaire 2

Example numbers correspond to those in the text.

(1) a. shachoo-ga   untenshu-ga
        president-Nom   driver-Nom
    b. okumanchooja-ga monbano-ga   yuubinbutsu-o
        billionaire-Nom   security guard-Nom mail-Acc

    c. senmu-ga   hisho-ga   shain-ni
        department chief-Nom secretary-Nom company worker-Dat
    d. eigahaiyuu-ga   koibito-ga direkutaa-ni   shutuen-o
        movie actor-Nom lover-Nom director-Dat   appearance-Acc

(2) a. yuukaihannin-ga seimeibun-ga
        kidnapper-Nom   statement-Nom
    b. taipisuto-ga konpyuutaa-ga joohoo-o
        typist-Nom   computer-Nom information-Acc
    c. yuumeisakka-ga   genkoo-ga siriai-ni
        famous writer-Nom draft-Nom acquaintance-Dat
    d. kaishain-ga   kyuuryoo-ga kodomo-ni omocha-o
        company worker-Nom salary-Nom   child-Dat toy-Acc

Index

Accentual phrase (APh) 224-229, 232-233, 236, 239-240, 244-247
accentual phrasing 223-225, 229, 231, 235-239, 248
adjacency constraint 177, 179
Agent 214-216
ambiguity resolution 57, 64, 72-73, 75-76, 239
automaticity 3-4, 13-14, 16, 18-19, 26

Blom Approximation 146
bunsetsu 96, 141, 146, 154-5, 164, 195

Canonical order/sentence 135, 138, 140-142, 144, 147, 151-160, 168-170, 173, 176-181, 183, 208-209
Cantonese 3-4, 7-8, 12, 18, 113-117, 119, 123-124, 126
Case Filling Strategy 212
Case Hierarchy 210, 212-214, 218
case information 191, 212, 214
Case Marker Processing Hierarchy 176
case marking/markers 99, 172, 175, 211, 214, 218
categorical ambiguity 54, 57-58, 60, 64-65, 67-68, 70, 72-73, 75-81
categorical grammar 183, 184

center-embedding/embedded (sentences) 86-87, 104, 140-142, 144, 147, 151-154, 156, 158, 160, 257-258, 260, 263, 275
Chinese 3-4, 7-12, 17, 19, 23, 26, 54-56, 58, 60-64, 69, 78, 80, 113-114, 119-120, 122-124, 146
cognitive processing 2, 4, 6
Consistency Score (CS) 196-200, 202-204
Constraint-Based models 230
context-dependency hypothesis 8, 113, 119, 125
context-dependent models 4-7, 26
context effects 111, 113, 124-125
context-independent models 4-7, 26
contextual ambiguity 56
contextual information 5, 11, 13, 72-73, 75, 79
control information 191
control sentence(s) 189, 199, 201
cross-modal gating task 16
cross-modal task/experiment/paradigm 16, 20, 21, 24, 113-114, 124
cross-modal lexical decision task 15, 19, 23, 26
cross-modal lexical priming experiment/ method 15, 191

289

290 / INDEX

cross-modal naming task 15, 17, 236-237, 247
cross-modal priming 139

Delay model 132
depth-first processor 240
difficulty rating 92, 143-144
Direct Access Hypothesis 193
direct association hypothesis 174, 179, 183
double center embedding/doubly center embedded 86, 257-260, 262-264, 274-275, 277
double embedding 267, 270, 276
Double Nominative Construction 90
Dutch 139

Empty subject 189-193, 196, 199-202, 212
encoding or storage interference 90, 99
Event-related brain potentials 191
Extended Possession Construction 268-271, 273-4, 6
exhaustive access account 4, 8, 112-113, 125
   See also multiple-access account
eye-movement monitoring experiment/technique 133, 140, 145-146, 156-158
exhaustive/multiple access 112-113, 125

Filler 193, 202
filler-gap 168, 175, 189, 192-194, 199, 204
first-in-first-out 197
first-pass gaze time (FGT) 146, 148, 151, 154
first-pass regressive eye-movement (FRN) 148, 153
flat structure 133, 136, 139, 157
form-driven account 4

frequency 4-5, 7-8, 26, 61, 65-72, 74-76, 78, 80, 136, 158, 170, 177, 179-182, 242

Gap 168, 174-175, 178-179, 182-183
garden path 33, 35, 38, 43, 48, 50, 104, 105, 214
Garden Path depth-first model 230
ga repetition 259-261, 263, 269, 274
Gating task/paradigm 16, 113-115, 119
gaze times 146-147
German 139
Goal 214-217
go/no-go (lexical decision) task 16, 17
Government and Binding 132

Heavy NP shift 142
head-driven approach/model/parser 89, 132, 135, 159
head-initial language 215
hierarchical structure 157, 159
homophones 9, 16, 112-114, 116, 119-120, 122-123, 125-126
homophone density 113, 115-118, 126
homophone frequency 113, 119, 121, 125-126
homophony 3, 8, 10
human cognitive system 53, 55
human language cognition model 76

Immediacy 3, 13-14, 16-19, 26
incremental model/processing 31-32, 39-42, 49-50, 132, 135, 158-159, 171, 175
information structure 225
interaction/interactive hypothesis/model 2-4, 14, 19
interactionist account 3, 6
interactive mechanism/model 112, 126
intermediate phrase 224-5, 245
isolation point (IP) 115, 118-120
intonation phrase (IPh) 225-228, 232-234

intonational structure 225-226

Japanese 87-89, 91, 94, 96, 99, 103, 108, 131-145, 157-160, 167-172, 175, 177, 180-182, 184, 189, 190-191, 194-196, 201-202, 207, 212, 215, 225, 230, 257-261, 263-264, 268-271, 275-277,

Korean 105, 223-226, 228-233, 236, 239, 241-242, 245-248, 251, 259, 263-265, 268, 275

Language-driven hypothesis 11
last-in-first-out 202
lexical access 2-5, 7-8, 11, 13, 15-18, 24, 26-27, 245
lexical ambiguity 1, 3-4, 7, 10-5, 17, 26, 56-58, 111-114, 124-125
lexical decision task 15, 20, 138, 212
lexical resolution 75
Location 217

Mandarin See Chinese
memory load 87, 169, 170, 178
minimal pair 191
Minimal Revisions principle 240
modified selective-access account 6-7
modularity 2-3, 27
modularity hypothesis 2-4, 12-4, 16, 18
modular system/theory/view 5, 13, 72
moving window 96, 102-103, 154, 172
multiple-access account 4-5, 7, 26
Multi-level Parsing Model 191

Nominative (case marker/marking) 89-90, 96, 105, 135, 140, 142, 154-155, 159, 168, 169, 176, 212-214, 216, 218, 257-259, 262-265, 267, 270, 273, 275-277
nominative case repetition 260, 263, 268, 275, 277

nominativeness 105
nominative preference 214
Nominative Object Construction 268-270, 273-274, 276
non-canonical word order 167, 168

Object-control (O-control) 190, 194-208, 211, 217
object preference 204
optional movement 138
ordered-access account 5-7, 26

Parallel Subject Construction (PSC) 268, 269, 272,-274, 276
parser 86, 94, 191-192
parsing 237-238
Patient 215
phonological repetition 105, 259
pitch accent 225
positional similarity 87-88, 92, 94-96, 101-102, 104-105
pragmatic information 238-239
pre-head parsing decisions 159
Preliminary Phrase Packager (PPP) 192
primacy effect 197, 209
Primary Location Hierarchy 217
PRO 183, 190-191, 193, 195, 198, 203, 212, 217
proactive interference 87, 88, 89, 90
probe recognition task 136, 183
prosodic disambiguation 224
prosodic information 229, 238-240, 245, 248
prosodic phrase/phrasing 223-225, 234-236, 238, 247
prosodic structure 223-224, 229, 233, 236, 245-247
Prosodic Visibility 239, 241, 244, 246

Questionnaire 91, 96, 99-101, 103, 143-145, 231, 260-261, 265-266, 271-272

Raising structure 193
random stochastic system 77
read-out sentences 201
reanalysis 31-34, 38-41, 48-52, 104, 238, 240, 243-244
reanalysis ambiguity 31, 51
recency 200, 202, 204, 209
recognition experiments/task 206-208, 210-213, 218
regressive eye-movement 146-147, 151
relative clause 31-36, 38-43, 45, 48-52
reordered access hypothesis 112,125,126
retrieval experiments/task 201, 206-208, 210, 218
retrieval interference 90, 95
retroactive interference 87- 90

Scrambling/scrambled 101-104, 131-145, 147, 151-160, 167-171, 173-184, 197, 200, 204, 208-209
selective access 112,125
self-paced reading (experiment/ method/paradigm/task) 36, 43-45, 133, 137-138 140, 146, 154, 156-158, 164, 168, 172, 174, 180, 184, 209
sentence completion (task) 268, 271
Sentence Structure Supervisor (SSS) 192
sentential context 4-5, 7, 24, 26
serial order 94
similarity-based interference 86, 87, 93, 95, 101, 104, 105, 275
Simple Subject Construction (SSC) 268, 270, 274
Sinica Corpus 54, 58-60, 62-63, 65, 69, 73-75, 77
Source 217
speeded-selection hypothesis 12
stack/stacking/stacked 91-93, 95, 97-104
strictly selective-access account 5
structureal ambiguity 56, 230

subject-control (S-control) 190, 194-204, 206-208, 211, 217
Subject-Object Reanalysis (SOR) 33-40, 42-43, 45-50
subject preference 197, 199, 201, 206, 213-214
Subject Reanalysis (SR) 33-36, 38, 40, 42, 45, 48, 50
subordinate meaning 113-126
syntactic disambiguation 224
syntactic similarity 87, 88, 91-93, 101, 104, 275

Taiwanese 19, 23
thematic compatibility information 31, 35, 38-40, 49-50
Theme 214-217
Theta-role Hierarchy 214, 216, 218
Theta-role information 191, 215
Theta-checking Strategy 214
top-down prediction 214
topic marker (-*wa*) 212-213, 258
total gaze time (TGT) 146, 148, 151-154
total number of regressive eye-movement (TRN) 148, 151-153
trace 175, 193, 198, 203
transparency 157
Two Stage Parsing Model 191

Visibility Hypothesis 239

Wait-and-see strategy 211
word order effect 204, 209
working memory 85-88, 94-95, 102, 105, 170, 174, 182